The Dog Trainer's Resource

The APDT Chronicle of the Dog Collection

Mychelle E. Blake, Editor

Dogwise™ Publishing
Wenatchee, Washington U.S.A.

The Dog Trainer's Resource. The APDT Chronicle of the Dog Collection
Mychelle E. Blake, Editor

Dogwise Publishing
A Division of Direct Book Service, Inc.
PO Box 2778
701B Poplar
Wenatchee, Washington 98807
1-509-663-9115, 1-800-776-2665
website: www.dogwisepublishing.com
email: info@dogwisepublshing.com

Graphic Design: Nathan Woodward, Dogwise Publishing
Indexing: Elaine Melnick, Our Index Lady
Cover Photo: Karen Hartman
Interior Photos: Mychelle Blake, Dale Burke, Don Hanson, Karen Hartman, and Adam Morrison

Library of Congress Cataloging-in-Publication Data:

The Dog Trainer's Resource : The APDT Chronicle of the Dog Collection / edited by Mychelle Blake.
   p. cm.
 ISBN-13: 978-1-929242-39-9 (alk. paper)
 ISBN-10: 1-929242-39-5 (alk. paper)
 1. Dogs–Training. 2. Dogs–Behavior. 3. Small business. I. Blake, Mychelle. II. Association of Pet Dog Trainers.
 SF431.D66 2007
 636.7'0835–dc22

              2006016840

Printed in the U.S.A.

Contents

APDT (Association of Pet Dog Trainers) membership brings a variety of benefits for dog trainers and others interested in canine behavior and training. Members enjoy tremendous educational and networking opportunities and get access to our e-mail list and a subscription to the award-winning *The APDT Chronicle of the Dog*. Full members also receive a listing on our Web site trainer directory, access to group discounts on medical, health, life and liability insurance, and discounts on our Annual Educational Conference and Trade Show and Cyber Trade Show. Please visit our Web site at www.apdt.com to join the APDT. Or, you can call 1-800-PET-DOGS or e-mail us at information@apdt.com.

Foreword

I am so pleased to have been asked to write the Foreword for *The Dog Trainer's Resource. The APDT Chronicle of the Dog Collection*—a selection of articles published in the newsletter for the Association of Pet Dog Trainers (APDT). Over the years, the Chronicle has provided a wealth of information for APDT members. In book form, these articles will remain available to veteran trainers as well as those who are new to the field and to their (human) clients.

During the 1980s, pet dog training was already a long-established profession, yet without professional organization or representation. Most dog training clubs and classes were governed by Kennel Clubs. Club members would train specialized breeds for years to perfect a number of obedience drills for competition. In a sense, the trainers knew the obedience rules and examination questions well before the examination. Pet dog training is entirely different—there are no rules, the questions are unknown, and the syllabus is literally huge—comprising all aspects of a dog's (and owner's) behavior, temperament, and training. Moreover, most owners—just like their dogs—are novices. And they want to train their dogs as quickly and as effortlessly as possible. Certainly, pet dog training is one of the most complicated, challenging, sometimes frustrating, yet most thoroughly rewarding of endeavors. Hence the endless quest for the quickest, easiest, most enjoyable and most expedient ways to produce equipment and gizmo-free reliability.

Pet dog trainers were howling for education and professional organization. Consequently, in 1991, I started organizing six APT (the original acronym) conferences in Canada, UK and USA, (two in each country during 1993 and 1994). (The acronym "APDT" was first coined by Roger Abrantes and myself at the 1992 World Congress of Kennel Clubs in Bermuda during a reception at the Bacardi Rum factory.) The first APT conference was held in Toronto in May 1993. The Canadian APDT, later to be renamed the CAPPDT, Canadian Association of Professional Pet Dog Trainers, was whelped at this conference. The topic was people training and the keynote speaker was Job Michael Evans. Sadly, Job died within the year and the 1994 US Conference was dedicated to his memory.

The APDT in the United States was founded at the November 1993 APT conference in San Mateo. Seventy trainers became members. The first APDT Newsletter (now a collector's item) was published in Spring 1994—edited and typeset by Doug Hostetter and Skooter his canine co-editor. Later that year, 307 people attended the second US APT conference in Orlando, where the APDT held its first Annual Meeting. (Perhaps this is why the Orlando APT Conference is now commonly regarded as the first APDT Conference.) The APDT held its first Annual Conference in Chicago in 1995 with 1,100 attendees. Under Kathleen Chin's superbly efficient guidance, the conference grew in leaps and bounds and in 1999, the San Diego conference drew over 1,500 delegates from 45 states and 10 countries. The membership grew accordingly, and now the APDT is the largest and most influential association of pet dog trainers in the world.

My intention in founding the APDT was threefold: to attract and organize the largest membership possible; to provide a forum for education, networking, and governance; and to design and implement a national accreditation program for pet dog training.

In various countries around the world, other doggy professions (veterinarians and psychologists), governing bodies, and governments were making noises about controlling pet dog training and behavior counseling. I felt so strongly that pet dog trainers were much better qualified to make decisions about the direction of pet dog training. A large membership, stellar education *vis a vis* the *applied* behavioral sciences, and a stepwise accreditation program were necessary, so that the APDT could protect the livelihood of its membership.

To this day, the APDT has remained an open educational group—open to all pet dog trainers. As such, it has attracted an extremely large membership and has a powerful and influential, concerted voice. Pet dog trainers have now secured their profession. Moreover, the large membership, 4,500 and growing, has evaluated the need and established the protocols for continuing education and accreditation (to maintain quality). The APDT Annual Conference remains the largest and most comprehensive, dog behavior and training educational extravaganza worldwide (www.apdt.com). As an offshoot of the APDT Education Committee, the Certification Council for Pet Dog Trainers (CCPDT www.ccpdt.com) has established the only international pet dog trainers certification program (CPDT). By working together and staying together as a group—the APDT has literally changed the face of pet dog training.

The APDT has tirelessly promoted dog-friendly dog training techniques, comprising lures and rewards, fun and games, and woofs and wags. The APDT has made living together so much more fun for both dogs and their owners.

Ian Dunbar PhD, BVetMed, MRCVS, CPDT
Founder of the APDT
Berkeley, California, June 2006

From the President of APDT

I was waiting him out. My foster Papillon, Mika, was spastically bouncing off the sliding glass door, while my other dogs waited patiently behind him. He had only been with me for a week, rescued out of a shelter after living with an animal "collector," and he acted as if he had espresso running through his veins. He had no clue how to be calm. The slightest sound, the slightest noise, launched him into the stratosphere. This time, the trigger had been my announcement it was time to go outside.

Sproing! Sproing! Sproing! He bounced. Minutes went by. I had asked him to sit, a cue which he knew, so I was waiting for him to plop his little fluffy butt on the ground before I opened the door. I was waiting him out. My three-legged Labrador Retriever, Cody, however, thought Mika needed some extra instruction.

Cody reached out with his nose, and gently pushed Mika's rear into a sit. I opened the doors, laughing, and released the dogs out onto the porch. Aren't dogs the best teachers?

If only dogs could pass on their knowledge to us in the written word! Since they can't, we have gathered knowledge from the world's leading dog trainers that has appeared in our association's newsletter over the years to benefit future generations of dog trainers. *The Dog Trainer's Resource, APDT Chronicle of the Dog Collection* is packed with useful tips, insightful articles, and the latest information on canine learning theory. Such a resource shouldn't be lost in a backlog of a dusty archive…it's meant to be shared. So we've compiled these highlights here in one place, to help rookie and veteran trainers alike better understand our canine friends.

Just as the Association of Pet Dog Trainers has grown since our inception in 1993, so has *The APDT Chronicle of the Dog*, from a manually copied newsletter to the full 40 professionally printed pages it is today.

Terry Long, CPDT, served as the Managing Editor from late 1999 to 2002, and deserves much credit for taking the *Chronicle* to new heights in professionalism. Terry now serves as a regular contributor with our "On Behavior" and "Reviewer's Corner" columns. Nicole Wilde, CPDT, also contributes to each issue with our popular "Member Profile." Thanks also to our former Submissions and Copy Editor, Judith Engstrom, for offering her talents to the mix.

Our current Managing Editor, Mychelle Blake, has worked tirelessly to deliver each issue, and the newsletter has prospered in her capable hands. Her efforts have helped us create a successful and respected publication. We consistently earn recognition as a finalist in the annual Dog Writers Association of America (DWAA) annual awards competition, and several of the *Chronicle*'s articles have earned DWAA Maxwell Medallions.

In this book, you will find the knowledge of many canine professional experts. Special thanks to all the authors who have contributed to our newsletter over the years—you are the reason why we've been so successful! Also, thanks to the APDT staff and Board of Directors for their efforts in making this book happen, along with our publisher, Dogwise, for suggesting the idea in the first place. And much appreciation goes to my fellow members of the Editorial Committee — Melissa Bussey, CPDT; Susan Smith, CPDT; and Eve Marschark, CABC, CPDT, for their hard work in shepherding each issue.

As I look at Logan, my newest lovable lab, lying at my feet while I write this, I think of all the dogs who helped shape who he is today. It is my hope that the wisdom in these pages will inspire you to become a better teacher and friend to the dogs in your life. So please enjoy…and learn…then teach.

Teoti Anderson, CPDT
APDT President 2004-2006

From the Editor

I remember my first experience of *The APDT Chronicle of the Dog* clearly. At the time, it was known as *The APDT Newsletter*. I was just like many of you who are reading this volume now—new to the field of working with dogs and unaware that there is a tremendous opportunity available for educating oneself about the profession.

I first spied a copy of *The APDT Newsletter* at a friend's house who was a professional dog trainer. *What's this? A newsletter that provides dog training and behavior modification information? There is actually an organization of dog trainers that promotes education and networking?* Within the pages of *The APDT Newsletter*, I found a goldmine of information on training and behavior modification and how to prepare oneself to not only see dog training as a hobby, but as a serious career path.

The APDT Newsletter not only sparked my quest for more knowledge about dog behavior, but gave me the tools I needed to learn how to become a serious and knowledgeable professional. APDT has been at the forefront of the movement toward greater education of the dog training community and increasing the validity and competence of dog professionals everywhere. It has also provided valuable information on such vital topics as how to set up one's business, marketing your services to the community, establishing relationships with veterinarians, and appropriately pricing one services.

This volume you hold in your hands provides valuable information for both aspiring and experienced dog trainers, as well as those who work with dogs in doggy daycares, veterinary clinics, therapy dogs, dog sports, and more. *The APDT Chronicle of the Dog* has featured a variety of authors and perspectives on dog training and behavior modifications, and touches on the broad spectrum of what is involved in the working professional's field of dog training and behavior.

Some of the featured authors in this volume include Jean Donaldson, Director of the renowned the San Francisco SPCA Academy for Dog Trainers and author of *The Culture Clash*, *Mine! A Guide to Resource Guarding in Dogs*, and *Fight! A Guide to Dog-Dog Aggression*; Donna Duford, author of *Agility Tricks for Improved Attention, Flexibility, and Confidence* and a frequent speaker at the APDT's Annual Educational Conferences; Trish King, Director of Animal Behavior and Training at the Marin County Humane Society and author of *Parenting Your Dog*; Dr. Karen Overall, author of the seminal text, *Clinical Behavior Medicine for Small Animals*; Terry Ryan, a well-known trainer and instructor of trainers and author of several books that every trainer should have on their bookshelf, including *Coaching People, Coaching Dogs*, *Toolbox for Remodeling Your Dog's Behavior*, and *Beyond Block Heeling*; shelter activist, author and speaker Sue Sternberg author of *Successful Dog Adoption* and *Great Dog Adoptions*, whose "Gimme Shelter" column garnered a prestigious DWAA Annual Writing Competition award, and are our most requested reprints from new and existing members; and Nicole Wilde, speaker and author of the popular books, *So You Want to Be a Dog Trainer*, *It's Not the Dogs, It's the People!*, and *One-on-One: A Dog Trainer's Guide to Private Lessons*.

Some of my favorite highlights of the book are:

- "Assessment and Treatment of Resource Guarding" by Jean Donaldson, should be required reading for trainers working with aggression cases;

- The "Levels System: Advance-at-Your-Own-Pace Classes" by Joan Guertin with Terry Ryan, featuring a unique new idea on structuring classes to best meet the needs of clients;

- Mardi Richmond's articles "Internships: Training the Trainer" and "Are You Searching for an Internship Program" which provide valuable information on how to find a mentor, as well as become a mentor to up and coming trainers;

- "Assessing the Alpha Roll" by Terry Ryan, an article that helped end the use of this damaging technique;

- Sue Sternberg's heartbreaking three-part series "Becoming a Shelter Dog." which follows the path of several dogs who come through a shelter's doors— some make it out to find a new home and family, while others sadly do not.

- All of the articles by the Bailey's, two of the most renowned animal trainers and applied behavior analysts in the world. Their wisdom and learning are vital elements for any trainer looking to understand the workings of classical and operating conditioning.

From how to run your dog training business, to working with our human clients, to modifying the behavior of fearful and aggressive dogs, *The Dog Trainer's Resource* is a compendium of the many thoughts and experiences of these trainers and more. It is a "must-have" for any serious student of canine behavior and training, whether you are a hobbyist trainer, just entering the field of dog training, or a seasoned professional.

Dog training has certainly changed over the last decade, and each issue of *The APDT Chronicle of the Dog* has been for me, and I hope for all of its readers, a vehicle to educate oneself on the advances in our field. Our goal with *The APDT Chronicle of the Dog* has always been to provide knowledge, inspiration, and pride in our profession. I am honored to be a part of the production of this book as well as of *The Chronicle*, one of the Association of Pet Dog Trainers main instruments for educating my colleagues. I look forward to the bright future of the APDT and *The APDT Chronicle of the Dog*.

Mychelle Blake, Managing Editor, *The APDT Chronicle of the Dog*

Puppy Training

Dog trainers deal with issues relating to puppy train-ing—or the lack of puppy training—frequently. Most trainers believe that socializing puppies at the right time and using the right techniques is critical to avoiding many behavior problems as the pup gets older. How long pup-pies should remain with their littermates, the importance of puppy temperament tests, and when to begin training are subjects of interest and debate among dog trainers. The articles in this section review current thinking on socializa-tion, weaning, and what some readers might find a surpris-ing take on the effectiveness of puppy temperament tests as they are commonly administered.

The Old Fears of Puppy Socialization: Let it Go!

Pia Silvani, January/February 2004

"Shall we get a puppy?" I asked my husband. The empty crates are in the basement, carefree days with no concerns about open doors and missing dogs, uninterrupted restful nights, and active canine vacations, with hiking, swimming, and no leashes! Were we ready to take the plunge?

In June a little bundle of cuteness danced into our lives. She's everything we could have hoped for—fearless, joyous, curious, and confident. Will this last? How many times have we lectured to our clients about the importance of socialization? We certainly want everlasting good spirit and "glee" for her.

Between the ages of 3 to 16 weeks, the average puppy will learn more than in her entire lifetime. What occurs during this critical period has an everlasting emotional and cognitive effect on the dog. What frightens me is the fact that we only had control over a certain portion of this critical socialization time. Guinn came home at seven weeks (49 days). We only had the back-end of the period to work with. We, the professionals, are the ultimate consumers: we select a good breeder, put faith in their knowledge about the proper raising of the litter, and we are careful in selecting the right pup. But what about average pet owners? Are they still picking the quiet one in the corner?

Development

Puppies are pretty helpless for the first 12 days of their life during the neonatal period. Their eyes and ears are not yet open and their motor capabilities are limited. The majority of their time is spent nursing and sleeping, and behavior is mostly reflexive. If puppies are handled and exposed to mild environmental stressors during this period, it can have a positive impact on them in later years. Pups left undisturbed can be emotionally reactive when they reach adulthood.

Pups begin to develop their motor skills during the transitional period (12-21 days). They begin to walk unsteadily, can eat soft meals once their first teeth come in and emerge into the world with an amplified amount of social and environmental stimulation.

From 21-84 days, a puppy's socialization period begins. It is a sensitive period in the dog's developmental stages. This is the optimal time for them to experience and learn without being fearful.

Between three to five weeks pups go through the primary socialization stage where a great deal of learning occurs. Much of this learning establishes a foundation for behavior patterns (good and bad!) later in life. Insufficient socialization during this time can lead to hyperactivity, over-reactivity, emotional rigidity, anxiety, and more. They may have problems with separation and exhibit fear or aggression toward strangers. When separated from the litter during this period, many pups are intolerant of other dogs later in life.

The secondary socialization period (6 to 12 weeks) is the "process of bonding and social conditioning within the context of the human domestic environment ..." (Lindsay, 2000)

As we've learned from the experts over the years, it is critical that puppies are provided with adequate social contact and as much exposure to as many things in the environment as possible during the socialization period. Having this knowledge can assist us in educating not only pet owners, but also other animal professionals, about the importance of developing good social contacts with pups. A pup will develop abnormally if the environment does not provide her with sufficient or adequate experience. When you see a potential problem, don't ignore it because you don't want to hurt the client's feelings.

The Issue of Poor Socialization

When asked to write this article, timing could not have been more perfect, with the new addition to our family. Furthermore, I had just received the July 2004 issue of *The Whole Dog Journal* where Nancy Kerns interviewed Dr. Ian Dunbar on this topic. Seeing puppies entering classes at 16 weeks with problems has bothered me for some time now. I wholeheartedly concur with what Dr. Dunbar expressed.

For the past years, I've been observing pups that have experienced what I perceive as poor socialization. The pups were probably deprived of early environmental exposures since they appeared to have unusual deficits and/or dysfunctional behaviors. If a puppy is isolated from the world early on, she will have difficulty enjoying companionships. She may exhibit distrust or even extreme fear of any social contact and appear to have behavioral disabilities. These dogs typically will exhibit poor learning and problem-solving abilities and are unable to cope since fear or avoidance overrides all.

Research has shown us that with concentrated remedial socialization, some pups can regain some tranquility, yet they may never reach their full potential had things been handled correctly from the onset. Many of these pups are entering the households of novice pet owners who are inexperienced technicians and not educated in canine social behavior.

Solutions

I asked myself three questions:

1. What should breeders be doing to make our jobs easier and give pet owners what they are looking for—a well-balanced puppy!

2. Why are we, the pet professionals, not on the same page about socialization and how can we get there? Pet owners are receiving conflicting advice from breeders, veterinarians, and trainers. Instead of helping them, we're making their heads spin!

3. What information should breeders and veterinarians give out in every puppy packet so clients are better informed about what socialization means and signs to look for that may cause potential future problems? As we know, without taking a proactive approach, the behaviors will "not go away with time" and are not simply "puppy behaviors."

What Breeders Can Do

Breeders are with puppies from birth giving them an opportunity to take advantage of early learning. By following some of the suggestions I've listed below, breeders can have an enormous impact on the future of the pups:

- At about three weeks of age, expose the pups to other friendly, healthy dogs and by five weeks, people.

- Take car trips, especially to the veterinarian's office. The pup's first experience with the veterinarian should not be a cold, motorized table and needle in the rump. Acclimate the pup to the motion of cars to avoid car sickness.

- Gradually expose them to different sounds starting at low levels (doorbells, vacuums, hair dryers, vehicles, horns, barking dogs, kids playing, etc.)

- Separate pups from their litter for short periods of time to help accustom them to being alone. What a shock to them after sleeping with seven siblings to then be put alone in a crate in a dark kitchen!

- Acclimate the pups to various substrates.

- Between five to eight weeks, familiarize the pup to grooming tools, ear cleaning, drinking and eating from a bowl, training with treats, wearing collars, leash walking, and much more.

- Acclimate pups to crates and ex-pens, leaving the pup with a "puppy pal" (soft toy to cuddle with) and proper chew toys.

- Allow pups to investigate in the yard, teaching them to walk up and down a stair or two as opposed to carrying them in and out.

- Take the pups out in the rain (they're dogs for goodness sake!) How many pups have accidents during inclement weather?

- Work on housetraining to help get the new owner off to the right start.

Socialization Pros and Cons

Many veterinarians and breeders are recommending early socialization and including this learning program as part of their total wellness plan for pet owners. Yet many are not. How can we all be on the same page to help us reach a unified approach to socialization?

- Both research and findings from various guide dog organizations show that fewer than a half a dozen, out of hundreds of thousands of puppies, became ill before their final set of vaccinations. All other pups that were taken into public places became successful guide dogs.

- Dr. R.K. Anderson states: "The risk of a dog dying because of infection with distemper or parvo disease is far less than the much higher risk of a dog dying (euthanasia) because of behavior problems. Are there risks? Yes. But ten years of good experience and data, with few exceptions, offers veterinarians the opportunity to generally recommend early socialization and training classes, beginning when puppies are eight to nine weeks of age."

- Isolating these puppies until they are 16+ weeks is detrimental to their behavioral health. Puppy classes have turned into behavior modification classes as a result.

- Purdue University Animal Behavior Clinic stresses the importance of early socialization by defining their recommendations for puppy class protocols. In their letter dated December 4, 2002, Drs. Andrew Luescher and Steve Thompson eloquently stated, "Let's welcome new puppies into our society by showing them what we expect, not dispose of them because we failed to communicate our expectations at a time when the puppies are most impressionable." A copy of this letter can be found on their Web site, www.vet.purdue.edu/animalbehavior.

Information for Puppy Packets

Veterinarians, breeders, trainers, shelters, and other animal professionals should join forces by educating pet owners about the importance of early socialization and understanding the critical development stages. Pet owners are unaware of early warning signs for potential future problems. Some suggestions might be:

- Socialization is about positive experiences.

- Define what normal vs. abnormal canine behavior is and what to expect as the puppy matures.

- Puppies that spend a lot of time "hiding" under furniture are not confident in their household. From what and whom are they hiding?

- Puppies that hide with their bones and toys—red flag! Is the family constantly taking things from the pup's mouth? Has she now reached a threshold? Can the owner remove items from puppy's mouth without being threatened?

- The puppy rarely responds to her name or other cues. Why?

- The puppy is not housetrained by five months. Are the owners not watching? What else is the puppy doing?

- The puppy does not tolerate grooming. The owner thinks the pup "fools around." Is it fooling around or becoming agitated?

- Neither the veterinarian nor groomer can handle the pup.

- The puppy is not enjoying socialization class (hiding, running away, quivering). Not all puppies belong in a puppy class and may not get over it.

- The puppy is threatening while eating. To whom or what are the threats directed? Let's not wait until a bite occurs!

- The pup has no interest in people or dogs, or avoids one more than the other.

- The pup has curled her lip, growled, snarled, or snapped at other dogs, children or adults. When and in what context?

- The pup is extremely timid when introduced to new people.

- Avoid dog parks and other areas where pups may become frightened by unsocialized adult dogs.

If we can join forces with our colleagues now, perhaps we can hope to see fewer problems in the coming years. ❖

References and Recommended Reading

Scott, J.P. & Fuller, J.L. (1965) *Genetics and the Social Behavior of the Dog*. Chicago: University of Chicago Press.

Fox, M. (1971). *Integrative Development of Brain and Behavior in the Dog*. Chicago: University of Chicago Press.

Lindsay, S.R. (2000). *Handbook of Applied Dog Behavior and Training*. Ames, IA: Iowa State University Press.

Overall, K.L. (1997). *Clinical Behavioral Medicine for Small Aanimals*. St. Louis, MO: Mosby.

Hetts, S. (1999). *Pet Behavior Protocols: What to Say, What to Do, When to Refer*. Lakewood, CO: AAHA Press.

Selling Early Socialization

Terry Long, January/February 2004

Elaine and Mark Dowell put a lot of thought into adopting their new puppy. They researched a variety of breeds, talking to breeders and owners of dogs they thought would fit their family's lifestyle. They visited shelters and talked to adoption counselors. They planned the arrival of the new pup for when at least one of them would have more time to devote to housetraining, and they hired a pet sitter to come by at noon every day so the pup wouldn't be alone for more than a few hours at a time. They bought a couple of baby gates, a crate, a variety of toys, and arranged their first visit with the veterinarian who had provided their previous dogs with loving care in the final days of their lives. Elaine and Mark looked forward to getting off on the right foot.

Finally, they made their choice and brought home a six-week-old puppy from a private rescue organization. She was adorable; a white German Shepherd and yellow Labrador Retriever mix, and they named her Callie. She passed their vet's health exam with flying colors. Although looking forward to taking Callie out for walks, the Dowell's followed their vet's admonition not to take Callie anywhere until she was at least four months of age, when all her vaccinations would be complete. Elaine and Mark settled for introducing Callie to the friends and family members who visited on occasion.

"But My Vet Said ..."

When they hired a trainer to start private training sessions, the Dowell's were surprised when the trainer recommended early socialization. This was in direct contradiction to what their veterinarian had told them. The trainer said that it was imperative that they expose their pup to a variety of people and animals before the tender age of twelve weeks. The trainer felt this was especially important because of the high percentage of German Shepherd she suspected comprised Callie's genetic heritage. In the trainer's opinion, German Shepherds needed more than the average amount of socialization. The Dowell's listened intently, asking questions, considering that socialization might not mean unnecessarily exposing Callie to contagious diseases. After the trainer left, they talked to their vet again who adamantly insisted that Callie remain restricted to the house. Mark and Elaine chose to follow their veterinarian's advice.

Callie developed into a striking dog. She would eventually reach 70 pounds and the size and shape of a German Shepherd. She was a bit on the timid side, backing away from visitors, and avoiding people and dogs on their walks and in the new group obedience class they joined. At about nine months of age, after being chased by a child trying to catch her off-leash dog, Callie began displaying aggression toward people and dogs. Her aggression toward dogs included growling, lunging, and barking even when a dog was over 200 feet away. The Dowell's were dismayed to discover that their once timid Callie now required expensive and time-consuming behavior modification. How did this happen, they wondered? Didn't they do everything right?

The Conundrum

Many dog owners like the Dowell's struggle to sort out conflicting information they receive from pet care professionals. It is very common for veterinarians to insist that dogs not leave their homes until close to four months of age. From a vet's perspective, this makes eminent sense. They want to avoid exposure to contagious viruses such as distemper and parvo. Vets spend four years (or longer) in vet school focusing on the treatment of medical problems. If they are lucky, they have a semester course on animal behavior. Trainers and behaviorists, on the other hand, want to avoid many of the behavior problems they see in their practices. Their education focuses on understanding the impact of canine critical developmental stages, learning theory, and how to best prepare a dog to meet life's psychological challenges through early training and socialization. With such diametrically opposed perspectives, it is easy to see why dog owners are torn between following their veterinarian's advice and their trainer's advice. Many trainers are reluctant to press their clients to ignore their veterinarian's advice. So, what can trainers do to help dogs get adequate socialization? There are a number of strategies that work.

Working with Veterinarians

First, remember that veterinarians receive very little education about dealing with behavior problems unless they pursue advanced course work and become a board-certified veterinary behaviorist. As a result, they are most concerned with keeping puppies from contracting deadly viruses. They are unlikely to radically change their advice simply because trainers point out potential behavior problems. Instead, they need to be convinced that protecting puppies from exposure to viruses can be accomplished—through careful planning—at the same time as a sound socialization program is implemented. The following strategies focus on starting a dialogue with veterinarians:

1. Letter From a Colleague—Dr. R. K. Anderson, the co-inventor of the Gentle Leader™ head collar, is the author of an open letter to veterinarians about the importance of early socialization. It can be downloaded from the "resources section" of the APDT web site (www.apdt.com), and distributed to your local vets, along with your business card and class schedule.

2. Fact Sheet—Create a one-page Socialization Fact Sheet that outlines the results of the study conducted by Scott & Fuller, as well as citations from more recent books. Veterinarians value strong evidence before changing protocols. Presenting them with solid information from board-certified veterinary behaviorists and applied animal behaviorists may help them consider alternatives to keeping puppies at home during the critical socialization period (i.e., three to twelve weeks of age). In the Socialization Fact Sheet be sure to address how to protect puppies from

high-risk situations (dog parks and other places frequented by unknown dogs), while still providing adequate socialization (puppy parties, controlled access to vaccinated dogs, etc.).

3. In-Service Programs—Offer to provide complimentary "in-service" educational programs for veterinary staff. Many veterinary clinics hold routine educational meetings for their staff. Offer to provide a brief presentation on a variety of subjects, including socialization. Many veterinarians still recommend outdated practices such as the alpha roll correction, "dominance exercises" (forcing a dog to stay on its back until it "submits"), etc. Providing brief educational forums can help them choose to remove this kind of advice from their client education, as well as understand the importance of early socialization.

4. Complimentary or Discounted Training—Invite veterinary staff to group classes, with or without their dogs. This will expose them to the benefits of early socialization and training.

5. Socialization Chart—Provide a one-page document that lists a variety of things puppies should be exposed to (children, adults, dogs, cats, motorcycles, skateboards, etc.). List these on the left side of the page and along the top of the page, running left to right, list the weeks, i.e., seven through twelve weeks (and beyond!). This chart can be handed out to their clients, along with the Socialization Fact Sheet described above.

6. Protocol for Pup's Veterinary Exams—Provide information about how a puppy's first veterinary visits can be made more of a positive experience. Dr. Lore Haug (College Station, Texas) wrote an excellent article on this topic in the APDT Newsletter (May/June 2000). Veterinarians may also contact Dr. Rolan Tripp (La Mirada, California), a veterinarian with a special interest in behavior, for information about how to establish clinic protocols that optimize a puppy's early experiences.

7. Veterinary-Sponsored Puppy Parties—Offer to hold puppy parties/classes at your veterinarian's clinic. This can provide a location that veterinarians are more comfortable with for young puppies, and can also have the beneficial value of providing the veterinarian a "value-added" service for his/her clientele.

Community Outreach
The following strategies focus on public education.

1. Shelter education—Training demonstrations can be offered at many local shelters, giving trainers the opportunity to educate the public, as well as shelter volunteers/ staff, about the importance of early socialization.

2. Public demonstrations/fund raisers—Many trainers are asked to participate in fundraisers for non-profit organizations. This is a great opportunity to provide

live training demonstrations, while also getting out the word about early socialization.

3. Community Forums—Develop a community outreach program that hosts a monthly forum for dog owners. Such a program can be held at varying locations in your community. For example, you can rotate the location from between several veterinary clinics, groomers, doggy day care centers, pet stores, etc. Each forum can focus on a different topic, but would always include getting the word out about early socialization. The Socialization Fact Sheet described above can be used as a handout at such forums. Often, local newspapers will announce your event for free since it is a community service.

4. Affiliations—Contact groomers, doggy daycare centers, pet stores, and other affiliated dog services about providing your Socialization Fact Sheet to their clientele. Most would be happy to provide free information to clients.

Puppy Parties

As a trainer, there are a number of strategies you can implement that will have a direct impact on providing opportunities for early socialization.

1. Puppy Classes and Parties—If you do not offer group classes yourself, find out who does and check them out. Many trainers will take puppies who have received at least one or two vaccinations, and many report that they have never had problems with parvo or distemper in their years of offering these classes. Refer your clients to classes that allow (even encourage!) interaction between puppies. Many classes not only do not allow this, they actively prevent puppies from interacting. As many trainers know, this can lead to fearfulness, frustration, and/or dog-dog aggression over time. Make sure that the trainers who run the class know how to appropriately match puppies for play time, not allowing puppies to bully or be bullied.

2. Puppy Roundups—If there are no good puppy classes in your area, consider creating an e-mail list for your puppy clients so that they can contact each other about getting their puppies together with each other. You can provide protocols to follow and leave it up to your clients to contact each other about getting together. (You may want to include a liability waiver as part of your written protocols.)

3. Controlled Exposure Protocols—Part of the Socialization Fact Sheet described above should include brief examples about how to expose puppies for socialization without risking disease. However, a separate, more detailed one-page document should be developed for your clientele. This handout would reference the scientific support for early socialization, but should also go into step-by-step detail about how to implement a safe socialization program. This would include the do's and don'ts. For example, for people who are very afraid of taking their puppies to public parks or other locations, the protocol can direct them to take a mat, exercise pen, hand cleaner, etc., to different locations and allow people to pet

their puppies after washing their hands and to allow people to bring their dogs up to the pen while the owner provides tasty treats to their pup. It may seem overly conservative to some, but for others, it may give them just the safeguards and peace of mind they need to move forward with a socialization program.

Conclusion

Trainers have a challenging occupation. We delight when we get calls from owners when their puppies are a few weeks old instead of several months or years old and have developed learned behaviors that are difficult to undo. How frustrating it is, then, to get to owners and puppies early only to find that others have told them not to start early socialization. Fortunately for the Dowell's, they worked with a competent trainer who helped them implement a desensitization/counterconditioning program to overcome Callie's fears. Now at age three, Callie, for the most part, can be trusted not to lunge on leash and even plays with some dogs off leash. The Dowell's learned the value of early socialization the hard way. By implementing a broad-based educational program as outlined above, trainers can help change the tide and ensure that puppies have a strong foundation that will serve them for life. ❖

This article was the 1st Place Essay Winner in the 2003 John Fisher Scholarship competition.

Whelping and Weaning:
Thoughts On An Ancient Process

Jodi Binstead, March/April 2003

My current relationship with dogs began about eighteen years ago. Of course, my family had dogs throughout my adolescent years, but I cannot really say I had a relationship with these animals. They were just there. It was not until I acquired my first dog as an adult that the dance really began. I soon became hooked on learning and teaching dogs as much as I could.

I learned to train dogs using punishment-based methods, and then twelve years ago I discovered the wonderful power of positive-based training. About that same time I began my search for the Jack Russell Terriers that would be the foundation of my breeding program. While researching the breed, I discovered that they came with a reputation for being "independent, naturally aggressive, cat killers, and not good with children." With my introduction to Chris Bach and her "The Third Way" training method came the knowledge that these characterizations were myths.

The JRT temperament I was looking for I found in England! What I did not realize at the time was that it was not just genetics that produced great temperaments. The dynamics of how these puppies were raised from birth to the time they went to their new homes had a major impact on their ability to interact with humans and other animals. This became even more apparent after I was asked to raise my last litter in a different manner than I had with previous litters.

Bach has a theory that breeder interference, while well intentioned, is actually creating many of the problems that instructors see in their classes every day. In both puppies and adult dogs, trainers see dogs who have no knowledge of self-imposed self-control, little or no bite inhibition, very poor dog-to-dog social skills, an inability to accurately read other dogs' signals and body language, and little regard for personal space, theirs or ours.

It is common practice for breeders to remove the bitch from the litter at about 4 weeks, allowing limited access to the puppies. In some cases the bitch is removed permanently once solid food is introduced. The belief is that most social behaviors are learned from littermates. As a result of this belief, breeders generally keep a litter together until they are eight to twelve weeks old, in the hopes that this will give the puppies the opportunity to learn bite inhibition and social skills from each other. I now believe that littermates are not necessarily the best or only instructors.

In my past litters there always came a time when the puppies would begin to nip at my chin, bite my fingers, grab and hold onto an earlobe, and use pant legs as a tug-of-war toy. In general they used their mouths inappropriately. They would approach any dog as if that dog were their long lost buddy, never looking for the signs that they were welcome; they just assumed they were. These puppies had to be taught self-imposed self-control. In other words, they had to be taught that there are times when things are not available to them and that they should go on to something else.

Bach's theory is that by not allowing the mother to wean the litter on her own we have effectively removed the puppies' opportunity to learn many of the skills necessary to live harmoniously with their new human families. Her theory maintains that by allowing the bitch to wean the puppies naturally the puppies learn these crucial skills from her. I agreed to raise my last litter in this manner and document any differences I observed between this litter and the past fifteen litters I raised. My only regret is that I will not be having any more litters in the near future to continue the observations. Here is what I found!

The Differences!!

I have always been very involved with my litters. They are raised in the family room and kitchen, in the midst of the household. They are handled, held, and cuddled from the day they are born. The prospective families are encouraged to visit right from the start as I feel that the puppies need to be exposed to many different smells and touches, even before their eyes and ears are functioning. Visitors are encouraged from the beginning.

With past litters, once the puppies began to experiment with solid food I would begin to separate the bitch from the litter for varying periods of time, lengthening the time as the pups aged, and eventually separating them permanently so that the bitch's milk would dry up. This usually began at about 4 weeks. The one constant I observed when I returned the bitch after any separation regardless of whether it was for a couple of hours or over night, was that the response was always the same—the puppies mobbed the bitch! I also fed the bitch and the puppies separately.

With this litter the bitch had constant access to the puppies, I adapted the whelping box so that she was able get in and out, but the puppies could not. Self-preservation on my part! While it might be even more advantageous to integrate the puppies into the whole household, I do have a husband that I want to keep! While she often took advantage of the opportunity to leave the puppies to go outside or to socialize with the family, she still spent the majority of her time in the box with the puppies, often sleeping on one side while the puppies slept on the other. This continued until the last puppy went home. I would also have the puppies out in the fenced yard with the bitch as much as possible.

Solid food was also provided when the family was together. The bitch was fed right along with the puppies. I made sure that there was dry kibble available at all times. In the beginning I fed kibble soaked in warm water, making sure that there was enough for both the bitch and the puppies.

If I had a puppy that tended to be pushy and hog all the food I would separate that puppy out and feed the puppy with just the bitch, as she tended to not allow this type of behavior. I continue to do this until the puppy is no longer exhibiting these behaviors. This is the only time I would interfere with the feeding routine.

The first difference I observed was that there were many times when the puppies would wish to nurse and the bitch would tell them that she was not available to them. She used the minimum amount of negative feedback necessary to deter the puppy. Some puppies were very sensitive and others were a little more persistent. As a result the puppies were not only learning self-imposed self-control, they were also learning how to approach the bitch and how to read her signals indicating when she was available and when she was not. After the first few attempts the puppies became extremely adept at reading even the subtlest signals from the bitch. Sometimes I was unaware of the signal the bitch gave that turned the puppy away. As they aged and their teeth became sharper and more damaging, the bitch would inform the puppy of what was too harsh, therefore teaching the puppy bite inhibition. I noticed that mouthing was generally not allowed and the puppies were informed that pulling on ears and biting back legs was not a good idea. I also observed that they were gentler with their littermates as well. The bitch continued to play with the puppies regularly, but she set the rules.

We, as humans, make poor dogs. Attempts to replicate how the bitch teaches the puppies are generally inadequate. Our timing is poor and our emotions get in the way. Leaving this task to the bitch makes our job as teachers much easier as a professional has already laid the ground rules!

In regards to human interaction, I found these puppies to be vastly different from past litters. They did not mouth as much as previous litters. They tended to be more patient and more able to focus their attention and relinquish unavailable resources. In other words, they understood self-imposed self-control.

The most dramatic difference was when the puppies were introduced to the other adult dogs in my family and subsequently other new dogs. These puppies were much more educated in how to approach a strange dog. Rather than just running up to the dog and assuming that their attention was wanted, the puppy would approach the dog, accurately read that particular dog and react accordingly. Depending on the signals given, the puppy would respond by turning away and looking for facilitation elsewhere or continue to approach and interact with the strange dog.

One trait that seemed common among previous litters was a phase where, when you picked the puppies up, especially while they were busy doing something else, they would protest, usually with a growl. I did not have a single situation where this occurred with this litter.

Once the puppy was placed with the new family the differences continued to become apparent. This was the first litter where I did not have at least one new owner calling with a problem involving mouthing, clothes grabbing, or excessive chewing. I have been able to follow this litter and can still observe the results of this experiment. They have retained the social skills in regards to their interaction with strange dogs. They are wonderful with other puppies and boisterous adolescents, not overly tolerant or overly intolerant—what I would describe as being fair.

I also came to the realization that this particular bitch, Hattie, had been raised in a similar fashion. She was whelped on an English sheep farm where they hold the National Sheepdog trials every year and their JRTs are raised for vermin control. Hattie's great-grandmother was 22 years old when we purchased Hattie. All the dogs lived together sharing resources. That is not to say they were not socialized, they were—by the family, the farm hands, and the neighbor children, as well as the other dogs and animals on the farm. I finally figured out why a friend had dubbed Hattie as the Jack Russell "antichrist." In his words, "she was way too sweet to be a Jack Russell." She has all the traits that this last litter of puppies has, and I have to attribute much of that to the fact that the breeder allowed the mother to do her job and raise the puppies with support, not interference!

There are other breeders who are conducting this same experiment with a variety of breeds. It is my hope that I can bring you further evidence that refraining from interfering in this ancient and natural process can have a profound effect on the puppies we produce.

Not every bitch will have these abilities and it is up to us to choose the bitches that are good nurturers. Eliminating bitches that do not exhibit these qualities from a breeding program can only improve that breeding program. By passing down, generation to generation, the ability to effectively raise puppies, I believe that we will be able to place puppies in their new homes with many of the important social skills and self-control traits already in place. These traits will make the transition into the human family a little smoother for both the new owners and the puppy.

If anyone is interested in raising a litter in this manner I would be happy to help you in anyway that I can. If you would be willing to provide written documentation of your observations I would be very grateful. ❖

This article was an Essay Winner in the 2002 John Fisher Scholarship competition.

Puppy Temperament Testing

Karen Overall, July/August 2000

Everywhere I travel in the worldwide veterinary community, veterinarians want me to talk about temperament testing and how best to use it. My answer—based on the data and on the appalling logic that implies that our dogs should be more reliable and predictable than we are—is almost always, "Don't."

The behavior of no social species is deterministic. Nothing is predetermined by breed, etched in stone by lineage, or totally open to manipulation by the physical and social environment. The latter invokes the tabulae rasae myth: If you start with the best material and do everything "correctly," you will have a perfect, predictable dog. Such myths subject dogs to extraordinarily cruel expectations and conditions while compelling their people to feel only grief and guilt.

Components of Temperament Testing

The temperament (or aptitude) test usually includes two segments:

1. Personality aspects—such as social attraction, following, restraint, social dominance, and elevation dominance

2. Responses associated with successful performance in obedience trials—such as retrieving, touch sensitivity, sound sensitivity, chase instinct, stability, and energy level.

Each category is evaluated on an ordinal scale, but there are no consistent, operational definitions that remove personal bias from the evaluations. These terms are not defined in a meaningful and unambiguous manner that would allow an observer to monitor changes in actual behaviors.

Testing Suitability for Specific Tasks

The paradigm in temperament tests is one of suitability versus unsuitability with respect to a specific task or function. Although breeders who use these tests are often pleased with them in regard to matching puppies to owners, and somewhat pleased with them regarding accurate predictions of temperament, no objective data has been collected a priori to test the validity of a posteriori claims.

There are some general problems with this approach:

- Because such tests are correlational, they provide no insight into factors that "cause" the behavior.

- Since the tests are conducted at seven weeks of age, there is a large potential role for environment to play in the dog's adult temperament.

- The tests evaluate the dog at one static period of life.

Summary of Studies

Behavioral medicine has often been perceived as a soft, non-scientific discipline because conclusions have been based on impressions rather than on quantification of repeatable, reliable, specific behaviors that allow observers to draw and test their conclusions. It is exactly this criticism that invalidates temperament testing as done to date.

Many studies have examined the results of an early, invariant temperament test and its ability to predict later behavior.

R. Beaudet and his colleagues looked at puppy behaviors at seven weeks and again at 16 weeks. Despite this short interval of time, they failed to find any association that would allow them to predict social tendencies at 16 weeks of age for any individual of the five breeds tested at seven weeks of age.

In one of the first and best studies of the utility of temperament tests to predict adult behavior, Margaret Young found no correlation between the results of the test performed on over 400 puppies at seven weeks of age and the adult behaviors of the dogs when they were socially mature two to four years later.

Erik Wilsson evaluated 1,235 eight week old German Shepherds at the Swedish Dog Training Center. When these dogs were re-evaluated at 64 to 71 weeks, only three of nine characteristics evaluated as adults statistically correlated to behavioral scores as pups, and—this is important—the correlational finding is no different than would be expected given a random association. Wilsson's conclusion was that puppy performance on the test did not predict any aspect of adult behavior.

Testing and Service Dogs

Wilsson also tested for "mechanism" by evaluating true genetic heritability and genetic maternal effects on offspring behavior. His findings should give pause to anyone breeding and evaluating service dogs: Individual variation in behavior among puppies could be explained by both heritability and common litter environment effects, but individual pups were more variable than could be explained by litter environment, and litters were more variable than could be explained by heritabilities and dam or sire effects.

For those who believe that dogs are tabulae rasae, this is a terrible blow. For those who believe that behavior is not deterministic and that dogs undergo profound neurochemical changes at social maturity, this finding is logical and expected. When service organizations tell me that they can reliably predict which puppies will succeed by the time the pup is 18 months of age, I am neither surprised nor impressed...but it does make me wonder, given the clear lack of success with mapping future performance on early evaluations, why anyone persists in this approach.

(continued)

Limitations of Testing

No questionnaires or puppy tests can hope to ascertain any predictability for future behavior unless these tools can map the trajectories of the behavior in a manner that allows us to understand the times of greatest change while suggesting factors that cause this change. If these factors are intrinsic—like neurochemistry and neuronal plasticity—any indirect assessment we make only suggests an area that we should further explore.

Designing a New Evaluation

This discussion does not mean that we are cast hopelessly adrift in evaluation and breeding programs in which most animals fail (75 percent of the dogs in Wilsson's study failed for any type of service work, a statistic not dramatically different from U.S. service organizations). First, before we say there is no way to predict who fails in service work, we should design an evaluation that examines specific behaviors rather than our interpretations and judgments of them. This evaluation must be administered using a repeated-measures design monthly or bimonthly so that we can learn when behaviors change. We can then look at physiological and neurochemical correlates of these changes in the hope of understanding which ones are receptive to molding to the types of tasks we want the dog to do.

After all, we don't care if the dog is normal, abnormal, or something we cannot define. We care that he or she can do the job well and reliably in a manner consistent with humane and caring guardianship of the dog. The latter criterion is important especially when applied to service dogs, who are now called upon to perform tasks for an ever more diverse set of humans and their needs.

The outcome of testing suggests that we should consider using shelter dogs for service dog training. If 75 to 80 percent of purpose-bred dogs fail at social maturity, all we need to beat the current paradigm is to have 30 out of every 100 two to four year old shelter dogs chosen for task work succeed or show aptitude for success. The fiscal savings are nothing short of dramatic.

Benefits of Temperament Testing

For pet owners, fanciers, breeders, and human canine companions, the primary benefits of testing temperament should be:

- anticipation of training problems.

- early recognition of problem behaviors.

- anticipation and understanding of behaviors as they change.

Understanding alone often modulates problems. There are serious concerns for the average pet owner or guardian who wishes to use any temperament test to predict the type of pet that a dog will become. However, if the individual wishes to understand how his or her dog is changing and how to best meet the dog's needs, a judgment-free evaluation repeated at frequent intervals could be the best early warning system that the dog needs help.

We put a lot of time into expectations of breed, genetics, and early exposure. Maybe some of that time could be more profitably spent learning if those criteria matter to the dog. ❖

Learning Theory

There is probably no field in which the dog training profession has progressed as much in recent years as that of understanding learning theory. Concepts like operant conditioning, negative and positive punishment, and latency were largely foreign to the dog trainers of ten years ago. APDT has been at the forefront in creating an environment and forum in which dog trainers can be exposed to the latest thinking in the field and learn how animals behave, how they learn, and the most effective ways to modify behavior. This section begins with several essays on learning theory by Marian and Bob Bailey who have served as mentors to an entire generation of dog trainers. Then there is a series of articles on clicker training following by information on how research concerning learning and behavior should be structured, conducted, and evaluated.

The Science of Animal Training

Marian Breland Bailey and

Robert E. Bailey, November/December 2001

Yes, Virginia, there is a science behind modern animal training. It's called operant conditioning (OC)—more precisely referred to as behavior analysis—and includes a method of behavior modification and therapy based on laboratory science.

Scientists who study behavior have been undertaking extensive science-based research and gathering volumes of data on behavior analysis since the early 1930s.

Although B.F. Skinner is the acknowledged originator of operant conditioning, the roots of this science go back to the turn of the century. Early researchers such as Edward Thorndike, Ivan Pavlov, and John Broadus Watson contributed to the evolution of our present-day understanding and application of behavior analysis.

From Thorndike to Skinner (1900 to 1940)

The experiments of psychologist Edward Thorndike addressed the mechanical problem-solving ability of cats and dogs and whether or not animals could learn through imitation, trial and error, or observation. By 1910 Thorndike had developed a law of psychology—the law of effect—that attempted to explain behavior in terms of stimulus response and satisfaction/discomfort associations. The law of effect stated that behaviors that lead to satisfying outcomes were more likely to be repeated, while behaviors that lead to undesired outcomes were less likely to be repeated. Psychology professor and researcher John Broadus Watson basically bypassed Thorndike's law of effect. Instead, Watson seized the Russians' (Pavlov and Bekhterev) work on the classical conditioning paradigm as the scientific cornerstone of his "behaviorism." (We are most familiar with classical conditioning as the type of learning made famous by Ivan Pavlov's stimulus-response (S-R) experiments with dogs.) With the 1919 publication of his major book, *Psychology from the Standpoint of a Behaviorist*, Watson became the founder of the American school of behaviorism.

During the 1920s, Watson became more involved with practical applications of psychology (in advertising and marketing) and did not extend his early work on behaviorism. However, the "behavioral genie" was out of its bottle and, during the 1930s, others pursued animal behavior and its consequences.

Chief among psychologists studying animal behavior at this time were the neobehaviorists, the "new" behaviorists, who adopted Watson's main principles of objectivity and the study of overt behavior while developing their own variations on Watson's theme. Most also tried to adapt Watson's model of classical or Pavlovian conditioning to the more important, everyday behavior of animals and humans.

While B.F. Skinner has become the most famous and influential of the neobehaviorists, others developed a following. Tolman, Hull, and others also studied animal behavior. For a number of reasons, behaviorism, led by the neobehaviorists, gained strength through the 1930s and 1940s, perhaps paralleling the general rise of science, and became the dominant "system" of psychology. Skinner's view was finally to prevail because he put aside the Pavlovian paradigm as the center of his system, developing his own scientific description of how behavior changes. His system also worked in the real world, a significant contrast to most other "psychologies" of the time.

The point of all of this is that behaviorism, and the neobehaviorists' view of behavior, is not monolithic. Operant conditioning, which we are discussing here, is not the only behavioral psychology. Behaviorism, and mostly Skinner's version—operant conditioning—dominated psychology until the 1970s and 1980s. In the 1980s, the so-called "cognitive revolution" began to color psychologists' thinking and teaching, but not their practical achievements. Today, practical applications of so-called "cognitive psychology" look suspiciously like operant conditioning with different wrappings.

In 1938 B.F. Skinner published *The Behavior of Organisms: An Experimental Analysis of Behavior*, arguably the most influential work of the century on animal behavior.

Skinner's approach focused on everyday behavior instead of involuntary physiological reflexes. Thus, he moved away dramatically from the behaviorism models of John Watson and Ivan Pavlov that had emphasized the psychology of stimulus-response, and embraced the theory of natural selection of successful responses through their consequences to humans and other species. This fact should be noted by those who dismiss OC as merely stimulus-response or as a simple extension of respondent conditioning.

Operant Conditioning According To Skinner

Let's take a look at the original basic principles of operant conditioning as laid out by Skinner's landmark book, *The Behavior of Organisms*.

Operant conditioning concerns the changing of motor actions and action patterns. These are fancy names for things that we do in our normal working day—our so-called voluntary movements. Keep in mind that this focus on voluntary movements is a big switch from earlier research that focused on involuntary physiological reflexes.

Skinner shrewdly reasoned that most everyday behavior—such as studying, mowing the lawn, or going shopping or to a movie—does not fit the Pavlovian S-R model.

There is no single, outstanding stimulus to which one can point that elicits, automatically, any of those behaviors. Rather, the responses that make up our everyday behavior grow stronger and survive as the result of our operation on the environment—hence, the designation "operant" for these responses. In other words, reflexes may allow us to control our blood pressure automatically, but learning operant behaviors allows us to cope with our surroundings.

Behavioral Consequences

Skinner recognized that an operant behavior could have three possible consequences:

- good (reinforcing)
- bad (aversive)
- neutral, or none (extinction)

This analysis of potential consequences is one of the beauties of operant conditioning, offering a simplicity and clarity available in no other behavioral methodology. Things can get better, get worse, or stay the same—all depending on the circumstances.

According to Skinner, behavioral consequences are measured by the rate of response; that is, how often a response occurs per unit of time. Skinner said that a reinforcer is any object or activity that causes a response to increase in strength (rate or probability of response). In other words, the occurrence of reinforced behavior increases (or sometimes maintains its rate), while the occurrence of non-reinforced behavior decreases.

Reducing Behavior

There are two ways of reducing behavior: ignoring it and punishing it. If a behavior is not reinforced in any way, it will decrease in frequency. Thus, if nothing occurs inside or outside the animal that reinforces a behavior, the probability is that the behavior will reduce in strength or happen less often. The process of reducing behavior due to lack of reinforcement is called extinction.

Applying an aversive stimulus (punishment) when administered by a human or another animal will also decrease behavior. Actually, the very definition of whether a stimulus is aversive or punishing rests on the decline of behavior. If applying the stimulus results in the decline of a behavior, that stimulus is classed as an aversive, or a punisher. It is also true that if a stimulus increases the rate of behavior, that stimulus is a reinforcer. Thus, the nature of a stimulus, reinforcing or aversive, is defined by the behavior of the animal and not by a decision of the trainer.

OC Is Simple

Are you grasping the point that OC is made up of simple concepts, practices, or principles? You might argue, "It can't be that simple." But it is. By combining these practices and some others, you can increase or decrease most behavior and selectively shape just about any behavior possible for a given animal. Operant conditioning is a science that has given us the tools to study and predict behavior and, ultimately, to influence, if not completely control, a given behavior.

Applied behavior analysis is not exactly synonymous with applied operant conditioning, anymore than behavior analysis is not exactly the same as operant conditioning.

Operant conditioning, as a science or as a technology, is the study, prediction, and control of operant behavior. Respondent conditioning has to do with respondent (largely reflex) behaviors, not operant behaviors. Behavior analysis includes both operant and respondent behaviors and their interactions. We, the Baileys, view behavior as more or less a continuum between what has been thought by many to be totally separate camps, operant and respondent. For this discussion, however, we do not wish to split hairs and will accept OC as synonymous with behavior analysis.

When we teach animal trainers, our position is that OC is "simple but not easy." The animal decides what is reinforcing and what is punishing. Not all reinforcers are under the direct control of the trainer (there are internal as well as external events leading to reinforcement). The animal decides the meaning of cues. The animal is always right.

The trainer's challenge is to observe the animal, communicate with the animal, and respond to the animal. Yet, all the while, the trainer must be in substantial control of the animal's behavior in order to ply his or her craft. This is the reason for our "simple but not easy" view of OC, and probably why many find OC difficult to apply.

OC Is Not a Theory

Many people believe that operant conditioning is just a theory. It is not. Operant conditioning is a naturalistic, scientific description of how animal behavior changes—in other words, how animals learn.

Skinner's book, *The Behavior of Organisms*, contains his observations of how rat behavior changes as circumstances change. Some of his later books were elaborations or extensions of the same observations. Skinner did not postulate or speculate on the reasons or mechanisms of such changes. As a personal aside, in our private conversations with Skinner, he did not hold theorizing in high regard, rather preferring the gathering and analysis of data.

As a science, OC is objective and open to the world, and it emphasizes quantitative data, replications, verification, and follow-up. As a technology, it is a powerful tool for changing behavior. On a personal level, we earned our livings using it for almost half a century. ❖

The ABCs of Behavior

Marian Breland Bailey and Robert E. Bailey,

November/December 2001

The "ABCs of Behavior"—meaning the antecedents, behavior, and consequences—is a shorthand expression used by behavior analysts since the 1960s. Before behavior analysts, or trainers, begin to build a new behavior or change an existing one, they carefully examine the content of each of these elements. This helps to determine what may be causing a behavior, as well as how to change it.

A Is For Antecedent

"Antecedent" refers to anything that precedes the occurrence of the behavior. In the dog training world, we are most familiar with antecedents that are stimuli—such as an odor, a high-pitched sound, or a trainer's verbal cue—in short, any change in physical energy that the dog can perceive or react to. Stimuli present themselves to the dog in different forms. Let's talk about two of those forms: background/context stimuli and salient stimuli.

Background/Context Stimuli

This form is the entire array of stimuli—the context—that greets the dog as he encounters a situation in which behavior is going to occur. These stimuli might include sounds, odors, and visual cues, or any combination of vision, hearing, touch, temperature change, pain, head movement, and balance. It includes the trainer and any other individuals present, and their movements. Of this total array of stimuli, most may be totally irrelevant or meaningless to the dog at a given time. In some situations, however, the dog may react to one or more important stimuli, which we call the salient stimuli.

Salient Stimuli

The word "salient" means outstanding or prominent. Stimuli can become salient in one of two ways:

- Natural salience: where the dog comes with a genetic tendency to pay special attention to certain stimuli (e.g., a German Shorthaired Pointer being stimulated by the rustling of a pheasant in a field).

- Learned or conditioned salience: where the dog is exposed to a stimulus that is paired with primary or strong secondary reinforcers or aversives (e.g., the sound of a kitchen can opener that precedes the dog's meal, the word "No!" shouted by an owner as his dog moves toward a ham sandwich on the kitchen counter).

Regardless of how stimuli acquire their salience, they can become the most important variable in a training scenario. For shaping or modifying a behavior, the trainer should have control over these salient stimuli. If a stimulus in the whole array of background stimuli is more salient than those being presented by the trainer, that trainer is in trouble because she is losing stimulus control over her animal.

For example, a trainer may discover to her chagrin that an incidental arm movement causes the dog to emit a response prematurely. In behavior analysis parlance, that arm movement is a context stimulus; however, it is more commonly referred to by trainers as a "secondary cue." Context stimuli are always present, so trainers should take precautions to stand or sit very still and supply no extraneous stimuli while training.

Previous Conditioning History

Another important antecedent of behavior is the dog's history. If you have raised a pet yourself, you more or less know what has happened to him in the past. But quite a different situation occurs when the dog has spent time in a pound, an animal shelter, or an abusive home. If you give a cue or command to sit and the dog responds, you can probably assume that this behavior was part of the dog's previous training history. Likewise, if the dog is fearful of specific objects such as sticks or walking canes, there is a good chance that the dog has encountered these objects in an unpleasant framework.

The more you know about the dog you are training, the greater your advantage in determining how to change behavior.

Establishing Operations

Yet another form of antecedent is an "establishing operation," also known as a "setting factor." The general definition of an establishing operation is a condition that changes the value of a reinforcer and, thus, increases the likelihood that certain responses will increase or decrease. For example, if a dog deprived of food becomes more hungry than usual, the value of the food will increase; the dog will perform behaviors that have resulted in food in the past. The dog also will work harder to get the food.

Other establishing operations may include availability of water, changes in climate, hormonal changes, and various health conditions (e.g., a dog with digestive tract problems might typically show no interest in food).

B Is For Behavior

When we talk about a dog's behavior that occurs in response to antecedents, we're referring to the behavior's function—what the behavior does for the dog or, in other words, the consequence of the behavior. We are also talking about all the responses and sub-responses that take place in the instance of behavior occurring.

For example, a dog trainer may have a problem with his dog not being able to clear a high hurdle. The trainer may analyze a behavior called, perhaps, "hurdle jumping." Clearly, such a behavior consists of a number of responses such as getting into the starting position, running toward the hurdle, gathering limbs into the jumping mode, springing over the hurdle, and landing.

The trainer's goal is to evaluate each response individually and try to identify a specific sub-response that's causing the problem. For example, he may videotape the jump and notice that one of the dog's legs is poorly angled for best propulsion of the body into the leap. In that case, he can use shaping techniques to work the leg into the proper position.

Regardless of the complexity of the behavior, analysis of the responses and sub-responses allows the trainer to plan the training periods and sessions. Planning of this sort can give the trainer a huge advantage over a haphazard trainer who may approach the problem with no analysis and no plan.

C Is For Consequences

As we mentioned in the "Science of Dog Training" article, an operant can have any one of three consequences:

1. reinforcement

2. aversives (punishment)

3. extinction

Reinforcement

Reinforcement, which can be either positive or negative, is the process of strengthening the operant that produces a desired consequence. The reinforcer can be the natural result of the dog's behavior in its everyday environment, or perhaps a treat given by a trainer for a properly executed response.

Positive reinforcement involves the presentation of a good consequence when the response is performed (e.g., you say "Come," the dog comes, and you offer a treat). It increases the likelihood that the behavior will occur in the future.

Negative reinforcement involves the removal of a bad consequence when the response is performed. Many dog trainers are familiar with the ear pinch used in a forced retrieve to compel a dog to take the dumbbell in his mouth; this is the use of negative reinforcement. When the dog takes the dumbbell, the ear pinch is stopped. As with positive reinforcement, negative reinforcement increases the future likelihood of the behavior that removes or avoids the aversive.

Aversives (Punishment)

Not all operants are so fortunate as to be followed by reinforcers that strengthen responses. One type of consequence—an aversive—not only weakens the behavior it follows, but can actually deal it a deathblow to the extent that the behavior may never reappear.

There are two categories of aversives: primary and secondary. Primary aversives, like primary reinforcers, have their roots in natural substances or occurrences (e.g., an event that causes tissue damage or an intolerable odor). Secondary aversives, like secondary reinforcers, become what they are by association with the "real thing" (e.g., the word "No!" paired with a slap).

Aversives in general, and punishment in particular, may have bad consequences for the dog and trainer. They can produce uncontrollable fear, not only of the trainer, but the entire training situation. Aversives can suppress virtually all behavior. They may also encourage aggressive responses. More acceptable alternatives, such as reinforcement, should always be considered before using aversives.

Extinction

Extinction refers to the gradual weakening of a previously reinforced response when it is no longer reinforced. This represents the surest, most permanent, and most humane way of eliminating a behavior. For example, a dog kept in a yard discovers that by pushing on a certain board near the gatepost, he can make the gate open. On several occasions the dog gets out this way and enjoys romping through the neighborhood. Finally, the dog owner fastens the board so that the dog can no longer open the gate with a push. The dog keeps pushing unsuccessfully at this board, time after time, until gradually the response of pushing disappears.

When using extinction to eliminate an undesired behavior, it is important to train a substitute behavior. Teaching a dog to sit instead of jump up on visitors is a good example.

Two things may happen in the course of extinction that sometimes discourage trainers who are trying to use this method to get rid of a problem behavior. The first of these is the "extinction burst," a sudden occurrence of several rapid emissions of the response in question. For example, the dog who has almost given up pushing the board may suddenly emit several quick pushes. This extinction burst can occur any time during the extinction process. In fact, such a burst often occurs at the beginning of an extinction period (or training session). Many novice trainers observe the burst and then conclude, erroneously, "See, extinction does not work. The response has become more frequent and faster."

The second thing that may happen is "spontaneous recovery." After an initial extinction session, the response may appear to be completely gone. A period of time later—a few hours, overnight, perhaps longer—the dog again offers the response in a training session.

Neither extinction bursts nor spontaneous recovery are incidences of the dog testing the trainer or being stubborn. Rather, each is a normal phenomenon that occurs in the process of changing behavior.

Extinction often encourages variability of behavior, allowing new responses to appear and receive reinforcement. Many experienced trainers take advantage of this phenomenon. For example, a trainer who wants to increase the energy a dog puts into a response may be able to "catch" some of the vigorous responses caused by an extinction burst, reinforce them, extinguish the weaker responses, and build to a generally more powerful response that can then be put under stimulus control, (i.e., on cue).

Extinction may occasionally induce a small amount of aggression, but nothing like that which occurs with the use of punishment. Extinction also does not seem to create the fear present in the animal after use of aversives. Hence, it is preferable as a means of weakening or eliminating behavior.

Operant Conditioning Definitions at a Glance:

Operant Conditioning: a naturalistic, scientific description of how animal behavior changes—in other words, how animals learn; an objective science that emphasizes quantitative data, replications, verification, and follow-up.

The ABCs of Behavior: these are the elements of behavior that are analyzed to determine how to best change an animal's behavior.

Antecedent: something that happens before the behavior occurs; the most common of these are stimuli, establishing operations, and previous history.

Establishing operation (EO) or setting factor: an operation or event that changes the value of a reinforcer and increases the strength of all responses pertaining to that reinforcer.

Behavior: anything an animal does.

Consequence: the result of an animal's behavior.

The Fundamental Principles of Operant Conditioning

Trainers who use operant conditioning apply five fundamental principles. Each of these principles listed below describes a process that alone, or in combination with others, provides trainers with essential tools in changing behavior:

Stimulation: a change in physical energy to which an animal can respond or that an animal can perceive with its sensory organs (e.g., vision, touch, hearing).

Reinforcement: the process of strengthening the behavior that produces a desired consequence; can be either positive or negative.

Extinction: the gradual weakening of a previously reinforced response when it is no longer reinforced.

Aversive: a consequence that weakens the behavior it follows; also called punishment when applied by a human (trainer, parent, etc.) or another animal (usually a conspecific, e.g., a mother bear cuffing her cubs).

Generalization: the ability of an animal to learn to respond to a range of stimuli rather to a single stimulus ("stimulus generalization") and the ability to learn to perform a certain behavior or group of behaviors in response to a specific stimulus ("response generalization"). ❖

Operant Conditioning: Dispelling the Myths

Marian Breland Bailey and Robert E. Bailey,

January/February 2002

Myth #1: All trainers are operant trainers because all training is operant conditioning.

If a trainer from time to time accidentally applies an operant conditioning (OC) principle or procedure, that does not make the trainer an operant trainer.

Few traditional trainers purposefully use all the fundamental and derived operant principles. Some traditional trainers who appear to be doing well make extensive, albeit unwitting, use of operant principles, while other less skilled traditional trainers make less use of these procedures. Those who do poorly often violate these principles.

While operant trainers base much of their training chiefly on objective experimental findings, the same is not true of traditional trainers. The traditional manner of teaching the apprentice trainer is to pass on—trick-by-trick, behavior-by-behavior— the secrets of the master trainer. In addition, many of the traditional trainers' methods are based on speculations concerning various dog "private events" and "drives," usually with little or no evidence. Such concepts as "prey drive" may seem to explain much, but in fact they explain little, and such terms mean different things to different people. Where people have agreed what prey drive is, it may serve as shorthand to describe certain behaviors, but it does little to explain behavior. Books on traditional training methods abound, some very old, but these books are simply collections of anecdotes and "how-to-do-its."

Myth #2: Operant conditioning and clicker training are new and untried inventions.

Clicker training is far from new, although it is newly popular with dog and bird trainers. Marian Breland (now Bailey) and her late husband, Keller Breland, were using clickers for animal training back in the early 1940s. (We had to make our own clickers in 1943 because clickers, called "crickets" then, were part of the World War II effort.) Later, Skinner mentioned using a clicker in his article, "How to Train Animals," in Scientific American (1952).

Wherever it came from, the use of the clicker simply creates a secondary reinforcer, one that possesses some unusual advantages. OC principles have been in continual use in the real world (e.g., by our firm, Animal Behavior Enterprises) since 1943. Most of our work used clickers or electric feeders that produced sounds similar in physical characteristics and function.

In the 1980s and 1990s, Karen Pryor popularized what is known as clicker training. The name "clicker training" and the label "clicker trainer" have taken on lives of their own. In the early days, clicker training was essentially a synonym, or perhaps slang, for operant conditioning. That is no longer the case. Karen Pryor now considers clicker training to be more of a subset of OC, where punishment plays little role, if any. Karen Pryor's definition is good enough for us.

Myth #3: Operant conditioning does not allow punishment during training.

We do not claim to be totally positive trainers (TPTs) or clicker trainers, although we tend to lean strongly in this direction. In our combined careers spanning more than 103 years, we have used positive punishment perhaps a dozen times. Properly applied positive reinforcement is so effective, so fast, and produces such well-behaved animals that we use it almost exclusively. We know how to punish effectively when necessary. In the rare event where we used punishment to suppress behavior, only a few applications of a selected aversive were necessary to make unwanted behavior disappear (even in the face of extreme inducements for the animal to emit the formerly punished behavior). We did not need continued or additional correction.

Myth #4 (by traditional trainers): Operant conditioning is "soft" and lacks control.

In spite of its emphasis on positive methods (yet not excluding aversives), behavior analysis, when properly applied, does not present a "soft" training system. Nor do we (or other behavior analysts) believe in permissive child or animal rearing. Children and dogs need limits to be set and standards to achieve. The notion that using positive methods in dog training arose from permissive child-rearing practices puts the cart before the horse. The long spell of excessive, permissive child rearing and education came more from the Freudians and the "progressive" education of the 1920s and 1930s (before Skinner) than from behavior analysts. Almost everyone now deplores this permissive aberration. Operant trainers set standards and limits (their criteria) and reinforce the animal's behavior when it meets those criteria.

Strong, effective stimulus control of behavior has been the rule in our work, but we accomplish this through positive means. Our free-ranging work with dolphins, ravens, pigeons, gulls, cats, and dogs demonstrates this control. We never punished a dolphin (nor a sea lion, whale, cat, gull, raven, or pigeon), nor corrected such an animal with any but positive means. Further, we never lost an open-ocean dolphin to a pod of free-swimming dolphins, a school of tempting fish, or other distractions.

Myth #5 (by clicker trainers): The clicker is forgiving.

The simplicity of OC concepts may be at the heart of some of its problems. Many clicker trainers are fond of saying that the clicker is forgiving, but they fail to finish the sentence by saying clicker training is forgiving if you don't want sharp behavior. You get what you reinforce or what you click, not what you want. Poor reinforcement yields poor behavior. If your clicks are ill timed, then the behavior will not be precise. There is no magic in the clicker.

Myth #6: Behavior analysts believe that animals do not think.

Please note that we have not said a word about the animal's thought processes. Skinner said simply that he did not know, and could not know, what an animal or another person was thinking. There were not then, and there are not now, any reliable ways of objectively measuring an animal's thoughts.

Skinner said he did not need to know what the animal was thinking in order to shape its behavior. Thus, "private events" (that is, thinking) are ignored, not disclaimed. In Skinner's view, and in ours, statements concerning what the animal is thinking are speculation that serves little purpose when attempting to study, teach, or train behavior. This may change as neurology advances.

Myth #7 (by clicker trainers): Ratios are mandatory and should be started early in training.

We have discussed this ratio controversy at great length in other venues, and there are e-mail posts on various archives putting forth our position on the matter. We have used ratios only when it proved essential or convenient to maintain fully developed, high-rate behavior resistant to extinction. Most of the time, we used continuous reinforcement and trained the behavior to fluency. Continuous reinforcement gives the greatest precision and sufficient strength for most purposes. We strongly suggest that ratios not be used until the behavior is fully developed to the trainer's criteria.

Myth #8 (by clicker trainers): Punishment does not work.

Of course it works, and it has done so for traditional trainers for thousands of years. Clicker trainers lose credibility when they make arguments to the contrary. However, the fact that it can work does not mean that it is the only way, or even the best way, to train today. Thousands of years ago, horseback was the fastest mode of travel. The new technology in mass travel is the automobile. The new technology in mass training may be operant conditioning.

Myth #9 (by traditional trainers): Reinforcement does not work.

Of course it works, because it increases the strength of responses. Proper application of reinforcement technology results in very reliable behavior. Efficacy means "cutting the mustard."

Operant trainers pretty much own the fields of marine mammal training, husbandry training in zoos, bird training, and some other exotic animal areas, but traditional dog trainers have claimed that OC can't hack it with dogs. However, OC practitioners are now entering the dog training areas devoted to obedience, agility, service dogs, field dogs, schutzhund, and elsewhere. The next few years will show whether OC practitioners can move beyond the present superficial application of the technology, abandon their myths, and achieve high levels of training complex, advanced behaviors.

Myth #10 (by traditional trainers): Control of an animal is impossible without corrections.

Wrong. OC practitioners have repeatedly demonstrated fine precision control over behavior with positive reinforcement alone. Our accomplishments at Animal Behavior Enterprises should be a testament to the potential power of reinforcement. And we are not alone—many others have successfully used OC.

Myth #11a (by traditional trainers): Many clicker-trained animals are not really well trained.
Myth #11b (by clicker trainers): Many traditionally trained animals are not really well trained.

Sadly, both camps are right, at least to some degree. Successful animal training, regardless of the methodology, demands good mechanical skills and basic knowledge. This requires years of diligent study and practice. Few people are willing to devote their lives in pursuit of such excellence.

As in other unregulated crafts and trades, many practitioners from both schools lack the basic skills needed for their profession. Because there are no generally accepted levels of performance, animal trainers are seldom measured for quality and productivity. Truly skilled practitioners, traditional and OC alike, are the exception rather than the rule. This should not be surprising, since there are relatively few truly professional animal trainers when compared to the total number of trainers in the United States.

Myth #12a (by traditional trainers): Most clicker trainers do not know what they are doing.
Myth #12b (by clicker trainers): Most traditional trainers do not know what they are doing.

Again, they are both right to some degree. Both the traditional camp and the clicker camp neglect the importance of mechanical skills, including precise timing. Few from either camp pursue advanced knowledge of behavior, especially the formal (academic) knowledge necessary to develop a true, widespread, sustainable, and teachable technology. Further, few from either camp use videotapes or coaching schemes to improve their training techniques.

Myth #13a (by clicker trainers): The more clicks (reinforcement), the better.
Myth #13b (by traditional trainers): The more corrections (punishment), the better.

Many traditional trainers believe that more corrections are necessary. Many clicker trainers believe that more clicking and treating are necessary. Indeed, a high rate of contingent positive reinforcement is a requirement for ensuring strong behavior. But to present a reinforcer—a click-treat sequence—for noncontingent (not related to the criteria) behavior accomplishes nothing. To be contingent, a reinforcer must depend on the behavior.

On the other side of the coin, corrections applied for no reason (i.e., noncontingently, randomly) do no good. However, these mythical beliefs can produce a lot of noncontingent correction and noncontingent clicking and treating. One can argue, with considerable supporting evidence, that noncontingent correction can do actual harm to an animal. Noncontingent clicking can result in a fat, not very well-trained animal or, at best, will produce no effects at all.

Myth #14a (by clicker trainers): The secondary reinforcer is just as good a reinforcer as a primary reinforcer.
Myth #14b (by clicker trainers): The secondary reinforcer is impervious to misuse.

In an experienced animal, a secondary reinforcer can be extremely powerful because of its numerous past associations with primary reinforcers. This may lead to the illusion that the clicker or other secondary reinforcer is every bit as powerful as the primary. There are trainers who believe clicking without treating is perfectly okay, that using the clicker as a keep-going signal is perfectly okay, and that using a clicker as an attention-getter to call the animal is also okay.

With the usual lack of precision prevalent with many clicker trainers, most do not realize the growing weakening of behavior that results from such practices. Less-than-ideal use of the clicker may succeed at a lower level in spite of the trainer, rather than because of him or her. In this regard, it is true that clicker training is forgiving.

Conclusion

Our abbreviated remarks in this article are not intended to be a complete technical treatise on operant conditioning or traditional training. We have not presented documentation, citations, or references. Furthermore, both training types support many myths and superstitions that we have not mentioned. Many more may be growing out there. Here, once more, knowledge of the science can spot these for what they are.

We can point out a way to reduce these myths and superstitions. The Internet offers a rapid, easy way for people to present and exchange data and information. This assumes that objective data, rather than casual anecdotes, become the focus of animal trainers everywhere. Trainers will have to learn new skills: quantification, unbiased observation, record keeping, and cautious interpretation. This last one is tough for all of us, but all trainers, regardless of methodology, will profit from such a universal sharing of valid information. ❖

To Click or Not to Click: The Role of the Marker Signal in Shaping Behavior

Lynn Loar, November/December 2000

Among dog trainers and animal behaviorists, we often hear the phrase "clicker training without the clicker." What people mean is that they use positive reinforcement primarily, if not exclusively, and probably use the word "yes" or "good" in place of the click or some other artificial sound to signal approval.

As a result of using language (the "yes") instead of an artificial sound (the "click" of the clicker), progress is slower than it might be for both the animal and the human. The reliance on spoken language, with its lack of precision in pinpointing incremental behavioral gains, not only reduces learning but also represents the trainer's failure to establish true empathy with the learner.

Limitations of Verbal Commands

It is hard for animals to sort out spoken language. Wild animals rarely hear language at all. Domesticated animals hear speech around them all the time, little of it directed at them and less of it intelligible without the expenditure of great effort. Animals' hearing is focused on sounds of predators and prey and on auditory indicators of safety and danger. Recognizing the speech sounds directed at them—and figuring out what the sounds mean—takes considerable work, more than learning the behaviors the commands are intended to trigger.

Verbal commands often create obstacles for people, too. Few people (just three percent of the population) are auditory learners. Children learn enormous repertoires of behaviors before they can produce language. Sequencing and retaining spoken information comes much later in childhood. Children with learning disabilities may have difficulty following verbal directions. People who have had harsh parents or teachers may also respond poorly to instructions given aloud, reacting affectively with recollections of past insults or humiliations rather than focusing on the task at hand.

Thus, while omitting the clicker may be convenient for the trainer who now has a free hand, it makes the dog deal from weakness rather than strength, from confusion rather than clarity. The trainer's behavior/intent may be positive and benign whether clicking or saying "yes," but the dog is clear in the first situation and working at a considerable disadvantage in the second.

The Impact of the Click

The marker signal provides a precise staccato indicator as the desired behavior occurs. Its sound carries clearly and distinctly above the surrounding din of verbiage. The brevity and specificity of communication with the marker signal cannot be equaled conversationally. Moreover, because the sound is extraordinary, it has a significant impact on both the dog and the trainer. Both participants are reinforced by the click: the dog for the act, and the trainer for the well-timed click.

Hearing "yes" or "good," the dog knows he pleased the trainer. Hearing a click, he knows he got the behavior right. Vague praise, while nice, is not as useful for learning as the specific targeting of achievement.

The click stresses the dog's role as the "behaver" rather than the trainer's role as the giver of praise. Thus, the relationship becomes more egalitarian, with both the dog and trainer trying to get the behavior and communication right. The click reinforces the efforts and precision of both participants. The resulting shared experience builds a collegial rapport that transcends age, language, and species.

Timing and Empathy

Perfect timing is required for the efficient shaping of behavior with a marker signal. To achieve perfect timing, the trainer must:

- be totally focused on and attentive to the dog's effort.
- understand the behavior being shaped.
- understand the dog's level of frustration.

A good trainer can anticipate possible misconstructions and streamline shaping so that the dog's energy is directed toward the goal with little effort wasted on irrelevant actions. The ability to anticipate the likely conceptualization of the dog—along with the desire to work swiftly to conserve the dog's energy, buoy his enthusiasm, and encourage learning—represents empathy. Clicking frequently constitutes altruism, as well as guidance.

Better Than Verbal Praise

The click works better than verbal praise for the dog because of the dog's innate auditory limitations and the click's clarity of communication. The click works better for the trainer because of the concentration and precision it requires of the trainer. The click works better for the relationship between the trainer and learner because it reinforces both of them, reduces the power differential, and increases the collaboration and enjoyment of a shared experience.

Clicker training without the clicker compromises achievement. Clicker training with the clicker maximizes learning. ❖

Getting Behavior...With a Click and A Cluck

Bob Bailey and Terry Long, January/February 2003

Using a conditioned reinforcer to get behavior is not new. The science and technology of operant conditioning (OC) began with B. F. Skinner's laboratory experiments in the 1930s. Later, during World War II, Skinner took the technology out of the laboratory and applied it to a U.S. Navy project that involved training pigeons to guide missiles. Two of Skinner's graduate students who assisted with that project became so inspired that they went on to make their living applying OC—with the use of a conditioned reinforcer called a clicker—to animal training.

Keller and Marian Breland (later Bailey) were the first to apply the technology commercially when they founded Animal Behavior Enterprises (ABE) in 1943. Their company went on to train over 150 different species (15,000+ animals) with operant conditioning, using the clicker as the primary training tool. (See "The Science of Animal Training," above.) In the last decade, Karen Pryor, Gary Wilkes, and many others accomplished what the Brelands could not in the 1950s: interest the dog training community in adopting the clicker to train dogs. Since then, many training teachers have been teaching dog trainers how to use the clicker, most using dogs as their primary vehicle for demonstrating and teaching behavioral technology. There is, however, a more efficient and effective method of teaching—and learning—precise training skills.

Chickens as a Training Model

Using chickens to teach trainers the skills required to train a variety of animals is not new, either. ABE first used chickens as a training model in 1947. All of the trainers who worked for ABE learned basic clicker skills by shaping behaviors in a chicken before they "graduated" to training other species.

Animal training, regardless of methodology, is mostly a mechanical skill, involving considerable hand-eye coordination. Operant conditioning and the broader but less well-known behavior analysis are sciences and technologies for studying and changing behavior. Applied operant conditioning and behavior analysis, including what is popularly called clicker training, have both a theoretical base, or fundamental principles, which can be taught in the classroom, and practices or methods (the mechanical skills) that can only be learned by doing, i.e., hands-on experience.

Because the fundamental principles do not change from one animal to another, it is possible to teach the fundamentals using simple animals. Once the fundamentals are mastered with simple animals, it is possible to extend them to the training of more complex animals. Thus, dolphin trainers, primate trainers, dog trainers, horse trainers, parrot trainers, raven trainers, and any other kind of animal trainer, can well profit from training a simpler animal model: a chicken.

Teaching with chickens can dramatically shorten the time it takes to teach the science-based principles and practices of operant conditioning and behavior analysis.

Shaping behavior of chickens can also develop basic mechanical and timing skills needed for efficient training. With chickens, behaviors come and go quickly, and more or less in direct proportion to the skill demonstrated by the trainer. Behaviors happen swiftly because the chicken learns and moves quickly. Days of learning with a dog are compressed into minutes and hours of training a chicken.

Chickens are simple and cautious birds. While chickens may be limited in their range of responses, they are not stupid. Chickens, as a group, have coped with the world for millions of years. Chickens survived by learning what to do and what not to do. As trainers, we simply take advantage of the chicken's power to learn. The chicken's very simplicity makes it an ideal model for teaching students the skills needed to shape behavior. Most higher animals are complicated by many levels of social, investigatory, or play behaviors. Chickens, on the other hand, seem dedicated to eating, avoiding being eaten, and reproducing, with very few diversions. This simplicity is a help when shaping behavior. The student can spend more time shaping behavior, and less time dealing with extraneous behavior patterns.

In addition, chickens are not only simple, they are fast. Though chickens are omnivores, eating both plants and animals, they have the speed and competitiveness of a true predator. It takes a quick and observant trainer to time the clicker correctly to coincide with desired behavior. In short, the ordinary chicken is probably the most ideal behavioral model available for teaching training skills.

Relevance to Dog Training

Many dog trainers express the opinion that training can be taught only by training dogs. Understandably, a dog trainer must eventually train dogs to learn canine peculiarities. However, for teaching the basic principles of operant conditioning and the skills of training, it is far better and faster to work with a simpler subject, where behavior can be shaped and molded depending on a trainer's new-found skills, rather than arising unpredictably from some highly specialized genetic predisposition.

As APDT member Mel Bussey observed of her workshop experience using a chicken, "Upon returning home, I discovered the extent to which my training skills had improved. I was able to split the dogs' behaviors into smaller increments, and be more specific in defining my criteria. And I was much more aware of my rate of reinforcement, allowing me to increase my criteria at the appropriate time.

I also found that my timing had improved tremendously. This resulted in much more accurate and efficient training because my communication with the dogs was much more clear.

"I was also able to apply what I had learned to teaching my human students. Breaking down the students' behaviors into small steps, as the Bailey's had done for us, increased the rate of learning for the human side of the handler-dog teams as well. As their mechanical skills of timing, criteria, and rate of reinforcement improve, their dogs' skills improve as a result."

Studying Behavior of Many Species

Training chickens is less forgiving of a trainer's mistakes than training dogs. Mistakes produce their effects quickly in a chicken. A dog, because of its higher general intelligence, may sooner or later learn what is wanted. Thus, in spite of a trainer's failure to select the proper behavioral criteria and to reinforce at the proper time, a dog will eventually "get it," although perhaps slowly and imperfectly. A chicken, under the same circumstances, would simply appear not to learn, or the behavior would be so slow in coming that it would be painfully obvious that there was a problem in the trainer's technique.

Dog trainers, like ethologists, can learn from studying the behavior of many species. And, in the case of learning the mechanical skills necessary for our craft as trainers, chickens are a likely training model. After all, if we can get a chicken to do an agility course, what next?

Getting behavior is what it is all about, isn't it? ❖

For Those Who Can't Wait...Generalizing Short Latencies the Bailey & Bailey Way

Terry Long, January/February 2004

This article is based on a lecture by renowned animal trainer Bob Bailey at The Bailey & Bailey Chicken Workshop in Hot Springs, Arkansas, in June 2002.

"Sit!" "S-i-i-i-t!" "SIT!" I said, "Sit!!!!" "Good dog! What a nice sit."

Sound familiar? Most dog trainers are all too familiar with students who can't resist giving their dog multiple cues for any given behavior. Many of us are used to solving this double-cueing problem by coaching our students to give a cue once, and only once. Although many students comply, their dog still doesn't sit any faster in response to their cue.

If our real objective is to speed up the dog's response to a cue, it really has little to do with giving a cue once and then rewarding the behavior regardless of how long it takes the dog to do it. What we want, actually, is short latency. Latency is the time between the cue and the animal's response to the cue, and preferably, it is sooner than later. One of the most innovative ways to shorten latency is one that was used routinely by Marian and Bob Bailey and Animal Behavior Enterprises (ABE), their company that trained thousands of animals from over 140 different species. This method relies upon tapping into an animal's ability to generalize and, surprising to many dog trainers, works quite well with dogs.

Starting Fresh

"If you don't demand short latency in the training of new behaviors, you won't get it," said Bob Bailey. "At ABE, short latency was a routine aspect of all of our training of any behavior we taught. All behaviors are now, not later. So when you start to train a new behavior and you get the rudiments of that new behavior and can say that the behavior is 75-80% the way you want it to look, interject latency as a criterion. Don't train all the way to fluency and then try and require short latency," he added.

Often, ABE would be hired to fix a training problem. They would be sent an animal that had been trained well to begin with, but over time had been allowed to develop slow responses to its new trainer's cues. It was in these cases that the Baileys developed their own way of retraining latency using generalization as a key ingredient.

Retraining: Keep it Simple

You start the retraining process by making the decision to set aside two or three days where you do not allow the dog to receive cues or reinforcement for any behaviors other than the one you are going to start with. In some cases this means crating the dog or managing the dog's environment in a way that ensures total control over the dog's interaction with anyone but you in these new training sessions. That means no cues for anything until you have completed the retraining process. "The key part of this is that you are not training anything else," said Bob. "The animal's life is built around this one behavior. You get a very strong response as a result."

"Another reason for not training other behaviors [during this process] is that the dog will learn to discriminate between the behavior you are working on to shorten latency and the other behaviors where you don't demand short latency," Bob noted, explaining, "Why not demand it on all behaviors? Well, consider the rate of reinforcement. You have upped the criteria on everything the animal does, thus likely reducing substantially the rate of reinforcement, possibly causing the animal to decide to not play your silly little game."

The following steps describe the retraining process. Bob advises, "Once you start this, don't wait a week [between training sessions] to do this. Once you start, don't train anything else. Get all current, well-trained behaviors on short latency with this process.

1. Pick a very, very simple behavior—You will start with a behavior that is on cue and is well known to the dog. One that Bob suggested was the "Touch" cue, i.e., the dog touches his nose to your hand or a target stick. (If the dog only knows more complicated behaviors, first take a few days to train three or four simple behaviors such as "Touch," "Sit," "Down," etc.)

2. Establish a reasonable latency—For the "Touch" example, a half a second may be a reasonable response time according to Bob (think "one thous" instead of "one thousand one.") However, the time criterion selected by the trainer should be whatever makes sense to the trainer. As Bob noted, "It is really more a matter of maintaining a high enough rate of reinforcement rather than some arbitrary interval between cue and response. The criterion should be high enough that the animal has enough failure to learn that what it was doing is not right, but not so high that the animal becomes discouraged."

When the dog responds within your established time criterion, click and treat. Counting that time starts when you have given the cue and ends when the dog starts the response. The click happens when the dog's nose touches the target.

3. Too slow, withdraw the opportunity for reinforcement—If the dog doesn't respond within the time you have set as your beginning criterion, withdraw the target and end that trial. Wait two to three seconds and begin a new trial. Don't be tempted to raise you voice or add other secondary cues to prompt the dog.

4. Keep training sessions short but frequent—Train for two to three minutes ten times a day. Remember not to provide any reinforcement for any other behaviors during this process.

5. Tighten your latency criterion—Once the dog is responding within the half-second period of time, raise your expectations to a third of a second or whatever you as a trainer are capable of shortening it to or whatever is reasonable for the simple

behavior you have chosen to work with first. Get this shorter latency as fast as you can. It could take one day, it could take two.

6. Pick another very simple behavior—Before you start another training session, pick another simple behavior. First, start out by cueing your original, simple behavior, e.g., "Touch," and after you have cued and reinforced that behavior with its short latency several times, smoothly interject the cue for your second simple behavior. Very likely, without thinking, the dog will give you the previously slow behavior very quickly. Click, treat, and cue the original "Touch" again, alternating between the two very simple behaviors. Gradually ask for more and more of the second simple behavior and less and less of the original one.

7. Pick two other simple behaviors—You are on the homestretch! Pick two more simple behaviors. You will now alternate between the second and third behavior until the third behavior is being cued the majority of time, and then start to interject the fourth simple behavior until the fourth behavior is being cued the majority of the time.

Generalization of Latency

"This short latency has generalized," explained Bob. "I'm not even going to offer a theoretical explanation about why. I have speculations, but I don't have any reason why it generalizes so well. Some things don't generalize, especially with dogs and some other animals. This generalizes very, very well. It you do it right, it's virtually guaranteed to work."

"What you don't want to do," he continued, "is try to combine training the behavior or changing the shape of a behavior and trying to do this process at the same time. And you want to be sure every behavior I have described is well trained before throwing it into the process. By the time you get to the third or fourth behavior this way, you are going to be absolutely amazed at what happens."

"Virtually all of the behaviors cued are going to start to come very, very fast ... as long as you require it! If you know that you have successfully shortened the latency on these three or four behaviors, now just give another cue, and if you don't get it right away, you give a timeout, withdraw the opportunity, and the animal catches on very quickly [that the new criterion applies to all other cued behavior]."

Latency as a way of life

For those who choose not to wait—or to re-cue—short latencies are something we can get from our own dogs and from our students' dogs. All we have to do is ask for it! ❖

Assessing Behavioral Research

Melissa Bain, March/April 2002

The field of animal behavior is in a constant state of progression due to the multiplying numbers of studies done in this area. With hundreds of research papers, review articles, and books published each year, how do we determine which are worthy of review?

Although most researchers put forth their best efforts, there are some pitfalls in performing research—especially behavioral research. In this article, I will review the basics of scientific research to help guide you in your quest for useful information.

Types of Published Reports

The many types of research and articles in the scientific and lay press fall into three general groups: observational or field studies, case reports, and retrospective and clinical studies.

Observational or field studies. These are studies in which the researcher observes animal behavior to gather information about the particular species or situation. The studies may involve free-living animal behavior, whether in a zoo or in the wild, such as that of wolf pack behavior. Or they may involve observations of household pets.[1]

Case reports. These are articles published in journals outlining a small number of cases (or sometimes just one case). They are reports of observations and/or results of the particular treatment or treatments performed. They bring attention to the problem or question at hand and are easy to draft since they are often related to everyday clinical practice; or, they may be about a situation that is relatively uncommon, with only a few illustrative examples. An example of a case report is the "Behavior Case of the Month," published in the *Journal of the American Veterinary Medical Association.*

A case or case series report is not a proper clinical trial in that there is no hypothesis (or question to be answered by the study), nor is there proper methodology. Case reports provide less information than clinical trials because the client and clinician knew the treatment, introducing the placebo effect.[2]

Unfortunately, many accepted beliefs in dog training and clinical behavior—such as desensitization protocols for treating fear-aggressive dogs—result from case reports. The practices resulting from these beliefs may work for the owners and clinicians (and the dogs improve), but how great is the improvement compared to a control group? Case reports do not help us answer that question.

Retrospective and clinical studies. These studies are the crux of clinical research. While some such studies in behavior are excellent, others are undertaken in a less-than-stringent fashion. So how can you determine which studies are worth your time to review, which ones are designed well, and which ones you can incorporate into your daily work?

As I review scientific articles for this newsletter's "On Behavior" column, I apply the following seven steps as much as possible to provide you with an educated review. You can use these same steps when getting ready to review a research article for yourself.

1. **Interest Level**. Does this study interest you? Can the study results help you grow in your education or career? If the answer is no, then do not spend your time on it.

This is a personal choice on your part. By reading the abstract (the brief overview that precedes a published study), you should have a good idea if you should spend more time reviewing the study.

2. **Clear Hypothesis**. Does the study state an objective or answer a question? This statement of what the researcher is looking (i.e., the question the study should answer) is called the hypothesis. If, for example, the study is on the effectiveness of a medication on separation anxiety, the hypothesis may be that "Medication X will help decrease the symptoms of separation anxiety in the dog." Some studies are not clear in their stated hypothesis and, thus, may not have rigorously defensible results.

3. **Study Population**. What is the study population? Is this population representative of a broader population? This question is important if, for example, you are reading a paper on the stray dog population in India, which may not be comparable to that in the United States because differing religious beliefs may reflect higher esteem for animals.

Another example is hypothetical research done on treatment for aggression in Akitas. Is this research applicable to other breeds, such as the whippet? There may be none, some, or a lot of applicability between the study population and your target population, and you should take this degree of applicability into consideration.

4. **Valid Study Design**. Is the design of the study valid? This is an important area to cover, and also the most confusing.

You will come across four major study designs: prospective placebo-controlled randomized trials, historical database trials, crossover design trials, and retrospective case studies.

The gold standard for trial design is the **prospective placebo-controlled randomized trial**. This type of trial is designed to minimize experimental bias, produce comparable treatment groups, and allow validity of statistical tests—all necessary in conducting sound clinical trials. These studies take the placebo effect into consideration. They are the trials that the Food and Drug Administration often requires for approval of treatment modalities.

There are ethical issues with this design in that some participants are not treated with the potentially "better" treatment, or they may not be treated at all. This issue can be overcome if the control group receives the currently proven and accepted treatment (if available), while the treatment group receives the new treatment. These studies are undertaken primarily in medical trials. (Be aware that it is difficult to have a control group receive a treatment in clinical behavior because there are few scientifically proven and accepted treatments.)

Also, this type of design is difficult to use for rare conditions, such as an uncommon disease in people, because of the limited number of test subjects with the condition.

The **historical database** provides a larger number of participants than the prospective placebo-controlled randomized trial. With the historical database study, the controls are taken from a database of people or animals who previously had been diagnosed with the problem and were either given no treatment or were given another treatment. All participants in the current treatment group are, theoretically, treated equally. However, there is a huge potential for bias in this design because all of the current participants are being treated.

Two other factors should cause us to look closely at the validity of this design. First, there may be a difference in the current patient population compared to the earlier control group. And second, there may be different methods of selecting the patients for the current treatment group compared to the earlier group.

The **crossover design** allows each participant to act as his or her own control. Half of the participants receive treatment A for the first part of the trial, and treatment B for the second part. The other half receives treatment B for the first part of the trial, and then treatment A for the second part. The treatment group is twice as large as if you did a randomized placebo-controlled study, and all participants have the opportunity to be treated. One potential downside of this design is if the treatment effect carries over into the second period of the trial (i.e., if it cures the problem, then theoretically there is no disease to treat). Also, statistically, the crossover study is not as powerful a design as a randomized trial.

A **retrospective study** or **case survey** can have a higher number of participants in both treatment and placebo groups, which is informative for gaining a general knowledge about the treatment's efficacy. For these cases, there is a specific diagnosis of the given problem at hand.

However, specific criteria for which cases are included or excluded may or may not be given. Also, the study is not controlled in that the participants (a) are potentially given slightly different treatments; (b) may be treated by different people; (c) may receive better treatment over time as the investigators become more comfortable with the treatment; and/or (d) are not "blinded" to the treatment. These factors lead to experimental bias on the part of the participant and/or researcher.[3]

5. **Blinding**. Are the participants and/or investigators blinded to the treatment? We wouldn't think this would be necessary when working with animals, but owners interact differently with their pets in all situations—and whether the treatment is medical or behavioral. The placebo effect is evident in a 1999 study[4] where similar percentages of drug-treated and placebo-treated animals improved during the

trial. The animals did not cognitively know they were being treated with drugs (they might have known physiologically, however), but the owners interacted differently with the pets just in the act of giving the treatment.

The three main types of blinding to treatment in trials are unblinded (open) trials, single-blind trials, or double-blind trials. Triple-blind studies are sometimes done in human trials, but there are no studies that I am aware of in clinical animal trials.

Unblinded trials or **single-blind trials** are easier to do than double-blind trials and may more closely reflect actual practice, but there is a huge possibility of bias on the part of the participant and investigator due to a perceived placebo effect. There may also be preconceived notions about the treatment if the subject and/or investigator know what treatment is being given.

The gold standard for blinding in trials is the **double-blind trial**. Neither the participant nor the investigator knows which treatment is being given. There is no possibility for bias on either part, and we are able to detect a placebo effect.[5]

Double-blinded studies are more difficult and expensive to carry out compared to other designs because twice as many animals are needed for the study. Care must be taken so that the investigator, as well as the owner and patient, does not become aware of what treatment is being given. Someone must also be available to decode the treatment groups as necessary, such as in the case of accidental ingestion of a medication by a child.

6. **Sample Size**. Is the sample size large enough to be statistically significant? This question is difficult to answer without a solid grasp of statistics. However, it helps to use common sense. If a grand conclusion is made based on treating two animals, take it with a grain of salt. It may be true, but further research with larger numbers is needed to have a stronger statistical power.

7. **Data Collection**. How was the data collected? Was it collected on a daily basis by the owner or investigator, or was the owner asked to recall the events over the past "x" amount of time of the trial? It is more accurate to have the data recorded on a real-time basis than to ask the owner to recall something that happened four weeks ago.

The seven steps listed above are intended as quick suggestions on how to review a scientific article. For more information, contact your local university and talk with someone in the statistics department. A qualified professional can discuss study design with you, as well as suggest helpful books for you to read. ❖

(References on next page)

References

[1] See, for example, Barry, KJ & Crowell-Davis, SL. (1999). Gender differences in the social behavior of the neutered indoor-only domestic cat. *Appl An Beh Sci.* 64(3); 193-211.

[2] The placebo effect is a perceived or real beneficial effect due to being treated with a placebo (i.e., a positive outcome in both subjective and objective measurements due to non-treatment). A placebo is a control treatment with a similar appearance to the study treatment, but without its specific action or activity; and the study participant, owner, or animal does not know he or she is not receiving the treatment being studied.

[3] See, for example, Hopkins, SG, Schubert, TA, & Hart, BL. (1976). Castration of adult male dogs: effects on roaming, aggression, urine marking, and mounting. *J Am Vet Med Assoc.* 168;1108-1110.

[4] See White, MM, Neilson, JC, Hart, BL, Cliff, KD. (1999). Effects of clomipramine hydrochloride on dominance-related aggression in dogs. *J Am Vet Med Assoc.* 215(9); 1288-1291.

[5] Ibid.

The Structure of Scientific Thought

Karen Overall, November/December 2000

Scientists who worry about medicine always want to know whether the treatment works. Is it effective? Is it better than supportive care or benign neglect? Is a very expensive treatment more efficacious than a less expensive one?

These important questions address two fundamentals of medical care:

1. Providing the best care possible.

2. Understanding the forces that have made the patient ill.

The Physical Model of Care

If a dog's leg is broken because a car hits him, we fix the leg knowing what caused the damage and that our treatment worked. We may not always have had a detailed understanding of how bones heal—at least not until the past quarter century—but we could see the dog get hit by the car, assess the break, and immobilize it. Such physical incarnations of illness allow us to hold the pathology in our hands and assess changes for better or worse.

The Infectious Disease Model of Care

Conditions involving infectious disease do not allow us to hold the culprit in our hands. However, as technology has become better, we can directly see and evaluate pathological organisms and their behaviors. We have the ability to study infectious diseases in a wonderfully logical way that allows us to evaluate what makes a dog ill and whether we can fix the condition.

Lack of Traditional Models in Behavioral Medicine

In veterinary behavioral medicine—where we deal with behavioral and psychiatric conditions, atypical viruses such as HIV, and non-single gene genetic conditions—we have no models like the two discussed above. We must work to develop the creativity and flexibility to understand anything that deviates from the physical and infectious disease models. If we cannot understand the mechanisms that have altered an animal's behavioral responses, how can we understand whether our intervention has worked? This is where adherence to logic and details of the behavior will help.

Deductive Thought

A fundamental distinction in any scientific endeavor is whether your observation is the "same" or "different." You recognize a problem because it is "different," meaning that you have your first clue that something might be ongoing. If, for example, you think a lesion is "different," you then have to decide if it is bigger or smaller, bumpier or smoother.

We may all agree on this assessment with a lesion we can see and touch, but dealing with behavior may be more problematic. When we watch and assess behaviors, we need to be nonjudgmental in our views and words.

Example: Consider a dog with separation anxiety who barks when left alone. Before we start a behavior modification program, we repeatedly tape-record and count the barks per minute when the client departs. After one month of behavior modification, we repeat the tape-recording and ask the question, "Same ... or different?"

We have now taken the assessment of the patient's condition from the realm of opinion and made it science. The dog is still barking, but not as much, so we add drugs and repeat the assessment in another month. Then we again ask, "Same or different?" If it's different, we usually assume that the drugs augmented the behavior modification.

The problem here is that we have actually changed two things—(1) the length of time the dog was treated, and (2) the addition of drugs—and we don't know which is responsible or whether their interaction is responsible.

Comparative Methods and Statistics

We have two ways of learning whether the drugs, the longer period of behavior modification, or some combination of both is responsible for the changes noted in the above example:

1. Use a large number of dogs and repeatedly reassess each dog's individual improvement with behavior modification over time.

2. Use a placebo.

Reassessment

In the first situation, we would compare our original group to one where all factors were the same, except at some point we add medication. Using statistics, we would then ask any number of questions that would allow us to assess "same" or "different," such as:

- Is the rate at which the dogs change their behaviors different among groups?

- Do the numbers of behaviors change among groups?

- Is the endpoint different among groups?

If we have a sufficiently large number of patients—and the number needed will depend on how variable the data are—we will now be able to do some type of analysis of variance that will let us learn the relative effects of drugs versus behavior modification and the effects of their interactions on each other. We will be able to determine if drugs make behavior modification easier to accomplish.

The Use of Placebos

In the second situation, it is difficult to create a behavioral placebo because the absence of specific behavior modification does not mean an absence of behavioral intervention.

For example, the group not assigned behavior modification cannot be considered a true placebo because the client could be beating the dog. The only possible behavioral placebo would detail both specific non-intervention and specific passive intervention strategies and require that the client is wholly reliable in these plans.

The easier situation is a placebo test with drugs where one group gets behavior modification and the other gets behavior modification and drugs. An improvement on this design is to add a double-blind factor: neither the person collecting the data nor the client knows if the dog is taking a drug or a placebo. Regardless, we still must collect specific data or evaluations to allow assessment of differences and then subject the data to statistical analysis. If the data are statistically significant, we know the following:

- The probability of the outcome being due to chance is small.

- The association is "real" rather than "apparent."

- The link occurs with great certainty (generally 95 percent) in a repeatable and non-random manner.

Subjective Impressions

Rating scales for behavioral improvements have been problematic in human psychiatry where the patient can communicate with words. The situation is even more challenging for veterinary behaviorists.

Even though we may tend to dismiss a client's opinion, that opinion could be the gestalt integration of all the parts for which a client does not have words or measurement scales. If we ask, in a repeated measures design, the "same or different" (i.e., "better or worse") question on a five-point scale with the midpoint being "no change," we can elicit information that has been collected in a systematic manner.

What this means is that the client must keep a log of what the animal does. In behavioral medicine, the dog's behavior—and not our interpretations, artificial labels, or categories—are the data. ❖

The Future of Dog Training: Moving Toward More Objective Inquiry

Jean Donaldson, May/June 2003

We have a rich and detailed understanding of the behavior of many parasitic wasp species. And the profusion of minutia on the asexual cloning of bdelloid rotifers is eye-popping. We have an increasingly profound understanding of the neurochemistry of learning and memory and roomfuls of research on genome mapping, embryology, and evolutionary psychology.

By contrast, if one attends a conference on domestic dog behavior, there are few presentations of empirical studies addressing even our most basic questions about our best friend. The research void is mostly filled with a stream of engaging speakers promulgating personal opinions, catchy anecdotes, and untested hypotheses based on their own experience. This free-for-all gives some the mistaken impression that we already have real answers and so may actually slow down the acquisition of harder knowledge.

The field of dog training and behavior is at a crossroads: to enter the domain of the natural sciences or to continue to sequester itself and keep the free-for-all alive. The road toward the natural sciences requires setting a standard for what kinds of theories and information are presented at professional conferences and in professional publications.

Where Dog Training Departs—and Radically—From Science

My overwhelming personal experience tells me that the earth is flat. And, if I presented my case—day to day visual and proprioceptal experience, and any number of other observations I and my friends, colleagues, and neighbors have had—to other people unversed in what science knows about the subject, my contention would align well with their own personal experiences. It could make good sense. It sure looks flat to me. Of course, we would all be dead wrong. And, most importantly, I would not be allowed to present my "findings" at a geological or astronomical conference.

There are actually flat-earth societies, by the way, along with creation-science "texts" and psychic friends networks. All might demand to be heard at geology, biology and psychology conferences, on the grounds of courtesy, freedom of speech, or popularity. However, mainstream science makes no apologies for not entertaining these ideas—they do not meet the standard of evidence. Period. In dog training, however, personal experience and conviction, along with being a sufficiently compelling or entertaining presenter, have been sufficient qualification to present at the annual professional conference or write for its professional publication.

The Pitch

Imagine attending an APDT conference five or ten years from now, in which objective evidence—real scientific research—is presented on questions such as:

1. What training techniques are successful on what types of behavior problems.

2. What human teaching techniques work to reach course objectives in public classes.

3. What are the collateral effects of the use of positive reinforcement and the use of aversives in dog training.

4. What current behaviors or profiles predict future aggressive behavior.

5. What kinds of practitioners— veterinary behaviorists, applied behaviorists or dog trainers— achieve the most success with which specific types of cases.

6. What kinds of educational content most helps prevent relinquishment of dogs for behavior reasons to animal shelters and rescue groups.

You may be thinking, "Hell, I know positive reinforcement works better because I've seen dogs trained with aversives and have been training R+ exclusively myself for 10 years with fantastic results! I used to train with aversives and my results are far better now!"

There is a difference between personal experience and objective research. Intuitions and knowledge based principally on collections of anecdotes may be on the money, partly right, or way, way off the money. The best way so far developed to determine the accuracy of anecdotal (or any other kind of) observation is science. And, interestingly, having spent a lifetime observing, interacting with, reading about, and training dogs can, in certain cases, even make me a less apt experimenter than if I had no strong personal convictions.

If we decide we really want our answers about the behavior and training of dogs on firmer ground, the tools of science are well developed and at the ready. Science provides means for addressing the plethora of factors that can interfere with our getting at answers: blinds, controls, replications, and peer-scrutiny of all ideas put forward and measurements of likelihood that results are due solely to chance.

How Science Does It

The first step is some sort of observation about the world that results in a hunch or question about how the world works. For example, I may ponder, "Hmm, does going through doorways before the dog influence the incidence or intensity of aggression directed at family members?"

The next step is to frame this question in a testable way. One way would be to do an epidemiological survey of many, many dog owners and take careful note of whether or not the humans precede dogs through doorways and also what kind of aggressive behavior they have experienced. Another way would be to take a group of dogs that are aggressive toward family members—or aggressive to family members in certain contexts that are believed to be related to doorway passage—and divide them into groups. One group would be taught to go through doorways after humans, another group may have their aggression treated with another technique and a third group might receive no intervention outside of some time spent training the dog to do tricks. This step would require formal blinds to ensure that neither the families nor the trainers knew what the study was about. The next step would be to compare outcomes. The people evaluating outcomes—or interviewing the families about their reports of whether the problem was solved— would also be "blind," i.e., have no idea which dogs received which interventions. Yet another experimental design would be to rear puppies to precede or follow their human family members through doorways and track them for a few years to see whether there are differences in frequency or intensity of aggressive behavior. Again, those evaluating outcomes would be blind to which group each dog was in. After this, the study would be published, including all the details of its design, statistical methods and conclusions. This would then be scrutinized by other professionals who understand study design, possible confounding variables, and statistical methods. Any flaws in the research would be noted and more research done to better get at the question. Interpretations of the results might be cautiously drawn, further questions raised and further studies designed. Gradually a body of tentative knowledge would be built.

The Difference Between Constructs and Observations

While waiting for the boom in dog behavior research, we can all start drawing a clearer distinction in our minds and in our communications, between constructs and observations. We can all count the number of times a dog barks or measure how long he growls and how far away a given stimulus was when he commenced. This is an observation. A construct, on the other hand, is an idea about unseen, unmeasurable mental or social processes that attempts to explain why he did it. These explanatory notions are "constructed," that is, inferred from the observations.

The value of constructs is in their ability to allow us to chunk behaviors into efficient units based on under-lying themes such as courtship, play, and predation. A serious problem with constructs is that they can not be easily falsified. Thus, if a construct is sufficiently appealing or compelling, or has simply been repeated enough, this alone can ensure its survival, even if it is completely or partly, as Friedman and Brinker say in their paper on the dominance construct in parrots, "an explanatory fiction." Dog behavior is chock full of constructs that have been repeated so often, they are accepted as gospel. Behaviors like effusive greeting, ease of training, and aggression directed at family members are lumped under constructs such as desire to please and dominance.

Making Dogs Sexy

There just is not much out there on dog behavior. We glean occasional bits of information when dogs happen to be used as research subjects for other purposes, but the interest—and attendant money available—in dog behavior and training per se has been paltry. So, we madly borrow constructs from wolf behavior. We (hopefully) bone up on and diligently apply what is known about the operant and classical conditioning of animals in general. The good news is that we acknowledge the importance of knowing something about these animals that are our family members. They often puzzle us and sometimes bite us. What's missing is properly funded regular research into their behavior and on which particular tools from operant and Pavlovian conditioning we should use at which times to modify it.

So, how do we make dogs a sexy research area? A post-graduate scholarship funded by APDT on domestic dog behavior and training research springs to mind. Also, foundations which grant money to research into all manner of inquiry and might be persuaded to fund existing research fellows to look into questions about dogs, the way a recent paper in the journal *Science* looked at the superiority of dogs to chimps in reading social cues. And, who better to make foundations aware of the knowledge void than our professional organization? In the meantime, there are things individuals can do. The San Francisco SPCA Academy graduate e-mail list recently began a research paper review project, wherein a paper is read by everyone and discussed until fully understood and then another is selected and the process repeated. This could be done on a larger scale. We could all demand tighter screening of conference proposals and newsletter submissions. And, of course, we could change the rallying cry of "every idea should be heard" to "what is your evidence?" ❖

ASSOCIATION of PET DOG TRAINERS

Dog Behavior, Training, and Modification

The bread and butter of a professional dog trainer's life involves working with owners to modify problem behaviors they may be having with their dogs and to provide basic training skills for the mutual benefit of both human and dog. The articles in this section cover a wide range of behavioral and training techniques of interest to dog trainers. First are two thought-provoking essays about what it is that dog trainers should really be trying to achieve as an end-result of their training efforts. Then Karen Overall sheds light on behavioral modification and how to analyze results scientifically and Ian Dunbar discusses lure-reward training and the subject of instructive reprimands. This is followed by articles on training challenges on a variety of subjects from alpha-rolls, to the unique problems associated with dealing with protection dogs and hunter-retriever dogs, to helping develop training skills for the popular sport of dog agility.

The K9 VIP Program: A New Way to "Talk Dog"

Terry Long, March/April 2002

Lassie Come Home, The Incredible Journey, Old Yeller, and 101 Dalmatians—all stories of extraordinary animal feats—have warmed the hearts of countless families for decades. These tales of canine devotion and courage evoke our compassion, love, and awe. Who among us does not dream of someday having a dog with whom there is that special bond, a bond reminiscent of these storied dogs and their human companions?

Unfortunately, these glorified stories of the human-dog bond contrast starkly with the reality being lived by many pet dogs and their families. Instead of Lassie, many of us get real dogs—dogs who dig, chew, bark, jump, and, in some cases, bite the hand that feeds them.

Champion, a seven-week-old yellow Labrador mix, was adopted by two young girls and their mother in an emotional moment outside a grocery store. When the father called a professional trainer for help a few months later, Champion had already been relegated to life as a backyard dog.

"He's just too wild. He jumps. He bites. He steals things. He's totally out of control," lamented the father, adding, "I don't even know if we can keep him if he keeps this up. Can you train him so we can go outside without getting beat up?"

When asked why they got a dog, many pet dog owners mention companionship, loyalty, protection, friendship, and family. No wonder so many owners become frustrated and disillusioned with living with a dog. Instead of a relationship, they get soiled carpets, excavated gardens, and complaining neighbors.

It would be easy to blame this disconnect with reality on the popular media. After all, aren't the movie and television producers at least partly to blame for their role in spreading these myths? Perhaps they are, but such stories sell because humans seem to have an insatiable appetite for them.

If we are to point fingers, perhaps we dog trainers should look in the mirror. With the best of intentions, we unwittingly may be contributing to a skewed view of what it means to share our lives with dogs. How? By selling control (commonly called obedience) instead of relationship building.

Every time we answer the phone and promote obedience training as the solution to prospective clients' problems, we miss an opportunity to change the way the public views their relationship with their dogs. Every time we tell clients to show their dogs who is boss, suggest ways to correct problem behavior, or push obedience classes, we unwittingly contribute a person's view of dogs as animals that must be controlled at all costs.

Change Through What We Call It

It starts with semantics. Just as our language changed to embrace all kinds of human rights movements, the words we use to talk about dogs are important in conveying our philosophy of "relationship" to our clients.

How often do we hear that a new puppy owner has been told that he or she needs to show dominance over the pup? Owners are taught to roll their puppies and hold them down until they submit, to scruff-shake, and to use other physical punishments for infractions such as puppy mouthing or jumping. These techniques and a host of others are meant to demonstrate human dominance, a.k.a., control.

How would it sound if we changed some of the semantics as in the table below? If instead of "correct," we used the word "show"? Or we replaced the word "obedience" with "manners"? Words matter. Subtle changes in semantics can mean the difference between a client deciding his dog is "blowing him off" or giving the dog the benefit of the doubt, going back to the basics, and working to bring the goal behavior to true fluency.

Table 1: Old vs. New Language

Old Language	New Language
Dominate	Influence
Control	Trust and teach
Obedience	Manners
Submission exercises	Handling exercises
Dominance	Deference
Setups/proofing	Evaluate training progress
Correct	Show
Command	Cue
Tell	Ask

Change Through What We Sell

Trainers have a challenging job. We work with many kinds of people who have differing perceptions of dog ownership. Some of us may cringe at the lost potential of dogs whose owners are satisfied simply to have their dogs not jump, bark, or dig. We are, however, in the unique position of being able to shape not only dog behavior, but also the attitudes and expectations of our clients.

Education starts with how we, and/or our staff, respond to phone inquiries. Using compassionate interviewing techniques, we can help prospects recognize that what they really want is close bonding with their dogs. We can help them realize that they've lowered their expectations because of frustration and exhaustion. We can help them understand that "controlling" or "correcting" problem behaviors is not going to be the full solution. We can help direct them toward training alternatives that rely on management, play training, reward-focused techniques and, most importantly, careful control of all the good things in their dog's life. By doing so, we can help each dog see his or her owner as a Very Influential Person (VIP)... which is the first step in building a lifelong bond with Lassie or Old Yeller.

Change Through What We Teach

Champion, the backyard Labrador, had quickly become canis non gratis because his family didn't know any better than to attempt to correct bad behavior. They tried everything: spankings, holding his mouth shut when he mouthed or nipped, kneeing him in the chest when he jumped, and a host of other punishments for behavior they didn't want. When none of these things worked, they felt they had no option but to banish the dog from the house. After increasingly frustrating interactions with Champion in the backyard, they seldom went outside and they walked him less and less. Sound familiar?

When Dave, Champion's owner, called to get professional help, his initial inquiry was about boarding and training while he laid new sod to repair the excavated backyard. During his phone discussion with the trainer, he began to understand that he would be throwing his money away. Instead of boarding and training, he was encouraged to spend his money on in-home consultation—in essence, a customized program that would focus on making each family member a center of influence in Champion's life.

After the first meeting with the trainer, Champion regained house privileges. Over the next several months, his family learned to rebuild the relationship through controlling not the dog, but his resources—such as food, treats, toys, and petting. At a particularly trying time, Dave was offered the chance to rehome Champion to an interested party. He declined. Even though Champion was a handful, Dave was now seeing another side to him, one that evoked feelings of canine companionship and camaraderie.

Influence Every Day in Every Way

Be captivating. So what does being a VIP look like to dogs? First and foremost, people must learn how to be captivating to dogs. Think of all the descriptions that come to mind when we describe a person to whom we are attracted:

- Charismatic
- Inspiring
- Irresistible
- Provocative
- Stimulating
- Exuding animal magnetism

How could you resist someone with all these attributes? Trainers may need to get down on the floor and show their clients what it looks like. Canadian trainer Susan Garrett demonstrates one of the best examples of being completely and irresistibly captivating when she plays a game she calls "Smoke Ya." This is a high-intensity game of tag, around furniture, throughout the house. What does it teach the dog besides being just plain fun? That finding and keeping up with his or her human is the best thing happening.

Games VIPs Play

VIPs use a multitude of fun activities to build influence with their dogs (see Table 2: Fun Activities and What They Teach). None of the activities listed below takes a lot of space or expensive equipment. They are mentally stimulating and teach essential skills to dogs cohabitating with humans.

Controlling Resources

VIPs are also astute at controlling resources. Here are two easy techniques:

- **Nothing In Life Is Free/No Free Lunch.** Everything the dog wants in life should be earned, especially in his or her formative months. By simply asking the dog to perform a task (e.g., sit, down, spin, bow, sit pretty) before being fed, petted, or walked, we establish our VIP role.

- **Umbilical Cord and Tethering.** Tying a clothesline to a pup's collar and attaching it to us can very easily teach a young pup to follow us and pay attention to us.

Tethering a pup to a stationery object and giving her a toy to play with while we are nearby develops settling—and allows us to supervise her activities.

Table 2: Fun Activities and What They Teach

Activity	What It Teaches
Hide and seek	Come and attention
Problem-solving games (e.g., get the treat out of the bottle)	Problem-solving skills and continual learning
Nose work	Develops a natural ability
Musical chairs	Stay
Eye contact game	Attention and the first step in loose leash walking
Tug with the 3 rules	1) Sit/down 2) No mouthing 3) Relinquishment
Retrieve (variety of objects)	Picking up and relinquishing items
Gotcher Body	Handling for examinations and grooming
Tricks (e.g., spin, rollover, crawl)	Mental stimulation and continual learning
101 Things	Mental stimulation and continual learning

VIPs Are Addictive

People who learn to be VIPs learn to play games with their dogs. They learn to be charismatic and captivating, rather than controlling and correcting. VIPs become addictive to their dogs in the best possible sense of the word—by behaving in a way that results in dogs' enthusiastic devotion and attachment to their owners.

Reward-focused trainers know what this addiction is all about. It's what they do with their own dogs because they've seen how successfully it builds influence and strengthens the human-dog relationship.

Isn't it time for us to teach VIP behavior to our clients? Isn't it time to help our clients realize their dream of having the best canine companion in the world? Even if the family dog may never behave like Lassie and rescue Timmy from the well, he or she can surely become a treasured and beloved pet. ❖

This article was the 1st Place Essay Winner in the 2001 John Fisher Scholarship competition.

Enriching the Life of Your Dog

Emily Keegans, May/June 2002

Is your dog is getting enough out of life? Are his physical, mental, and social needs being met? Dog owners are asking themselves these questions more and more. Given our spreading urban environment and increasingly busy lifestyles, we worry that there will not be room for our dogs or that they will suffer from boredom, anxiety, or worse. Many of us are in search of ways to allow our dogs to fulfill their natural instincts and drives safely and appropriately. Others are seeking to curb or prevent unwanted behaviors.

Jean Schinto, author of *The Literary Dog*, says that "to deny [dogs] their nature is to do them great harm." Many dog behavior problems are actually normal dog behaviors. We have expected dogs to stop being dogs, to curb their natural instincts regarding the ways they interact with humans and other dogs. Instead, we expect them to understand this foreign world of ours—and to value the same things we do, such as furniture and carpets.

Dog trainers looking at behavior issues see patterns in the reasons why problem behaviors are occurring. One behavior that often arises is understimulation. We leave our dogs alone for an entire workday, with only a squeaky toy for company, and yet we're surprised when the dog helps himself to a more interesting activity such as dissecting the couch or excavating the back yard.

Along with obedience training and behavior modification, many trainers are recommending something extra to their clients. Trainers are encouraging owners to engage their dogs with challenges, training games, or puzzles—in order to find or earn dinner, for example. Dinner can be stuffed into a Kong toy, which is then tied in a knotted sock and hidden somewhere in the house or yard. The hunt is on! Dinner—now a "work-to-eat program"—becomes more interesting, with predatory energy burned in the process. Imagine that your dog has a fuel tank full of energy, and each time you burn up some of that energy with a game, exercise, or mental challenge, there is a little less fuel left for chewing the molding or chasing the neighbor's cat!

Zoo animals who live in understimulated environments often begin to display abnormal behavior patterns or compulsive, repetitive behaviors known as stereotypes. These are behaviors such as pacing and excessive grooming of self or others. The solution that many zookeepers have turned to, one that has become an art in itself, is enrichment. What is enrichment, and how can it make a difference in the lives of the dogs we have chosen as companions and working partners?

To enrich is "to make fuller, more meaningful, or more rewarding." Zookeepers have identified many ways to improve the quality of life for the animals in their care. The type of enrichment a zoo chooses is dependent on the species of animal and how it would naturally interact with the environment. Zoos try to provide some of the natural elements missing in that animal's life by adding activities and challenges similar to those met by his wild counterparts.

Because much time and energy in a wild environment is spent finding and securing food—and because feeding time in captivity often passes far too quickly—many of the zoo's enrichment activities are focused around food. For example, when a chimpanzee in his native Africa finds a termite mound, he pokes a stick into one of its holes. Termites swarm onto the stick, and the chimpanzee licks them off the stick as if it were an ice cream cone.

Several zoos have made artificial termite mounds with holes into which the chimpanzees can poke sticks and come up with applesauce, tomato ketchup, or other treats. In the mongoose enclosure at the Oregon Zoo, a hidden insect dispenser drops mealworms into the sand for the mongoose to dig.

Varying the animal's living environment is also important. Placing novel items in the enclosures, providing new sounds and smells, and rotating toys all help to keep things less predictable. One dog caretaker hides pieces of a freshly baked pumpkin muffin around the house each evening. She describes the building excitement of Casey, her Golden Retriever, as he waits behind a baby gate, then bursts forth and races through the house searching for each piece. (She admits, however, that some of her family members view her as "mean" for hiding the food and they will move it to make it easier for Casey to find.)

We may needlessly worry that we are making things too hard for our dogs when they actually seem to enjoy the challenge, especially if it involves interacting with their human pack. A zookeeper I spoke to told me that, because stress is part of a natural environment, they often try to replicate incidents that may happen in the wild in order to produce healthy amounts of stress in the animals. Some zookeepers place tiger urine in the elephant enclosure, or they may set a controlled fire in an enclosure. So, although it doesn't sound as though Casey is too stressed over having to search for the hidden muffin pieces (it may even be the highlight of his day!), consider that some stress and the bit of extra mental and physical energy that he puts into the hunt is healthy and natural.

It has long been known that dogs are descendants of wolves. And, while they are not wolves or wild animals, they retain many wolf-like traits. One way we can discover appropriate enrichment for our dogs is to look at wolf behavior. We know that wolves are predators, scavengers, and highly social creatures that investigate their world primarily through their sense of smell. So how do we fulfill the needs of the wolf in our den?

Social needs may be highest on the list. Isolation from the pack can be devastating for a dog and can lead to behavior problems. Social interaction must include time with members of the dog's human pack, as well as members of his own species. The time you spend with your dog doing training, playing games, walking, or just being couch potatoes together will help fulfill his social needs. Training your dog to become a therapy dog is an excellent way to satisfy the needs of a gregarious dog. Visits to off-leash dog parks, play dates with Fido's favorite friends, or living in a multiple-dog household will help keep a dog's canine social skills well tuned. When dogs who have been isolated from their own species do have a chance to socialize, they often seem overwhelmed and may appear too strong or act intimated and fearful. Working with a trainer can help address these issues and give your dog his doggy time back!

Wildlife biologist David L. Mech breaks down the hunting sequence of wolves into seven stages: search; stalk; rush/chase; grab; kill; dissect; and eat. Other genetically programmed activities may be digging (for a den, food storage, or predation) and scavenging.

Hiding toys or treats around the house, yard, or park would be an excellent way to address the instinct to search and scavenge for food. Hide-and-seek can be a fun game for both you and your dog. Ask Fido for a sit-stay or have someone hold him as you run off and hide. Call his name or use your cue for "come." When he finds you, reward him with a play session or a treat. Not only will this satisfy some of his drive to search and stalk, but it is a great way to strengthen your recall and stay commands.

Flyball, Frisbee™, and fetch are all fun games that help to fulfill a dog's urge to chase. This instinct is usually very strong, and finding appropriate channels for it can help prevent problems. The sport of lure coursing, which involves dogs chasing a lure around a track, is enjoyed by various breeds (particularly sighthounds). If you have a dog with a high prey drive, you can even use the opportunity to use chase as a reward. If your dog goes wild when he sees a squirrel, ask for a behavior such as down or heel, then release him and let him chase that squirrel up a tree. This is an excellent way to help your dog learn to control his impulses and look to you when he wishes to access his environment, rather than just going straight for whatever he wants to investigate or chase. You are also harnessing a potent reinforcer to use for obedience work or behavior modification.

Tug-of-war is usually a doggy favorite and, when played with rules, can be a fun game for both of you and can help burn some of that predatory energy. Tug-of-war replicates the act of the cooperative kill. Imagine that you and your dog are part of a wolf pack bringing down a bison; you are a team working together, tugging on the large beast!

Many toys can address the instinct to kill and dissect. Toys that squeak and have floppy parts are great for shaking to death. Pulling the innards out of a stuffed toy is an enjoyable dissection project for many dogs, or you can use old pieces of fabric or socks to tie knots around squeakers and cookies.

You can use these ideas to prevent behavior problems. For example, if your dog knows that you hide a peanut butter-stuffed Kong tied in a sock somewhere in the house just before you leave, it can help to ease the anxiety of being left alone. As it becomes obvious to the dog that you are leaving for the day, you can ask for a stay, hide the Kong, and release the stay just as you walk out the door. That way, your exit predicts the beginning of the hunt and can cease to be such a dreaded event.

Additionally, look at the breed of dog and consider how domestication has affected his instincts and drives. What was he bred to do, and how close is he to working stock? Do you have a hound bred to follow his nose? Perhaps setting challenges for him to search for food or objects using his sense of smell would appropriately engage him or, for the more serious, there is the sport of tracking.

Is he a terrier bred to hunt animals that live underground? For small terriers, the sport of "Earthdog" simulates that activity. Or a digging pit containing buried squeaky toys to unearth and attack may enhance the terrier's life, at the same time satisfying his need to dig and confining the location of the digging.

You should make the designated area very tempting by burying some chew toys or bones in easily diggable soil or sand. Set up a few easy finds so that discovering the toys will encourage your dog to return to the same place for digging next time. Examine the tendencies your dog already displays; you can tailor your enrichment choices to fit your dog's needs by watching what he is already doing and finding appropriate outlets for the behavior.

In *When Elephants Weep*, Jeffrey Masson discusses a concept known in Germany as *funktionslust*: the enjoyment of one's abilities. Perhaps a sport would foster some of your dog's natural abilities, allowing him to develop his skills and talents. There are many organized dog sports and activities. In addition to the ones already mentioned, consider sledding and weight pulling, hunting and field trials, herding, and agility.

I surveyed some dog owners on what forms of enrichment they are providing their dogs. It seems that enrichment is limited only by your creativity and the preferences of the specific dog. Kong™ toys were probably mentioned the most, with stuffings that included cookies or kibble "cemented" into the Kong using peanut butter, cream cheese, or wet dog food. Your dog will really have to work to get all the food out. He may toss the Kong around, roll it, or shake it in order to dislodge those last remnants. Freezing the Kong makes the extraction that much more challenging and can also be wonderful for soothing the gums of a teething puppy.

Other popular enrichment activities are digging pits, wading pools, running through the sprinkler, teaching new tricks, massage sessions, and dancing around the house. Toys hung from trees by rope or other fabric make great targets for jumping and tugging. Jumps and other equipment keep agile dogs occupied in the back yard. Nicholas, a Keeshond, loves to dunk his head in his water bowl for frozen tortellini, an activity that reportedly keeps him occupied for at least an hour. Your imagination is the limit!

As our understanding continues to expand regarding the complex social structures, rituals, and drives of dogs, a growing respect for their natural qualities forms the basis for our interactions. Trainers are seeking to understand normal dog behavior and provide outlets for it rather than suppress it.

New ideas in training and a commitment to using gentle methods are changing our relationships with dogs. For example, the training method of free-shaping, in which we wait for the behavior and reward it when it happens, stresses a very different role—that of observer. The more we observe our dogs and give them opportunities to naturally express themselves, the more we can learn about them.

Be aware of your dog's body language and learn to observe patterns in it. Watch the way your dog plays—and the objects and games he chooses—and you will have a wonderful tool for enriching both his life and yours. ❖

This article was the 2nd Place Essay Winner in the 2001 John Fisher Scholarship competition.

Defining Dog Behavior, Training, and Modification

Karen Overall, May/June 2000

One of the most common misconceptions we have observed at the University of Pennsylvania's School of Veterinary Medicine Behavior Clinic involves our clients' understanding of what constitutes behavior modification. Most people come to us after working on a behavior problem under the guidance of other dog training and behavior professionals. Often, they have expended great effort to resolve a behavior problem by teaching obedience commands to their dogs. My nurse practitioner, Jenny O'Connor, and my assistant, Alison Seward, work very hard to explain to our clients that obedience has nothing to do with behavior modification, and that valuing obedience above all else can actually get in the way of helping the dog.

The Underlying Physiological State

We make sure that each client understands the important distinction between behavior modification and obedience training. While many of the same behaviors (sitting, lying down, etc.) are used in both behavior modification and obedience training, the focus is wholly different. Behavior modification programs are not obedience exercises and, unless the behavior modification emphasis is on rewarding the physical signs that parallel the dog's underlying physiological state, the dog won't get better. This is why a dog who has done well in obedience classes may still have problems. Any dog can sit and still not be relaxed; if he is not relaxed and, instead, is complying under duress, he is not learning to change his behavior. This distinction may sound incredibly simple, but it is both elegant and complex.

Behavior Within a Context

Another obedience-related pitfall is thinking that the dog should perform the requested task blindly, regardless of context. This bothers me for a few reasons.

First, it assumes that dogs are automatons, or *tabulae rasae*, and their job is to do only what we command. Many of my clients say, "But he is supposed to..." and I have to stop them and help them understand that the criteria assumed by the word "supposed" are theirs (not the dog's), and such complaints are about their power and not about the dog. In these interactions, the dog must be considered at least an equal participant. No living thing is an unwritten slate, and blind compliance leads to trouble in most social situations. (One exception might be military combat.)

This leads to my second concern. If blind adherence designed to void personality differences and ensure task completion is desired in combat, do we promote a combative, adversarial role when we expect such responses from our dogs? I think that we do, and that says a lot about us.

Third, a demand for absolute obedience encourages us to do things to our pets just because we can. Such approaches encourage and justify violence and abusive training methods.

Finally, the point of having a dog should have something to do with what we find appealing and joyous in dogs. We can only experience this joy if we think of training and guidance as separate from abuse and discipline.

Rules For Behavior Modification

So what is distinctive about behavior modification? At our Behavior Clinic, we focus on encouraging and enforcing deference. Because behavior modification approaches involve some behaviors commonly encouraged in obedience classes, there is a real risk that clients will assume that they have already tried such approaches without success. This fundamental misunderstanding about behavior modification needs to be overcome if behavioral approaches are to be implemented. At the outset, we need to make the following salient points with our clients:

1. Behavior modification exercises are not obedience exercises. Clients should be disabused of the notion that this is fancy obedience. Obedience training, while sharing many similarities with behavior modification, differs in premise, interactive reward structure, goal, and outcome. Most dogs who undergo behavior modification have been through some form of training and most know how to sit. For a dog to sit successfully in a class (or even a show) situation, the dog does not have to be relaxed. That is not true for behavior modification. Dogs who are stressed or anxious cannot successfully learn a more appropriate behavior, and they certainly cannot associate that behavior with having fun or with good things happening.

The goal of behavior modification is not just to have the dog sit, but to relax and be receptive to changing his or her behavior while doing so. It is critical that clients understand and appreciate this difference. If the client perceives that all we are doing is trying to teach the dog what he or she has already learned in obedience class, the client will not see the need to comply.

2. The client's biggest challenge will be with appropriate timing of rewards and corrections. Dogs read non-vocal or body language far better than most humans. It is easy for them to subvert the exercise and shape the client's behavior (problem dogs already do this). Someone outside the relationship needs to be able to comment on timing problems and instruct the client when to change his or her posture, tone, or quickness of praise or reward. If the dog cannot relax for the client, but is able to do so when behavior modification is instituted by some outside party, the client is doing one of three things:

- pushing the dog too hard, too fast.
- giving confusing signals.
- demonstrating bad/wrong timing.

This is hard work—it is not magic.

3. Practice behavior modification at first in quiet, non-distracting environments. Do not use clickers, whistles, bells, or hand signals. Once the dog masters the behavior modification programs, he will have no problem coupling the learned vocal cues to visual ones. Until then, the dog should work in calm, quiet circumstances for vocal cues and a consistent reward structure.

Hand signals, which are commonly used in obedience, are not recommended during the initial phases of behavior modification. They can be a needless distraction and, for very aggressive dogs, such signals will put the person using them at risk. Without exception, dangling body parts in front of an aggressive dog is not recommended and will make the animal more anxious. In a worst-case scenario, hand signals can be seen by the dog as threats.

If we can teach clients the above rules about behavior modification, we can begin to use classic counterconditioning and desensitization to change behaviors. But, to be successful, clients need to understand that the goal is not only to teach the dog not to react in some circumstances, but also that the dog can always look to the client for cues about the appropriateness of his or her behavior. For this to work, the clients must be clear, consistent, humane, and reliable. In and of itself, that's a laudable goal. ❖

Lure-Reward Training

Ian Dunbar, July/August 2006

In pet dog training there is an endless quest for the quickest, easiest, most enjoyable, and most expedient route to produce equipment-free and gizmo-free response reliability.

Recently, some trainers have criticized luring, stating that dogs are trained "better" if they have not been lured. This, of course, is learning theory heresy. Behavior is consequence-driven, not antecedent-driven. By tautological definition, once a dog has been trained to criterion, he's been trained to criterion. A dog is not trained better depending on whether he was lured or not. If he's trained, he's trained, and if not, he's not.

However, the choice of training technique will have a huge influence on "time and trials to criterion." As the quickest and one of the simplest of all training techniques, lure/reward training is the technique of choice for most owners to teach their dog basic manners. For behavior modification and temperament training, food lure/reward training should be mandatory. There is extreme urgency to prevent and resolve behavior problems. Simple behavior problems, such as housesoiling, destructive chewing, and excessive barking, kill dogs. Time is of the essence. Similarly, biting, fighting, and fearful dogs are hardly happy or safe to be around and so there is simply no time to mess around with time-consuming techniques. We must resolve the dogs' problems, relieve their chronic, yet acute, stress levels, and improve their quality of life using the most time-efficient methods available.

Other techniques are championed in other specialist training fields, wherein the syllabus is finite and the trainer knows the rules and questions (criteria) before the examination and especially, when time is not an issue—knowledgeable, experienced, and dedicated handlers will train for hours to perfect a desired behavior. However, pet dog training differs markedly from teaching competition or working dogs, from training marine mammals, and from computers autoshaping rats and pigeons in laboratories. With pet dog training, the questions are unknown and the syllabus is infinite—comprising all aspects of a dog's (and owner's) behavior, temperament, and training. But the most important difference—owners are not dog trainers; they seldom have a trainer's education, interest, dedication, experience, or expertise.

Trainers should never underestimate their own expertise. Characteristically, techniques that we recommend for owners to train their dogs are entirely different (easier, quicker, and less complicated) than techniques that we might use to train our dogs.

In pet dog training, the two most expedient techniques are lure/reward training and all-or-none reward training. This article will describe a comprehensive lure/reward training program, which comprises five stages:

I. Teaching The Dog What We Want Him To Do

II. Teaching The Dog To Want To Do What We Want Him To Do

III. Enforcing Compliance without Fear or Force

IV. Refining Performance Precision and Pizzazz

V. Protecting Performance Reliability and Precision

The first three steps focus on establishing response reliability and are all-important in all fields of dog training. The last two steps—for refining precision and for protecting precision and reliability—are primarily for obedience, working, and demo dogs and will only be summarized in this article.

Teaching The Dog What We Want Him To Do

Stage I involves completely phasing out food lures as they are first replaced by hand signals (hand lures) and then eventually, by requests (verbal lures).

Given the prospect of the plethora of rewarding consequences for appropriate behavior, most dogs would gladly respect our wishes and follow our instructions, if only they could understand what we were asking. In a sense, Stage I involves teaching dogs ESL—English as a Second Language—teaching dogs the meaning of the human words that we use for instructions. Dogs need to be taught words for their body actions (sit, down, stand, etc.), and activities (go play, fetch, tug, etc.), and for items (Kong®, Squirrel Dude®, car keys, etc.), places (bed, car, inside, outside, etc.), and people (e.g., Mum, Dad, Jamie, etc.).

The basic training sequence is always the same:

1. Request

2. Lure

3. Response

4. Reward

This simple sequence is all that there is to the "science" of lure/reward training. After just half a dozen repetitions, the food lure is no longer necessary because the dog will respond to the hand-lure movement (hand signal). After twenty or so repetitions (with a half-a-second interval between the request and the hand signal), the dog will begin to anticipate the signal on hearing the request, i.e., the dog will respond immediately after the request but before the hand signal. The hand signal is no longer necessary, since the dog has now learned the meaning of the verbal request.

The "art" of lure/reward training very much depends on the trainer's choice and effective use of an effective lure. The lure can be any item or action that reliably causes the dog to respond appropriately. Obviously, the trainer and the trainer's body movements are the very best lures (and rewards), with interactive toys coming a close second. However, for pet owners, food is generally the best choice for both lures and rewards. Again, pet owners are not yet dog trainers, but they need to train their dog right away using the easiest and quickest technique.

Food lures should not be used for more than a half dozen trials. The prolonged use of the same item as both lures and rewards comes pretty close to bribing—wherein the dog's response will become contingent on whether or not the owner has food in her hand. Either completely go cold turkey on food lures after just six trials, or use different items as lures and rewards. For example, use food to lure the dog to sit but a tennis ball retrieve as a reward. Or, use a hand signal to lure the sit but an invitation to the couch as a reward. Regardless of what you choose as lures and rewards, always commence each sequence with the verbal request.

For pet owners, dry kibble is the standard choice for both lures and rewards. Weigh out the daily ration each morning and keep it in a screw-top jar to be handfed as lures and rewards in the course of the day. Freeze-dried liver is reserved for special uses: rewards for housetraining, lures for Kongs, lures for shush, occasional lures and rewards for men and children to use, and for classical conditioning (to children, men, other dogs, motorcycles, and other scary stuff).

Teaching The Dog To Want To Do What We Want Him To Do

Stage II involves phasing out training rewards as they are first replaced by life rewards and then eventually, by auto-reinforcement. Just because a dog "knows" what we want him to do does not mean to say that he will necessarily do it.

Puppy responses are pretty predictable and reliable but with the advent of adolescence, most dogs become more independent and quickly develop competing interests, many of which become distractions to training. Given the choice between coming when called and sniffing another dog's rear end, most adolescent dogs would choose the latter.

To maintain response reliability, all of the dog's hobbies and competing interests must be used as rewards. Training must be completely integrated into the dog's lifestyle. Training should comprise: short preludes before every enjoyable doggy activity (a la Premack) and numerous short interludes within every enjoyable long-term doggy activity. For example, the dog should be requested to sit before the owner puts on the leash, opens the back door, opens the car door, takes off the leash, throws a tennis ball, takes back the tennis ball, allows the dog to greet another dog or person, or offers a couch invitation or tummy rub. And of course, the dog should sit before the owner serves supper. Additionally, walks should be interrupted every 25 yards and play with other dogs should be interrupted every 15 seconds for a brief training interlude, (e.g., random position changes with variable length stays). Each interruption allows the resumption of walk or play to be used again as a life reward. As a cautionary note, if walks and play are not frequently interrupted, the puppy/adolescent will quickly learn to pull on leash and no doubt will become an uncontrollable social loon or bully.

Food rewards are no longer necessary for reliable performance, but it is smart to occasionally offer kibble rewards prior to life rewards during training preludes and interludes, so that the presentation (and eating) of kibble (an average-value primary reinforcer) becomes a mega secondary reinforcer. Supercharged kibble is useful when teaching subsequent exercises.

The ultimate goal in dog training is for the response to become the reward so that the dog becomes internally motivated and the response is auto-reinforced. This is similar to what happens when people are effectively taught to play tennis, dance, or ski; external rewards are no longer necessary.

Enforcing Compliance Without Fear or Force

Stage III involves teaching the dog that he must always respond promptly and appropriately by enforcing compliance without fear or force.

Just because a dog really, really, really wants to do what we want him to do does not mean to say that he will always do it. Internally motivated dogs usually have response reliabilities around 90%. I have always thought that dogs are pure existentialists—they revel in the here and now—and that squirrel, that dog's rear end, or that little boy on a skateboard is right here, right now. In a flash, reliability goes down the toilet.

There are times when a dog simply must follow instructions to the letter. A pet dog requires an ultra-reliable emergency sit or down, a rock-solid stay, and a healthy respect for doorway or curbside boundaries. Once we have used just about every conceivable life reward under the sun to internally motivate a dog to want to comply, we must also teach the dog that there are instances when he must comply.

In all the fields of dog training, enforcing compliance is perhaps the most misunderstood aspect. When discussing punishment, training tends to change from a science to a religion and some trainers express emotional extremes. Some trainers hold the view that compliance must be enforced by physical (often painful) punishments, such as leash corrections or electric shock. Other trainers abhor the use of positive punishment and negative reinforcement. And yet other trainers even eschew the use of negative punishment and no reward marks, deeming them to be too stressful.

Regardless of where any trainer lies on the continuum of relative use of rewards and punishments:

1. Minor stressors are essential during early development for an animal to develop confidence as an adult, and certainly to develop sufficient confidence to live with humans. Learning, training, and development are often stressful. Adolescence is extremely stressful. It's a simple fact of life.

2. It is essential to consider, "What to do when Plan A fails?" What to do when the dog dashes out of the front door and into the street to chase the boy on the skateboard? What is the Plan B and Plan C?

3. For the dog's safety, compliance must be enforced to raise response-reliability to 95% (within two seconds after a single command) and to 100% (following Plan B or C).

Compliance may be effectively enforced without fear or force. Technically, a punishment decreases the immediately preceding behavior. A punishment need not be physical, painful, scary, aversive, or unpleasant. A punishment needs to adhere to eight criteria (see next article). Most important, punishments need to be effective (another tautology), instructive, and immediate, yet not overbearing.

Personally, I dislike using any gizmo or permanent management tool. Instead, I like to rely on the things that are always readily available: voice (for requests/commands, praise, and instructive reprimands), food and toys (as lures and rewards), and hands (for rewards and control). In those instances when the dog does not respond following a single command, the dog will eventually respond (100% of the time) after any number of instructive reprimands delivered in a negative reinforcement format (see On Using Instructive Reprimands at the end of this article).

Once a dog has been trained (exclusively via positive reinforcement) to 90% response reliability, whenever it fails to respond within two seconds, I instructively reprimand the dog. The volume of the instructive reprimand is lower than normal and the tone is soft and sweet, yet insistent. Once the dog sits, for example, I say "thank you" and then the dog has to immediately repeat the exercise to meet the original criteria. Once the dog sits within two seconds of a single request, I praise the dog, offer a couple of treats, and say "go play." If the dog does not sit following the instructive reprimand, the instructive reprimand is repeated in a negative reinforcement format until the dog complies, whereupon the dog has to immediately repeat the exercise and meet criteria, before "life as the dog knows it" continues once more.

Recently, I have been working with a Level IV biter (deep punctures of more than 1/2 the length of the canine tooth, with lacerations and/or slashes in both directions from the puncture). I elected to take the case because the owners are responsible and compliant and will crate the dog when visitors come to the house, but they desperately want to normalize the relationship with their dog. By my fourth visit, the wife had learned how to keep the dog in a long-term settle-down on his mat (for five and a half hours), while she cooked dinner and went about other household duties (and her husband observed in awe). In the course of the five and a half hours, the dog briefly left his mat a total of 22 times. Each time, the wife instructed "Rover, go to your mat, go to your mat, go to your mat." Her voice was always soft, sweet, and insistent. As soon as the dog returned to his mat and lay down, she praised. Periodically, she would visit, praise, and reward the dog for lying on his mat. At no time during the procedure did the dog display any obvious behavioral or physiological concomitants of stress, even though we were using occasional positive punishment and negative reinforcement in conjunction with copious positive reinforcement. On the contrary, the owner is regaining control and the dog is being reintegrated into family living. I have videotaped this session to show at the upcoming APDT Educational Conference in Kansas City. Positive punishment and negative reinforcement can be sweet and soft, yet extremely effective.

I seldom recommend negative punishment because doing so often allows the dog to get away without responding appropriately.

Refining Performance Precision and Pizzazz

Once response-reliability tops 95%, it is time to shape and differentially reinforce performance precision and pizzazz For example, fronts and finishes and stays are refined by improving attention, expression, and exact location (forwards/backwards, closer/away, etc.) and body position (e.g., five types of down stay). Recalls are progressively accelerated and heeling is fine-tuned by teaching speed-up and slow-down.

Protecting Performance Reliability and Precision

Stage V requires a substantial time-commitment and so it is essential to "protect" the dog's superior performance. Snazzy obedience is quickly destroyed when obedience commands—most commonly "heel" and "down" are used to control the dog in stressful situations, e.g., around dodgy dogs or people. Much worse is when obedience commands are misused by family and friends. For example, when a husband instructs five dogs to "sit stay" at the front door, when admitting three buddies for pizza, beer, or while watching televised sports. One dog barks, one dog jumps up, one dog gooses the guest, one dog lies down (knowing that husbands don't know the difference), and one dog sits and stays … and is forgotten. When the obedient dog eventually breaks his sit stay and creeps into the living room, he is rewarded by laughter and pizza.

Training is best protected by having three command levels: DogCon One, DogCon Two, and DogCon Three. The dog is given a different cue, or perhaps easier—a different name for each command level: an informal pet name, a formal name, and a competition/working/demo name respectively. The choice of name informs the dog which level of obedience is required: the pet name prefix signifies a mere suggestion (which may be ignored), the formal name prefix requires 100% reliability, and the demo name calls for ultimate reliability, precision, and pizzazz. It's showtime!

The notion of allowing a dog to ignore a command used to shock trainers. But this is what happens most of the time around the home, anyway; giving commands and not enforcing the dog's response is the major reason why reliability goes downhill. By acknowledging and formalizing "disobedience" and allowing a dog to ignore pet-name suggestions, we can better protect formal-name reliability. All we have to remember is that on those occasions when we use the formal-name prefix, we must insist on 100% compliance.

As T. S. Eliot might have said, "A dog requires three different names."

On Using Instructive Reprimands

When communicating with dog owners, I use the term "punishment-training" simply to mean, using punishments when training—most usually short-duration punishments but occasionally, long-duration punishment (positive punishment and negative reinforcement), adhering to the eight criteria (see next article), and preferably, predominately using well-timed, soft and sweet instructive reprimands. Similarly, I use the term "reward-training" simply to mean, using rewards when training—most usually short-duration rewards but occasionally, long-duration rewards (positive reinforcement and negative punishment), adhering to similar criteria for the use of rewards, and almost entirely using soft and sweet praise and mega life-rewards.

The use of punishment-training and reward-training are not mutually exclusive. On the contrary, the vast majority of pet dog trainers occasionally use punishment-training after first teaching the dog via reward-training.

Obviously, the time is long overdue for pet dog trainers to completely and utterly revise the ridiculously ambiguous and emotionally inflammatory terminology of learning theory. ❖

Eight Criteria for the Effective Use of Punishment in Pet Dog Training

Ian Dunbar, July/August 2006

1. Tautological—Punishment should be punishing

Punishments must effectively reduce the likelihood and future frequency of the immediately preceding behavior.

Repeated "punishment" is the best evidence that the "punishments" were ineffective and therefore, not punishments at all. Instead the dog perceived the so-called "punishment" as inconsequential, annoying, or abusive. On the other hand, when punishment is effective, the dog will no longer misbehave. Indeed, one definition of a dog trained to criterion could be, that punishment is no longer necessary. Checking the effectiveness of punishment (or any training technique) should be ongoing process, via a Test-Train-Test format.

2. Immediacy—Punishment must immediately follow the unwanted behavior

Ideally, both "crime and punishment" should occur in less than a second. The relevance of punishment depends very much on its immediacy.

3. Instruction—Punishment should also indicate the desired response

In addition to indicating "What is Wrong" (i.e., the immediately preceding behavior), a punishment should also inform the dog "What is Right."

Often, the desired behavior is evident from the specific environmental context. For example, a punishment in the vicinity of a closed door, or another on-leash dog, usually indicates that we would like the dog to sit. Even better, the desired response may be re-emphasized by the wording of the reprimand. For example, "outside!" would be a suitable instructive reprimand for a puppy caught in the act of eliminating indoors

4. Strength—Punishment need not be unpleasant, painful, or scary, it just needs to be effective

It is a huge misconception that punishments are necessarily unpleasant, painful, or scary and need be administered using some training tool or gizmo. On the contrary, a dog may be effectively punished using soft and sweet instructive reprimands. Otherwise, it remains an exacting art to precisely estimate the exact optimum strength of a punishment in any given training scenario; trainers constantly walk a knife edge—either they are too lenient and have to up the ante, or they are too severe and the dog becomes fearful. Again, for nearly all training exercises, a dog may be effectively punished using soft and sweet instructive reprimands. Occasionally, when proofing for life-threatening situations (e.g., honoring open doorways, curbside boundaries, and an emergency sit/down response), stronger instructive reprimands are used.

5. Duration—Punishment should be of extremely short-duration

Extremely short-duration punishments are most effective, wherein a dog starts to misbehave, is immediately punished, and stops misbehaving (starts behaving as desired), all in less than second.

Continued misbehavior, however, usually requires continued punishment. Long-duration punishment is less commonly used, and comprises two separate psychological processes: positive punishment and negative reinforcement. The instructive aspects of a long-duration punishment are the onset and the offset: commencing punishment informs the dog he is making a mistake and terminating punishment informs the dog he is back on track again.

6. Warning—Punishment should be preceded by a warning

If not warned beforehand, the dog cannot learn the meaning of the warning, which would be inane. And if not warned beforehand, the dog cannot avoid the punishment, which would be inhumane.

A dog must have adequate opportunity to avoid punishment by acting appropriately as previously trained. For punishments to be really effective, the dog must first be taught acceptable alternatives, and, in all instances, the appropriate instruction (request/command) must be given before the dog is punished for not responding as desired. In a sense, the request (command/stimulus/antecedent) now becomes a warning, as we now enforce (without force) a previously learned response.

7. Prior Training—Punishment should be preceded by adequate prior training

Before being punished, the dog must know what the owner expects him to do, i.e., if this is wrong, what is right? Therefore, before punishing the dog for making mistakes, the owner must first teach the dog the appropriate response.

Because there is only one right response, teaching a novice dog what we want him to do takes only a very short (finite) amount of time. On the other hand, there are an infinite number of "wrong" responses and so, attempting to teach a novice dog by punishing undesired responses takes an infinite amount of time—the Myth of Sisyphus! Hence, with novice dogs, punishment-training is much less time-efficient than reward-training. And time is of the essence in pet dog training.

8. Consistency—Punishment must be consistent

In order for punishment-training to be effective, the dog must be punished each and every time she misbehaves. A dog only has to get away with misbehaving once to learn that there are times when she is not punished. Henceforth, the dog will reserve her misbehavior for times when the owner is absent—either physically, mentally, or functionally.

The eighth criterion illustrates why punishment-training is less effective than reward-training. Most learning theory experiments on the use of punishment were performed by computers training laboratory rats and pigeons. However, no owner is 100% consistent 100% of time. Whereas some experienced competition and working-dog trainers may achieve close to 100% consistency during an intense short-duration training session, most dog owners are highly inconsistent living with their dogs at home.

Because of the difficulty in satisfying the eighth criterion, punishment-training methods are seldom expedient for pet dog training. Punishment-training is reserved for highly specific and short exercises (during which we hope the owner/trainer can at least approximate 100% consistency) for enforcing (without force) previously learned commands, and for absolute proofing in life-threatening situations.

But...the most wonderful aspect of reward-training is that inconsistency does little harm, and often does a lot of good. Occasionally, a dog may be rewarded for incorrect responses (temporarily increasing time and trials to criterion), but the mis-timed rewards still serve to cement the bond (classical conditioning). And of course, inconsistently rewarding a dog for correct responses cements the reliability of the de-sired response. Variable reinforcement ratios, and even utterly random reinforcement, are excruciatingly effective. ❖

Recognizing Multiple, Related Diagnoses for Treatment Success

Karen Overall, September/October 2003

Citation: Overall KL, Dunham AE, & Frank D. (2001). "Frequency of nonspecific clinical signs in dogs with separation anxiety, thunderstorm phobia, and noise phobia, alone or in combination." *JAVMA*. 219:467-473. This article is based on the presentation by Dr. Overall at the 2002 APDT Conference in Portland, Oregon.

It was a "treatment failure" that first inspired me to examine an area that is frequently not examined in veterinary behavioral medicine: incidence of co-morbid diagnoses and the effects on nonspecific signs. I realized that some portion of my population experienced "treatment failure" when treated with a benzodiazepine alone for noise and thunderstorm phobias. Like many busy clinicians, I had the jargon 'treatment failure' fully etched in my unconscious. Then I had a Eureka! moment. Given that the benzodiazepines (e.g., diazepam, alprazolam) work only by augmenting the inhibitor neurotransmitter GABA, if the dog truly had a noise or thunderstorm phobia and the dog did not respond to a benzodiazepine, something about the mechanism of the condition must be different. Either the dog's reaction was not a phobic one associated with responded changes in GABA (and possibly glutamate, the excitatory amino acid from which GABA is made) or something else was ongoing diagnostically. Simply, I had abused the most fundamental question of all science: is the response the same, or is it different? If it is different, you can ask why that is so, and now you are doing science. But to just write off the result as a "treatment failure" is akin to alchemy and disposes of all the important information.

The result of this query was publication of my co-authored paper cited above on separation anxiety and noise phobia, which generated huge amounts of attention in both the human and animal medical fields. Psychiatrists and psychiatric geneticists were interested in it because it represents one of the few papers with excellent data on a population of patients consistently screened for related diagnoses, and for whom other demographic data, including which signs they exhibited, were known. Veterinarians have been enthusiastic about the data because our findings allowed them to ask relevant questions about which they would not have previously thought, and which would provide them with answers about why their treatment for separation anxiety, alone, would sometimes fail.

Discrete Definition of Behaviors

Before we could start to ask about co-morbid diagnoses and shared diagnostic signs, we had to discretely define diagnoses in a way that did not rely on nonspecific signs. If you are going to use presence or absence and intensity of signs as an indicator of different types or intensities of one condition, you cannot commit a logical violation and also use them to define the condition or make the diagnosis. So, we used a set of previously published criteria (Overall KL. (1997). *Clinical Behavioral Medicine for Small Animals.*, St. Louis, MO: Mosby):

1. Separation anxiety—Necessary condition: Physical or behavioral signs of distress exhibited by the animal only in the actual absence of, or lack of access to (virtual absence), the client. Sufficient condition: consistent, intensive destruction, elimination, vocalization, or salivation exhibited only in the virtual or actual absence of the client; behaviors are most severe close to the separation, and many anxiety-related behaviors (autonomic hyperactivity, increased motor activity, and increased vigilance and scanning) may become apparent as the client exhibits behaviors associated with leaving.

2. Noise phobia—Necessary and sufficient conditions: Sudden and profound, non-graded, extreme response to noise, manifested as intense, active avoidance, escape, or anxiety behaviors associated with the activities of the sympathetic branch of the autonomic nervous system. Behaviors can include catatonia or mania concomitant with decreased sensitivity to pain or social stimuli. Repeated exposure results in an invariant pattern of response.

3. Thunderstorm phobia—Necessary and sufficient conditions: Sudden and profound, non-graded, extreme response to thunderstorms or any aspect of them (e.g., wind, noise, lightening, changes in barometric pressure, rain, darkness, ozone level changes, etc.), manifested as intense, active avoidance, escape, or anxiety behaviors associated with the activities of the sympathetic branch of the autonomic nervous system. Behaviors can include catatonia or mania concomitant with decreased sensitivity to pain or social stimuli. Repeated exposure results in an invariant pattern of response.

Preliminary Data

A preliminary study I conducted found that there was high concordance between dogs who exhibited signs of separation anxiety and those who met the criteria for noise or thunderstorm phobias. These preliminary data suggest merit in three avenues of exploration:

1. That the development or expression of noise/thunderstorm phobias and separation anxiety are not independent, and the extent to which they co-vary may suggest differences in mechanisms for thresholds of anxiety-related disorders;

2. That reactions to noise may predispose dogs to other anxiety related conditions; that the interaction may have time penetrance, and the longer an animal has been affected with one condition, the more at risk it might be either for a more complex form of the conditions (e.g., a greater number or intensity of signs); and

3. That incidence and co-morbidity of both conditions may be underestimated or incompletely represented, even in a tertiary care behavior clinic, in the absence of a questionnaire or evaluation tool that systematically explores all responses to both related situations in all patients.

By examining patients who had complaints associated with any of the three conditions we were able to evaluate avenues 1 to 3, above. Our findings indicated that for the combined data, the frequency of separation anxiety as the sole diagnosis was significantly higher (G test; P #0.05) than expected under the hypothesis of independence of diagnoses. The observed frequency of noise phobia as the sole diagnosis was significantly lower (G test; P #0.05) than expected under the hypothesis of independence of diagnoses. The observed frequency of a diagnosis of separation anxiety + thunderstorm phobia and of separation anxiety + noise phobia was significantly (G tests; all P #0.05) lower than expected under the hypothesis of independence of diagnoses.

Finally, the observed frequency of a diagnosis of thunderstorm phobia + noise phobia and of separation anxiety + noise phobia + thunderstorm phobia was significantly (G tests; all P #0.05) higher than expected under the hypothesis of independence of diagnoses. The null hypothesis that individual diagnoses (SA, TP, NP, SA+TP, SA+NP, TN, and SA+TP+NP) are independent was rejected (likelihood ratio chi-squared test, Q = 28.17, df = 6, P= 0.0001).

The conditional probabilities for each association are shown in Table 1. It is important to note that if separation anxiety and either phobia were the same, or if both phobias were equivalent, the related paired probabilities would be identical, and they are not. Not only are all three of these different conditions but the extent to which they affect each other varies with condition in my clinical population.

Summary Findings

In summary, the finding that separation anxiety occurs significantly more often as a solitary diagnosis than would be expected under random conditions, and that noise phobias occur significantly less often as a solitary diagnosis under the same conditions, supports the concept that although they share nonspecific signs, the diagnoses are separate entities. Furthermore, the finding that the observed frequency of a diagnosis of separation anxiety + thunderstorm phobia, and of separation anxiety + noise phobia was significantly lower than expected were they independent, but that the observed frequency of a diagnosis of thunderstorm phobia + noise phobia, and of separation anxiety + noise phobia + thunderstorm phobia was significantly higher than expected, were the diagnoses independent, supports two important conclusions.

First, noise and thunderstorm phobia are different from each other and affect the frequency and intensity of related behaviors in co-morbid diagnoses differently.

Second, the interaction of multiple pathological responses to noise likely either reflect an altered, dysfunctional, underlying neurochemical substrate, or is the result of one. While not definitively tested here, the extent to which such dynamic interactions shape expressed behavioral phenotypes is supported by differential responses to behavioral medications. Interestingly, a recent paper on human obsessive compulsive disorder in the *American Journal of Psychiatry* (Saxena et al., (2003), 160;3:522-532) supports the role for co-morbid diagnoses and treatment outcome, and demonstrates that treatment responsiveness may act as a "marker" to identify when aberrant neuro-chemistry is more complex than originally thought. Troubled dogs have a lot to offer in the way of teaching and science for both veterinary and human medicine.

Table 1		
Probability that a dog had separation anxiety, given that it also had a diagnosis of thunderstorm phobia	0.8701	(87%)
Probability that a dog had thunderstorm phobia, given that it also had a diagnosis of separation anxiety	0.6147	(61%)
Probability that a dog had separation anxiety, given that it also had a diagnosis of noise phobia	0.8804	(88%)
Probability that a dog had noise phobia, given that it also had a diagnosis of separation anxiety	0.7364	(74%)
Probability that a dog had thunderstorm phobia, given that it also had a diagnosis of noise phobia	0.7609	(76%)
Probability that a dog had noise phobia, given that it also had a diagnosis of thunderstorm phobia	0.8974	(90%)

Glossary

Benzodiazepine: A group of drugs used as anti-anxiety agents or tranquilizers. Trade names include Valium, Ativan, Xanax, and Klonopin.

Chi-squared test: The sum of the quotients obtained by dividing the square of the difference between the observed and the theoretical values of a quantity by theoretical value.

Co-morbidity: The coexistence of two or more illnesses.

Concordance: Correlation; in genetics, the occurrence of a given trait in both members of a twin.

Conditional probability: The probability of an event given that another event has occurred.

GABA: A neurotransmitter, gamma-aminobutyric acid, thought to play a role in influencing schizophrenia.

Glutamate: An amino acid that plays an essential role in the body's metabolism.

Invariable: A trait or factor that does not change.

Neurochemical substrate: The neurochemical substance upon which an enzyme acts.

Neurotransmitter: Chemicals in the nervous system that facilitate the transmission of impulses across synapses between neurons.

Null hypothesis: A hypothesis that is assumed to be true, and is tested in an experiment for possible rejection.

Phobia: A persistent and irrational fear of a particular object or situation.

Penetrance: The frequency with which a heritable trait is manifested by individuals carrying the principle gene or genes conditioning it.

Phenotype: The outward, or physical, appearance of an animal in all of its anatomical, physiological, and behavioral characteristics. ❖

Assessing the Alpha Roll

Terry Ryan, July/August 2001

The alpha roll is a frequently mentioned technique in canine behavior and training literature. In general, the roll is implemented by turning the dog onto his back and pinning him until he assumes a state of submission. However, there is usually no clear definition of the term "submit," nor is there an explanation of what to do if a dog doesn't submit.

Similarly, there appears to be no standard definition of "alpha roll." In fact, there are many variations demonstrated by trainers and instructors. One popular variation starts with a scruff shake—grabbing the dog on either side of the neck—and then lifting the dog's weight off the front feet and staring into his eyes until he submits.

Why are dog owners encouraged to do the alpha roll? Supposedly, it simulates the natural methods of the following canine behaviors:

- establishing leadership
- dominating a dog
- correcting a dog
- punishing an inappropriate behavior

Alpha roll advocates often justify the technique because "it's the way wolves do it," but that rationalization is weak. As professional dog trainers, we—and ultimately our clients—would benefit from an explanation grounded in critical analysis rather than habit or myth.

If we could successfully interview a wolf (or a dog, for that matter) we'd be light years ahead in training. In the absence of such communication, we must rely on the careful observation and astute second-guessing of experts with strong backgrounds in wolf behavior.

For this article, I called upon the expertise of four team members who teach a "Wolf and Dog Behavior" course with me every summer at Wolf Park, Indiana: Dr. Ray Coppinger, Professor Erich Klinghammer, Pat Goodman, and Ken McCort.

The Wolf-Dog Parallel

According to Erich Klinghammer, PhD, an ethologist and professor emeritus at Purdue University and the president of the North American Wildlife Federation, "the so-called alpha roll overpracticed by some is nonsense." Klinghammer believes that there is a big difference between wolves and dogs, and to "simply extrapolate from wolves to dogs is at best problematical."

Dr. Ray Coppinger, a biology professor at Hampshire College and a co-founder of the Livestock Guarding Dog Project, concurs. He says that, in evolutionary terms, "to be descended from a wolf doesn't mean dogs are wolves or behave like wolves." Furthermore, he states that dogs develop in "very different environments and acquire very different social behaviors than wolves."

85

Do Wolves Do The Alpha Roll?

These experts are skeptical that the alpha roll is a uniform and routine dominance behavior in wolves. "In watching the wolves," says Pat Goodman, MS, a resident ethologist at Wolf Park, "I find it is rare for them to forcibly push down and hold down a subordinate, a rival, a youngster. In the overwhelming majority of cases, rather than being pushed down, the wolf who ends up on the ground is already going down in response to psychological pressure...I have seen the alpha roll 'work' in wolf-wolf and in wolf-human encounters, but I have also seen it backfire."

Klinghammer notes that the preferred strategy of one wolf establishing dominance over another is "usually a drawn-out series of encounters that eventually convinces a wolf to submit and run away." In fact, says Ken McCort, a dog training and behavior consultant, "with wolves the inguinal presentation behavior is usually volunteered by a lower ranking wolf as sort of an appeasement to a dominant animal in the face of some threat or altercation"... and leaders in packs "control assets (possessions, territory) more often than physically controlling individuals."

Does The Alpha Roll Work On Dogs?

According to Goodman, there is probably no peer-reviewed literature that addresses testing reactions of dogs to variations of the alpha roll. Even without such research, Coppinger takes a clear position against alpha rolling: "I cannot think of many learning situations where I want my learning dogs responding with fear and lack of motion," he says. "I never want my animals to be thinking social hierarchy. Once they do, they will be spending their time trying to figure out how to move up in the hierarchy."

So What Should Trainers Do?

In general, I believe that "down" is a good position to teach your dog, if for no other reason than physical control. I frequently use downs at a distance instead of a recall, and I use downs and belly rubs as a relaxation technique. The down cue is also a means to reduce barking and establish control of overly excited dogs in my classes. (Yes, they can have too much fun playing games!)

I have observed situations in free-playing dogs where one dog will stand over a dog who's lying in a submissive position and there seems to be communication in this interaction. For me, it boils down to this: With some dogs, I want to catch them in the act of standing up, in the owner's presence, and reward that "I'm okay" behavior. For other dogs, I want them to volunteer (or I will cue or lure) a relaxed or tummy-up position so I can give them a belly rub or get them to relax.

All of my anecdotal, nonscientific experience with dogs reinforces the reality that dog training is an art, a science, and a mechanical skill. Deciding which dog needs what is the art of dog training. ❖

The Settle ("Relax") Behavior

Diane Sullivan, January/February 2002

A tool that every trainer should possess is how to aid in settling a puppy or dog. I use this exercise as a cue to calm down or relax a pup in a potentially stressful situation—such as a visit to the vet, a first car ride, having toe nails clipped, having ears cleaned, or during thunderstorms. In addition, this exercise helps the puppy or dog become comfortable with handling during bath time, teeth brushing, and mini-inspections (e.g., finding ticks and burrs). Here are the basic steps:

- First, start with a puppy who is already tired from a long play session or exercise.

- Find a quiet space for you and your puppy. An eight-week-old pup is ideal, but the exercise can certainly be done with a willing older dog.

- Sit on the floor with your legs open in a V shape.

- Move the pup close to your body and gently put her on her side. While giving calming sounds, begin to introduce your cue word. I use "settle," although "easy," "relax" or "be calm" will work as well.

- Cup the pup's shoulder area with one hand so as not to allow her to nip or bite your hand.

- Gently but firmly drape your other hand (or a leg) over the lower half of the pup's body so she cannot wriggle free.

- While holding the pup in place, repeat your cue word. Within 30 seconds or so, the pup should make what I call a resignation sigh.

- Keep the pup in this position for 30 to 60 seconds the first time. And don't forget to heap tons of praise on the pup when you let her up. If the puppy becomes agitated during this exercise, use some yummy treats to entice her to remain still...or keep the exercise to a five to ten second time period. Be firm, but not overbearing, in keeping the pup in a relaxed position. Once your pup understands this exercise, you'll want to use it when she is stressed or overexcited. I tell my clients to practice this every day until the pup is calm and quiet for a full five minutes.

The Ear Massage

After you have established your squirm-free time (which should occur relatively quickly) and repeated the exercise for a few days for the initial 30 seconds, you can work on my expanded version of the settle exercise: the ear massage. With your thumb and forefinger, start massaging at the base of the ear leather and work your way down to the end of the ear, as if trying to smooth out imaginary wrinkles. Repeat these motions as long as needed.

The ear massage works well if your dog is seriously injured in an accident or is bitten by something that causes her to go into shock. Its effect seems similar to that of one person holding an injured person's hand and asking the injured person to stay awake so he or she doesn't go into deep shock. It's calming and supportive...and it may save a dog's life. ❖

Are You Ready to Take on Behavioral Cases?

Pia Silvani, January/February 2004

Before you put your reputation on the line, think twice about taking on behavioral cases—the dog's life and relationship with the owner could be at stake.

No matter how simple the case may appear, there is usually no quick, easy solution to most behavior problems. Owners typically do not seek help until they are frustrated, concerned, and at their wit's end. They may have exhausted all other avenues—nothing has worked. You get the call! You might be the dog's last chance.

Knowing this should not put pressure on you to take the case, however, one of the universally recognized principles in professional practices is that it is difficult to know what you do not know.

Self-Evaluation

Consider a self-evaluation:

- "Can I adequately handle the case?"

- "Am I ready?"

Some things to think about:

1. **Knowledge?** Evaluate how much time you have spent educating yourself through reading, attending lectures, and mentoring under experts. A few quick reads and attending a seminar here and there is not sufficient.

2. **Communication?** When you take on behavioral cases, you become a translator, or go-between, for two different species who desire to live harmoniously together. Can you be effective? You will need to find a common ground so they can tell each other their needs, desires, and limitations. To effectively accomplish this both dog and owner must find you trustworthy. You will be asked questions far beyond the arena of dog training. Can you clearly identify the scope of your role?

3. **Competence?** Are you prepared to take a history, knowing exactly what questions to ask to help determine what is causing the problem? Prepare a detailed history sheet, including a liability waiver, and make sure you have adequate liability insurance. Plan on developing a systematic way of extrapolating information from the client without making them feel unworthy. Can you get information without the client becoming defensive? Are you fully familiar with the possible triggers that might be involved in the particular case? Can you be well balanced in your thinking and sustain a professional relationship with the client, regardless of how you feel? These owners are counting on success, no matter how difficult the problem may be. The wrong advice can backfire, causing the owner to be upset and making you legally liable as a result.

4. **Ethical Beliefs?** There are two important considerations here:

  • Do you understand the difference between punishment, discipline, and abuse?

  • There are various forms of punishment that are non-aversive and effective. On the other hand, there may be times when positive punishment is necessary. If this is your choice, are you fully familiar with the limitations, risks, and benefits of using punishment to effectively implement a treatment program in a humane and effective manner? You must be familiar with what influences the effectiveness of a consequence, or it can cause more harm than good.

5. **Success?** Can you resolve the problem and make recommendations that will help treat the underlying cause as opposed to treating the symptoms? If a client called regarding house soiling, is a crate always recommended as your first option? What if the soiling was a result of separation anxiety and the owners took your advice only to find a bloody dog when they returned?

6. **Honesty?** What if the situation becomes much more then you had anticipated? Can you be honest? Can you be truthful and fair to the dog and owner? You will receive more respect by being honest than by misleading the client about your abilities. Let the client know you cannot go beyond your scope of practice, while assuring them that you will continue to provide them good services by directing them to someone with "different specialties." You can teach the value of training while providing support and education.

Dr. Suzanne Hetts' book *Pet Behavior Protocols–What to Say; What to Do; When to Refer* (AAHA Press, 1999) is a "must have" for anyone interested in expanding upon self-evaluation when starting out and furthering their education in behavior problems.

Taking on the Case

Since you will be paid for this service, do not spend an hour on the telephone giving advice and getting information. Compare behavior problems with a chronic illness: you would not diagnose or troubleshoot a serious condition over the phone. There is much to see and know before making conclusions.

1. **Pre-Visit.** Explain to the clients in advance:

  • Cost of session;

  • Length of session (one to two hours depending upon the complexity of the case);

- What the visit entails:
  Getting a history;
  Learning about the dog's background;
  Household environment and influences;
  Family dynamics;
  A verbal and written summary;
  Giving options to help resolve the matter.

- You will not be training the dog; and

- *No guarantees.* We cannot guarantee our own behavior, never mind the behavior of a dog.

2. **Professional Etiquette:**

   - Be prompt. Your time and your client's time is valuable.

   - Dress for success—neat and clean. You only have one chance to make a first impression.

   - Establish rapport—be approachable, courteous, attentive, and friendly.

   - Refrain from making disparaging remarks about other animal care professionals—they could have been your referral or a source of future business.

3. **Avoid Distractions.** Give the client your undivided attention and avoid disruptions. Try to make in-home appointments during school hours unless you need to see the dog and child(ren) interact.

4. **Avoid Being Judgmental.** Be sympathetic to their problem, no matter how you feel. If you do not have patience and do not enjoy working with people, then you should probably not be involved in behavioral work. The more understanding, compassionate, and caring you can be, the more the client will open up. If you come across as insensitive, the client may develop the same attitude.

5. **Stay Focused.** Keep the client focused and on track. Ignore the "yes, but" client since it is unrealistic to expect a pet owner to share your understanding of why the dog is behaving the way he is and how to resolve it. Clients are very often releasing some of their anxiety. They feel responsible, guilty, angry, ashamed, embarrassed, frustrated, and/or anxious about the future. You are there to support and help them find a way to improve the relationship and resolve the problem.

6. **Observation Flags:**

   - Relationship between dog and owner;

   - Behavior of dog to owner;

   - Behavior of owner to dog;

   - Dog's behavior and reaction to you and the environment;

   - Family dynamics;

- Early background and reinforcement history.

- Does the owner want to really change the behavior (including both owners?)

- What are they looking for you to tell them?

- What are the most important things for the client to accomplish? Can you satisfy their needs and wants? What is a want? What is a need?

Summation Overview

You have digested all of the information given to you. The discussion of the information collected in your session can be extremely touchy and sensitive. Perhaps the owner wanted you to recommend re-homing the dog, yet you feel the dog can do quite well in the present environment with limited work. Or, re-homing the dog is not an option for the client, yet you feel the dog is far too dangerous to continue to live in the home.

Most owners are unaware of the depth, time, and commitment involved when attempting to alter behaviors. What happened to the "magic wand?" Can't you just make it go away? Your goal is to show flexibility and attempt to come to a mutual conclusion by making recommendations that meet their criteria and ability. The key is to find a way for them to be satisfied and successful.

Depending upon the severity of the case, there are four options to discuss with your client. Be careful to give them time to decipher and think through the options before making a quick decision: (1) management; (2) behavior modification; (3) re-homing; or (4) euthanasia.

Management. Management means that the owner must control the environmental triggers to help alter the dog's behavior. In certain situations, this can be very effective by itself. In other instances, it may need to be combined with behavior modification. Management is not as easy as it sounds, especially when children are involved.

Behavior Modification. Behavior modification typically entails a systematic desensitization and counterconditioning program, using a combination of classical and operant conditioning. The hope is to change the conditioned emotional response (CER) of the dog. Once the CER is altered, changing the behavior becomes easier. This path requires a dedicated client, willing and able to spend many months on accomplishing a goal.

Re-homing. Re-homing generally only comes as an option when there are children or other family dogs involved, and the dog's bite threshold is high. Keep in mind that re-homing the dog does not necessarily resolve the core problem.

Euthanasia. The decision for euthanasia should *only* be made by the owner(s). It is not your place to tell the owners what "you" would do; they do not have your level of experience or education in canine social behavior. When presenting euthanasia as an option to consider, *always* recommend a second opinion. This is a gut-wrenching option that can leave the owner feeling panicked, grief-stricken, confused, angry, and guilty. *Never* recommend euthanasia over the phone.

Summary

Taking on the responsibility of a behavioral case can be difficult and challenging. To be successful, it is essential that you are confident in, and comfortable with, the preparations you have made. Experience is an important teacher! Consider too, the value of your time spent providing early education and devising intervention programs to help prevent future behavior problems. Working with shelters can provide important educational information to new and potential pet owners! ❖

Training the Hunter/Retriever: An Emerging Challenge for Positive Trainers

Jim Barry, September/October 2004

Training hunting dogs poses a special challenge to positive trainers. The tasks that gun dogs perform are physically demanding. Hunting dogs must search fields for hours on end, locate and flush game and retrieve over long distances, across difficult terrain and in uncomfortable weather. And they must remain focused in the face of major distractions, including wildlife and gunfire.

What Gun Dogs Do

In addition to being hunting companions, gun dogs compete in tests and trials to earn titles. Many breed clubs sponsor a basic Working Certificate (WC). For a Labrador Retriever to earn a WC, for example, she must retrieve shot birds on land and in the water out to about 50 yards. There are higher level tests that involve longer distances and distractions such as boats and decoys. Dogs at these levels must also do "blind retrieves," delivering birds that the dog did not see fall, following whistle and hand signals from the handler.

Field trials, sponsored by the AKC, are structured events in which dogs compete against one another. They often involve multiple long retrieves, distant blinds, and very heavy cover (brush). A few years ago, some gun dog trainers, dissatisfied with what they perceived as a disconnect between field trials and real hunting, organized hunt tests, in which dogs gain titles by performing a specific set of tasks. The tasks increase in complexity as dogs move from Junior to Senior and Master levels (or the equivalent title, depending on the organization.) The AKC, the UKC, and two other organizations—North American Hunting Retriever Association (NAHRA) and North American Versatile Hunting Dog Association (NAVDHA)—offer hunt test programs.[1]

What is "Force Fetch?"

Historically the training of hunting dogs in the U.S. has been dominated by professionals who use force-based training. This approach is epitomized by the "force fetch" method. Most professionals use electronic collars, so that they have become the norm in training gun dogs. While the professionals have developed coherent and systematic training systems, their reliance on negative reinforcement and positive punishment is a turn-off to many who prefer positive reinforcement methods.

Force fetch is both a training method and a philosophy. As a method, it relies on negative reinforcement to train a dog to take, hold, and release an object. The trainer starts with an appropriate retrieving object, usually a dummy or a paint roller. A stimulus is then applied to the dog, usually by pinching the ear or by inserting a dowel between the toes. When the dog opens its mouth, the object is inserted and the stimulus is ended. The dog is then required to hold the object for longer periods of time or to move forward to take it before the stimulus ceases. Eventually, the object is moved to the floor and the dog learns to end the stimulus by picking it up on the command "fetch." The command is then generalized to other objects and the distance is increased. According to Evan Graham, one of the most articulate proponents of this method, the objectives of force fetching are appropriate mouth habits, including hold and delivery, compliance with the retrieve command under demanding conditions in the field, and increase in momentum.[2]

As a philosophy, force fetch is the foundation for "force" or "pressure" training. The concept is that, because hunting requires such difficult work, the dog must learn to tolerate discomfort at each stage in the training process. Force fetch is followed by such exercises as "stick fetch," "force to pile," and "water force." All involve using "pressure" from an ear pinch, a stick, or an e-collar. The goal, as John and Amy Dahl put it, "is a matter of teaching the dog that nothing that happens as a result of going on a retrieve will be as bad as the consequences of not going."[3]

Positive Training Proponents

Fortunately, positive trainers have begun to take an interest in training gun dogs. Several have developed alternatives to force fetch, employing shaping and clicker methodologies to train a retrieve on command. Susan Smith, who moderates the Positive Gun Dogs discussion group, described below, has a clicker technique to teach a retrieve. Shirley Chong's approach is described at http://shirleychong. com/keepers/retrieve.html, and Morgan Spector has a method in his book *Clicker Training for Obedience*.[4]

For other areas of gundog training, resources on positive approaches are slim. Steve Rafe wrote a book on *Training Your Dog for Birdwork*.[5] Although it is outdated in some respects, Steve has pamphlets that provide more current information on positive techniques available from his Web site, www.starfire-rapport.com. The American Hunting Dog Association (www.ahda.org) has a basic book on gun dog training, however many of the methods have to be modified for a positive reinforcement approach.

There are now several good sources of gun dog training information on the Internet. They include the NAHRA and NAVHDA Web sites, *Working Retrieval Central* (www.working-retriever.com), and two periodicals, *The Retriever Journal* (www. retrieverjournal. com) and *The Pointing Dog Journal* (www.pointingdogjournal. com). Two resources merit particular mention. The first is the Positive Gun Dogs e-mail list on Yahoo. The list now has more than 300 members, all of whom are interested in positive training methods for hunting, tests, and trials. Some are very experienced; others are novices. But all are very supportive and willing to answer questions from "newbies." To join, send an e-mail to positivegundogs-subscribe@ yahoogroups.com

Another excellent resource is the Gundog and Bird Dog Forum, managed by British trainer Eric Begbie. British gun dog training methods, while not entirely "positive," are much gentler than those used in America. Eric's "broadsheets" on training are available on the forum. To join, go to www.less-stress.com/discuss2/. Some of the British members have even begun to experiment with clicker training a retrieve!

For training in the field, most regional gun dog breed organizations have field training and test programs. Check the national breed club's Web site for the locations of regional clubs. When you take your dog to a training session, you probably will be the only person there with a clicker on your lanyard. Be prepared to explain what it is, and also to take a little heat for using "soft" methods.

Many members of the Positive Gun Dogs list have trained their dogs successfully through the Senior Level in hunt tests. To our knowledge, no dogs have become Field Trial Champions based on positive training methods, but the experience of positive trainers in other dog activities augurs well for the future of gun dog training. To paraphrase Margaret Mead, "Never say a dedicated group of positive trainers can't change a dog sport. How else was it ever done?" ❖

References:

1 See www.akc.org/dic/events/hunting/index.cfm; www.hrc-ukc.com/; www.nahra.org/; and www.navhda.org/.

2 Graham, E. (2003). *Smartworks for Retrievers*, 2nd ed. Liberty, MO: Rush Creek Press.

3 Dahl, J. & Dahl, A. (2001). *The 10-minute Retriever. Minocqua*, WI: Willow Press, p. 178.

4 Spector, M. (2001). *Clicker Training for Obedience*. Waltham, MA: Sunshine Press.

5 Rafe, S. (1987). *Training Your Dog for Birdwork*. Fairfax, VA: Denlinger's Publishers, Ltd.

The Ubiquitous Labrador Retriever: Has Success Spoiled Our Number One Breed?

Beverly Hebert, July/August 2003

No doubt about it—Labrador Retrievers still reign supreme as America's most popular dog. According to the AKC there were 154,616 registered Labs in 2002—56,124 Golden Retrievers in second place and 46,963 German Shepherd Dogs in third place do not even come close. Therefore it may seem surprising that many APDT trainers who responded to an informal survey said they no longer include Labs among their top recommendations as family pets.

Those trainers who still place Labs high on their list give the same reasons as the Lab-loving public: good looks and an easy care coat; high intelligence and responsiveness to training; an outgoing, affectionate nature; mellowness with other animals; rugged stamina and awesome retrieving instincts. These characteristics contribute to the breed's ability to function as a versatile working dog fulfilling a variety of important roles in society. Today the breed's reputation as the ideal family and hunting dog is superimposed with the angelic image of Labs working as service and guide dogs, and as members of search and rescue teams. In addition, law enforcement agencies have discovered that Labs make ideal bomb and drug detection dogs. No other breed is more often in the media spotlight, portrayed as the dog for all seasons.

However, many pet dog trainers and shelter staff workers are seeing another side to the Labrador's personality that leads them to wonder if the match between this high energy dog and today's busy urban family is not a match made in Heaven after all.

The Angelic Labrador Retriever's "Evil Twin"—Demolition Devil Dog

"People get Labs because they want great family dogs but they wind up with the 'dog from hell' that has to be managed constantly," said trainer Sue Conklin (Denver, Colorado) while working with an adolescent male Lab named Brody. Although Brody's owner took him for long daily walks, he was too destructive to be trusted in the house, barked for hours if left alone, continued to jump up in spite of attempts to train him to sit politely for petting, and worst of all, would sometimes nip wildly at his owner's clothes and grab at her with his paws. Brody sounded like a prototype for the hard-to-live-with Lab, mismatched with two working owners.

Even having a seemingly ideal family situation wasn't enough to keep a Lab named Tess out of harm's way. After conducting extensive research into the best kind of dog for their family, Paige and John Contreras decided upon a Lab. They obtained Tess from a breeder they found on the internet when she was six weeks old. Her owners said they tried to properly train her, first working with a trainer at home, then eventually sending her to a board and train facility as a last resort. John Contreras worked out of their home and Paige was a stay-at home mom, so all along puppy Tess got plenty of company and supervision. However, they found Tess difficult to potty train and she peed whenever she got excited. She also had to have expensive knee surgery when she was about six months old, followed by a long period of constant crating. Paige says jumping up and play biting were things Tess never really outgrew and soon it became impossible for the children to play with her. By the time she was 85 lbs. she was too big and strong for Paige to handle, even on a head halter. John was the only one who could walk her, and one day after Tess threw what he felt was a "temper tantrum" on leash, John came home and announced he was done with her. Paige, tired of cleaning up the dog's pee, agreed with relief. Exit Tess.

Meanwhile in Long Beach, California a pair of Labs named Maggie and Jake were wreaking havoc on the life of owner Karen Frakes. Karen had found Maggie difficult from the beginning. "Every day when I came home from work, it was another disaster to clean up or fix or get repaired. There were times I thought, I'm going to have to give her away… before she was a year old I would just stress out over this everyday—then I thought, maybe part of her acting out is that she's alone all day, so… I went to the pound, and there was this beautiful six month old Lab, just about Maggie's age. I brought him home and… they broke out the windows in my French door and ripped the redwood slats off the outside of my house. When I had a computer installed, they ripped off the outside electrical wiring so I had to have an electrician come and put a steel box around it. They dug a four foot deep hole in my newly landscaped yard, ripped down small trees and bushes, would chew on everything—my antique furniture, my shoes, lots of clothes—they chewed a hole in my bathroom wall—it just went on forever. One day when I was walking them, they saw another dog and were so excited—they were going one way and I was going another and I tripped and broke my arm. Then one night I opened the door and they rushed behind me and knocked me off the steps and I got a concussion and had to go to the hospital."

Brody, Tess, Maggie, and Jake's behavior, not untypical of undertrained, underexercised Labs, explains why so many with less committed and patient owners end up in shelters, usually during or shortly following adolescence.

"Most of the owners that I deal with are giving up their Labs because they don't have time for them," says Sheridan, Wyoming breed rescue volunteer Barb Walset. "We end up with a lot of Labs that have excess energy and the need to work, and owners want them to lie on the floor in front of the fireplace. That doesn't come until much later with this breed."

Trying to bridge the gap between owner expectations and the reality of rambunctious Labs has become a full time job for Joel Walton (Prince Frederick, Maryland), author of *Labrador Retrievers for Dummies* and *Positive Puppy Training Works*. "Labs or any breed bred to do certain kinds of work are generally going to be very active dogs…while most owners want a dog that doesn't do anything at all, except wag his tail and look at them with love in his eyes and maybe walk with them," says Walton. "When I'm talking to owners, I say, 'When you got a puppy you didn't want to learn to be a dog trainer, did you? You already have a full time job and hobbies and a family—you probably even go places on vacation where you can not take your dog with you, right?' "

"The good news for the dogs is they're pretty adaptable. Labradors…have been bred to pay attention to human beings and follow their directions and that's certainly a good start for a pet dog. Also, there's a vast activity range in Labradors and the most important thing people can do when they're looking for a puppy is to get the right fit. For those who want just a pet, that means finding a breeder whose goal is to produce good pets. If you go to a breeder who specializes in field trial champions, you're going to get an Olympic athlete type of dog bred to have enough energy to do tremendously demanding work!"

Sally McCarthy Munson, who breeds Shamrock Acres Labradors in Waunakee, Wisconsin, agrees that Labs from field lines tend to both act and look different from Labs produced by conformation breeders. Munson says those from field backgrounds are a little more streamlined and lighter in weight, with longer legs and narrower heads. "Most conformation dogs have some English bloodlines, and because of this, people call me and ask, 'do you have American Labradors or English,' but that's not the right question—what they should be saying is, 'Do you have dogs with a field or with a show background?'"

Another thing to know, says Marianne Foote, owner of Winroc Labrador Retrievers and a director in the Labrador Retriever Club, "is the trend now is that everybody's a specialist. Basically we have three groups—the high performance field trial and obedience trial breeders and competitors who fall into the same category because they're demanding a lot of energy, a lot of focus, and a lot of trainability; those are probably dogs that are labeled hyper by the average pet owner. Then there are the straight conformation breeders … and third, there are the hunt test dog show crosses."

It is these field and show combination lines that McCarthy Munson says are most likely to produce the ideal Lab temperament—which she describes as a dog with enough brains, drive, and focus to succeed in sports like hunting or agility, but also a dog who can also turn that energy on and off and be very manageable around the house. "These are my favorite litters! We have pet people who get these dogs that may never hunt—but they enjoy hiking, water sports, or running with their dog."

However, it is not safe to assume all show line Labs are couch potatoes. Since low and high activity level and hyperactivity are all subjective terms, the best way someone can end up with the kind of puppy they want is to take a good long look at the parents. It is also wise to go to breeders that can give references from people who already have purchased dogs from them. Conversely, Juxi Burr of Albuquerque, New Mexico, who has produced many champion Labradors, says the most likely way to end up with a problem puppy is to get one that has been randomly bred by a high volume breeder or a private party "backyard" breeder, contributing to what Burr terms a disastrous overpopulation problem.

Marianne Foote concurs. "Unfortunately, what's happened is that everyone is blaming (hyperactivity) on field trial dogs, but very few field breeders have constant litters, and most of their dogs go to those who are going to be competitive with them.

The phone calls that I get about behavior and soundness problems come from people who have bought dogs off the internet. Of course, there may be some poor field line dogs too—but good field trial dogs can't be out of control! A good performance dog has to have a long attention span and ability to learn…but what I call the internet breeders, basically puppy mills breeding dogs for public consumption, are selecting dogs for color only. It's significant that phone requests I get about puppies are generally prefaced by color preference; the public perception is that yellows are sweet and kind, and chocolate is rare, but neither stereotype is true. What I'm saying is not that dogs of these colors don't carry these good qualities, but that Labs of any color can have an incorrect temperament if they come from breedings based on color alone."

An interesting corollary to the pet owner's preference for yellow Labs is the fact that the majority of dogs with hunting or field trial titles are black. According to Candlewood Kennels breeder and producer of several field champions Mary Howley, this is because "those lines that carry the black coat color have traditionally been the most successful, so there is still the perception that the best competitive dogs are black." However, Howley says that in the past 25 years it has become possible to get equally good blood lines in dogs with yellow or chocolate coats.

All this may be helpful information to pass along to clients planning to get a puppy, but what about those who are already in trouble with a Lab they may have bought from a puppy mill dealer? Given that trainers are going to be meeting a lot of these folks, what help can they offer these pet owners and dogs like Brody, Tess, Maggie, and Jake?

Trainers to the Rescue—Keys To Successful Interventions

For starters, here is what three trainers who work with many Labradors think others should know about what makes them tick:

- Connie Cleveland: "What people need to remember is, this is an incredibly social breed! They really want to be somebody's dog. When they're not getting the attention they need, their response is hyperactivity. Other breeds may become shy or aloof, but Labradors get physically active, jumping up and knocking people down. They are so strong and physically tough that without early training, many owners lose the ability to control them at a very young age. If you combine big, strong, and gregarious, you have a dog who is going to be dragging his owner around."

- Barbara Demarest: "Labs are very powerful and also easily stimulated—not so much prey driven, but just excited by other people and dogs. For almost every owner, I suggest the Gentle Leader™ head collar. For Labs, a lot of the solution lies with exercise. That's probably true of many breeds, but it's phenomenally true of this breed."

- Sue Conklin: "The thing I find with Labs is, where other active dogs may tend to pester you, dropping balls at you, Labs are more likely to body slam you."

All of this is not to say that the same training methods that work with out-of-control Labs will not work with other dogs as well, which brings us back full circle.

"Dogs are dogs are dogs," says Joel Walton. "If everyone approaches it that way, we know a lot about training dogs and about building proper relationships. If anybody says 'yes, but Chows, or yes, but Jack Russells, or yes, but field bred Labs'—just remember, dogs have more things in common than differences, and if you manage them correctly, they can die of old age in their homes."

Elements of a good training program begin with good interviews and histories. For difficult to control dogs, the next steps usually include:

- A plan to meet the dog's real needs, including companionship and mental stimulation.

- A management plan (i.e., teaching owners what to do when visitors come, etc.)

- Use of proper equipment: crates, tethers, head halters, etc.

- Basic obedience training: owners whose dogs will sit, stay, and come when called have control over their dogs.

- No Free Lunch/Say Please Program: This helps owners establish the right relationship and gain control over the dog without resorting to physical bullying.

- Gentle mouth exercises to encourage bite inhibition.

- Rewarding calm behavior.

- An individually designed exercise program.

Possibilities for exercise programs include: excursions to a dog park, doggy day care, or back yard play dates; stuffed Kong™ for chewing; using treats to send the dog downstairs and recalling him back upstairs; and playing tug, retrieving, and catch games. Recalls in the back yard over a series of low cavaletti jumps will also provide a good work-out. Teaching the dog some tricks and short sessions comprised of fast sits, downs, and targeting can provide both mental and physical stimulation and relieve stress.

Brody's trainer began by obtaining a detailed history. By carefully questioning the owner, and observing and interacting with the dog, she discovered that his seemingly unprovoked episodes of wild grabbing and nipping was not aggressive attention seeking, but rather related to stress over having his neck or collar grabbed. "When he was a puppy, he was sometimes hooked up to a cable runner between posts—and he would repeatedly get himself wrapped around the end post (tightening his collar) and panic and scream until somebody came out to get him." Desensitizing exercises helped Brody overcome his negative reaction to having his collar touched. In addition, integrating Brody more into family life by placing him on a leash while his owners watched TV and allowing him to sleep in a crate in their bedroom, helped satisfy his needs for companionship. At last report, Brody's owner has been able to slowly allow him more freedom in the house and is happy with his progress.

Maggie and Jake, who could have been voted most unlikely to have a happy outcome, are doing fine now. They are still in their homes and Karen, their owner, was recently able to call her handy man to come and make repairs because they are not destructive anymore. Things started to turn around for this trio when Karen began working with a trainer. "Every day, rain or shine, I had walked them religiously," Karen recalled, "but Terry Long, my trainer, said that kind of walking just wasn't enough for these dogs—they needed to be able to run—so now they go to the dog park every day!" In addition to the chewing and digging problems, Jake also had some fearful behaviors that needed to be addressed. "He seemed to be uncomfortable in his skin, poor little guy. He was afraid of cars and of leads; when I'd take him for walks he would hyperventilate." Jake was put on medication, and the medication plus daily outings to the dog park for both Maggie and Jake have made all the difference.

Tess also ended up safe and sound in a new home. Tess was adopted by Erica Pints (Stanton, California), her trainer from the boarding kennel. Tess' original trainer, Terry Long (Long Beach, California), believes that many Labs like Tess simply overwhelm their unsuspecting owners. "Good-intentioned owners like the Contreras family are often woefully unprepared for the day-after-day, week-after-week, month-after-month reality of meeting the needs of a young Labrador. They expect to do some training and feel that they are doing a lot, but the reality is that these dogs need much, much more than the owners ever imagined. As a result, management—crating, tethering, etc.—start to comprise a large part of their dealings with their dog. And that just doesn't meet the dog's needs."

Erica says she never had trouble handling Tess and ended up falling in love with her. When Erica noticed that Tess was wetting herself in her sleep, a vet check found she had a weak bladder, and the problem was solved with a medication called Phenylpropanolamine. As for the temper tantrums on leash, Erica says, "What was happening was that on the way home from a walk, the dog would start to jump and bite at the owner because she didn't want to end the walk. Her home was not a bad home, but because her owner couldn't trust her enough, Tess was always stuck in the crate. I never had that problem with her. She had a history of knowing how to walk with me on a buckle collar and leash with treats—if she pulled, I would say 'let's go' and we'd change directions. Tess is about two now and she's a great dog! I have a blast taking her to the beach because she just dives in the waves and I love to see that! She loves to retrieve too so I taught her to go fetch a toy when she wants to be petted; this was also to stop the biting and jumping up, and it did! It's so funny—sometimes when I come home from work before she even comes near me she goes and grabs her toy and then comes back to me for petting. She's a really good dog!" Tess is living proof that one person's surrendered dog can turn into another person's best friend.

Joel Walton has evolved an especially amusing way of getting that important point over to potential puppy buyers right from the beginning. "They come to visit and everyone is looking for the perfect family pet. I tell them how much work they will have and I introduce them to a big black male who jumps up. I watch to see if that freaks them out and I tell them, this is how your dog will be if you don't have time to train him. Then I put that dog up and I bring out another big black male with good manners that sits politely for petting, and I tell them, this is what the dog can be like if he's properly trained. And after they chew on that awhile, I tell them that the first dog and this dog are the same fellow!" ❖

What Every Trainer Should Know About Protection Trained Dogs

Dan McNally, May/June 2004

The phrase "protection training" invokes different images to different people: out of control dogs inflicting severe injuries to passers by, a dog that is a danger to visitors and/or children, junkyard dogs, police dogs taking down suspects, Schutzhund dogs in competition, or a family dog that can protect when the need arises. What is myth, and what is reality? Are these dogs really a danger to the public in general, or only if they are not trained properly?

History

Dogs have been used for varied jobs for thousands of years: hunting, herding, droving, livestock and estate guarding, war duties, police work, and personal protection.

Breeds traditionally used for personal protection are ones that are found in the working group (AKC) such as the Doberman Pinscher, Rottweiler, Giant Schnauzer, and Boxer. Some dogs have been used for dual purpose work, such as the large herding breeds. The traditional job of these breeds is to herd stock and protect it from dangers such as wolves and poachers. These are the larger breeds that can be found in the herding group (AKC) such as the German Shepherd Dog, Briard, Bouvier des Flandres, and the Belgian Sheepdog.

Why Own a Protection Dog?

There are several reasons people desire protection trained dogs, personal protection being the most obvious reason. Depending on where someone lives, works, or travels, this may be the best protection option for them. Some people want to protect themselves and are not comfortable with owning a firearm, or are not physically able to perform self-defense techniques. For these people, a protection dog may be a good choice.

There are also protection sports, just as there are human sports involving firearms and martial arts. The best known of these is Schutzhund, a sport that originated in Germany. Schutzhund involves obedience, tracking, and protection. Other protection sports are French Ring and various personal protection competitions.

Types of Protection Dogs

Image or Threat Dog. These dogs are taught to react to a threat by barking, growling, and snarling. They are not taught to bite. The goal is to project a threatening "image." This is the type of dog that most people seeking protection training really want. This is fairly simple to teach and almost any trainer can do a good enough version of this by teaching a bark, growl, or bark/growl on cue.

Area Guard. This is the stereotypical "junk-yard dog." The dog is taught to protect a specific area. For the dog, the rules are fairly simple: go into protection mode when someone enters the specified area and go out of protection mode when they leave the area.

Protection Dog. These are multi-purpose protection dogs. They are taught to display as image dogs do, attack on cue, or in specific situations they have been trained to stop attacking and shut down on cue. These dogs require a very high level of training, stability, and temperament. This level of training also requires a dedicated owner willing to put forth the time and effort that this level of training entails.

"Attack Dog." This is really not a type of protection training but needs to be discussed. I would categorize an "attack" dog as a badly trained, unstable, out of control, dangerous dog, and these are the dogs that give protection training a bad name. Unfortunately, this is the type of dog that a majority of the public perceives when they hear the phrase "protection dog." These dogs are created by misinformation, bad training, and/or the wrong dog used for this type of training. They carry all of the risks and liability concerns of any other dangerous dog, perhaps even more so.

How We Train

In a nutshell, protection training involves taking a dog's natural protective instinct, bringing it out, reinforcing it, building it to the desired level, and forming/controlling it to the degrees we want. We put biting on cue and "cease biting" on cue. The dog is presented with a visual threat, and when the dog reacts, it is reinforced by the threat retreating.

Many people are surprised to learn how much time is focused on not biting, on controlling the protective instinct, and teaching the dog to only bite when asked or only in the very specific situations that it has been trained for. The control level for a safe protection trained dog needs to be extremely high.

The Right Dog

You need to have the right dog for protection work. The dog needs to have a very high confidence level. There can not be any fearfulness, shyness, or hesitation around people. What we like to see in a protection prospect is a very outgoing personality to the point of being pushy and annoying. We look for dogs and puppies that will not take no for an answer and keep pushing until they get what they want. This can be modified with basic training of course, but this is the basic mindset we want to see. It is this confidence and persistence that will be a great asset for protection training. Good protection prospects can be a handful for the average dog owner and need to start basic training as soon as possible.

The dog cannot have any aggression problems, although due to a higher guarding drive, resource guarding can be more common in protection prospects than other dogs. Resource guarding does not eliminate a dog from being a protection prospect, but it does need to be addressed before protection training starts.

The dog's training level needs to be very high. I will not even start protection training until the dog is reliable off-leash. If the owner does not have the commitment to train their dog to an off-leash level, they most likely will not have the commitment needed for protection training.

Common Perceptions and Misconceptions

Socialization will ruin a protection prospect.

This is probably the most prevalent and the most dangerous misconception regarding protection training. The theory goes that if the dog likes people, he or she will not protect you, and the way to create a protection dog is to not socialize it with humans. This could not be further from the truth. The dog needs to be more heavily socialized than most dogs. If the dog is not comfortable with humans, it should not be protection trained. A large, powerful, under-socialized dog can be a huge liability and a danger to the public, period.

If I love my dog, he will protect me.

Maybe, maybe not. It is not unusual for a dog to not bite during a protection test, even if it looks like he or she wants to. It is also not unusual to teach these dogs to bite in a very short time. It simply requires forming the protective instinct to a higher level. There is a difference between wanting to protect and having learned the physical skills to do so. This is no different with humans: a human may very well want to protect him or herself, but may not be able to if they do not possess self-defense skills.

Although a protective instinct is part of a dog's natural make-up, it may or may not be at a high enough level for the dog to protect when needed. It also takes a high confidence level that some dogs simply do not possess.

They are inherently dangerous/they are not safe around children.

Protection-trained dogs are not inherently more dangerous than other dogs. However, there are extra things that need to be considered when owning one. You cannot send a stranger into your house if someone is not already in the house. You need to be aware of where you are and pay attention to your dog to make sure he or she is not reading something wrong. Even with these caveats, a protection trained dog is much more stable and controllable than the fearful dogs we see all too often.

If you have the right dog and he or she is trained properly, the dog will not be much different from any other dog. My own protection trained dogs have been used as therapy dogs in nursing homes and in schools for safe-dog programs with no problems at all. Most police dogs, when not on duty, live in the officer's home with their children.

Harsh physical corrections are needed in protection training.

As with any other form of training, there are different techniques used by different trainers. These can range from positive techniques to very harsh ones. With protection training, most of the use of corrections and force revolve around teaching the dog to shut down, or "out." Some trainers maintain that corrections are needed to teach this. The reason is that some trainers wait to teach the "out" until the dog has a high bite skill. As with most things, the more we let a behavior strengthen, the harder it is to control it later. It is much easier to start teaching the out in the beginning of protection training. This way, the out level will coincide with the biting level. It is certainly possible to protection train a dog without physical or collar corrections.

You need to beat the dog to get it to bite.

Some people believe that protection trained dogs are beaten or otherwise abused to cause them to bite. Although some people may do that in the name of "training," it is not necessary or desired to do this. You may have seen "bad guys" swinging sticks at a dog in Schutzhund competitions. This is not done to hurt the dog but to give the dog a bigger visual threat to deal with. The dogs are not hit hard with these sticks— they simply get a tap on the ribs. There are some sticks that make a loud sound when they strike the dog. These sticks are hollow and split so they sound loud with very little force. I have hit myself harder with these sticks than I would a dog.

Only certain breeds can do protection training.

As with other doggie endeavors, you can certainly increase your chances of finding a suitable dog within certain breeds that have been traditionally used for protection work as mentioned earlier. Although this can increase your chances, it is no guarantee of a good prospect.

This is not to say that other breeds are incapable of protection work. It is more about instinct, attitude, and confidence than it is about traditional breed usage. Some breeds I have seen used are Standard Poodles, Border Collies, and Australian Shepherds. One of the best dogs I have personally trained, and a good example of why not to pigeonhole a breed, is a Labrador Retriever. She is also a top-notch horse herding dog.

Insurance Liability Concerns

Homeowner's Insurance. This can be a bit tricky. On the one hand, most insurance companies will not insure a home that has a protection-trained dog. On the other hand, an insurance company's idea of a protection dog is that of an out of control, dangerous dog. When I am asked, "Do you own a protection trained dog?" the question I hear is, "Do you own a dangerous dog?" I can honestly answer no. A fearful dog can be much more dangerous than a properly trained protection dog.

Liability Concerns. A properly trained protection dog does not bring a significantly higher liability risk to the owner, although there is an increased risk. The liability concerns are more in line with owning any other dog. However, you do need to accept responsibility in the event something goes wrong. If a protection-trained dog bites, it will generally be a much deeper bite than the more usual grab and release of most dogs. As with most things, the key to reducing liability is the knowledge of what you have, what it does, what it doesn't do, and how it works.

There have been parallels made between protection dogs and guns. In one sense, there is a similarity and in another sense, not. Both dogs and guns are potentially lethal forces, although a protection dog is much more controllable. You can not call back a bullet, but you can call back a protection dog. You can teach a dog to only bite certain parts of the body and to hold on to that part without inflicting major damage. You cannot direct a bullet to inflict a desired level of damage to a particular body part.

However, a comparison between protection dogs and guns is not without merit. This is a good barometer of an owner being able and willing to accept the responsibilities that come with owning a protection trained dog.

What Does This All Mean to Non-Protection Trainers?

There is a perception among some dog trainers that protection dogs are dangerous and should not be owned by anyone. They dismiss clients who express an interest in protection work. As with any other type of training, there are good trainers, bad trainers, and trainers who are somewhere in between. The difference here is that a bad trainer can very well produce a truly dangerous dog.

The more proper information owners receive, the less chance they will end up with a dog that is far beyond what they bargained for. I myself have worked with too many dogs with aggression problems that were caused by bad protection advice.

Not every dog is suitable for protection work, not every owner should have one, and not every trainer should do protection training. If you, as a trainer, are not interested in protection work, that is just fine. We all have our own interests and preferences. However, with a better understanding of what these dogs really are and how we get them there, even trainers who only work with puppies can be a big help to those of us who do protection training and the general public. There are many things, especially socialization, that can be done in the puppy and basic training stage to help the owner produce a better, safer dog.

Even if you personally feel someone should not have a protection dog, if someone really wants one, they will seek out that training. If an owner does not receive proper information about protection training, they may end up with a bad trainer and a dangerous dog. What I have also found is that the more information people have about protection training, the less likely they are to go through protection training with their dog.

The same rules apply here as with any potential referral. Visit any trainer who you are thinking of referring an owner to for protection training. Ask them how they train, how they screen clients, and ask to see an example of a dog they have trained. This can be even more important with protection training, given how badly things can go wrong. ❖

Immersion or Deprivation

Edited by Terry Long, featuring comments by Suzanne Clothier and
Deborah Jones, March/April 2003

As agility training becomes more and more popular, many trainers are faced with
the dilemma posed in this hypothetical case, which we presented to two respected
professionals. They were challenged to give us their best ideas in 700 words or less.

Ginger, Agility Socialite

Gary has come to you with a vexing problem. His dog, Ginger, is a high-energy
two-year-old English Shepherd who has been taking agility classes at a local school
after completing a basic group obedience class. They did quite well in the beginning
agility class and have just finished an intermediate class.

Ginger does all the obstacles with speed and confidence—when you can get her
to concentrate on Gary and the equipment. Most of the time, Gary finds himself
challenged to keep her attention away from the other dogs. All Ginger wants to do
is play with the other dogs. He has consulted two of the trainers at the school about
what to do. One says to take the dog on a regular basis to the dog park so that Ginger
can get her "doggy fix," and know that the agility field is not where you play with
other dogs. The other trainer told him to drop out of agility class, not to let Ginger
play with any other dogs at all but to, instead, work on "making Ginger pay attention
to you regardless of what else is going on" before coming back to class.

How would you suggest Gary proceed with Ginger?

Suzanne Clothier

There is so much missing here! Without more information, here are the basics
of my approach, which always addresses the relationship between dog and handler, a
foundation that sets the stage for both problems and their solutions.

Communication—Of particular interest to me is how Gary and Ginger communicate with each other. This can be seen in the use of or reliance on equipment and
whether or not there is tension/pulling on the leash. Show me a dog who pulls, and
I will show you a higher level of arousal, mutual disconnection, and a handler who
substitutes leash restraint for attentiveness, all of which set the stage for performance
problems.

Commitment to the conversation—Gary needs to learn that each time he steps into
Ginger's presence and asks her to be with him, he has begun a conversation with her.
If he expects a high quality conversation that can continue even in the face of other
things competing for Ginger's attention, he needs to practice that in every possible
way. This includes no pulling, his own unfailing attention to Ginger, and also the
generous reinforcement of Ginger's attentiveness to him.

Earn her respect—Gary may also need to learn to control resources which are meaningful to Ginger, with clear, consistent rules for how she needs to cooperate with him in order to enjoy those resources. When Gary acts like someone who deserves a dog's respect, he will receive more respect.

Self control—The description "high energy" is all too often code for "fast, reactive, volatile," a difficult combination if the dog is not taught self-control. I begin at the precise point where the dog is aware of the stimuli yet still responsive. I ask the dog to sit quietly on a loose leash. If she gets up, I ask her to sit again, and then we do it again, and again, and again. And we practice in countless situations. The dog learns that there is another option beyond reaction: control yourself!

Key elements are time and space. Ginger may be able to control herself for a specific amount of time, say for ten minutes in a class setting, before she needs a brief walk outside to lower her arousal level. Or she may need space between her and the stimuli, say 50 feet away from other dogs. When in doubt, use less time and more space, and build incrementally on success.

The goal of self-control training is a dog who is able to sit quietly, watch the world around her without reacting to it, and remain aware of and responsive to her handler if he asks for her attention. I do not want a dog who simply watches the handler.

Skill—Ginger and Gary both need new, specific skills. For Ginger, avoidance, i.e., "never let her play with other dogs," teaches nothing and may even intensify her desire/need. Equally ineffective is unstructured satiation, i.e., letting her play in the misguided hope that she will get "enough" and thus be willing to work after her desire has been satiated. This also teaches nothing. Instead, I would teach Ginger how to disengage from playing with other dogs. And far from discouraging it, I would be actively using play with other dogs as a real-life reward.

I would teach Gary how to deliver rewards in a timely, interesting, generous way and be FUN for Ginger in order to effectively compete with an intensely reinforcing activity. It is always difficult to instruct an inattentive/unaware handler who is neither fun nor generous, and hard to train a dog who does not respect her handler, who has no self-control, and who does not know how to stop playing when asked. To force the dog's attention and to restrain her, the handler becomes reliant on equipment and possibly the use of force, or simply loses control of the dog. It is a delight to instruct an attentive handler who is fun and generous with rewards, and easy to train a dog who has self-control, who respects her handler, and who can move easily between playtime and work.

Overall, don't stick band-aids on surface problem(s). Resolve training and performance problems at the foundation level of relationship...it is often where they begin.

Deborah Jones, PhD

Gary and Ginger have a problem that is fairly common in agility training. While Ginger is capable of performing the required behaviors, she is not focused on the activity. Instead, she becomes distracted by something else in the environment. In this case the distraction is other dogs.

Ginger is a young and highly energetic dog. As they progress to more difficult agility sequences and exercises, Gary needs to set up her training sessions so that she can be successful. For many dogs, an hour-long group class is less than ideal. The excitement of having to wait while watching other dogs run can be highly arousing and frustrating for certain dogs. Being asked to perform a specific sequence repeatedly (sometimes so that the handler can get it right) can be stressful and de-motivating. And being asked to pay attention for long periods of time can be quite difficult for young, distractible dogs.

Class Structure—Even though "Ginger does all the obstacles with speed and confidence…," she must not find doing agility as rewarding as playing with other dogs. If she were truly enjoying the activity, she would not feel the need to do something else instead. It would be helpful to change the class environment to make things easier and less stressful for Ginger. For example, working with Ginger for only part of the class time, and only working short, quick sequences, will help to maintain her enthusiasm. Crating her away from the activity between her turns would help as well. Also, Gary could practice and play focus games and tricks with her between their runs. One way to start this would be to wait for attention, even a slight look from Ginger toward Gary, and then click and treat. Gary is not giving a cue for attention, he is waiting for Ginger to offer it, then reinforcing that. In this way he is teaching Ginger that focusing on him can be rewarding.

Instead of a treat Gary could use the reward that Ginger has clearly told him she wants, a chance to interact with another dog. Gary could set up a training session with another friendly dog and owner. Again, Gary is going to wait for attention, not ask for it. When Ginger glances in his direction he will click, and allow her a minute to interact with the other dog ("Go play!"). He would then move Ginger away from the dog, wait for attention, click and allow interaction again. This process will allow Gary to control Ginger's access to other dogs. He is establishing control of the situation by requiring something of her (attention), then allowing her what she wants.

Deprivation—It would be a mistake to keep Ginger away from other dogs. Taking away her chance for social interaction will only make her want it even more when other dogs are around. On the other hand, allowing her unlimited free play is a bad idea as well. Instead, making interaction with other dogs dependent on working for Gary will help solve the problem. In addition, contrasting the use of "Go play!" as a reinforcer with a positively trained "Leave it!" will help Ginger understand that sometimes it is appropriate to play with other dogs, and sometimes it isn't.

Other Skills—Tricks such as spin, sit up, and bow would give Ginger a chance to stretch her muscles and use up a bit of her energy while in class. Having her touch Gary's hand (either with her nose or paw) would focus her on him and give them a fun and easy activity to do together. Working with Ginger in a familiar setting, such as her own backyard, to practice more difficult sequences and exercises, will allow her the opportunity to learn without the high level of distraction she experiences in class. Once in class, Gary should be aware that Ginger's performance will be poorer quality until she is able to withstand the distractions present. He should lower his expectations and reinforce easier versions of the required behaviors. Rather than waiting until the end of a sequence to reinforce, Gary should click and treat (or play) after one, two, or three obstacles, then continue on. Also, randomly rewarding with a wide variety of reinforcers will keep Ginger interested in the agility game. Using jackpots for good performance and surprising Ginger with special toys and treats will help keep her focused on Gary and on agility. ❖

Aggression

Aggression in dogs is a vitally important subject for dog trainers to understand and be able to treat. Many clients first come to trainers for help solving a wide variety of aggressive behaviors that are or could become potentially dangerous to them, other dogs, and of course the trainer herself. Getting the treatment regimen right is critically important as it often is a life-or-death issue for the dog in question. This section includes articles and panel discussions on how aggression can develop, training recommendations, and an in-depth look at resource guarding.

An Examination of the Use of the Ethological Perspective for Resolving Inter-Dog Aggression Problems

Wendy van Kerkhove, May/June 2004

Minimizing or eliminating inter-dog aggression in the home of owners of multiple dogs is a matter of paramount importance. Many instances of dog-on-dog aggression involve bloody fights that leave the owners feeling emotionally distraught and helpless. There are two commonly recommended interventions in these instances: 1) spay or neuter both dogs; and 2) have the owners determine the dogs' dominance status relative to one another, and then have the owners support and maintain this dominance relationship. Behavior management is often also advised. This treatment protocol can be found in the books of many well-known behaviorists (e.g., Dodman, 1996; Overall, 1997; Hetts, 1999). For the most part, this advice is based on the firm conviction that the dynamics of social order at work in wolf packs is directly relevant to the social behavior of domestic dogs. Central to this belief is the concept that a wolf pack consists of individuals continually competing for higher rank but ultimately held in check by the alpha male and alpha female. It is believed that these social hierarchies effectively reduce and minimize overt aggression between individual members of the pack (Scott & Fuller, 1965). It is further assumed that what is true for wolves is also true for dogs, and it follows, therefore, that if a stable social hierarchy is established among the dogs in a family home, peace, and tranquility will prevail.

My concerns about the wolf model's practical utility emerged as the by-product of seeing first hand the effectiveness of alternative interventions in which information about social dominance was irrelevant. Specifically, I have found the existence of alternative and well-tested approaches for diminishing unwanted behavior and increasing desired behavior via principles of operant conditioning (OC) and classical conditioning (CC) to be effective in treating these aggression problems. Although the behavior modification approach does not preclude a role for ethological social dominance processes, neither does it specifically require one or explicitly recognize one in its treatment prescriptions.

My misgivings about the use of the dominance hierarchy model led me to research the primary literature on wolf and dog social behavior and dominance hierarchy theories in general. My initial understanding of wolf interactions was that little bloodshed occurred between wolves once a hierarchy was established, as most conflicts are resolved through a repertoire of no-contact body-language, vocal signals, and social conventions. However, in a study of a captive wolf pack Zimen (1975) describes extremely violent interactions between two female wolves, and later two male wolves engaged in battle, which he presumed to be over the alpha position. These fights were intense and bloody, and the wolves involved sustained major injuries. Zimen concluded that aggressiveness in wolves is modulated by numerous factors, including the season of the year, the social relationship between each wolf, and rank. With respect to rank, the higher the wolf ranks in the pack, the greater the display of aggression.

As it turns out, much of the research done on wolves has involved wolves in captivity. These observations dramatically contradicted the non-violent conventions that I had come to believe occurred within wolf packs. During observations of captive wolves clear dominance hierarchies are established and many of the challenges and altercations involving the establishment of the hierarchy involve serious injury and bloodshed.

David Mech's (1999) research of the social order within wild wolf packs contradicts most of the widely held beliefs regarding dominance hierarchies. After observing wolf packs in nature during thirteen summers on Ellesmere Island in Canada, he concluded that the behavior of non-captive wolf packs is quite different from that of captive wolves. These packs consisted of a breeding pair and their offspring from the previous one to three years. Within these packs, as the offspring become one to two years old, they leave and attempt to breed with other dispersed wolves, produce pups, and start their own packs, thereby becoming alphas. In the wild, all young wolves (regardless of temperament characteristics that might imply otherwise) are potential breeders and therefore potential alphas. Under these conditions, if a wolf lives long enough to breed, then he/she does. In non-captive packs there is a natural order based on age, which is seldom contested. In his thirteen years of observations, Mech saw no dominance contests within the packs he watched. He did observe a consistent demonstration of rank between these wild wolves, however they only involved the animals' postures during social interactions.

Clearly, there is more to the story of wolf behavior and social hierarchies than the conventional understanding, but exactly how that story should be related to the behavior of pet dogs is far from clear. Additionally, wolves and dogs are not exactly biologically or behaviorally the same. Indeed, because of their differences, when it comes to seeking information about the "natural dominance hierarchies" of dogs, perhaps feral dog behavior would be a better model. Five studies on feral dogs were located: Beck (1973), Nesbitt (1975), Fox (1987), MacDonald & Carr (cited by Serpell, 1995), and Boitani, Ciucci & Andreoli (also cited by Serpell, 1995). In reviewing each of these studies it became abundantly clear that urban and non-urban feral dogs tend not to live in socially structured packs, but rather form amorphous group associations. Often groups of two or three are observed developing a loose association and then dissolving it within a short period of time. It is believed that ecology has a lot to do with this. Urban feral dogs are scavengers, getting handouts or knocking over garbage cans; they are not hunting large prey. Additionally, the survival of pups is almost nil, and, unlike wolves, when pups are born, usually only the mother cares for them. The primary method for feral dogs maintaining their numbers is by the "recruitment" of stray pet dogs. Thus, the natural pack behavior of dogs appears to be very loose, changing, and unstructured, as opposed to tight, constant, and highly structured. The question that begs to be asked is this: If wolves in nature (not captive) develop social structures completely different from feral dogs (not captive) in nature, should one assume that captive wolves will develop the same social structures as dogs in captivity?

When studied scientifically, social dominance is defined with reference to repeated conflicts between conspecifics over a scarce resource whereby the same animal always gains access to the resource. The "winning" animal is said to be dominant over the "losing" animal with respect to that specific resource only. Thus, social dominance is often quite fluid and contextual. Additionally, for there to be a meaningful formal test of dominance, both animals must be equally motivated for the same resource, in order to rule out differential motivation as a confounding factor contaminating the results. If Buffy continually assumes the best resting place outdoors, and rushes out the door before Jody when exiting the house, can we unequivocally state that that Buffy is dominant to Jody in this context? Not necessarily. It could simply be that Jody is not particularly motivated to occupy the resting place or to get out the door. Or maybe Jody is just not as quick on her feet as Buffy. The presumption of unwavering and equal motivation or motor facility among dogs for all potentially contested resources seems quite unfeasible. Yet, this presumption is obviously made whenever pet owners are instructed in how to determine their dogs' social dominance status. As a result, determining dominance status is often exceedingly difficult. This makes implementing a plan involving the reinforcement of the known hierarchy equally difficult.

So, where does this leave us with companion dogs that are fighting in the home and sending us to the emergency vet on a Sunday evening? In my opinion, the body of work done on the social structures of wolves reflects a subject that is too complex and incomplete to give us a reliable model for understanding the behavior of domestic dogs living in a home. In addition, it is clear that with captive wolves, the alpha pair is most concerned with the suppression of breeding by other animals in the pack. However, many of our domestic dogs are spayed or neutered and show little in the way of sexual behavior, and yet they are still fighting. The fact that feral dogs do not behave as either captive or wild wolves behave casts further question on the appropriateness of any wolf model for dog behavior. Add to this the fact that the objective definition of social dominance can make determining which dog "should be the top dog" difficult at best has led me to look for other alternatives in tackling this problem.

One can make the argument that captive wolves and captive dogs do behave similarly and therefore the dominance hierarchy model is a good one to follow. I would argue that wolves clearly have the capacity to develop strong dominance hierarchies in unnatural conditions of captivity. However, this doesn't appear to happen under the natural conditions in which they live and have evolved in the wild. Clearly, wolf behavior is quite sensitive to the constraints imposed by the captive environment. In essence, wolves learn to behave differently when their environment is changed. An extremely persuasive argument can be made that living in captivity provides contingencies that provide learning experiences to these wolves. It may simply be the case that these contingencies of reinforcement and punishment have modified the behavior of these captive wolves. In essence, their behavior in captivity may simply be a product of learned responses.

In treating inter-dog aggression within the home, behavioral interventions based on OC and CC can work quite well. A well-established empirical fact is that consequences are contingent on behavior, and that behavior changes as a result of these contingencies. In treating inter-dog aggression, the behavior modification portions of the plan involves reinforcing behavior that is appropriate in order to make the response stronger, and punishing behavior that is inappropriate in order to diminish that response. The use of negative punishment, positive reinforcement, and CC are the fundamental tactics used.

The role of negative punishment is to reduce inappropriate responses. For example, Buffy will growl at Jody if Jody approaches Buffy when Uncle Bill is petting Buffy. If Jody gets too close, Buffy will attack Jody. The goal is to allow Jody to approach Buffy and Uncle Bill with impunity. Uncle Bill might have a leash on Buffy and allow Jody to approach. As soon as Uncle Bill detects any unwanted response in Buffy (low growl, body tenses up etc.), Uncle Bill says to Buffy, "Too bad, you blew it" and leads Buffy by leash to the bathroom and leaves her in there for thirty seconds. After repeated trials, Buffy will start to learn that her response has led to the unwanted march to the bathroom. Buffy likes Uncle Bill and doesn't want to leave him nor be left in the bathroom. As a result, she might try and change her response as Jody approaches.

The role of positive reinforcement is to strengthen appropriate responses. For example, after repeated trips to the bathroom, Buffy is now just looking away as Jody approaches. This is not something that was taught to her. Looking away is just an alternative response that she is offering, and it is an appropriate response. Now, not only does Buffy not get marched off to the bathroom, she gets to stay next to Uncle Bill and she gets cookies!

Perhaps, after a few days to a few weeks of this training, Uncle Bill notes a very interesting response in Buffy. Now, when Buffy sees Jody approaching she no longer looks away, but rather wags her tail and looks quite excited and expectantly at Uncle Bill. Why has this change occurred in Buffy? Because along with the OC that Buffy endured, she also learned an association between Jody's approach and the receipt of cookies. This is an example of associative learning (CC) that occurred as a result of the repeated pairing of the approach of Jody with the delivery of cookies.

What is important to understand is that respondent and operant conditioning principles work in dealing with dog-on-dog aggression in the home, and they do so without having to speculate about instinctive social forces and organizational structures and competitive motivations from the dogs' ancestral past. This is not to say that there isn't such a thing as "essential dogness." It is simply to say that the individual animal's personal history of experience may be at least as important if not more so than its ancestral history and any alleged instinctive behavioral imperatives. ❖

(References on next page)

References

Beck, M.A. (1975). "The ecology of "feral" and free-roving dogs in Baltimore." In W. M. Fox (Ed.), *The Wild Canids: Their Systematics, Behavioral Ecology and Evolution* (pp. 380-390). New York, NY: Van Norstrand Reinhold Company.

Boitani, L., Francisci, F. Ciucci, P. & Andreoli, G. (1995). "Population biology and ecology of feral dogs in central Italy". In J. Serpell (Ed.) *The Domestic Dog: Its Evolution, Behaviour and Interactions with People* (pp. 217-244). Cambridge, UK: Cambridge University Press.

Dodman, H. N. (1996). *The Dog Who Loved Too Much*. New York, NY: Bantam.

Fuller, L. J. & Scott, P. J. (1965). *Genetics and the Social Behavior of the Dog*. Chicago, IL: The University of Chicago Press.

Fox, W. M. (1987). *The Dog: Its Domestication and Behavior*. Malabar, FL: Robert E. Krieger.

Hetts, S. (1999). *Pet Behavior Protocols: What to Say, What to Do, When to Refer*. Lakewood, CO: AAHA Press.

MacDonald, W. D. & Carr, M.G. (1995). "Variation in dog society: between resource dispersion and social flux." In J. Serpell (Ed.), *The Domestic Dog: Its Evolution, Behaviour and Interactions with People* (pp. 199-216). Cambridge, UK: Cambridge University Press.

Mech, L. D. (1999). "Alpha status, dominance, and division of labor in wolf packs." Can J of Zoolog, 77, 1196-1203. Jamestown, ND: Northern Prairie Wildlife Research Center Home Page. www.npwrc.usgs.gov/resource/2000/alstat/alstat.htm (Version 16May2000).

Mech, L. D. (2000). "Leadership in wolf, canis lupus, packs." Can Field Nat, 114 (2), 259-263. Jamestown, ND: Northern Prairie Wildlife Research Center Home Page. www.npwrc.usgs.gov/resource/2001/leader/leader.htm (Version 09Mar2001).

Nesbitt, H. W. (1975). "Ecology of a feral dog pack on a wildlife refuge". In W. M. Fox, *The Wild Canids: Their Systematics, Behavioral Ecology and Evolution* (pp. 391-395). New York, NY: Van Norstrand Reinhold Company.

Overall, L. K. (1997). *Clinical Behavioral Medicine for Small Animals*. St. Louis, MO: Mosby-Year Book, Inc.

Zimen, E. (1975). "Social dynamics of the wolf pack." In W. M. Fox, *The Wild Canids: Their Their Systematics, Behavioral Ecology and Evolution* (pp. 336-362). New York, NY: Van Norstrand Reinhold Company.

Dog-Dog Aggression Panel

Edited by Terry Long featuring comments by Nina Bondarenko,
Morgan Spector, and Karen Overall, November/December 2002

For this issue, we posed several dog-dog aggression questions to three respected professionals who specialize in behavior modification. They were challenged to limit their responses to approximately 300 words for each of the three questions.

The questions are:

1. What are some *preventive steps* you have clients take when they report squabbling between two of their dogs? Assume that no bites have happened and that what has happened has been loud, but limited to one dog (Dog A) always being the one to pounce on the other (Dog B), driving it away from toys, the owners, and going through doorways. Do you ever recommend preferential treatment (elevation in status of one dog over another)?

2. What are some of the *critical interview questions* you pose to clients who report that their two dogs have had fights resulting in trips to the vet for one or more dogs? Assume your goal is to determine whether a behavior modification program could be successful or whether you will suggest rehoming. What information do you receive from clients to those critical questions that would make you suggest rehoming as opposed to behavior modification?

3. For those clients who want to pursue behavior modification, what do you consider the *most critical aspects of a program?*

The panelists:

Nina Bondarenko, Hants, England, owns and operates Dog Development Systems, a multi-service training business that specializes in aggression training, counseling, and helping people find the right companion dog for their lifestyle.

Karen Overall, MA, VMD, PhD, Diplomate, American College of Veterinary Behaviorists, ABS Certified Applied Animal Behaviorist, is the author of *Clinical Behavioral Medicine for Small Animals.*

Morgan Spector, Lancaster, California, has been training dogs since 1989 and has been a clicker trainer since 1993. He consulted for two years to Canine Companions for Independence on how to apply operant conditioning to service dog training, and he is the author of *Clicker Training for Obedience.*

Nina Bondarenko on Preventive Steps

- Initially, isolate the dogs and initiate simple behavior response training programs for each dog (i.e., teach the "Listen to Me" cues such as recall to target, down, and retrieve using clicker or bridge and target training). Then use positive reinforcement for all relaxed behavior, and put this on a cue such as "Calm down" or "Easy does it."

- Keep Dog A on a long line or extending lead, use the "Calm down" cue, and reinforce all relaxed behavior by both dogs whenever they are near each other. Ignore the dogs when they are not near each other. You should be interested in the dogs only when they are calm and in proximity to each other. Interrupt any potentially rough behavior by Dog A by standing on the longline (or putting the brake on the extending lead).

- Teach Dog A to respond to John Fisher's Training Discs. Use the discs to interrupt any unwanted behavior.

- Hand feed only when the dogs are interacting calmly without aggression, so that you can build up a stronger association with the "Calm down" cue and the rewards are more reinforcing for the dog. This ensures that you reinforce strongly and intensively, and the dogs look forward to interactions with each other. Do not feed from a bowl at regular mealtimes.

- If any dog begins an aggressive display over toys or other resources, the owner needs to interrupt and indicate to both dogs that the toys are out of bounds because they belong to the owner, not the dogs. Dogs can then be put on a timeout (i.e., withdrawn from the social interaction) as a consequence of this behavior. Do not attempt to raise the status of either of the dogs nor change the hierarchy situation, except to raise the leadership of the owner over both.

- The key to successful prevention is a high level of consistent and varied positive reinforcement whenever the dogs are interacting calmly and positively, as well as a quick interruption of any unwanted behavior.

Nina Bondarenko on Critical Questions

- Ages of the dogs; gender (or, if neutered, at what age); length of time in ownership; origin of dog and at what age.

- What training approach, if any, has been used already? When did the behavior start? Can the owner think of any events that are possibly related?

- Lifestyle of owners (e.g., time available, routines, any children).

- Owner's current expectations of the dog.

- Minimum requirements of clients from any training program.

- Extent of damage to the dogs; how many trips to the vet to date.

I suggest rehoming if the people state that they have no time to train, or if the dogs have caused deep, tearing bites requiring more than a couple of stitches and have been to the vet more than twice for the same problem. I also suggest rehoming when the people only want to hear ways to stop the behavior and have no interest in implementing a program to change or reshape behavior.

Nina Bondarenko on Critical Aspects of a Behavior Modification Program

- **Owner compliance and support.** You need to ensure that the dogs respond quickly and positively to some initial training to reinforce the owner's commitment to the program. By teaching the dog a simple response on cue, (down on a hand signal, or recall to target of two outstretched fingers, for example), the owner can feel pride and reassurance that the dog is clever and worth the effort needed to follow a behavior-shaping plan over several weeks.

- **Safety first.** Ensure that owners are given enough resources to keep their dogs and themselves safe throughout the rehabilitation program. I will suggest any equipment that may protect the owner from accidents with the dog. It is also important to reduce any chances that the owner may lose patience with the dog and act either aggressively or thoughtlessly, which may cause the dog to defend himself. Teaching simple responses on cue will help this.

- **Reality checks.** Provide frequent review and reassurance for owners during the program. By building in frequent reviews (by the owner in the form of a weekly questionnaire/tick box; scoring the times the dog responds correctly; or by a phone call or visit from the trainer), the owner can maintain a sense of progress and improvement, which encourages commitment to the program. It is important to reinforce the owner so that the owner will be encouraged to reinforce the dog.

- **Step in to help out.** Be prepared to step in quickly if the situation deteriorates, and offer extra training assistance. This may sometimes be all that is needed to ensure success in a program. Constant reassurance and reinforcement for the owner, while offering additional expertise and knowledge in a specific situation, will demonstrate confidence in the owner's ability to eventually resolve the problem successfully.

Morgan Spector on Preventive Steps

- Some of these situations can be relatively benign. The dynamic will produce lots of noise and some fur will fly, but no real harm will be done and the dogs will work it out for themselves. If the dogs are not widely separated by age or size, and if the owner can tolerate the process, it's probably the best way to go.

- In a situation where Dog A is younger than Dog B, or Dog A is the newcomer, I would first look to some interventions that would generally have the effect of announcing to Dog A that Dog B has preference. This might include feeding Dog B first, playing with Dog B first, etc. The risk is that Dog A might escalate his challenges. I'd want to make sure that Dog A had his own "special time" with me. If the situation is escalating, I would consider management (including kenneling one while the other was in the house) and being sure to give both as much equal time as possible. I'd also look to options such as feeding them in separate areas and making sure they each have their own crate.

- One response to Dog A taking toys away is for the owner to then take the toy from Dog A. This has its risks, so the owner has to spend time conditioning Dog A to surrender items to the owner. This sort of thing is a "top dog" maneuver; if the owner can do it successfully, it can help define the pecking order in the household and may help ease the situation generally.

Morgan Spector on Critical Questions

- What are the relative ages of the dogs? Is Dog A younger or older than Dog B?

- Are they the same breed?

- Are they the same sex?

- Is there a typical context in which the incidents happen such that one can predict with reasonable certainty when (or where) the conflicts arise?

- Does Dog A exhibit aggressive tendencies in other situations?

- Assuming that you didn't get the dogs at the same time, was Dog A in the home first, or Dog B?

- Is the situation escalating in intensity?

I would also be particularly interested in whether the owners can and will devote the time and energy needed to make a management program work. The single most important hurdle for these owners is to understand that this type of situation will never really be "fixed," but will require constant attention.

I would also want to know whether there are children in or around the house, since the agitation between the dogs could easily spill over to a human in the area. The greater that type of risk, the more rehoming looms as the most reasonable alternative (although, as a practical matter, rehoming is all too often not a viable option).

Morgan Spector on Critical Aspects of a Behavior Modification Program

- The first and most important aspect is the owner's willingness to see the program through.

- Second, give the owner tools both for intervening with the dogs and managing the situation if conflicts occur. In other words: "Here is something you can do if you see the dynamic starting" (head it off whenever possible) and "Here is something you can do if it gets away from you and you need to put them each in solitary for awhile."

- Emphasize that if you isolate one dog, you need to isolate them both. Don't put one in a crate and leave the other traipsing around the living room. That's a recipe for disaster.

- Make sure to not leave the dogs loose in the same area without supervision. Ever.

- I would want to make sure that the owner can handle each dog safely and confidently, as physical management may involve being able to move the dogs physically when they are starting to get into it.

- I would want the owner to spend a lot of time working each dog on basic control cues. These would cue behaviors that could, by the simple act of being performed, head off the impending confrontation. These might include the dog's name as a recall, establishing a "leave it" cue, and the sit or down. It is most important to establish these with Dog A because if you can call off Dog A from the conflict, it's unlikely that Dog B will take advantage.

- If you are a clicker trainer, be sure to reinforce any response in the direction of breaking off the engagement (i.e., shape incremental changes in behavior). If you are able to get Dog A to cease and desist and, for example, lie down, have Dog B also lie down. If you are delivering treats, start with Dog A.

Karen Overall on Preventive Steps

As a specialist in behavioral medicine, I see dogs who are referred to me because of an escalation in aggression or because of serious injuries. I almost never see dogs who have not been injured. My advice is therefore different in a pathological situation versus a "normal" situation, where dogs may disagree or be changing their relationship. Many of my clients are concerned about any rough play, tussling, or vocalization that may erupt from their dogs and, if they have had a problem with serious interdog aggression in the past, the client's concern moves to terror quickly.

At the outset, whether the dogs are exhibiting rough play, pushy behavior, or true pathological aggression, I always ask the question, "Are both of these dogs behaving appropriately, given the context?" If the answer is no, then some intervention is necessary. Preventive intervention is similar, in some respects, to a behavior modification program in a case that has escalated.

- Teach each dog to sit and be calm before providing any human attention (e.g., walks, tick removal, play, food, headcollar placement). I instruct clients to follow my "Protocol for Deference." (Overall (1997) Appendix B-1).

- Reward the dog who is behaving most appropriately (e.g., the dog who sits first, defers sooner). The reward structure means that the most appropriate dog is fed first, played with first, let out first, etc., and the least appropriate dog, last. Size, age, and health are second-order concerns unless the differences are extreme.

- Put a bell on the aggressor (Bear Bells, Silverfoot, Squamish, BC, Canada). The bell helps the other dogs know exactly where the aggressor is. It should be noted that in households that follow these preventive rules, some dogs may be able to spend time with the victim and aggressor and never be attacked. When this is true, that dog can go back and forth and all lives will be enriched.

Karen Overall on Critical Questions

- If clients come to me with a dog who is pathologically aggressive (see "Social Systems and Pathological Aggression," below), I tell them that one of their dogs can be killed, and it will likely be the sweetest one. If they want to treat the dogs, I strongly recommend doing so. If they refuse to treat, they must either live with the dogs separately or they must place one dog.

- The people—as the guardian of the dogs—must put their needs aside and address those of the dogs. The dog who is placed is generally the sweet dog. The client can place the aggressor only in a single-dog home that will remain a single-dog home. The client can have no fantasies. (One of my most successful placements involved a Rottie about whom the new owner had no illusions...the Rottie hates other dogs, particularly females, but she now has a record store on the Atlantic City Boardwalk named after her and she loves the customers who come to pay homage daily.)

- The biggest deterrent to fixing or controlling the problem is the client who wants to have a "peaceable kingdom." These clients believe that they can love and reason with the dogs enough and the behavior will stop. This client behavior is generally followed by the most serious attack yet.

- Clients who are committed to keeping their dogs and keeping them safe can live well and happily with baby gates, doors, and rotating car, play, training, and access schedules. The dogs, as well, can live happily with these rules. These rules are almost impossible to enforce if you have young children, and the smaller the house, the harder it is to succeed. However, before time-share cohabitation can happen, people have to realize in their gut—not intellectually, but at the gut level—that they can be responsible for the needless death of one of their dogs. People don't generally get this at once. But when they do, they often comment on what a "nice" dog the aggressor has become, and how calm the rest of the dogs are. Of course, they are calm. They now have a rule structure that guarantees them safety, whereas before they had a totally unpredictable, mobile explosive device in their midst.

Karen Overall on Critical Aspects of a Behavior Modification Program

- If the clients implement preventive steps early enough in the ontogeny of the conflict, the conflict will stop. If serious fights have occurred, this alone will not be sufficient. Medication (generally a selective serotonin re-uptake inhibitor) and active behavior modification (to desensitize and countercondition the dogs to each other on lead and then off lead) must be included, and the behavior modification must be intensive and consistent. Among my client base, those with serious fights more often opt for some behavior modification, +/- medication to decrease anxiety, and separation of the dogs. These clients know, to their sadness, that the victim often now needs medication, too.

- Regardless, if the clients are at all worried about the dogs, or if I am worried about the dogs, I want the dogs separated behind locked doors when no one supervises them. Threats can be as debilitating as an actual blow and, when a dog cannot escape a threat (as in most kennel situations), he or she can become profoundly debilitated. By putting on "hold" the artificial concept of the peaceable kingdom, clients can have a different kind of harmony and develop a deeper understanding of, and relationship with, their dogs.

Appendix: Karen Overall on Social Systems and Pathological Aggression

There are many pushy dogs who must go through doors before other dogs, must be able to take toys or rawhides from other dogs, and who are always able to blackmail some poor canine housemate from his or her morning biscuit. These same dogs control all dog play and all access to people. The conventional wisdom views such dogs as normal.

In fact, these dogs are often hailed as the "alpha," "top," "boss," "head," or "leader" dog, and clients who express concern are instructed to encourage the other dogs in the household to take this dog's lead. These clients are then encouraged to reinforce the lower "ranks" of the other dogs by a reward and reinforcement schedule. This is truly appalling logic and, with genuinely pathological dogs, can be profoundly dangerous advice.

Unfortunately, we know so little about dog behavior that we have no idea how many pushy dogs go on to develop truly pathological behavior. If they stay pushy without truly threatening the lives of their downtrodden housemates, they're socially obnoxious but survivable. In fact, most normal dogs will learn to avoid the circumstances that cause the pushy dog to exert his or her forcefulness, which has the effect of lowering the overall level of reactivity and socially ostracizing the bratty dog. The bratty dog likely barely notices this because his or her attention from humans comes when he or she is alone. The close, supportive, playful relationships that the other dogs will share are not truly enjoyed by this dog, but we have no idea if they know this. If the dog goes on to be truly pathological, it is not sufficient that the other dogs get out of the aggressor's way and allow him or her first access to everything. Even if these dogs defer to everything the "boss" dog wants, it is not sufficient. The aggressor targets a dog that he wishes to banish from the social hierarchy, and he continually attacks that dog, looking for an opportunity to kill. (For those who do not believe death can result from such interactions, I have a file of cases they may want to read. Some come with graphic pictures.)

The key to understanding the difference in these two types of dogs—the truly dangerous, aggressive dog and the socially undesirable, pushy dog—lies in understanding why social systems evolved in the first place. Social systems evolved because, by distribution of effort and clear, redundant signaling, everyone in the group does better than he or she would alone. Is the behavior exhibited by the pushy dog described above consistent with a social network where tasks are shared, responsibilities are distributed, and play is likely to be about learning to make mistakes successfully? Absolutely not. No one should have to control everything.

The thing that makes most social interactions work is the pattern of deference found in every true social system: individuals defer to those who may make more appropriate decisions, given the context. If clients are allowed to watch their dogs without preimposed labels, they usually cannot identify an alpha dog. Instead, they note that one dog is more outgoing with new people, another with new dogs, and perhaps yet another in situations when the dogs aren't on their own turf. Status is always conferred by a group: it cannot be taken and maintained and, when it is conferred, it is given to the individual who makes the most contextually appropriate decisions. All members of groups are not all good at the same things.

In such social systems, people often fail to recognize the elegant dance that maintains order because, by using terms like "alpha," we have convinced clients that dogs fight for status. Nothing could be further from the truth. Unless a dog is defending itself against an attack, fights are the exception and a signal that there is social breakdown. Normal dogs can accommodate pushy compatriots. They have trouble accommodating truly pathological bullies because, by definition, that's not on the agenda of the aggressor. With a video or a few observant minutes, clients can tell the difference. If behaviors involving deference (e.g., looking away, turning the neck, disengaging by rolling on the back, trying to leave) are given to the aggressor and the aggressor continues to block access, intensify the threat, or bite, there is a pathological problem here. Dogs who are working out relationships grab around the ears, sides of the neck, and shoulders, and although the noise is terrible, there is almost never any damage. True aggressors go for the front legs, the throat, the belly, and the eyes. The recipient of such aggression may grab the aggressor by the ear and hold on, because the aggressor then cannot get hold of the recipient's throat. ❖

References

Overall, Karen L. (1997). *Clinical Behavioral Medicine for Small Animals*. St. Louis, MO: Mosby, Inc.

Dog-Dog Aggression and Abandonment Training

Trish King, July/August 2002

When I began teaching dog obedience at the Marin Humane Society 14 years ago, we were pretty ruthless about dogs who showed dog-dog aggression. We would politely ask those dog owners to leave. There was no place for dog aggression in a normal obedience class.

There still isn't. It isn't fair to the owners or the dogs.

However, back then I felt as though we were abandoning the very people who needed us the most. So I made a promise to myself that I would try to find a way to help those owners and their companion animals. While I think we still have a long way to go, we have made great strides, and, if nothing else, have helped people come to terms with the animals they love.

What Causes Aggression?

Over the years, we have identified and are beginning to understand some of the reasons for dog-dog aggression. Here are four common reasons why such aggression might occur.

1. **Expectations.** People today have greater expectations for their dogs' social behavior than they had 20 and 30 years ago. Back then, it seemed as though there was more tolerance of a wider range of behaviors. In the neighborhood where I grew up, for example, there were several dogs we simply knew to avoid because they bit. Nowadays, dogs are expected not only to interact with their humans, but also to get along with any and all other dogs who come their way.

2. **Lack of or improper socialization.** Sometimes owners are encouraged to not socialize their dogs at all until after the full series of puppy shots is completed, which may mean that the pup is four months of age or older before beginning socialization. While this delay helps guarantee the pup's physical health, it can be detrimental to his or her mental health. (Can you imagine doing that with a child? Sorry, but your kid can't play with others until all her shots are complete... about age 12!) The earlier puppies are exposed to the real world, the more likely they are to tolerate it.

3. **Leash laws.** Leashes are required in most towns near where I live, so we see a great deal of on-leash aggression. In my experience, this type of aggression is often not serious. Many dogs who look terribly aggressive on leash play happily in dog parks or with doggie friends. The roots of on-leash aggression lie in frustration; the animal tries to get to another animal, hits the end of the leash, gets frustrated, and throws a tantrum. The owner buys into the energy, yells at the dog, pulls at the leash, and pandemonium reigns.

4. **Dog parks.** Although dog parks are great if properly used, they can be breeding grounds for poor social skills. Going back to the human model, imagine a playground in which three-year-olds and 12-year-olds play together with little or no adult supervision. Think about the bullying, ganging up on, and general out-of-control stuff that would take place. It would be reminiscent of the Lord of the Flies.

What Motivates Aggression?

We have learned that dog-dog aggression is sparked by a variety of motivations, some of which are much more easily modifiable than others. Here are eight common motivations.

1. **Fear.** Life can be frightening for a dog who thinks he's abandoned or helpless. Dogs are social, with an overriding need to be with other dogs or people. One of the more common causes of fear-based aggression is a traumatic episode in early life—such as being jumped by another dog. Occasionally, the victim will tend to attack all other dogs who look like the original attacker.

2. **Frustration.** Dogs who tend to lunge at the end of a leash, race up and down a fence line, or pull frantically from a tie-out (e.g., a leash wrapped around a tree) are very frustrated. They are probably also afraid—or they were, sometime in the past, before they learned to scare away anyone or anything that appeared threatening to them.

3. **Protection.** Because dogs are social, they tend to protect and defend other members of their group. They may place themselves between a threatening individual and their owner, and they may often rely on other pack members to defend or back them up. We sometimes think dogs are protecting us when they're really counting on us to protect them.

4. **Territoriality.** Most dogs are intrinsically attached to a territory. Dogs defending their territory can be extremely dangerous; it is instinctive for them to chase away intruders, and it is also instinctive for the intruders to allow themselves to be evicted. The territory owner (the dog) has a built-in predilection for success. Success then builds upon success, and dog bites are often the result.

5. **Status.** Dogs of higher status believe they have certain rights, such as first access to food, sleeping places, and territory. A high-status dog who feels that a low-status pack mate (human or canine) is acting out of its rank might attack. This behavior is usually a quick disciplinary move. In a family, the dogs most likely to fight are lower-status animals. Major disputes within a household are often extremely difficult to reconcile or diffuse.

6. **Redirected aggression.** This is a common phenomenon in which a dog wants to bite one thing, but, when that thing is unavailable, he or she attacks the nearest

object, dog, or person. For example, two dogs are fence fighting and one of them suddenly bites the other.

7. **Bully behavior.** This phenomenon has surfaced with the popularity of the dog park, in which dogs learn that they can overpower other dogs by physically running into them, mounting them, and otherwise terrorizing them.

8. **Predatory behavior.** This is instinctive hunting and feeding behavior, not aggression. It is usually distinguished by its speed and lack of warning.

What Is Abandonment Training?

Abandonment training is a quick way to teach a dog that, as soon as he becomes aggressive toward another dog, his owner is leaving. This type of training is done by using two leashes, one held by the owner and the other by the trainer. The technique itself was adapted from methods described by the late John Fisher and John Rogerson. Abandonment training works on the first three types of aggression—fear, frustration, and protection—as long as the relationship between the owner and the dog is appropriate. Abandonment training is only one of a variety of techniques we use to help clients whose dogs exhibit dog-dog aggression. Other forms of behavior modification can be used for the remaining problems.

Identifying Good Candidates

A good candidate for abandonment training will meet the following criteria, as determined through behavior consultation:

1. He is attached to the owner and becomes anxious when the owner leaves.

2. He has a tendency to defer to the owner, to act sorry when the owner gets angry.

3. He has some doggy friends.

4. His aggression manifests primarily when he is on leash or behind a barrier.

5. He has had a little obedience training (i.e., he knows cues such sit, leave it, and come).

If the initial consultation shows an inappropriate relationship, we don't try abandonment training at that time. Instead, the client goes home with a program to develop a relationship in which he or she is seen as the ultimate authority. We call it the People Empowerment Program (PEP).

During the initial consultation, we also pay a great deal of attention to other areas in which the dog shows a lack of control. The two major areas we have pinpointed are over-arousal in a house or yard (e.g., barrier aggression) and in a car. The correlation seems to be the speed at which the dog can reach a state of extreme excitement. While it's hard to know exactly what's going on in the dog's brain, it would seem that the chemical flooding that takes place is extremely reinforcing. Our goal is to get the dog to calm down whenever we ask, and to manage his environment so that this is possible. We have a wide variety of suggestions for clients, most of them relating to environmental controls such as blocking off doorways or crating a dog while in the car. We have found that retraining a dog without these controls often does not work or does not last.

Most clients go home with a recommendation to work on PEP for three weeks before returning to try abandonment training.

The Training Process

Here are the basic steps involved in the first stage of abandonment training:

- The client picks a word that will be used in conjunction with a physical cue. We use both physical and verbal cues because, when a dog is going off at another dog, the last thing he or she is thinking about is the human. So we have to do everything we can to make an impact. The verbal cue is often "Hey" or "Bye" or "Oops." We discourage the word "No" because it typically holds too many connotations from the dog's past. The physical cue is the feeling of the leash hitting the dog's rump.

- The client holds a six-foot leash on a regular flat collar. We hold a 20-foot leash, also attached to a flat collar. We don't use a Gentle Leader because things get pretty exciting pretty quickly, and we don't want anyone getting hurt. The actual training is done outside in a large yard. The client walks her dog toward a calm, well-behaved dog or two. We're carefully watching her dog's body language. At the very first sign of arousal—such as the lowering of the dog's head, the ears pricking forward, a hard stare, a sudden forward pull on the leash—the client yells her cue and throws her leash at her dog. The leash is supposed to hit the dog (but not hard, of course).

- As soon as the owner throws the leash, she runs away, calling the dog as she goes. If he turns and follows her, she rewards him with a vast amount of praise and a jackpot of treats. If he doesn't, all action stops. I hold the long line, preventing her dog from moving toward the benign dogs. The benign dogs stop (and get fed for being so cool).

- At this point, the dog usually decides that going to his owner is a great idea. If he does, he's rewarded. If he doesn't, the owner leaves, hides, and then calls him.

- We repeat the process three or four times. Most dogs get very good very quickly. If they don't, we stop the exercise. There is no point in trying to get the dog to go to an owner he doesn't need.

If we're successful, our clients are usually pleased (often jubilant) until they realize that we won't be going on walks with them! We then teach Stage 2 of the process, which we call "Knotted Leash Walking."

Knotted Leash Walking

1. Choose a signal word. Pick a word that tells the dog you're going to go (such as "Hey," "Bye," "Oops," "Run," "Yuck," or "Oh, oh." I prefer not to use the word "No" because it has a variety of emotions already attached to it.

2. Get a leash. Use a six to eight-foot leash. Knot the leash about 18 to 24 inches from the clasp that goes on the dog. Assuming the dog is on the left, hold the knot with your left hand. With your right hand, hold the loop at the end of the leash. The dog should be able to walk beside you and about a foot behind or ahead of you without pulling the leash.

3. Practice. When you practice, walk the dog in a safe place where there are no other dogs. As you walk him, watch his head and other body language very carefully. As soon as he loses attention in you—for example, he walks a little ahead of you, or to the side, or even looks away—give your signal word (see #1 above), and let the knot go. Hold on to the looped end with your right hand, and change directions. If the dog keeps going in the original direction, he will feel the tug when he hits the end, turn around, see that you're now somewhere else, and try to catch up to you. When he does, reinforce heavily—such as with lots of praise or maybe a jackpot of treats.

4. Practice some more. Do this exercise many times. As the dog begins to understand that he cannot lead you any more, and that, in fact, he really doesn't know where you're going next, he'll start watching you to see where you go. This is exactly what you want.

When done properly, and in conjunction with other behavior modification techniques, abandonment training can be quick, dramatic, and successful. ❖

The Success of Treatment Outcomes

Karen Overall, Published in two parts,

January/March 2001

PART I

Studies that examine the success of treatment outcomes in veterinary behavioral medicine routinely comment on two sets of related factors:

1. The predictability, danger, damage, and "trust."[1]

2. The number of "things" that the clients are expected to do to help the dog get better.[2]

The first set, which is the focus of Part 1 of this article, reflects the physical, legal, and emotional aspects of risk and its management. The second set, to be addressed in Part 2, reflects the extent to which clients acknowledge and address how their lives would be affected by living and dealing with a troubled pet.

What is seldom appreciated—and even more rarely acknowledged—is that these factors are based on understanding and knowledge. The more understanding and knowledge we can give our clients, the greater the chance or probability of a successful outcome.

Predictability

Let's address the predictability aspect first since it's what gets pets killed. Predictability is an outcome of knowledge. If a dog bites you every time you brush his head, he's totally predictable regardless of his behavior's undesirability and whether it makes sense to you.

At my clinic, clients often tell us that the dog is unpredictable and then they list every circumstance in which the dog reacts. What they are really saying is that the dog's behaviors are out of context. Yes, of course, that's what makes these dogs abnormal.

Once we clarify with clients that their pets are exhibiting truly out-of-context behaviors, they can use that predictability to avoid eliciting the behaviors and to stay safe. To get to that point, we need the owners to list all the circumstances that provoke the dog, along with the dog's responses.

Danger

Danger is based, in part, on the predictability of a behavioral sequence. If a behavior is truly predictable, then it is avoidable. Lots of things can make situations unpredictable: the stress of holidays, the stress of illness (yours or the pet's), additions or deletions in the family, and other unpredictable factors (e.g., small children).

Any animal who has any problem associated with anxiety—in other words, all pets and humans with behavioral problems—will become worse as stressors are added.

The risk of danger then increases. The easiest way to decrease danger is to realistically assess the risk and avoid problematic situations.

Your dog hates strangers and you want to have the family (all 29 of them) for Christmas? Board the dog. But you wanted an L.L. Bean Christmas? Too bad. Board your dog, then rent the L.L. Bean dog and bed. Even though we cannot always have the peaceable kingdom, we do not need to experience trench warfare.

Damage

Damage, which is tightly coupled with liability but not necessarily with danger or degree of aggression, concerns almost everyone. How realistic are our concerns? I always tell clients that if an 18-month-old child is knocked over by an exuberant Lab and hits her head on a curb, she is just as dead as if that dog ripped her throat out. Harsh? Perhaps, but damage is a function of a few seemingly unrelated factors:

- frailty of the victim (older and younger persons are more frail than typical adults).

- physical location of the bite or assault (hand bites may interfere with function but are seldom fatal; neck bites and skull fractures can more easily be fatal).

- force of the bite or assault (this is affected by the dog's mass, the victim's mass, the direction and mobility of each, and the dog's teeth size and head/neck musculature).

- pattern of the bite or assault (warning snap, graze, bite and release, repeat bite).

Severe wounds can be the result of accidental contact and the two parties moving away from each other. The number of sutures doesn't matter. Facial sutures are small and more numerous than torso sutures; female children are more carefully sutured than male children; and most punctures are never sutured to minimize the risk of debility due to infection.

Trust and Risk

Trust is an emotional component that is difficult to assess with dogs. I prefer the term "reliability" in that, as abnormal dogs improve, their behavior becomes more reliably good instead of reliably bad. Predictability allows us to avoid damage, danger, and risk by knowing and understanding the dogs. The fact that their behaviors make no sense given the human response does not matter; if they made sense, the clients wouldn't be seeing me.

The dog who always bites is wholly trustworthy: You can trust that he will always bite. If what you wanted was Lassie, the biting dog will disappoint you because of your preconception. In fact, much of what my clients call "lack of trust" reflects this sadness and let down.

If we can move beyond our preconceptions, the dog can get better and the relationship can be altered. I have loved all my dogs, but my troubled dogs are the ones to whom I am indebted for making me a better person.

PART II

We try to make behavior modifications fit the clients' and patients' households. To meet those goals, we need a rationale for our instructions, an understanding of a desired or expected outcome, and an accurate assessment of time allocation.

Teaching Clients about How We Learn

We try to teach our clients a little bit about how we all learn (but not to the point where we bore them to death with learning theory). One of our first instructions when treating any dog is to "stop exposing the dog to any circumstance that elicits the behavior or makes it worse."

We discuss with the clients that this directive is common sense. For example, a client may find it peculiar that he cannot push a dog off a bed without having the dog growl, but the reality is that the dog *will* growl if pushed off the bed. The client must understand that any time an animal repeats a behavior, that behavior and the associated sequence get reinforced whether or not the outcome is desirable.

Clients need to understand that we learn a response best by getting rewarded every single time we exhibit the response, and that we best maintain such learning through intermittent reinforcement. If a client struggles with her dog every time the dog is on the bed, will the dog growl more or less frequently? More. If the dog is allowed on the bed, is the client making the situation worse or better? Worse, if the client then insists that the dog must get off the bed.

Some clients cannot avoid provoking the dog's undesired behavior because they can never control the stimulus (e.g., thunderstorms) or they cannot always control the stimulus (e.g., leaving the house). However, they do not have to reinforce the dog's anxiety associated with those things. So we ask clients with dogs who are in stressed situations to not say to their dogs, "It's okay." Why not? Because the dog clearly does not think it's okay...and, by using a signal the dog associates with rewards, you may have inadvertently encouraged the anxiety. Also, if you are saying one thing and the dog is saying another, is that conflict likely to make the dog's anxiety worse or better? Worse.

This type of discourse saves time because the clients understand it at the gut level and can then apply the same logic to other parts of the dog's treatment program.

The Relaxation Exercise

In the next step of our treatment program, the client asks the dog to sit quietly and look at the client for anything the dog wants. Most clients tell us that their dogs already know how to sit. Terrific! That saves time, but it's not what this is about... this is about relaxation.

We want the dog to sit or lie down quietly and calmly and look at the client in all situations when he or she wants something (e.g., food, walks, love, attention, belly rub, tick removal). The goal is for the dog to be calm and look to the client for cues about appropriate behavior. If the dog is in motion, vocalizing, or not looking at the client, he's not attending and relaxing and cannot be rewarded for being calm.

Sitting is a starting point. Every time a butt hits the ground or the dog is quiet—even if it is accidental—the dog is told he is brilliant. Now the dog can transfer this behavior and look to the client for cues about how he should react in distressing circumstances.

Abolishing Punishment

The next treatment step involves the abolition of corrections and punishment. Distraction, avoidance, gentle guidance away from a situation, and intervention to prevent damage are fine, but there is no place for correction. How are you going to correct a growling dog? Growl (or yell) back? Will this make him better or worse? Worse, because if he was trying to find out if you were a threat, you just convinced him; and, if he was anxious, you worsened his anxiety and reinforced the inappropriate response.

The dog will get better if the client:

- does not provoke the dog.
- rewards relaxed behaviors associated with looking to the client for cues.
- avoids further distressing and confusing the dog through corrections.

Whether the situation gets sufficiently better is a judgment the client has to make.

The Time Commitment

Our active behavior modification programs require commitments of time for desensitization and counterconditioning. If a client wants her dog to actively change a behavior, doing so will take a lot of effort and require a maintenance program. We are frank about this at the outset—that active behavior modification is hard to do well, that it is not obedience work, that it will drive the client nuts because it is simultaneously hard to do and deadly dull, and that—done correctly—it works.

We emphasize that getting it right is more important than spending hours doing it. If the client has only five minutes twice a day, make those five minutes count. Will it take longer for that dog to ignore passing dogs as compared to a dog whose people work with him for 30 minutes four times a day? Of course, but this is not a contest. If a client only has short times available per day, we give her segments of programs to work on, and—and this is critical— we give her gauges with which to assess the dog's improvement.

By getting the clients to reward the physical signs associated with improvement in the underlying physiological state (e.g., relaxation and biofeedback for dogs), we engage the clients in actually watching the dog and responding to his or her needs. We emphasize that the dog's behaviors are the gauge by which each client can learn if his or her dog is improving or needs more help. Suddenly, behavior modification may be time consuming, but it's not so boring.

When clients admit to being less than avid in their commitment to the program, they almost uniformly report that their dog is improving but they feel crunched for time. Whether or not this is okay doesn't matter—it happens, it's reality. So have the clients doomed their pet to total relapse? Not if we explain to them that they now have a tool that they can use in the future for touch-ups, when they have more time, when the dog seems particularly tense, etc. The client's life with his or her pet is a journey, not an outcome.

The Drug Factor

So what works? And what about drugs? True psychopharmacological intervention (e.g., anti-anxiety and anti-depressant agents, not tranquilizers) acts by redressing underlying neurochemical abnormalities, thereby altering threshold levels for reaction and rates at which improvement occurs. The patients still have to learn other ways of responding.

Meeting the Dog's Needs

Behavioral medicine, unfortunately, has no equivalent of ruby slippers where just wishing it were so makes it that way. If a client is truly and deeply committed to getting the dog better, that dog will get better because the client will meet the dog's needs; and, while the client minimizes danger, he or she will also minimize things that adversely reinforce the dog.

Ultimately, the client has to decide what he wants and what's best for the dog. If the client doesn't want to live with a dog who has to be fed behind a locked door, that dog is out of the household. What the client does and whether the dog can get better are often two entirely unrelated issues. If the client can do what's truly in the best interests of the dog, then behavior modification programs such as the ones we offer at our clinic can help.

We have many clients who complete only the above-described steps of the behavior modification program (with or without medication) and decide that their dogs are so much better and so much happier that they couldn't care less if their dogs ever like other dogs. These clients will gladly avoid dog-dog situations, which is kinder to the dog and easier on the client.

What makes our behavior modification techniques so popular with our clients is that they can be incorporated into everyday life, they take minimal overt effort (although they do take a lot of thinking ahead), and they generalize to just about every situation. The dog gets a consistent, humane rule for living, not one just for interacting with the dog next door. ❖

References

[1] Reisner, IR, Hollis, NE, and Houpt, KA. (1994). "Risk factors for behavior-related euthanasia among dominant-aggressive dogs: 110 cases." (1989-1992). *JAVMA* 205:855-863.

[2] Takeuchi, Y, Houpt, KA, and Scarlett, JM. (2000). "Evaluation of treatments for separation anxiety in dogs." *JAVMA* 217:342-345.

Assessment and Treating of Resource Guarding

Jean Donaldson, November/December 2002

Scores of generations of dogs have been bred for specific conformation, work functions, and temperaments. These same dogs enjoy the luxury of steady provision of food and other resources. One would think, then, that the relatively expensive behavior of resource guarding would be rendered obsolete. After all, guarding behaviors take energy and put the animal at risk of injury and even death. Yet, many pet dogs guard things, both from other dogs and from people— including the people who do all the providing!

It is easy to see how, in a natural environment, a group-hunting carnivore who guards would have reproductive advantage over one who gladly relinquishes. It's a good trait, like a well-developed immune system or legs that can run fast. In a domestic environment, however, it is an undesirable trait that results in bites to family members and owner relinquishments.

Fallacies about Resource Guarding

There are several common fallacies about resource guarding that cloud our understanding and, thus, our approaches to treatment of this common behavior problem.

1. **It is abnormal behavior.** Guarding food, coveted objects, mates, and physical space are highly adaptive traits in a natural environment. If dogs had to fend for themselves tomorrow, guarders would have the survival and reproductive edge over non-guarders.

2. **Because it is largely genetically driven, rather than learned, it is immutable.** This fallacy is not limited to resource guarding. While it is true that genetics can make certain behaviors easier to learn in some cases, or interfere with learning in other cases, there is no neat correlation between how much a behavior is thought to be genetically influenced and its susceptibility to behavior modification.

3. **It can be cured by making the dog realize that resources are abundant.** The idea behind this fallacy is that all we have to do is convince the dog that there are no reasons to guard because resources are plentiful (by providing a plethora of toys, treats, and chewies). Alas, it would seem that dogs were snoozing in logic class. They do not learn this way.

4. **It is a symptom of dominance.** This fallacy is largely a legacy of the pervasiveness of social hierarchy models as explanation for dog behavior, as well as springboards for treatment techniques. Most dog owners have sketchy, if any, understanding of the most basic techniques of operant and classical conditioning. Yet virtually all owners throw around the word "dominance" with abandon. Rank as the reason for resource guarding has also provided decades of quasi-justification for the use of aversives in training. In actuality, resource guarding responds well to desensiti-

zation, counterconditioning, and well-executed operant techniques, which raises questions about dominance:

- When the dog stops guarding, has he become less dominant as a result of the desensitization and counterconditioning? If so, by what mechanism?

- Is rank, therefore, not a fixed trait? If not, can one still say a dog is a "dominant" dog?

- If dominance is a relationship rather than a trait, how could simple desensitization/counterconditioning exercises change the relationship?

The behaviorist paradigm provides a much simpler way to describe post-treatment behavior. That is, rather than expending energy on why the behavior exists, the behaviorist concentrates on changing the behavior.

5. **It is a result of "spoiling" the dog.** Guarding crops up in dogs with all kinds of life histories. "Spoiled" is also a very subjective term. I am dismayed that some people label dogs spoiled simply because the dog's basic needs are being met, they are well loved, and their lives are relatively free of aversives.

Get Out Of the Black Box

Dog training and behavior modification are fields full of camps with different biases. One well-known distinction is between trainers who use primarily or exclusively techniques that are free of aversives (e.g., pain and startle) and those insist that aversives are necessary and benign.

Another less-publicized difference is whether one's focus is on observable data or on interpretations of what might be going on inside the dog's mind. Where a more traditional trainer might see observable behavior as a symptom of an underlying problem, syndrome, or illness (such as dominance aggression in the case of resource guarding), the behaviorist sticks to what the dog is doing—in this case, guarding—and modifies that behavior without trying to guess what is going on "in the black box." I can't know what is going on in the mind of any dog at any time. I can, however, observe, measure, and modify behavior using operant and classical conditioning. This is not to say that I don't have opinions, gut feelings, or an entertaining time speculating about what I think is going on in a dog's head. It's just that, when it comes to behavior modification, a focus on what the dog is doing is more fruitful.

Prognostic Indicators

Prognostic indicators include:

- number and clarity of triggers.

- owner commitment and compliance.

- bite threshold and presence of protracted warning.

- dog variables such as impulsivity, size, and learning ability.

Of these indicators, one of the most important is determining a dog's bite threshold and early warning signs. Clearly, dogs with soft mouths have rosier prognoses than dogs who inflict damaging bites. Dogs with bite inhibition are less of a liability risk. They also can be treated more aggressively because the worst-case scenario is more bearable (a less damaging bite) should the dog offend during or between training sessions.

To assess bite severity, obtain a thorough history of all the dog's bites. The most important feature is the degree of damage per bite. It may require some sleuthing to extract this information from the flood of other details you may receive during history taking. Do not be distracted from your task of finding out, for each incident, exactly what kind of injury occurred to what person, on what body part, through what kind of clothing and, what, if any, medical attention was given. There is no absolute standard regarding what kind of bite severity equates a treatable case. It is a judgment call made by the counselor prior to deciding to treat aggression cases.

Many qualified trainers and behaviorists opt to not take on aggression cases at all. Some will only treat cases where there is minimal damage (e.g., shallow abrasions to occasional shallow punctures) or no damage, or cases where dogs have demonstrated protracted threat but have never actually bitten anyone due to gloriously high bite thresholds. Some counselors will treat harder mouths, although they may examine other history features such as protracted warning, the owner's management capabilities, and presence of children in the home before committing to the case.

The important thing is that you decide which types of cases you are comfortable with and qualified for before fielding inquiries, and that you refer appropriately when you encounter a case that falls outside your scope.

Use of Muzzles, Tethers, and Gloves

There are advantages and disadvantages to the use of any tool in behavior modification. One disadvantage is always the necessity of weaning the dog (and owners!) off the tool unless dependence on it in real-life situations is immaterial. In the case of resource guarding, muzzles, tethers, and Kevlar gloves provide safety during exercises, especially in those cases where a mishap could result in a hard bite. These tools are often used in early exercises until the dog is well rehearsed with new behaviors. Then, tools are dispensed with so the training can be generalized to increasingly real-life situations.

Treatment Overview

A typical resource guarding rehabilitation program will center on direct desensitization and counterconditioning exercises to modify any known guarding. Extensive interviewing is often required to ensure that all objects subject to guarding are listed, as well as each item's relative importance (i.e., an object hierarchy).

Great attention will be paid in most cases to getting the new behavior generalized so that the dog is safe around people in general, rather than only those who have done exercises. Adjunct measures—such as impulse control exercises, the provision of vigorous exercise, and mental stimulation—are also common.

Management

Management means avoiding the problem or trigger for a behavior through environmental control. It can serve as a valid alternative to behavior modification or be used in conjunction with behavior modification. Management during treatment serves the dual purposes of preventing mishap while the dog is in training and protecting the program.

Principles of Desensitization and Counterconditioning (D&C)

Systematic desensitization is a technique that was originally developed to treat people with anxiety and phobias. The subject is exposed to a fear-evoking object or situation at an intensity that does not produce a response. The intensity is then very gradually increased, contingent upon the subject continuing to feel okay. A hierarchy is developed at the beginning of treatment, ranging from the easiest to most difficult versions of the stimulus.

Desensitization is most often performed in conjunction with counterconditioning, a technique which is an application of classical conditioning. In classical conditioning, when one event becomes a reliable predictor of another event, the subject develops an anticipatory response to the first event. The association between the two events is particularly evident if the second event is relevant or potent.

Counterconditioning is about changing associations. It's called counterconditioning rather than simply conditioning because the dog already has an unpleasant emotional response to the thing we're trying to condition, so we counter that by establishing a pleasant conditioned emotional response (CER).

How this looks in actual treatment is the presentation of a low-enough intensity, a sub-threshold version of the stimulus/trigger, immediately followed by a potent, pleasant counterconditioning stimulus. This process is repeated until the dog is evidently and eagerly anticipating the counter-stimulus when the trigger is presented. Then, the intensity of the trigger is increased slightly and the procedure is repeated. If, at any point, the dog shows the original reaction to the trigger, it means the intensity of the presentation is super-threshold. It is important to then back off to a reduced trigger intensity and work back up gradually again.

Troubleshooting Hierarchy Problems

Trainers sometimes announce that a certain technique—operant conditioning, for example—didn't work in a given case. Before making this assumption, make sure that there were no compromising, or even lethal, technical errors that, if resolved, would allow progress. In the case of D&C, proper execution of the program is vital to get a good result.

There are two common execution errors in D&C for resource guarding:

1. Going too fast. An all-too-common execution error is progressing to the next level in the hierarchy before the dog is demonstrating the desired CER. This is called "skating on thin ice." Pushing the dog to super-threshold by advancing too quickly up hierarchy rungs (using the object hierarchy list you developed from interviewing the owner) before the CER is well established at the previous level can seriously compromise the program.

2. Order of events errors. Another key to either establishing a beautiful CER or literally achieving nothing is how well the trainer orchestrates the order of events. In order for a dog to have an anticipatory response to the first event, it must have high predictive value that the second event is coming. This predictive relationship can be muddied by simultaneous conditioning, backward conditioning, or inadvertently presenting a compound stimulus.

Simultaneous conditioning refers to the second event occurring simultaneous to the first so there is no predictive relationship. Backward conditioning refers to the two events occurring in reverse order so that the predictive relationship is also reversed. Dogs get excited at the sight of their leash coming out of the cupboard because the walk comes afterward. If the walk happened simultaneous to or before the leash came out of the cupboard, the leash's appearance would not be a very good tip-off.

Similarly, if events in a resource counterconditioning procedure are not in the correct order, conditioning won't take place. The first event is the sub-threshold approach of a person or other "threat" to the resource (such as, in later exercises, touching it, removing it, or touching the dog while he is in possession). The second event is the fabulous payoff, along with the dog retaining the original resource or getting it back.

Another common problem is the CER resulting from an association with some other element in the stimulus package that preceded the payoff. Instead of being associated with the element you wanted (the approach, touch, or resource removal), the CER became associated with something like the training context itself.

For example, if trials are delivered in too rapid a manner from the beginning to the end of the session without any down time, the dog might develop a stronger or exclusive CER to the exercise set-up, smell of the bait, and/or to the trainer. If trials are delivered in too steady a manner, the inter-trial interval can actually overshadow the approach. The dog learns a rule such as "treats are arriving every eight seconds" rather than attending to the approach or exchange that precedes the treat. Finally, if some other thing the dog is already familiar with as a predictor of good stuff (the reach of the trainer's hand toward the bait pouch) occurs simultaneous to the approach, touch, or removal, that element could block what you are trying to condition.

A carefully crafted, methodical treatment plan that details the dog's object hierarchy list, as well as critical attention to the order of events, will help tremendously in effective execution of a D&C program for resource guarding.

A Resource Guarding Case History: Food Guarding

Buffy, a stray Chow foster puppy, presented with object and food guarding against people and dogs. I elected to not touch the dog-dog issues as long as her socialization and play skills came along and she was clearly developing good acquired bite inhibition. The guarding against people, however, needed to be actively resolved.

The following is a summary of Buffy's food guarding exercises. The rapid pace of progress and aggressive increment jumps were due to her age. Adjunct measures included impulse control (stay, off, and wait) and soft-mouth training. I also addressed Buffy's socialization deficits, severe body handling problems, and object guarding.

Baseline

When approached while eating from her dish, Buffy would freeze and, if approach continued to the dish, growl briefly and then lunge and snap. If touched while eating, she would growl and simultaneously whirl and bite. Due to the independent body handling problem, this had to be partly resolved prior to combining it with food bowl exercises. Buffy did not guard an empty dish.

Hierarchy

Step 1 (Day 1): Installment feeding of canned food. I sat next to Buffy's dish and spooned in one mouthful. Once she had swallowed, I spooned next mouthful into dish. By the end of the second meal, Buffy showed clear orientation to the can/spoon/hand after each swallow.

Step 2 (Days 1 & 2): Overlap. Same as Step 1, except the next spoonful added to the dish was while Buffy was still consuming. Continued for three meals without evidence of guarding.

Step 3 (Days 2 & 3): Approach overlap. I now stood instead of sat next to Buffy. I spooned a larger installment, withdrew two paces, re-approached, and added the next spoonful while Buffy was still consuming. Continued for three meals, at the end of which time conditioned emotional response (CER) had become evident: Buffy wagged her tail and looked up on approach. Repeated for one more day (five small meals) with larger withdrawal distances and intervals.

Step 4 (Day 4): Trumping. I spooned her entire ration into the bowl. Withdrew five paces, paused 15 seconds, approached, and added (hidden) marble-sized dollop of goat cheese (this treat had been "pre-auditioned" out of context and ascertained to be in Buffy's Top Five All-Time Foods). Withdrew to six paces and waited for Buffy to continue to consume. This was not immediate, which is typical of trumping; the dog orients to the handler rather than back to the dish. Repeated. Clear CER on the third trial evidenced by her withdrawal from the bowl on approach, orientation to the approacher, and a tail wag.

Step 5 (Days 4 through 6): Covering high-value base. I approached while Buffy was consuming a high-value food, rather than normal meal ration-level food, and trumped it with higher-value food. While the higher-value food was being consumed, I added a different but equally high-value food, or more of the same. It only took one to two trials of each high-value food introduction to result in clear CER from Buffy.

Step 6 (Day 4 onward): Cold trials. I introduced random trumping. At least once per meal, from a random direction, at a random time, and with one of Buffy's top foods, I approached and added the bonus. Clear "yippee" CER.

Step 7 (Day 8 onward): Generalization. Introduced random trumps by different people, with careful monitoring for any evidence of regression, including absence of "yippee" CER to approach. Had this been an adult dog, the hierarchy—and, notably, a much more gradual one—would have been recommended at the beginning by each new recruit, with likely accelerated progress rate for each successive person.

Step 8 (Day 15 onward): Body handling. It was only here that I commenced patting, grabbing, or pushing her around while she was eating. In most cases, this would come earlier; however, it took me this long to get the independent body handling problem up to speed. The handling-during-eating exercise consisted of the body touch (later handling) followed by a trumping addition, and repeated until the body touch/handling elicited the "yippee" CER. For this exercise, Buffy's CER consisted of a wag as well as orientation to my other hand or face when my delivery hand was blank or behind my back (bonus food was stored in my mouth or pocket).

Conclusion: Buffy is now on maintenance, with a cold trumping or body handling trial usually once per meal, and the use of other people whenever an opportunity presents itself. I ended up adopting her. ❖

ASSOCIATION of PET DOG TRAINERS

Class Tips and Curriculum

While dog trainers need to be well-versed in learning theory and training techniques, all that knowledge goes to waste if the trainer cannot deliver this information effectively to students in a classroom setting. Simply put, dog trainers must be good *people* teachers. The best teachers create excellent learning environments with interesting classes as well as class levels and structure that are appropriate for any given group of dogs and humans. They also make learning fun and entertaining by learning the best techniques to make sure that lessons are well-received. Here are a series of articles that will hone your classroom teaching skills while making learning reinforcing for your dog and human clients.

The "Levels" System:
Advance-at-Your-Own-Pace Classes

Terry Ryan and Joan Guertin, September/October 2003

In many parts of the world, group dog training is conducted as a drop-in-at-will format. The training group might have an "intake class." At this entry level, any person with an inexperienced dog can join at any time. In the U.S., on the other hand, we are more apt to hold a class by announcing a starting and ending date. The students start and end the class together. In recent years I've thought about the pros and cons of these two extremes. In an attempt to formulate an outside-of-the box curriculum that takes the best of both approaches, I interviewed Joan Guertin. Joan is a long-time APDT member who had the same idea and was putting it to the test. She is Director of Common Sense Dog Training School in Springfield, Missouri.

The article that follows is the result of my Q & A with Joan.

What encouraged you to make a radical change in your teaching format?

There has long been a need for a class structure system that would more effectively meet the needs of pet dog owners. The "Levels" system attempts to meet those needs. The dedicated dog owner is committed to developing a working relationship with his or her pet and will most likely block out the time to do a traditional class. However, the average pet owner is busy, often having little spare time, and generally is not dedicated to training or solving problems. Therefore most trainers find themselves constantly confronted by the first time owner who has neither time nor inclination to block out weeks of dates to make a tough situation better. These are the animals that will ultimately be tied to a tree in someone's yard or turned in to a local shelter.

Like most trainers working in a traditional, week-to-week format, I was frustrated by absentees and the drop-out rate. I realized that although most people meant well when they enrolled in a class, life would just simply get in the way, and the more classes they missed, the more likely they were to drop out completely. The dogs were often dogs at risk of losing their homes if they were not trained. Even though I had several classes during the week and on weekends to which I could steer clients for make-ups, it was many times not enough to keep them in a class.

I introduced the Levels system in Sacramento, California, in 1995. My training team groused at first, but soon they understood the benefits and swore they would never go back to a traditional format again. Veteran dog trainers who were training with me swore they would never waste their time on a traditional class format again. I found that beginning students, who probably would not have done more than a basic class in the traditional format, were enjoying the Levels system so much and developing a great relationship with their dog that they either went on to competition, or continued to come back to play the games and proof their pet dogs' skills.

How do you format and schedule your "Levels" classes?

I offer four skill level classes for adult dogs. Level One, for example, meets at 6:30 p.m. on Tuesday evenings. New dogs can enroll on any Tuesday. Therefore, no one has to wait in order to join a class. They can come right away after they call me. They will spend at least two weeks at Level One. This means that I will have dogs that have already worked on the skills for a week. Coming back helps the owners clarify any issues concerning the exercises. Since all of my classes are family classes, I really encourage families to participate in Level One. Students in Level Two spend anywhere from three to five weeks at this level, or however long it takes them to learn how to walk the dog on a loose leash and communicate body language with the dog. It takes a while to get to where you have Level Four dogs—I try to save at least four weeks for the Level Four dogs so we can polish the CGC exercises and get a good long-distance down.

There is no minimum or maximum number of students per class. I have assistants work with me in Levels Two and Three, the two levels where dogs will spend the most time. Attendance is noted on each student's enrollment card.

What exercises are taught at each level?

In Level One, the following exercises are taught:

- Name Recognition. I check to see if the dog responds to his or her name said in a friendly tone of voice, or has the dog "tuned out." This allows me to see how the owner has conditioned the dog through voice and attitude. Sometimes a name change is warranted.

- Attention. I teach food lure exercises such as sit, stand, down, roll over, crawl, and sit up.

- Jumping Issues. I teach the sit as an alternative to jumping. Students learn the value of moving into their dog's space for this versus moving away from them.

- Come When Called. We play games including running between family members, tossing a treat for them to find, and hide and seek.

Students leave class having successfully taught their dogs some tangible skills. Students leave that first level excited and feeling empowered. They have found a non-aggressive and fun means to gain their dog's respect and attention. In the process, the dog's attention span increases and focus improves.

In Level Two, we work on:

- Stroll in the Park (loose leash walking). As we go from week to week, there will be new dogs coming into this Level and this changes the dynamics of the class. The owner has to work harder to get and keep the dog's attention while walking on leash.

- Leave it and Watch me!

- Canine Good Citizen (CGC) test exercises 1 through 4:
  - Accepting a Friendly Stranger
  - Sitting Politely for Petting
  - Appearance and Grooming
  - Out for a Walk

This is the level where I get lots of questions about behavior problems and I can begin developing strategies for helping owners solve them.

In Level Three, the class focuses on:

- Formal competition heeling exercises.
- Stays: sit, down, and stand.
- Formal competition recall exercises.
- Supervised separation for exercise #10 of the CGC test.

Finally, in Level Four, we work on:

- Proofing and raising the bar on training challenges, including all of the CGC exercises, particularly #10 Supervised Separation.
- Quick downs, distance downs, and drops on recall as safety exercises.

My students have six months to complete the four levels. The course culminates with the CGC test administered by a guest judge in a location other than our training room.

How do you charge for the classes?

I charge a fee for the entire program (all four levels of training). I will allow students to make payments in installments if need be. I also have a Puppy Levels class for puppies from eight weeks to five months of age. In addition to the classes, students receive a training manual with information on behavior and learning principles.

You've been doing this for a few years! Does it still appeal to you as the most successful way to structure your classes?

Oh yes! Since we allow six months to work through the levels, an instructor can really get to know the dog and family and therefore be of greater service. Obviously dogs that attend often will accomplish more. Even if attendance is sporadic, at least the student does not have the pressure of "trying to catch up." Absenteeism places a burden on the students. Once they fall behind, they never catch up. Levels allows for random participation without guilt, thus a lower drop-out rate.

I teach Levels One and Four on Tuesday evenings (6:30 p.m. & 7:30 p.m. respectively) and Levels Two and Three on Monday evenings (6:30 p.m. & 7:30 p.m. respectively). This means that I have income every Tuesday night when I have new students. It also allows the newbies to hang around and watch the Level Four students!

It is great motivation when they hear that these dogs began with all the same problems their dogs have!

Students can drop in to any of the levels where they need to work on the skills taught. I have no problem with them working two levels, dropping in at the middle of Level Two and staying on and working in Level Three.

The "Levels" system has proven to be a good response to the "I can't attend class on a regular basis" problem. It offers success to those with hectic schedules. It offers alternatives to shift-workers, people who work alternate weekends, and those whose work requires travel or frequent meetings. It allows freedom to take vacations and holidays and not "fall behind." It eliminates the stress of missed classes and it allows for the events that get in the way of things we want or need to do such as Fido's training class.

With this method, there is not as much pressure to attain goals in a short, limited time span. Wouldn't this lead to a lack of motivation for training?

Not necessarily—lack of pressure can be helpful! The "Levels" system makes it possible to keep a dog and owner where they belong until they have mastered a level's requirements, or until the owner feels comfortable in tackling the challenges of the next level of training. For example, if a Level Three dog is starting to pull on the leash, the owner can opt to drop back to Level Two to work on the fundamentals of leash work. I have no problem with the pair working in both levels, one for review and the other to learn new skills.

Do you have any words of wisdom for trainers thinking of developing a similar program?

Introducing the "Levels" program is not for the faint of heart. It takes commitment to make change and to move beyond our comfort zones as teachers. However, given the sad statistics of pet overpopulation and the numbers of dogs finding their way into shelters, we owe it to ourselves to risk trying new ways to allow the concerned owner an opportunity to be successful in developing a relationship with their dog.

What are the drawbacks of using the "Levels" system?

Creativity is required with record keeping! A system to follow up in the event of absences is important. A good assistant is the answer to this problem. Making the leap from the traditional class format is not easy. It takes planning, a willingness to change from the tried and true, and it does create other pressures. However, no system is perfect and I have found that this approach appears to increase the options for success for both student and instructor! ❖

The Benefits and Drawbacks of Holding Dog Training Classes in a Retail Environment

Wendy van Kerkhove, September/October 2004

Training in a retail setting can be hell, and it can be magical as well. One thing is certain: it requires every trainer to add tools to their toolbox in order to be successful.

Most of the larger pet store chains offer training classes and have a designated area where the training is held. At my store, the training areas are usually in the middle of the store; the area with the most exposure and highest foot traffic. This is a smart tactic because it exposes many shoppers to the training program. Teaching a one-hour class is tantamount to running a continuous infomercial for the service. From a trainer's perspective, however, it stinks because the distractions are relentless.

Challenges

Here are some of the problems that many retail store trainers have encountered and the solutions that we came up with to deal with them.

The average training center is only about fifteen feet square and some are much smaller! Consider dumping eight adult dogs and about fourteen people into that space and you are faced with the reality of a trainer who holds classes in a retail store.

Most of us use the training center as a congregation place to take attendance and ask for client questions at the beginning of class. We also use the space for passive exercises (settle and massage) and for off-leash play. We use another part of the store (a larger aisle) for all other training activities. This might seem like a simple solution until you realize that every part of the store contains a constant flow of shoppers, but that will be addressed later!

It is common to have children shoppers reaching through the training barrier to pet unsuspecting dogs. Then there are adults that ask your students about their dogs. And, let's not forget the customer who stands five feet away from your training area to watch your class with his dog-reactive dog! Finally, there is the shopper that thinks it is appropriate to yell, "Hey lady, can you tell me where the cat litter is?" while you are teaching! Talk about a trainer's hell!

In a retail setting, a trainer must learn to tune out the noise and stay focused on the training. Getting frustrated is not an option; it is not professional and your students will be affected by your attitude. Learning to maintain your composure involves accepting the situation and acquiring an understanding that those pesky shoppers are not aware of how they are affecting your job. It is okay to explain to a shopper that you cannot help them because you are teaching a class, but you've got to do it with a smile on your face.

At my store, we are taught a trainer's mantra: short on lecture, long on practice. This advice could not be more critical than in a retail setting. Lectures need to be short and concise so that the students can start to practice and you, as the trainer, can coach them. Keeping lectures short and practice sessions long keep your clients engaged and give you the opportunity to personally teach, coach and praise them.

Distractions cause another problem. It makes practicing the exercises extremely hard for the clients. Imagine trying to teach loose leash walking in an aisle full of cat food whose corners have been peed on by numerous dogs! Even practicing a basic stay can be difficult because of the level of distractions. What is a trainer to do? Explain to clients that they will probably never train in a more difficult setting and if they can do it here, they can do it anywhere! Then praise them for getting their dog to do even the most basic exercises in such a tough setting. Make your client feel proud, not frustrated. I often find myself saying to clients, "Don't worry, you don't live here! All you need to do here is to learn how to teach the behavior to your dog so that you can go home and practice." Sure enough by the following week the dog has learned the behavior and can perform it in the store.

Benefits

Along with all the challenges come distinct benefits to training in a retail setting. If you are a new trainer looking for a place to learn and hone your skills, a large retailer can fit the bill. Many offer well-developed "train the trainer" programs that can prepare new trainers very well.

Distractions can be turned into benefits. In advanced classes, I often use shoppers and their dogs as distractions to make my stay exercises more difficult. I've never had a shopper turn me down; they are often happy to be involved.

Marketing classes is much easier in a retail setting. With customers filing in and out of the store, there is a captive audience. I've overheard a student in class talking to a shopper who is watching from the outside telling the shopper how much fun the class has been and what they have learned. You can't get a better advertisement than that!

There are very few places where you can get health insurance, a 401K plan, and paid vacation for dog training. I'm not sure about other retailers, but with mine, if you are a full-time trainer, you can take advantage of all of these benefits. Even as a part-time trainer, you can get catastrophic health insurance.

The magic of training in a retail setting occurs when a dog does something extremely funny or clever and a large audience is watching. I was teaching a puppy class and a crowd of shoppers was watching the pups play off leash. They were still watching when we got back to "work." I chose an especially cute pup to use as a demo dog to teach sit. The dog never stopped moving in class and was a ball of fire. I got to the part of the lesson where I added the cue "sit" and when I said it, the dog whipped around and sat in a flash. The whole crowd erupted in applause and laughter. It was a great moment!

There are pros and cons to teaching in any setting. If you want a true training challenge and an assurance that every single experience will be different, consider taking a position in a retail store, you won't be disappointed! ❖

Improving Class Performance with Fun and Games

Sue Pearson, March/April 2003

Spring has arrived in the Midwest, it is a beautiful afternoon, and the air is thick with the tension of competition. The teams take their respective positions and the spectators, bursting with anticipation, begin to chant the names of one of the players. Raising his head to acknowledge the sound, the crowd favorite saunters out of the group and turns to face the roaring fans. Drinking in the attention, he takes a bow, and it brings the house down. Wrigley Field? Hardly. It is "Relays with Rover" night at the local dog obedience training center!

Games and competition are a part of everyday life and can play a powerful role in dog training classes as well. Add games and relays to your list of training activities and you have the potential to increase class attendance, improve dog and handler performance in measurable ways, and make class time more fun for students and instructors.

The savvy trainer will find a way to reinforce the most critical obedience and handling skills and make sure that everyone is a winner. Owners are busy people these days with over-scheduled lives, and an owner who has fun while learning is more likely to return to class each week. Return students put in more time training their dogs, develop better handling skills, and during the process create a solid relationship and bond with the dog. It is no small prize at stake—some dogs get one chance at a good, lifetime relationship and may take their first steps toward that goal in your dog training class.

Like technology, sometimes the simple ideas are the most successful ones. When devising new games and competitions for class, think of easy ways to change or create an activity to reinforce a different skill. Want pups to have a quick sit? Play "Sit Around the World," or as some trainers fondly refer to it, "Sit Happens." Tell the group their dog must be in a standing position when it is their turn, designate a starter dog, and then "ready, set, go!" The first dog sits, and when she is sitting, the second dog may sit, continuing around the circle. Keep track of the time it takes to get all the way around the group each week and let the class know how they are doing. Better yet, if you have children attending the class, designate one of them as the stopwatch person, and they will love keeping track of time for you. Not only do handlers become more efficient at getting their pups to sit quickly, they can learn how to encourage pups into a standing position as a by-product of this game. An easy modification is to have owners get their puppies to sit by using a hand signal instead of a verbal cue—or to get their pups into a down position. You can get a lot of training mileage out of a game like this!

Fast, reliable recalls may be one of the most important skills we can teach dogs in our classes, but it can be difficult to accomplish when the dog is more interested in the busy, colorful environment of the training class than in their quiet, inhibited owner. Practicing recalls in a competitive relay race will make even the most self-conscious handler get in the spirit to ensure the feisty little Dachshund does not beat his Rottweiler in the next round of races. Throw in a few ribbons or prizes and you have an instant recipe for motivation and success.

In addition to reinforcing basic obedience skills and increasing owner enthusiasm for training, playing games in class can also provide a tangible way for owners and instructors to measure progress. This can range from keeping track of time spent on a sit-stay; the number of sits and downs a dog can perform in 30 seconds; or how quickly a team can "settle" their dogs.

Not all games and competitions have gone to the dogs—some can be set up to encourage more efficient and effective handling. We notice that many novice trainers tend to repeat cues over and over with little success. This often puts the dog on audio overload and may teach him that the first seven cues do not count. Reminding (or nagging) owners to limit their instructions to the dog does not always work, so we can create a game to reinforce the owner or team that gets the job done with the fewest cues.

In "Doggie Golf," owners are divided into teams and one by one they approach a designated person. When they reach the person, the dog is asked to sit. They receive a point for every "sit" cue given to the dog. The team with the lowest number of points wins the competition. This quick and easy game not only reinforces sit (don't jump) but has the capacity to help owners see the effectiveness of limiting their cues.

Can good games do bad things? Absolutely. Games that eliminate dogs and handlers one by one are not much fun for the duo eliminated first. And, once eliminated from the competition, students are no longer practicing the skill unless you devise a way to keep them included in the activity. Similarly, few of us enjoy being the person on display with a dog who does not have the necessary skills to compete. And, the slower moving dog or owner who constantly brings up the rear in a team relay is probably not having much fun either. In these cases, instructors can look for ways to level the playing field by adjusting for the individual differences of dogs and their owners. If you have a dog in class who has trouble with a particular skill like "stay" or "down," and that skill is a cornerstone in one of the competitions, instructors will need to think ahead and develop rules that allow the owner and dog to participate without losing face. Instead of doing a "down," perhaps that dog and one from the other team will have to sit three times for their turn. Or, you can require one dog from each team to demonstrate a parlor trick instead of doing a "down." The well-prepared instructor can hand pick the "trick dogs" for each team, drawing class attention to their strengths instead of their weaknesses. If you notice that one person consistently has trouble keeping up with the group activities, try to identify a skill or strength unique to that dog and handler, and build an activity or competition around it so they can shine once in awhile.

When dividing up the class for teams, you might have them number off by ones and twos, or you can skillfully mix the faster and slower dogs on each team so that the odds are a little more even for winning. No one can truly appreciate the finer points of competition during "Run for Your Life Recalls" when you pit a cast of hyperactive Border Collies against a team composed of a Basset Hound, two Bulldogs, and a mighty laid back Mastiff.

Emphasizing team wins will help take the pressure off of individual owners whose dogs may not be performing as well or as fast. Team members tend to encourage and cheer each other on when they are working together. And, it is not beneath some instructors to surreptitiously assist a losing team by accidentally spilling the contents of their bait bag in the path of the opposing team. A good, close contest is always a lot more fun and exciting.

Competition is a part of our everyday life, and when incorporated wisely and fairly, usually works to our benefit. The effect is no different in dog class, where busy people with busy lives are more likely to go home and practice a few minutes a day with their dogs if they have a team or individual goal to work toward. A good instructor will know their students and be able to identify strengths and weaknesses within the group so that everyone can be a winner sometime in the class. Every dog and owner should leave class each week having heard something positive about their handling and their dog!

Games that are well designed have the potential to make classes more fun, increase owner enthusiasm, and reinforce basic obedience skills in the process. So what are you waiting for? Ready... steady... GO! ❖

Running a Class for Reactive Dogs

Ali Brown, November/December 2003

Most trainers have a story about a special dog that launched their career. I suppose I am no different. When I spayed Acacia, my Belgian Sheepdog breed champion, she not only gained weight, she also became what we call "reactive." She reacted to people and dogs, becoming progressively worse. It started as barking, went to growling, and when she started lunging at people and attacking other dogs (with little damage thankfully), I knew I was on a road to nowhere.

Enter Carolyn Wilki (Bangor, Pennsylvania), my herding instructor and mentor. She calmly suggested we switch from herding to a reactive dog or "growl" class. I was skeptical because of what I had heard about growl classes, and I did not think it was constructive or appropriate for Acacia, but I trusted Carolyn's judgment.

Ten months later, Acacia had done nearly a 180° turn in her ability to focus on me and deal with outside stimuli, and I became a much better trainer than I could ever imagine. She is not perfect, nor will she ever be, but she is calmer and much more manageable now.

Getting Started

In order to run a reactive dog class, you need space—lots of space—and you need dogs that love their own cars! During my reactive classes, dogs stay in their cars much of the time because the car acts as a crate. It is a safe place to be (crating inside the car is optional) and allows maximum distance from other stimuli that a crate in a training room cannot afford.

You need to decide who can attend a "reactive class." My definition of "reactive" is a dog that responds more intensely to external stimuli than the situation dictates. Dogs can be reactive to people, dogs, noises, motion, or smells, and they can react to those broad categories or just to one or two subsets of those categories. For example, Acacia reacts very much to motion, minimally to smell, only to hyper or confrontational dogs (Labs in particular), and to people, especially running people, pre-teens, and people wearing hoods. I know that some of this has a genetic component (motion), a socialization component (pre-teens), and a reinforcement history component (Labs and other jumping dogs). While I note all of this information on the intake for each dog, I usually treat the issue the same way regardless of the source.

Next, we need to decide how to start each dog in the class. My class is ongoing—students come into the class, work for as many weeks as they can or want to, and leave. I find it easiest to charge everyone a fixed rate for a six-week module. If a new dog starts, I prorate for the weeks left of that module. It is very difficult to start a dog/owner team in a reactive class without prior instruction, so I always insist on a minimum of three private sessions first. During these private lessons, I do my intake and explain to the owner about canine reactivity, including information on stress hormones, health issues (making sure the dog has a full physical evaluation by a veterinarian), management, and nutrition. I start them on some focus and name recognition activities using clicker training. The owner is instructed to keep the dog calm and quiet for at least the first week to reduce stress hormones in the body. Usually this takes up the bulk of the first 90-minute session. They leave with an information packet on reactive dogs and homework assignments.

During the second session, we build on the focus and targeting exercises, and begin to apply them to entry and exit points such as doors and cars. The dog must learn to look at the owner within a specified period of time (i.e., 5 seconds) or return immediately, without talking, to the car. The dog is then left in the car until he is quiet and calm, at which point the owner comes back and tries again. There are many nuances to this process, and many opportunities to discuss such concepts as calming signals, benevolent leadership, primary versus secondary reinforcers, and life rewards. We also continue discussing management tips (Kongs™, handfeeding, crating), and add skills such as leave it, sit, down, stand, and the usefulness of tricks. By week three, the dog/owner team has a good grasp of targeting and other skills, and it is time to decide whether they are ready to join the group.

The severity of the dog's challenges dictates the timing of entry into the group class. I currently have four dogs in the group class, none of whom have bitten a person. They completed their three private sessions and entered class immediately. I am working privately with a cattle dog who bit me (a level 2-3 bite) the first time I met him; he is so easily aroused that he will not be a candidate for the class for some time.

During the Class

Now let's go back to the dogs in the cars! We use a very large parking lot during off-business hours. We occasionally see a person walking or waiting for a train to pass, but for the most part it is quiet and predictable. The cars arrive and park as far away from each other as they can. Students have been instructed to reward calm and quiet behavior with food on the drive over. Once everyone has arrived, the humans get out of their cars and we have a powwow in the parking lot away from the dogs. We review what everyone has done since the last session, share successes and frustrations, and decide what each team is going to work on during this session. Initially I instruct each person as to what they will be doing, but as students become veterans, they learn to judge for themselves.

We then go back to our cars and take turns getting dogs out of the cars. Each dog should get two to three sessions per lesson, depending on the dog's emotional state. At the beginning, the dog may not make it out of the car without trembling, sniffing, or barking, so the owner rewards the dog with food for calm and quiet behavior through the car window. The next step for that dog might be that the reactive stimulus (person or dog) is visible at a distance. In future sessions, the stimulus is brought progressively closer. Then the dog is exposed to different people. When the dog is able to be calm and focused on the owner through several variations of this pattern, we start getting him out of the car, and the stimulus is again at a distance. The distance is dictated by the dog's emotional state. This can take anywhere from one to several dozen sessions before the dog can be close to the stimulus.

Once this dog's session is finished, the next dog gets out of its car. If the dog has reactive issues to dogs, we may get two dogs out of their cars at the same time at a distance. The owners work on focus using targeting and other obedience skills to keep the dogs' attention on the owners. I personally like to see a dog look over at the stimulus, then look back to his owner for reinforcement—this tells me that the dog is learning that outside stimuli are not as important as paying attention to his or her person. After all, the owner will take care of everything! Should the dog stop and stare for more than three seconds, the owner repeats the focus command. Should the dog lunge or bark, it is put back in the car with no discussion.

Once all the dogs have a turn, they get to go again if they are not exhausted from the first session. This type of learning is very stressful and exhausting for the dogs, and we must not be greedy trainers! The dogs progress at their own speed, and often have setbacks that can be very frustrating. But that is the beauty of these classes—they have a wonderful effect of being a support group for people who love their dogs dearly and can share their concerns with others who understand their frustrations.

Management and Expectations

I use lots of management, and educate the owners so that they learn to make their own decisions for all the other times I am not with them! I spend a lot of time teaching about tricks, luring, and free-shaping. The more skills a dog has, the more variety we can use in keeping the dog's attention on us! It also means we will be less predictable because we have so many more tools from which to choose. I do not use muzzles in these classes as the dogs do not interact directly with each other at all.

I make sure my students understand that their dogs will never be "Lassie." They must commit to following the recommendations and working with their dog with every interaction they have. This is one of the areas where I am truly insistent with my students—there is no room for unrealistic expectations in these classes. To date, I have found tremendous personal fulfillment through running these reactive dog classes—as a matter of fact, at the time of this writing, we are working on getting all the dogs in the same large room together. Slowly but surely, we are getting there! ❖

Breath: Your Most Important Training Tool

Paul Owens, March/April 2004

We were holding our dog class in a school parking lot and it was the second week of the session. A woman—not signed up for the class—drives by and promptly enters the lot. As I go to intercept her, her 50-pound Labrador bounds out of the car window before the woman can attach his leash. The woman is running after the dog screaming "Come!" while the dog makes a beeline for the Maltese across the lot.

The Maltese handler is trying to help her dog, but the scared little dog is wrapping the leash around her legs. The woman trips and falls to the ground. I grab the excited Labrador and quickly return him to the car. The people in class are upset and the woman with the Maltese is crying. I have my assistant start the class while I escort the woman a distance away. She wasn't hurt but it seems she was four months pregnant and previously had two miscarriages. This incident understandably had a tremendous impact. I spoke to her at length and she actually returned to class the following week. Everything turned out fine. She went to her doctor to make sure everything was okay, and she had her baby five months later with no problems. Talk about stress!

How does a teacher handle such a situation and turn it into something positive? I returned to the class and explained how such occurrences are part of real life. What we do as individuals in such situations dramatically impacts how we and our dogs will act in the future. Safety and getting the situation under control are the first concerns. Breathing is the next most important step. Breathing. That's what I did, that's what I had the pregnant woman do, and that's what I had the class do.

In our Paws for Peace children's classes where students learn to train and care for their dogs, we say, "If you expect your dog to be in control, you have to be in control first." Breathing is the single most important tool in a trainer's toolbox to develop and maintain focus and control. Certain breathing patterns can instantly relax you, your class, and their dogs. Breathing can change the way a situation is perceived. Yet breathing is the last thing most teachers or their clients think about when they come into a dog training class.

You have a stressful day and you still have two classes to teach that evening. You're dragging physically and emotionally. Your energy level is on reserves and your awareness is dulled. In the dog training business, where things happen in microseconds, this can be a potent recipe for disaster. At the very least, your students aren't getting what they paid for because all of you isn't there teaching.

Trainers have a wonderful opportunity to inform owners how their dogs interpret breath, or the lack thereof, in tense situations and how this can improve or worsen an already tense situation. It makes sense, if you consider how sensitive we are to one another's moods, and how we sometimes give a wide berth to people whose body language suggests aggression. We all make associations.

When a person is stressed, breathing becomes shallow, the person's body, especially the facial muscles, tighten and there is a chemical reaction from the adrenal glands in the body. To a dog whose senses are much more acute and highly sensitive, these become signals that can trigger the dog's fight-freeze-or-flight syndrome.

If you relax and focus your energy through breathing exercises, your students will mirror your attitude. They will begin to look at the situation as you do for what it was—a single moment, and nothing more. You can then explain that the dogs have an issue and demonstrate how positive dog training can resolve the issue. You have done all of this in seconds without anger or the use of aversives. You are in control. Your affect of understanding, leadership, and control—coupled with your step-by-step resolution to the problem—leaves a dramatic, empowering impression.

Practice the "Easy Breath"

Three things are required for the "easy breath:"

- The breath must be relaxed and not strained.

- The breath must be equally measured during inhalation and exhalation (e.g., three seconds in, three seconds out.)

- There should be no "holds" at the top or bottom of the breath. In other words, make the transitions at the top and bottom gentle and continuous. Ideally, this breathing is done through the nose with the mouth closed. There are hundreds of breathing methods. This particular one uses nostril breathing. If you cannot breathe in and out through your nose, don't worry about it. Just do your best.

You can practice three or four breaths whenever you remember—while driving, watching television, when you wake up, and before bed. The more you practice, the better the results. Easy breathing oxygenates your blood and energizes every cell in your body.

Breathing to Enhance Concentration and Relaxation

As you continue to practice, you'll be able to extend your inhalation and exhalation. This will happen automatically and naturally. Within a few days or weeks you'll be able to comfortably breathe in and out for ten to twenty seconds or more. Length of time is not of primary importance—increasing your depth of concentration and relaxation is. The length will take care of itself.

How can you energize your class presentation so that students leave feeling empowered? How can you sharpen your awareness and improve reaction time? How can you facilitate the human's and dog's learning? How can you reduce stress for yourself and those around you? And how can you improve safety? Breathe.

How you feel affects your breath. Fortunately, the reverse is also true: your breath affects how you feel *and* your ability to perform. Changing your breath pattern changes the way you feel and what you do. In addition, breathing affects the way dogs feel and what they may or may not do. Before every class, before every in-home training session, and during a class itself, remember to breathe.

The key to relaxation is to listen to yourself breathe. As an experiment, gently close your ears and listen to familiarize yourself with the sound. Then consciously relax your breath more and more. With practice you'll get better and better until you'll eventually be able to relax at will. You and your students, both dogs and humans, will benefit. ❖

The Dog Trainer's Voice

Michelle L. Romano, March/April 2003

Standing in a room with a twenty-five-foot ceiling, with eight barking dogs and their twelve screaming or shushing owners, it occurred to me that the voice of a dog trainer can get a little strained. As I tried—with little success—to make sure they all heard what that vital piece of the homework was, I found myself screaming, "Don't yell at him…Just ignore it, I'll repeat what you don't hear…You're just barking with him…Try turning him around…I said, I'll repeat what you don't hear."

Sound familiar? I have recently heard several dog trainers talking about losing their voices after instructing a class. I have not actually lost my voice as a result of a loud class, but I may have a slight advantage: seven years of formal voice training. The principles used in vocal coaching can be slightly modified to apply to frequent performances of speaking, rather than singing, in front of an audience. This article describes some simple suggestions on how to optimize your vocal "performance" in class and after.

Vocal Care and Nutrition

Your vocal chords are situated in your throat, adjacent to your esophagus, so what you swallow can have an effect on how well your voice performs. You can help open up your throat with hot tea. Herbal teas are excellent, as well as herbal throat lozenges. Soups, for the most part are also nice and soothing, and easy to swallow. Water is absolutely essential to lubricate your vocal chords. It is good for your overall health, and beneficial for your voice, to drink two to three liters of water each day. Have a bottle of water with you during your classes to sip throughout your lecture.

On the other side of the coin is the stuff you should try to avoid on days when you will be working your voice. Smoking is severely detrimental to the vocal chords. Don't believe me? Have a listen to Kathleen Turner, Joan Rivers, or Betty Davis. Alcohol should be avoided before and during lectures, as should caffeine, due to the dehydrating properties in both. Carbonated soft drinks can be irritating to the sensitive skin around the vocal organ. Finally, you will certainly want to stay away from milk and dairy products on the day of a lecture. Dairy creates phlegm, which can create friction on your vocal chords, which can lead to sore throats, loss of voice, nodules (nodes), and polyps.

In addition to the food and drink aspect, you will want to care for your voice in your daily interactions. When you speak, try to maintain a calm and quiet tone in your conversations with others. Avoid competing with other loud noises, like in a loud restaurant or at a sporting event or concert. Something I have found helpful is to try to give your voice a break for a few hours before your class.

Practice Breathing and Posture

When you speak for an audience, you should breathe through your mouth. You should take deep breaths concentrating on using your diaphragm; that is the muscle below your lungs that helps you breathe. If you use your diaphragm for the entire breath, from inhale through exhale, you will find you are taking deeper breaths and you will be able to control the air, so it will last longer. That involves holding back the air just a bit when the sound comes out. You will also want to breathe first, and then speak. This seems like common sense, but we often will just begin speaking without taking a full breath first.

Practicing good posture while you are speaking will not only make you look better, it will improve the quality of your voice and help you project it too. You should stand with your feet shoulder-width apart, with one foot slightly in front of the other; your shoulders should be pressed slightly back and your chin slightly up. This stretches your spine and gives your diaphragm more room, as well as creating a straight, unobstructed passage for the air to travel through. All of this will help create a full sound that projects easily throughout the room with very little effort on your part. Both proper breathing technique and posture will help to reduce the stress on your vocal chords.

Breathing Exercise

Get a heavy phone book, or a medium-sized volume of an encyclopedia. Lie down on the floor on your back and place the book on your stomach, just below your belly-button. Take deep breaths and watch the book rise for five seconds, and then lower for a full five seconds too. This exercise will strengthen your diaphragm muscle. You can increase the weight of the book as it becomes easier, or you can try to take seven seconds for each half of the exercise to increase the difficulty.

Practice Placement and Articulation

Correct placement of the sound is important to ensure that you project your words clearly to your audience without losing your voice in the process. You will need to do some visualization here. You need to send the sound up from your diaphragm, past your vocal chords (it bypasses them), and up to the hard palate, or the dome in the roof of your mouth. Take this one step further and visualize the sound going all the way up to the dome of the inside of your head—it resonates better against a bigger dome. In order for the sound to make this journey, you need to open your throat, relax the muscles, and let the sound bypass the vocal chords. Do not force the sound to happen. Your vocal chords vibrate when sound is produced.

The trick is to have them vibrate, but not touch each other in the process. You can accomplish this by keeping your throat open when you make sound; this is how you bypass your vocal chords. Now, think of an echo—that is what you want to create in the "dome." You should feel the vibration in your head, almost like a dizzy feeling. The sound should be full in your mouth, not breathy, throaty, or nasal sounding.

Articulating the vowels correctly, or not mumbling, will help your voice project easily and, in turn, be less stressful on your vocal chords.

Placement Exercise

Begin humming. Now open your mouth as wide as you can, continuing the sound. Now breathe. Now begin making sound with your mouth open again, using the sound "AH." Close your lips, while keeping your mouth open, still making sound. That is humming with an open mouth inside. Now breathe. Next, you are going to do the open mouth hum, with different vowel sounds: "mmaaa," "mmeehhh," "mmEEE," "mmoohhh," and "mmuuu." Remember to visualize the sound traveling up and bouncing off the dome and it will then project forward. The different vowels will help you project in this fashion while your mouth is actually speaking, through all the different shapes your lips make.

One final suggestion is using some sort of amplification or public address system. Many trainers are using wireless microphones and find them extremely helpful in avoiding vocal strain. The type of system you choose should take into consideration the size and shape of the space you are using. The best source to purchase a system would be a music store, where the equipment will be of a good quality and the staff will be knowledgeable enough to help you find the right setup for your situation.

You only get one voice. Losing your voice after a class is a warning that you have abused it in some way. These techniques will help you get the most out of the voice you have, so you can keep it, and keep it healthy.

Helpful Hints

- Drink two to three liters of water per day

- Give your voice a rest (do not talk) for the two to three hours preceding class.

- Have a cup of herbal tea about a half-hour before class to open up your throat.

- Do the placement exercises about a half-hour before class to warm up your voice.

- Periodically, during your lecture, put your hand on your diaphragm to make sure you are breathing properly.

- Check posture periodically.

- When the dogs bark and owners try to quiet them, just stop talking and smile. The owners will look at you and then you can gesture to them to turn their dogs around.

- If there is one instigator, walk over and block him yourself.

- After class, have a glass of ice water to re-hydrate your throat and reduce any swelling.

- Do not forget to breathe. ❖

(References on next page)

Voice Care Resources

www.singingvoicelessons.com. One can purchase a set of CDs on vocal care by vocal coach Shelley Kristen.

www.voice-center.com/maintain_ voice.html. Information on maintaining optimal vocal performance.

www.myvoiceteacher.com. Online voice lessons.

http://www.thehealthyvoice.com. Vocal tips e-newsletter, instruction, and seminar schedules.

Clients and the Community

Many dog trainers focus exclusively on becoming experts on dogs and training techniques. While expertise with dogs is critical, trainers also need to pay special attention to the wants and needs of their human clients and to the community in which they live. The articles in this section begin with a focus on making sure that the client's needs are being met in order to have a great outcome for the dog. That is followed by articles on some great programs that trainers have brought to their communities that promote goodwill and build business. Who knows, maybe you will become the local expert who is called upon to get involved with local leash and "dangerous" breed laws, the formation and management of dog parks, and working with community outreach programs that utilize dogs. Focusing on clients and the community at large is good for you, good for business, and good for the dogs.

The Dog Trainer's Resource

What Do Clients Want?

by Michael Baugh, March/April 2004

Most of us have a feel for what our clients want and need from us. As trainers and behavior counselors, we offer certain services, particular ways in which we structure those services, and unique styles and methodology. It makes sense that clients who want what we have to offer will seek us out.

As our industry matures and competition increases, it's important that we look more closely at what our clients really want from us as trainers. What are they really asking for when they call for our services? If you can answer that question and meet your clients' expectations, then you are tapping into what some business advisors call your "x-factor." This is the hard-to-define, special quality that sets you apart from the rest. It's that extra something that makes your clients not only appreciate your services, but love you as a trainer.

Finding out what your clients want is as simple as asking and then listening. This process begins with the first phone call. Dig for the right information to determine what the caller is asking for. Most of our callers at North Coast Dogs are looking for solutions to specific problem behaviors. We always ask, "What exactly is your dog doing?" or, "What would you like to see improve in your dog?" Then listen—don't jump right in with your "pitch." Be quiet and let the client talk. You'll find that they hand you the exact information you need. We keep intake calls under 15 minutes using this method because we don't have to describe all our services. Instead we say, "Thank you so much for the information, here's how I think we can help."

That brings us to the one thing we know for sure clients want: someone who not only understands their situation, but who cares about them as a person. That first phone call tells a potential client a lot about how you treat people. Some clients appreciate the simple fact that you answer the phone. (I'm still surprised by how many trainers don't answer or return calls.) There's nothing really complicated about listening to a client and asking them how you can help. Caring for your client is what a former boss calls "good home training." Use your manners. Be polite. Listen. Show compassion. Help. We've had clients tell us that they like North Coast Dogs just because we don't make them feel bad about how their dog is behaving. The number one emotion our clients say they have in relation to training their dog is shame and embarrassment. Some say they came to us because other trainers had actually shamed and embarrassed them even more. That's bad people skills and bad business.

The client is not your enemy—she's your friend. Authors Leslie Yerkes and Charles Decker call this "making it personal." They wrote a great business parable called *Beans* about a coffee shop owner. "Making it personal" is grounded in the development of genuine and lasting relationships with customers. The coffee shop owner learns each of his customers' names and has their favorite drink ready as they reach the counter. He gets to know his customers personally.

This is not difficult, nor is it high-end thinking. Learn your customers' names, not just their dogs' names. Then greet them by name. Ask them about their families or check in on their dog's training progress. We have weekly play groups for dogs. It's a great opportunity for our trainers to "make it personal" with clients. We see people who may not have been in class for months. For us, it's a chance to ask, "How are you and Bailey coming along with that barking-at-the-front-door situation?" For Bailey's guardian, it's a chance to see that we really do care about his personal goals and needs. And isn't that what we all really want—for someone to care?

After I'd had my wisdom teeth extracted, the oral surgeon called me from home to see how I was doing. That doctor decided to make it personal. Follow up is a great way to discover and satisfy what your clients want from you as a trainer. In a recent survey of our clients, we found out that our attention to follow-up is what people liked most about us. All of our in-home clients get at least one follow-up call from us. Aggression clients get a case manager who calls once or twice a week! And everyone who misses more than one class gets a call from the trainer "just to see how things are going." We think this policy shows top-shelf customer care. It's also an excellent way to ask people what they really want. If we're letting a client down, we know it immediately and we fix it fast.

In fact, I recommend you encourage your clients to complain. How's that for a mind-blower? Janelle Barlow and Claus Moller wrote the book on this concept, *A Complaint is a Gift*. Every client complaint is an opportunity to improve your service or product. And every complaint is a chance to heal a relationship and potentially keep a client. Barlow and Moller report that for every one complaint you get there are more than two dozen other clients who have complaints but never speak up (at least not to you). They may tell their friends how awful you are. Some tell everyone. But you never reap the benefits of their complaint. You never learn what they really wanted. And you can't heal the relationship with that client. They're just gone.

At North Coast Dogs we are complaint friendly. It's part of our company culture and every one of our trainers has bought into it. At every class meeting I say, "I want to make sure we're meeting your individual needs and goals in this class. So, are there any questions?" I'm asking them to complain. I've had classes where one person says they want to spend more time on a particular skill and then everyone else in class chimes in with agreement. Had I not asked, "Are we meeting your needs?" I would have missed a chance to better serve the entire class that day.

There are lots of ways to encourage clients to tell you what they want. The most effective way is to handle complaints well. Barlow and Moller suggest we thank our clients for complaining, then apologize for the failure and offer possible solutions for setting things right again. We have very liberal policies for handling complaints and each of our trainers is empowered to do whatever is necessary to satisfy clients. As a result we benefit from client feedback. And, surprisingly, clients do not abuse our generosity by lodging frivolous complaints.

Make it easy for clients to tell you what they want. Feedback forms are a great way to do this. We provide them for in-home and group class clients with hard copy and online options. Every issue of our monthly e-mail newsletter includes a link to the feedback section of our web site. We have signs posted at each of our learning centers (even in the bathrooms) asking, "How are we doing?" The signs list three easy ways to "let us know what you think." We also issue an annual survey of all our clients past and present. It's a great way to gather statistical data on what your clients want and if you are satisfying them.

So, let's "bottom line" our plan for determining what our clients really want:

- Ask what the client wants and then listen to their answers. He or she will give you the information you need.

- Make it personal. Learn about your clients and form relationships.

- Follow up. Make sure you are meeting (and continuing to meet) your clients' wants and needs.

- Encourage complaints. It's just a different way for a client to tell you what they want.

- Make it easy for clients to continue telling you what they want.

None of this is complicated. All of it is easy and inexpensive to put into action. What may be different for us trainers is that it's a blueprint for human-centered customer service. We're zeroing in on what Patricia McConnell calls "The Other End of the Leash"—the human end. Most of us have never met a dog we couldn't love at some level—even if they behave poorly sometimes. The challenge for each of us is to see that same inherent goodness in human beings. Now, there's your x-factor. ❖

Treat Your Clients Like Dogs!

Nicole Wilde, January/February 2003

When working with a client's dog, I often hear comments such as, "Oh, you are so patient!" Although what I want to blurt out is, "Hah! You should see me in traffic!" when it comes to training, they are right. When I am centered in that Zen-like, cosmic Training Zone, I have infinite patience. I am the person I want to be in real life. Interspecies Communication flows as dog and trainer perform an intricate dance of body language and firing mental synapses. Do I have that same patience with people? I try.

Ask any trainer who is harder to train, dogs or people, and you will get a vote for the two-legged. It is a sad fact of life that many professionals, myself included, understand and accept the canine learning curve, but get frustrated and annoyed with the human half of the equation. Let's face it—we are human too, and there are times when it is very difficult not to lose our cool. Treating our clients the way we treat dogs can help.

Establish Rapport

Imagine someone you have never met before is coming to your home. This person will be judging you on your dog's behavior and manners, your behavior and ability to learn new things, and perhaps even your housekeeping skills. Oh, and let us not forget, you will also be expected to learn a new skill and practice it for the first time in front of this stranger. Do you feel nervous? It might seem silly to you, but that is just how many clients feel when a trainer arrives for the initial visit. Some are afraid of looking inept or incorrectly answering your questions while others worry that their dog will do something embarrassing. Some have had a bad experience with another trainer, or training in general. For everyone's sake, let's put him or her at ease. Just as we would not jump into working with a dog without an initial greeting and a short getting-to-know-you session, we should not start firing off questions at a client without first establishing a rapport.

Since we each have a unique personality, how we put clients at ease will vary. I often use humor. If the client apologizes for the mess when I walk in, I might reply, "Ah, you should see my place; yours looks like *Better Homes & Gardens*!" If they apologize for Buddy the Lab's exuberant greeting, "Aww, Buddy's just trying to help by reminding me of what we need to work on" usually elicits a smile. Of course, forced humor will not help anyone, but if it comes to you naturally, use it.

Offering a compliment is another way to put someone at ease. I often find myself in a home where it is no stretch to exclaim, "Your home is beautiful!" Or perhaps the blouse your client is wearing is worthy of comment. (Be careful about comments regarding physical appearance if you are a male trainer working with a female client as you don't want to put her on the defensive.) Don't be insincere, but do let the person know there is at least something you like about them, their house, or their dog. A compliment lets the person know you approve of something from the get-go. If you are a true dog lover, it should not be hard to find something complimentary to say about Fido. After greeting a particularly adorable, wriggling bundle of fur, I might smile at the person and say, "Ah, I see the problem. This puppy is obviously suffering from excessive cuteness!" Again, only make the comment if you are sincere. If you are, your client will most likely feel more at ease, which will improve your chances of getting candid responses to your questions. It will also help to increase the level of success of your training as we all know that learning cannot take place when a being is stressed, be it human or canine.

Minimize Distractions

By the time you are done taking a history, both client and dog should be feeling relaxed. Now it is time to start training. Just as we set dogs up to learn by minimizing distractions, we must do the same for people. It is entirely appropriate to suggest the client let the answering machine pick up phone calls. Otherwise, many will feel compelled to answer, and "Stay, stay, stay, RING!" is not conducive to progress. Clients with small children are not always adept at redirecting them from running around, interrupting, or showing off for visitors, all of which can create frustration for everyone. Help them by suggesting the children watch a video in another room, play a game, or do homework in the meantime. You could even bring along "activity sheets" such as connect-the-dots or coloring pages and crayons for small children. If the television is on in the area you are planning to train, suggest it be turned off. I have had clients who wanted to leave a football game on during the session. I politely explained that yelling "Touchdown!" as the dog lies down was not the verbal cue we were looking for. Sometimes it is hard to insist on these things and you might feel you are being pushy, but both client and dog will ultimately benefit.

Break It Down

As Bob Bailey says, training is a mechanical skill. We trainers have, over hundreds or thousands of repetitions, become proficient at performing precise training maneuvers. How many times have you heard, "It looks so easy when you do it!" The trick is not to forget how it felt when we were first learning. I strongly suggest every trainer periodically learn a new skill. I recently took a belly dancing class. Who knew that moving your upper body one way while your lower body gyrates in a completely different fashion was so hard! I felt more than a bit foolish, and at times, frustrated. It certainly gave me a whole new empathy for clients who are trying to juggle a clicker, leash, and treats.

Just as dogs learn better when things are broken down into small pieces, so do humans. While many of us are meticulous about splitting a behavior into tiny increments so a dog will succeed, we downplay the human learning curve. Let's make it easy. When client Anna is having trouble managing the clicker, Roxy's treats, and the leash, let her hold the leash and click while you give treats, until she gets the hang of it. Or, when Bob attempts to put a Gentle Leader on Rudy for the first time, break it down into getting the muzzle piece on first; then, when he is comfortable doing that, add the fastening of the straps around the head. I often remind clients that when they first started driving, it seemed there were endless things to remember and coordinate, but eventually everything gelled into one fluent operation. Assess your client's skill level and observe minute movements as you would a dog's. Keep adjusting your program accordingly to ensure success.

Positive Reinforcement

As trainers who rely heavily on positive reinforcement, we understand the need to reward a dog for a job well done. But how many of us apply that same level of reinforcement to people? How many "jackpot" the client for a breakthrough performance on a training exercise? A big smile along with an enthusiastic, "Yes! That's it! You've got it!" can make a client feel every bit as reinforced as a dog receiving a shower of hot dogs.

Some people need more reassurance than others. But everyone, regardless of their confidence level, wants to hear that they are doing well. When I was a teenager, my very first job was teaching at a health spa. It was back in the days when aerobics was still called calisthenics. (That tells you how old I am.) Part of my job was to lead women through their exercises, show them how to use the equipment, and give feedback on their performance. I have never forgotten what we, as instructors, were told to do if a person was doing an exercise incorrectly. We were never to "correct" them, but instead to frame suggestions in a positive light. Instead of, "Sorry, that's wrong," we would say something like, "Very good, Dolores! Now, the next time, let's try bringing the bar down a bit slower." That lesson stuck with me. It is our job as trainers, no matter how inept the client might be, to stay cool and encouraging. After all, they are probably frustrated enough for both of us, and embarrassed as well. Find something the person is doing right and comment on it. Then suggest a better way. For example, "Your praise voice is excellent, and I love the animation you're putting into this. Now let's work on the timing of the click."

Reality Check

All of us have good days and bad. We might not be as pleasant and helpful with clients on some days as we would like. That's okay—we are human. But if you find yourself becoming impatient or callous to your clients' feelings on a regular basis, take a step back. Assess the problem as you would a training challenge. Perhaps you have been working too many hours and it is time for a vacation. Is there stress in your life that needs to be dealt with? Address the issue so you can remain a truly positive trainer for your clients as well as their dogs. Remember to take time in your own life to relax. (And yes, I know that is easier said than done!) It really is an investment in keeping your business successful.

Keep It Simple

In addition to breaking things into small steps so dogs and humans can learn, we must apply the Keep It Simple rule to both species. Just as you would not ask a dog to "sit" and then the next time to "sit down," be sure to keep your language straightforward when addressing clients. Although you might be a walking encyclopedia of learning theory, your client will not be served by your spouting terms like "Premack principle" and "cognitive dissonance."

No matter how complicated a theory might be, it is our job to present it to the clients in a way they will understand. Analogies can be helpful. Sure, I explain to clients that behaviors that are rewarded are more likely to be repeated. But contrast the dryness of saying, "According to the Thorndike principle …" with telling the client to imagine that each time I call them over, they will receive a $50 gift certificate; then asking what they think they might do the next time I call them over. Most people grin when answering that one, and they definitely "get it." Yes, we should explain desensitization and the need to manage the dog so as to not encounter trigger stimuli during the process, but I use a scorpion analogy. "Let's say you're afraid of scorpions. You could probably handle it if, while we sat in your living room, I pointed one out to you on the far garden wall. As you looked at the scorpion, I would give you a piece of chocolate. Each time I visited, we would decrease the distance of the scorpion in tiny increments, maintaining your comfort level, giving you that piece of chocolate every time. But what if, during this training period, you woke up and there was a scorpion on your pillow? Aaack! That would certainly set the process back." Using analogies makes theories accessible and memorable.

How Humans Learn

Everyone has his or her own learning style. Some people prefer to listen to new information, some like reading, and some are more visual. But regardless of an individual's learning style, almost everyone does better when they go through the motions rather than just listening, reading, or watching. As we teach a dog a new behavior, most of us explain to the client what we are doing. However, that is no substitute for the person actually going through the motions. Let's face it, a triple axel looks easy when Nancy Kerrigan does it, but I doubt any of us could pull it off on the first try. So regardless of how much head nodding and "Mmm-hmm-ing" is going on, have the client practice with the dog so you can give feedback. If more than one family member will be working with the dog, have each person try it so you can individualize feedback and instructions.

Last But Not Least

The bottom line is, training should not be all about us. Sure, our clients should think we are wonderful, hopefully enough so to recommend us to others. But ultimately, training should be about the client working effectively with their dog, and feeling good about themselves, their dog, and training in general. Treating our clients like dogs makes that possible. ❖

Knowing When to Ask for Help

Janine Pierce, May/June 2001

One of a professional dog trainer's most important skills, regardless of level of experience, is knowing when to ask for help. There will always be that occasional dog you can't quite figure out—the dog who doesn't improve or, worse, whose behavior seems to be deteriorating. With some dogs, as could have been the case with Buddy, it's a matter of life or death.

I had been working with Buddy, a very large Greater Swiss Mountain Dog, since he was four months old. When I first saw Buddy, he was more fearful than almost any other dog that age I had ever seen.

Through many private lessons and two classes, we made some progress. Buddy, however, wasn't relaxed. He moved cautiously and stiffly and hadn't progressed as much as I'd hoped in his ability to be handled. I felt as though his people were doing at least some of their homework, and I tried to think of new ways to help both the canine and human sides of the equation.

When Buddy's owners started to show their other dog, they dropped out of Buddy's Saturday class. I did my best to convince them of the potential seriousness of Buddy's problems, and they promised to work his program and come back soon.

They returned to class about seven months later and, to my dismay, my fears were coming true. Buddy had learned to growl. He was also discovering the effect of his growl on his environment.

During a private lesson at the owners' home, I observed that Buddy was tense most of the time and had developed an arsenal of problem behaviors. In addition, Buddy was having some trouble at the veterinarian's.

How could this happen to a dog I'd started working with at four months of age? I referred the owners to another veterinarian who wouldn't even be in the same room as Buddy. Double whammy! The next weekend, his owner confided that he was considering returning Buddy to the breeder, who wanted to put the dog on a choke chain to correct his behavior. I was certain that harsh training methods would not be the right approach for Buddy's fear-based behavior, not to mention that such methods probably wouldn't work. And if this huge, unaltered dog bit someone, it could be pretty serious. Determined to save Buddy, I decided to get help.

One of the things I like most about the APDT, regardless of the politics or disagreements, is that its members are determined to help the canines on this planet. They are usually open to sharing methods and ideas, and many do so without much ego clashing.

So I contacted my friend, Laura Bourhenne, who had been very supportive over the past few years and had introduced me to the APDT. I thought it would be a little galling to admit I was in over my head, but I couldn't have been more wrong. Instead, I felt immediate relief in being able to share this burden with Laura. She came to class, met Buddy, and witnessed his actions firsthand. We booked a private lesson, and I met Laura at Buddy's house later that week. Not only was she fantastic in her encouragement, but I honestly felt my clients gained respect for me as a trainer because I brought in a consultant. They knew I had Buddy and their best interests at heart.

Did I get paid for my time? Absolutely! I was paid tenfold in a very valuable commodity: education. I learned that the major reason why I wasn't being effective with this dog and his family was that I was too familiar with them. Laura seldom made eye contact with Buddy, and she moved more slowly than I with both the dog and the clients. Buddy stayed more relaxed during that session with Laura than I'd ever seen him before. I left feeling rejuvenated...there was hope for Buddy!

I learned a lot that day about anxiety-based aggression and about communicating with people. Laura and I will be continuing Buddy's treatment (and my education) in the weeks to come, and I consider it a win-win-win situation. Knowing when to ask for help is indeed an important and rewarding skill to keep in your bag of tricks! ❖

Meeting the Challenge of Teaching Clients with Special Needs

Veronica Sanchez, March/April 2004

As dog trainers, we are used to juggling a wide range of dogs' needs. However, the humans in our classes have many different needs. According to the 2000 Census, about 19 percent of the population in the United States has a disability.[1] Additionally, the number of people with limited English proficiency grows steadily. This increasing diversity challenges us to develop instructional strategies that effectively address clients' special needs.

Overcoming Language Barriers

Communicating complex concepts is difficult when we do not share a common language. In public schools, educators succeed in teaching abstract ideas to limited English proficient students using strategies that include verbal communication techniques and visual aids. A dog training class can be an ideal environment to learn new vocabulary because it provides a meaningful context with opportunities for demonstration to enhance understanding.

Many strategies for facilitating communication with limited English speakers are easy to incorporate. When we are not understood, our tendency to repeat the same words louder stresses the listener. A better approach is to speak slowly, without distorting your words, or to change your word choice. Some of my Hispanic clients with limited English proficiency have been confused by the word "treat," for instance, but have known the word "cookie." "Trick" is another word that may be difficult for English language learners. Demonstrating a few tricks is a simple way to clarify meaning.

Visual aids promote understanding for clients with limited English proficiency and make class more interesting for everyone. For example, if you would like your students to purchase specific treats, show some of the packages. Handouts are terrific, but unless students read them during class, they may not associate the words with the concepts. Consider using a chalkboard or posters to support your teaching as well. Because people acquire different language skills at different rates, it is not unusual for someone receiving formal instruction in a new language to have stronger reading than oral comprehension skills. Written visuals may be invaluable for these clients.

Non-verbal communication through body language, facial expressions, and gestures also fosters comprehension. Modeling is essential not only for teaching limited English speakers, but for all visual learners. Be conscious of your body language and use gestures that convey meaning. Do not forget to smile and maintain your sense of humor about misunderstandings!

A language barrier can make assessing learning difficult too. Adults are often embarrassed to admit that they are confused, and may nod or say "yes" when they do not understand. On the other hand, a client may respond abruptly, or appear to lack an understanding of dog training concepts, when this actually reflects their vocabulary limitations. Allow volunteers to answer questions instead of putting students on the spot. Observing a client's handling skills may provide a better assessment of their learning than their answers to questions.

Clients from diverse backgrounds enrich your class environment. It is important to be open to learning about cultural differences. Try learning a few words in another language—it will reflect your strong commitment to making students from different backgrounds feel welcome.

Accommodating People with Disabilities

Flexibility is the key to meeting the needs of people with disabilities. Remember that some disabilities are "invisible," and people may prefer not to disclose their disability. Do not ask clients to tell you their diagnosis or other medical information. Instead, provide a space for students to indicate special requirements on the class enrollment form. An accommodation may be as simple as having a chair available so the client can take a break. While accommodating people with disabilities may require a little creativity and effort, the dogs in your class will benefit from the opportunity to socialize with people who may look different.

As a person who uses a power wheelchair, my first question when looking for a dog training class always regards the physical accessibility of the training facility. Adaptive equipment varies in clearance requirements and knowing the measurements of door widths, curbs, and threshholds is very helpful. Being ready to give information about parking and curb cuts on the phone saves the client's time. People who have medical conditions that are worsened by temperature extremes may need to take classes indoors. Keep alternatives in mind when accommodations for regular classes are impossible. Are services at the client's home or at a different location an option? If you are totally unable to accommodate a client, provide a referral to a trainer who can and who uses dog-friendly methods.

When clients with disabilities enroll in your classes, some additional safety precautions may be needed. Be prepared to safely manage dogs that react with fear or aggression to adaptive equipment or to the appearance of a person with a disability. During playgroups and lectures, I turn off the power of my wheelchair to prevent animals from accidentally moving it, and people using manual chairs need to secure the brakes. Clients using crutches or walkers may be more comfortable seated in class. Remember to clear the floor of leashes and other objects for people with visual or mobility impairments. If necessary, provide additional lighting for people with visual impairments.

Additionally, some tools and strategies that minimize the physical demands of dog training may allow owners with disabilities to participate fully in your classes. For instance, head collars and no-pull harnesses can lessen the strength needed to control a rambunctious dog. Free shaping and targeting can be valuable training techniques for a student with limited mobility, and a target stick can facilitate training by reducing the need to bend over or reach down. Students with disabilities that impair the use of their hands may find leashes that wrap around the body and collars with quick release clasps helpful. Attaching a clicker to a wheelchair or walker with velcro can also make training easier. There are a wide variety of clickers that may help people with disabilities, such as Karen Pryor's i-Click™ or Gary Wilkes' Mega-Click™. Alternatively, clients may use a verbal bridge or a whistle. With a little creativity, many training tools and techniques can be adapted, enabling people with disabilities to enjoy training their dogs.

Teaching People with Disabilities

I have noticed that some people alter their tone of voice and slow their speech when talking to me—naturally this is frustrating! If you feel awkward, try to relax because there are some simple strategies that can make a big difference in facilitating your students' learning.

Even if you do not know sign language, you may be able to teach people with hearing impairments effectively. The techniques described for instructing people with limited English proficiency by using facial expressions, body language, visual aids, and handouts will also promote learning for students with hearing impairments. Make sure that clients who read lips can see your mouth while you speak. The background noise of a dog training class may even make hearing difficult for people with mild auditory impairments and increasing proximity can help. Some people with hearing impairments may be unable to hear a clicker. Allow the client to see you click by ensuring that the client has a clear view of your hand and the clicker when you give demonstrations.

People with speech impairments may need only a few accommodations to participate in your classes. Give clients with speech impairments extra time to talk. Repeat what the client says when you are not sure you understood to prevent misunderstandings.

When teaching people with vision impairments, describe your class demonstrations in detail and use directional terms to indicate the dog's position. Be aware that your student may not see your gestures or facial expressions. If your client uses a screen-reader, you may be able to e-mail your handouts or reprint them using a larger font.

People with mobility impairments vary in their physical limitations and in their needs for accommodations. Some clients who use wheelchairs and scooters may be able to stand, walk short distances, or transfer to another chair to train their dog. Sit down to communicate comfortably with clients using wheelchairs or scooters. Remember not to lean on adaptive equipment, and ask before pushing a wheelchair or giving assistance. People with disabilities often prefer to do things for themselves, although it may take more time.

Techniques that address different learning styles can help students with disabilities that impact their ability to learn and people with psychiatric disabilities. Frequent reviews, handouts, visual aids, and extra opportunities to practice in class promote learning. For students with memory impairments, keep instructions succinct and give students opportunities to practice immediately after demonstrations. ❖

Summary

These are only a few of the many ways to accommodate people with disabilities. People with multiple disabilities may benefit from a combination of teaching strategies. Do not hesitate to ask your students for ideas on how to make learning easier for them.

While teaching a diverse population of students can be challenging, many of the instructional strategies discussed facilitate learning for everyone. Furthermore, your ability and sensitivity to meet the needs of a range of clientele is certain to reap financial rewards for your business!

[1] See U. S. Census Bureau. Facts for features: 12th anniversary of Americans with disabilities act (July 26). July 12, 2002, http://www.census.gov/PressRelease/www/2002 cb02ff11.html.

Special thanks to Christy Hill and Kathy Minnick, CPDT for their feedback on this article.

Resources

The Americans with Disabilities Act Information Line staff will answer questions about laws, accessibility, and related issues at 1-800-514-0301 (voice) or 1-800-0383 (TTY) or you can research the ADA website at www.usdoj.gov/crt/ada/.

The Checklist for Readily Achievable Barrier Removal is a guide by the Adaptive Environments Center Inc. to make public accommodations accessible. It can be found online at www.usdoj.gov/crt/ada/checkweb.htm or ordered by phone at 1-800-949-4ADA.

Unsure of the "right" words to use when talking to people with disabilities? Read the U.S. Department of Labor's fact sheet: Communicating With and About People with Disabilities, at www.dol.gov/odep/pubs/fact/comucate.htm.

The Educational Resources Information Center has current research at www.eric.ed.gov, including articles on teaching people with disabilities and people with limited English proficiency.

The Operant Conditioning Assistance Dogs e-mail list at www.groups.yahoo.com/group/OC-Assist-Dogs/ is focused on the training of service dogs using positive reinforcement, but ideas and strategies discussed may be very helpful for people with disabilities training their pet dogs.

Take a Bow Wow Take 1 and Take 2 is a DVD by Sherri Lippman and Virginia Broitman on clicker training that demonstrate how to train behaviors, such as opening and closing doors that may be helpful to people with disabilities. Their new DVD, *The How of Bow Wow,* includes trainers working from wheelchairs while teaching foundation behaviors. The positive training techniques are easy to implement for people with disabilities. All three DVDs are available from www.dogwise.com.

Understanding Dog Restrictions—A Resource Guide for Trainers and Their Clients

APDT Legislative Affairs Committee, March/April 2004

Dog ownership in the United States and abroad has come under a myriad of restrictions in recent years, due in large part to an increasing fear among the general public of dog bites and dog attacks, and a fear of specific "aggressive" breeds. As dog trainers, it is not unlikely that we will encounter such restrictions, either placed on our clients' dogs, or on our own. This article will review some of the most prevalent dog restrictions in the U.S. and provide resources for trainers and owners.

Homeowner's Insurance

If you or your client owns a dog from a certain list of breeds, you may find it difficult to obtain or keep your homeowner's insurance policy. An increasing number of insurance companies are restricting their homeowner's liability policies to exclude some or all of the following breeds: Dalmatians, Rottweilers, Doberman Pinschers, Chow Chows, Akitas, Siberian Huskies, German Shepherd Dogs, American Pit Bull Terriers, Presa Canarios, Wolf Hybrids, and Staffordshire Terriers, among others. Insurance companies argue that these breed restrictions are necessary in order to keep costs down, and their actions reflect the rise in the dollar amount of claims paid out to dog bite victims. Restrictions on breeds vary: some companies will only exclude dog bite claims, others will refuse to write policies for owners of certain breeds, and others will refuse to write policies for owners of any type of dog. Although breed specific homeowner's insurance is becoming more and more common, there are still some companies that do not have breed specific exclusions. See our list of three companies that the Legislative Affairs Committee (LAC) has verified as non-breed specific, at the time of this writing, in our Resources section below.

If you or your client find yourself in this predicament, the American Kennel Club advises several steps:

- Call other insurance agents and companies in your area to discuss policies. Even different insurance agents for the same company may differ in the policies they will write. Ask friends who own dogs for recommendations, as well as your particular breed's national breed club.

- Contact your state's insurance commissioner for a list of companies in your state. Ask as well about your state's laws regarding breed discrimination. In some states, such as Pennsylvania and Michigan, it is illegal for insurance companies to discriminate by breed.

- Contact your state government officials to suggest introducing legislation that prohibits breed discrimination.

- Some insurance companies such as Nationwide Insurance are writing policies when the dog has passed the AKC Canine Good Citizen test. Discuss your dog with your agent and provide proof of training to see if they will make an exception.

- There are companies that will write separate liability policies just for dogs (in this case the dog can be excluded from the homeowner's policy) or you might be able to add a separate rider to your policy that covers your dog, depending on the insurance company.

Co-Op and Homeowner's Association Restrictions

One out of every six Americans lives in a home run by an association, and approximately 80% of all new housing built in the U.S. is administered by such a group.[1] Dog owners living in such housing often face weight and breed restrictions, as well as limits on the number of pets one can own. Dog owners who wish to purchase condominiums and apartments in ritzy areas like New York City can actually find their own pets subject to an interview process with the board association.[2] Weight limits tend to run small, with maximums running from about 40 pounds down to as low as 15 pounds per dog. Specific breed restrictions in place tend to focus on pit bull type dogs (as weight limits automatically disqualify the rest of the majority of the so-called "dangerous breeds"). Dogs with barking problems, as well as separation anxiety, can lead to owners being evicted.

In the event of such restrictions and possible eviction, some possible avenues an owner and their trainer can pursue are:

- Discuss legal action with an attorney who specializes in contractual cases to determine if the association by-laws can be challenged, or if they have been changed since the owner first purchased the property.

- Some owners may be covered under the Americans with Disabilities Act if their dog is a recognized service animal or if the owner can demonstrate a legitimate need for this particular animal due to their disability.

- Some associations can be swayed to allow a dog who can demonstrate good manners and training, usually through the AKC's Canine Good Citizen program.

Airline Restrictions

In August 2002, American Airlines introduced a policy restricting the transportation of pit bull type dogs, Doberman Pinschers, Rottweilers, and any dogs exhibiting "aggressive" behavior. This new limitation arose out of an incident in July 2002 when a pit bull broke out of its kennel in the cargo hold and chewed through part of a wall and some electrical wiring. Other airlines followed suit, although most have since changed their policies to prohibit dogs not by breed, but based on the exhibition of "aggressive qualities." If you or one of your clients find you need to transport your dog by air, a list of Web sites with different air carrier policies is in our Resources section.

Limit Laws

Some local communities have enacted legislation limiting the number of pets an owner may have in one household. These are known as "limit laws" and the impetus for most of these laws is puppy mills, collectors, nuisance barking dogs, and dogs kept in unsafe and unsanitary conditions. The limits vary by municipality: the most common number is four per household although some communities have imposed limits as low as two companion animals per household, and some limit laws include weight limits as well. Some laws restrict the number of dogs one can own, while some restrict the number of animals. While some laws allow a grandfather clause for owners who already own pets over the newly imposed limit, others do not and owners in these situations may find themselves forced to give up some of their pets, or move.

The problem with limit laws, aside from their unreasonable restrictions on our right to own as many dogs as we wish to, is that they often do not address the conditions that dogs live in. An owner may have a large property with many dogs over the limit that are properly housed and well cared for, whereas another owner in the same community may only have one dog that is kept in squalid conditions or is in the yard barking all day. Limit laws can be of particular concern to dog trainers, as we tend to own more dogs than the average pet owner, and some of these dogs may be fosters from a shelter or rescue. Some limit laws can also negatively impact a trainer's business if they do board and train, unless a kennel license can be obtained. Economically, limit laws also lead to less dogs in a given community, which leads to less client opportunities for trainers within that community.

Breed Specific Legislation

Breed specific legislation (BSL) is the enactment of restrictions on the ownership of certain breeds, or outright bans on any ownership of the breeds in question at all. At the time of the writing of this piece, 42 states in the U.S. alone have BSL in place, although most of these laws are at the local, city or county level and are not statewide. These laws ban or restrict the ownership of several different breeds or their mixes. A partial list of typical breeds listed in these bans is:·

- American Pit Bull Terrier
- American Staffordshire Terrier
- American Bulldog
- Bull Terrier
- Chow Chow
- Doberman Pinscher
- Rottweiler

- Staffordshire Bull Terrier

- Presa Canario

Restrictions on ownership can include special licensing policies and fees, mandatory muzzling in public, mandatory signs on one's property describing the breed of dog(s) in the home, mandatory spay/neuter, and insurance liability requirements that can be financially prohibitive. Some restrictions even preclude the owner from allowing the dog around children, even small puppies in need of socialization.

BSL is inherently unfair and most often does not take into account a real understanding of canine behavior and breed traits. Responsibility for dangerous dogs is placed on the dogs themselves, rather than their owners. A dog cannot choose to socialize itself, or train itself, or manage its access to other dogs and people if it has displayed aggressive behavior in the past and present. Only a dog's owner can do this, and this is where responsibility and accountability should lie. BSL also is faulty in that a dog is judged on his appearance, but pit bulls in particular are widely misidentified, even among seasoned animal professionals, and can be mistaken for a variety of breeds that are not part of the BSL in place. BSL is also inherently unfair in that it penalizes dogs that have never had a history of aggressive behavior, and are often friendly, outgoing, well-adjusted dogs. These dogs may even have obedience and other competitive titles, CGC certificates, or perform as therapy or SAR dogs.

BSL can affect trainers and their clients in several ways. An owner may be forced to either give up his dog, or move to a new location, in order to keep his dog from being confiscated and euthanized. In addition to the threat of losing one's dog or dogs, BSL can lead to a negative impact on one's income, as the numbers of dogs in the area may drop due to the laws, and owners who keep their dogs secretly will fear exposure and not seek the help of a private trainer or attend a group class. Clients who own breeds where socializing the dog to small children as a puppy violates the law will have to be counseled not to expose their dog to children, advice that goes against the better judgment of all of us who work with dogs day in and day out.

Homeowner's Insurance

At the time of this writing, the LAC has determined that the following companies do not have breed specific restrictions in place. Note that this is based on the parent company national guidelines and may vary from state to state or from agent to agent. Check with individual agents to find out their policies and procedures:

- SAFECO, www.safeco.com. To find an agent, go to www.safeco.com/safeco/agentsearch.

- State Farm, www.statefarm.com. To find an agent, go to www.statefarm.com/jscript/easysrch.htm

- United Services Automobile Association (USAA is a specialty company that insures federal government workers and members of the military) www.usaa.com; 1-800-365-USAA.

There are also companies that will write separate liability policies just for dogs, such as Prime Insurance Syndicate (www.primeis.com, 800-456-4576, ext. 7801). In these cases, the dog is excluded from the homeowner's policy.

The AKC Web site, www.akc. org, contains a Homeowner's Insurance Resource Center with tips on dealing with breed and dog discrimination and sample letters to contact your local and state officials. A list of insurance commissioners by state is available at www.akc.org/life/homeins/statesins_links.cfm.

The Humane Society of the United States' web site discusses issues affecting pet owners with a specific page on insurance company discrimination at www.hsus.org/ace/18624?pg=2.

www.dogbitelaw.com, owned by lawyer Kenneth Phillips, has information on dog bite statistics, as well as contacts for homeowner's insurance companies that do not discriminate by breed.

The APDT's "Position Statement on Breed Specific Homeowner's Insurance" can be found at the APDT Web site, www.apdt.com.

Airline Restrictions

If you or one of your clients find you need to transport your dog by air, the following web sites list different air carrier policies:

- www.akc.org/pdfs/canine_legislation/airline_chart_0406.pdf

- www.hsus.org/ace/11860

- www.adoa.org/reference/traveling_with_dogs.php

Be sure to contact individual carriers to ensure that you have the most up to date information on their shipping policies.

Limit Laws

The APDT's "Position Statement on Limit Laws" can be found at the APDT Web site, www.apdt.com.

The AKC's Web site has a downloadable informational brochure on limit laws at www.akc.org/canine_legislation/brochures.cfm.

Breed Specific Legislation: Web Sites and E-mail Lists

- www.dogbitelaw.com - This Web site contains statistics on dog bites, legal information on dog bite incidents and breed restrictions, and a resource list of articles available on the Internet.

- www.amrottclub.org/dogbite.htm - This Web site contains information on "How to Respond to a Dog Bite Incident."

- http://rott-n-chatter.com/rottweilers/laws/breedspecific.html - This Web site contains a list of municipalities in the U.S. with breed bans and sample letters to contact one's legislators to overturn breed bans.

- BSL Updates - An e-mail list with updates on BSL in the U.S. To subscribe, send an e-mail to BSL-UPDATES-subscribe@onelist.com.

- Find the Pit Bull - www.pitbullsontheweb.com/petbull/findpit.html - This Web site features a number of "pit bull-like" dogs with a quiz to determine the breed of the dogs in question.

- Pit Bull Rescue Central - www.pbrc.net - Pit bull rescue site which features information on breed specific legislation and a current list of municipalities with BSL in place. Also sponsors Positive Pit Bull Press, http://pbrc.net/petbull/pospress.html, which features positive examples of pit bulls.

Breed Specific Legislation: Organizations

- The American Kennel Club www.akc.org - The AKC's Web site features the Canine Legislation Center, informational materials on preventing dog bites and community education, the CGC Test, and a legislative alert e-mail list.

- The American Dog Owners' Association www.adoa.org - National organization of dog owners and fanciers that opposes restrictive dog laws. Web site has state news on restrictive legislation and informational brochures.

- Humane Society of the United States www.hsus.org - The HSUS Web site contains information on various canine issues and a government affairs section with information on state and federal laws affecting pet owners.

- American Canine Foundation http://acf2004.tripod.com - Organization active in pursuing legal challenges to BSL around the United States.

- Animal Legal Defense Fund - www.aldf.org/ - Provides information on legal actions involving companion animals, as well as wildlife.

- Assistance Animal Access Consulting Services - http://animalaccesslaw.tripod.com/ - Provides information on legal issues involving access for service dogs and compliance with the ADA.

- The Centers for Disease Control - The CDC Web site contains statistics and articles on dog bites in the U.S.:

  - Dog Bite-Related Fatalities - United States, 1995-1996. ftp://ftp.cdc.gov/pub/Publications/mmwr/wk/mm4621.pdf.

  - Dog Bite-Related Fatalities from 1979 through 1988. www.cdc.gov/ncipc/duip/dog1.pdf.

  - Causes of Nonfatal Injuries in the United States, 1986. www.cdc.gov/ncipc/duip/causesof.pdf.

  - Nonfatal Dog Bite-Related Injuries Treated in Hospital Emergency Departments - United States, 2001. www.cdc.gov/mmwr/preview/mmwrhtml/mm5226a1.htm.

- Which Dogs Bite? A Case Control Study of Risk Factors. www.cdc.gov/ncipc/duip/dog3.pdf.

- Breeds of Dogs Involved in Fatal Human Attacks in the United States between 1979 and 1998. www.cdc.gov/ncipc/duip/dogbreeds.pdf.

- Dog Bites: How Big a Problem? www.cdc.gov/ncipc/duip/dog4.pdf.

- Fatal Dog Attacks, 1989-1994. www.cdc.gov/ncipc/duip/dog50.pdf.

Books

Delise, Karen. *Fatal Dog Attacks: The Stories Behind the Statistics*. Manorville, NY: Anubis Press, 2002. Author Karen Delise compiles an impressive array of statistics and background information on fatal dog attacks in the U.S. over the course of four decades. Her book refutes the notion that specific breeds are dangerous and examines the determining factors that lead to a dog or dogs attacking and killing humans.

Randolph, Mary. *Dog Law: A Plain-English Legal Gguide for Dog Owners & Their Neighbors, 4th edition*. Berkeley, CA: Nolo Press, 2001. This well-organized book provides legal information on all aspects of dog ownership, including dealing with one's landlord, barking dogs, assistance dogs, traveling with your dog, and dog bites, among other topics. This book is a "must have" guide for anyone involved in a legal situation or case involving a dog.

Wynn, William J. *It's the Law! Pets, Animals, and The Law*. Sun City, AZ: Doral Publishing, 2002. A resource guide for state and federal statutes relating to all types of animals. Written by a former circuit court judge, the book surveys the legal world and its effect on dogs and their owners.

Bradley, Janis. *Dogs Bite, But Balloons and Slippers are More Dangerous*. James & Kenneth Publishers, 2005. This book provides arguments against unreasonable restrictions on dog ownership. The book covers the comparative risk of death and injury due to dog bites compared to other common hazards, and the poor quality of most research on biting dogs used to support badly thought out dangerous dog laws and inflated civil liability, in addition to unreasonable insurance practices. ❖

References

[1] Tanick, Marshall. "Homeowners association rules curtail freedoms." *Dog World*, March 2004, p. 20-21.

[2] Schneider-Mayerson, Anna. "Dogs have ruff time getting past co-op boards." *The New York Sun*, August 31, 2003.

"Freedom" Poodles

Audrey Schwartz Rivers, March/April 2004

"The opposite of hate is indifference." Elie Weisel, Winner, Nobel Peace Prize, Holocaust Survivor.

Every Sunday afternoon, neighborhood dogs and their humans gathered at a school playground for a makeshift dog park. The dogs rumbled in the fenced yard for an hour while their people gossiped.

Then Sammy came. The young American Staffordshire Terrier was a wiggle worm of energy—and a love muffin. He greeted every person with a slurpy hello and a roll-over request for a tummy rub. He bowed to all the pooches urging chase. His humans introduced themselves but received a cold shoulder as the regulars broke into small whispering groups. Several dogs ganged up on the submissive newcomer.

"That pit bull is fighting our dogs!" the regulars cried. They untangled their rambunctious charges and examined them for nonexistent pit bull bites. "Next week, we're going to the other playground," the regulars whispered.

Poor Sammy, he did nothing wrong—the tussle with a newcomer was just a dog thing. But the sweet pup forever would be stigmatized as the local pariah.

Dogs have been targets of ignorance and prejudice for centuries. During the world wars, anti-German sentiment caused the German Shepherd Dog to be renamed the "Alsatian" in Britain and nondescript "shepherd dog" in the United States. Thanks to Cold War tensions, the Russian Wolfhound morphed into its original "Borzoi," so its fanciers would not be considered Communist sympathizers. After the September 11th attack, Afghan Hound owners received threats and feared walking their flashy pets in public. Some suggested they revert to the breed's early name, "Tazi" to distinguish it from the Taliban. As recently as last year, politicos christened the "Freedom Poodle" to protest France's unwillingness to join the Iraqi War coalition.

While such politically correct nom de plume seems laughable, dog trainers need to be concerned for several reasons.

Breed Prejudice Leads to Breed Bans

Public outcry against so-called "dangerous dogs" have led many communities and states to legislate against certain breeds of dogs based solely on visual breed identity (and, in some cases, mis-identity). Depending on local ordinance, restricted dogs cannot be bred, even for show purposes; must be muzzled at all times; cannot reside within city limits or risk being confiscated and euthanized. Breed bans, like apartheid, usually result from ignorance and fear following sensational, albeit isolated, stories of certain dogs severely injuring or killing innocents.

Breed Bans (and Prejudice) Hurt Business

If blatant discrimination doesn't worry a trainer, maybe a ding to the pocketbook will. What if a forbidden breed shows up in class? Does a trainer have a legal obligation to refuse to train that dog and notify authorities? Must trainers enforce muzzle laws and are muzzles appropriate in class? Even if no ban exists, will other students not participate with "one of those" dogs in the same room, even if "Killer" is relatively well behaved? Does a trainer have a right to refuse training to any dog because of its breed (let alone the "breed" of the handler)?

Breed Bans Create a Liability Conundrum

Do trainers face any legal ramifications for consulting (even by phone) with an owner of a banned breed? Could the trainer be held responsible if the dog behaves in an aggressive manner with a person or animal, even if provoked? Increasingly, insurance companies restrict coverage of certain breeds in homeowner and professional policies. Can a trainer afford the risk of training, boarding, rescuing, or educating a banned breed? How does it help protect the public if a certain breed of dog is not allowed to be trained by law or insurance?

Ignorance of the Law is No Excuse

The controversy over the 2004 APDT Annual Educational Conference in Denver, a city with breed specific laws, highlights a catch-22 for many unsuspecting dog owners, trainers, and enthusiasts. Imagine taking an American Staffordshire Terrier to a Rally-O, agility, obedience, flyball, conformation, or other sponsored event that just happens to be held in a city with breed restrictions. Must Fido wear a muzzle while running weave poles? Could Bosco be confiscated? How do people know if their beloved pet is a persona non grata in a place they visit?

Where's a SAR Dog When You Need One?

Ironically, breed specific legislation often hurts the very folks who demand it. Many of the targeted breeds such as Rottweilers, German Shepherd Dogs, American Staffordshire Terriers, Doberman Pinschers, and American Pit Bull Terriers serve as therapy, assistance, service, and search and rescue dogs. Many of these harassed hounds have received medals for heroism, which is more than can be said of many breed ban supporters. Remember that the next time a natural disaster or terrorist attack strikes a city, and the FEMA-certified Rottweiler cannot come to the rescue.

Dogs Don't Fight, People Do

Those who believe banning breeds will end the evils of dog fighting, take note of the success of the war on drugs or curfews for teens. The grotesque excitement of dog fighting comes not as much from animals torturing each other, but the gamble, particularly the risk of getting caught. There is also the money factor, as there is a significant amount of money wagered on dog fights. Bans only make fighting dogs more valuable and riskier to own, propagating the thrill. Rather than outlaw fighting dog breeds, lawmakers and law enforcers must crack down on the outlaws who promote this deadly, sadistic "sport."

Who Needs Dog Trainers Anyway?

Our society shuns responsibility. We sue McDonald's because of spilled hot coffee. Corporate boards know nothing of accounting irregularities. We blame the bartender for pouring the last round that led to a DUI citation. The dog ate my homework.

Breed specific laws take the responsibility for an animal's behavior off the owner and place accountability solely on Fido for any misdeeds. Nature, not nurture, becomes destiny. If genetic markers alone predispose an animal to aggression, then obedience training must be a waste of time. Canine behavior is hot wired, so why should a human be responsible for keeping a trained, civilized pet? Perhaps in this blameless universe, dog trainers only can temporarily bandage an already cursed canine's character. So why spend the cash training Fido when dogs will be dogs?

Who's Next?

Today, governments legislate against pit bulls, American Staffordshire Terriers, Staffordshire Bull Terriers, Bulldogs, Bull Terriers, Dobermans, Rottweilers, Akitas, Chows, German Shepherd Dogs, Shar Peis, and Mastiffs, as well as mixes of these. What breed is next?

Perhaps size, not just genetics, should make a dog verboten. After all, mammoth dogs such as Great Danes, Great Pyrenees, and Newfies can easily injure children, the elderly, and the feeble. One community currently outlaws all dogs with unspecified "dominant traits." Does that mean that terriers (a.k.a. "terrorists") like feisty Jack Russells are next on the hit list? What about the scruffy Chihuahua or Yorkie down the block who challenges every other dog and human ankle in sight? How about dogs like Pugs or Boxers who just look mean? The city of Auburn, Washington proposed a law that would ban any dog above 30 pounds as potentially dangerous.

Discrimination against any sentient being should set off warning flares not just for dog trainers and lovers, but for all freedom-loving Americans. Prejudice in any form speaks of an abhorrent, equally vicious flaw in the human psyche. Through BSL, we perpetuate a legacy of hate for another "breed or creed." Today, we hate the pit bull. Tomorrow, the Afghan. The following week, Lassie. Next year, you and me. ❖

Dog Parks: The Good, the Bad, and the Ugly

Trish King with Terry Long,
September/October 2004

They're called dog parks or dog runs. Sometimes they're official, sometimes they're formed by a group of people who want their dogs to play together. Some dog parks are large—acres or miles of paths—but most are less than an acre in size, and some are tiny. Some are flat gravel or dirt, while others have picnic tables, trees, and other objects.

What all dog parks have in common is the reason for their existence. Dogs (and their owners) need a place where they can run free, sans leashes, and do "doggie" things. Many of their owners have no yards and the dogs would otherwise spend their entire outdoor lives on leash.

The fact that we even need dog parks is a reflection on American society, which is fragmented, with many people living solitary lives. Dogs and other pets are sometimes the only family an owner has. At the same time, municipal laws have been inexorably pushing dogs further and further away from acceptance in our culture. Thus, they're seen as nuisances by half the population, and as family by the other.

In a perfect world, dog parks would not have to exist. Well-behaved dogs would have the privilege of being off leash (and well mannered!) in many different areas. However, the world is not perfect, and so we must make the best of what we have.

Advantages of Dog Parks

The advantages are simple and powerful. Dog parks provide a safe space in which people can exercise their dogs, and watch them play (something I love to do!). Our culture is becoming less and less tolerant of our canine companions, and often they are not welcome elsewhere.

At their best, dog parks can facilitate socialization with a variety of breeds and breed types. They can be a wonderful resource for adolescent dogs that have too much energy and no place to put it. Many also function as a social center—a place where people gather to chat, to exchange news, and to commiserate with one another's problems. For many, it replaces family conversation and for some, it is their only contact with fellow human beings. This is probably why, when I recommend that a client not visit dog parks, some cannot bring themselves to do it. They miss the camaraderie too much.

Disadvantages of Dog Parks

The disadvantages are not so simple, but can be even more powerful, depending on the dog and its owner. Some of these are exacerbated by the layout of parks (see below). The real problems, both short and long-term, are behavioral. And often, owners unwittingly contribute to these problems because they don't recognize—or don't interpret correctly—what their dogs are actually doing and learning. Some of the problems cause difficulties only when dogs are meeting and interacting with other dogs. Others can cause future behavior to deteriorate. And still others directly impact dog/owner relationships.

Defensive Aggression

Dogs are social animals, but they—like us—tend to like familiar faces. Just as we do not routinely meet and chat with everyone we meet on the street, dogs do not need to meet with all other dogs. It often takes some time for one dog to feel comfortable with another; and they need that time to decide how they should react. As we know, time is not always available in a dog park situation. Thus, even friendly dogs that feel uncomfortable can give people the impression that they are "aggressive," especially when they meet a dog for the first time. If an overly exuberant Labrador Retriever, for instance, approaches a herding mix, the latter dog may snarl or air bite to make the Labrador retreat. After that, as far as the herding dog is concerned, they can meet nicely. However, people are likely to label the herding dog "aggressive," and punish her (or at least ostracize the owner!). This is a bad learning experience all around. The Labrador hasn't learned to inhibit his greeting style—which he would have if he hadn't been interrupted by overreacting humans—and the herding dog has learned that (a) normal warnings don't work; and (b) her owner won't back her up.

Learned Disobedience

When owners are not careful, dog park play quickly teaches a dog that the owner has no control over him. I'm sure we've all seen an owner following her dog, calling vainly as the animal stays just out of range, looks at her from afar, or just totally ignores her. And this is after the dog has learned to bark hysterically in the car all the way to the dog park, followed by pulling the owner through the parking lot, and then bolting away from her as soon as the leash is off.

Owner Helplessness

Dogs learn that their owners cannot keep them safe from harm when owners stand by and allow other dogs to play overly roughly, and to body slam and roll them over. When discussing this point, it's important to understand that the dog's perception of safety matters even more than the human's. This can be difficult for owners, who may dismiss their dog's obvious fear as unwarranted, since they "know" the other dog(s) mean no harm. A dog that is chased or bullied by another dog is not only learning to avoid other dogs, he is also learning that his owner is completely ineffective. A Chihuahua may very well be thinking he's destined to be a meal, but his owner doesn't seem concerned. This can have a serious impact on the human-dog relationship.

Problematic Play Styles

Dog play styles can be radically different, and sometimes they are not compatible with each other's. This can cause misunderstandings, or even fights, and it can also exacerbate certain play styles. Dogs that tend to be very physical in play often overwhelm other dogs. No one is inhibiting their play style. In fact, owners often laugh at concerns with "don't worry, he's only playing." Playing he may be, but he is also learning, and what he's learning is not necessarily what we want to be teaching. When bully type dogs play with similar dogs, the only unwanted outcome is that they don't learn how to be polite with other dogs. If they bully weaker dogs—which often happens—they learn that they can overpower other dogs, and they tend to repeat the behavior. The weaker dogs learn that cut-off or appeasement signals do not work, and they learn to be afraid of other dogs...sometimes all other dogs, sometimes just dogs that look like the bullies.

Resource Guarding

Resource guarding can become very problematic in a park, where resources are often few and far between. Some dogs will guard their own toys, some will try to take items from other dogs. Some keep the items, others just want to taunt the dog who "owns" the toy. Squabbles over resources, including humans sitting at a picnic table or on a bench, can easily erupt into nasty fights.

Frustration Aggression

Interestingly enough, leash frustration—a canine temper tantrum—is sometimes an offshoot of dog park experiences. There are a couple of reasons for this. Leash frustration often begins when a dog is so excited at the prospect of playing that he pulls his owner all the way to the park, lunging and barking—sometimes for blocks. His agitated owner pulls back and yells at the dog, thus increasing the arousal. By the time the dog gets to the park, he's all fired up for something very physical—like a fight.

Leash frustration also occurs because dogs that frequent parks mistakenly believe that they can meet any other dog they see. Once again, when thwarted, they tend to pull on the leash, and the owner yanks back. As the frustration builds, the dog appears to be aggressive, thus causing other owners to pull their dogs back in fear. Eventually, leash frustration can lead to real aggression. Often, owners of these dogs will be very confused because their dogs are so good off leash, and holy terrors on leash.

Facilitated Aggression

Many dogs are very attached to their owners, and will hang around near them. Often these dogs are worried about, or afraid of, other dogs, and will growl or display their teeth when they're approached. The owners unwittingly "facilitate" this behavior by remaining next to their dog, who then counts on them to help if a fight ensues. If this behavior is repeated often enough—if they feel threatened by a variety of dogs—they may default to that behavior.

Another form of facilitated aggression occurs when two or more dogs in a family visit the dog park. The two may well gang up on a third dog, possibly frightening him or her—or worse.

Age

While many dogs enjoy playing with others throughout their life, a substantial number do not once they have reached social maturity. These dogs will slowly lose interest in other dogs, and may signal them to go away. Some dogs become very reluctant to go into dog parks, which—as we have noted—can be out of control. Others will snarl or snap to indicate their displeasure.

Arousal

Dogs playing in parks sometimes are unable to calm down, and some can get into a state of sustained arousal that gets them into trouble. A dog that has been involved in an incident in which the excitement level is very high, might inappropriately and uncharacteristically start other incidents, often with unwanted outcomes.

Trauma

Finally, a traumatic experience can make an impact on a young dog that cannot be fully understood nor erased. A puppy or adolescent who is attacked may well show aggressive behaviors that begin after that incident. Sometimes a young dog can be traumatized by what the owners think are minor events. I liken that kind of trauma to that suffered by a child who is traumatized, perhaps by getting stuck in an elevator. After the first experience, all elevators are bad—even though she knows intellectually that all elevators are not bad. Pity the poor puppy who doesn't have the reasoning to know that what occurred once does not always happen again.

The Power of Knowledge

Owners, of course, play an important role in dog parks, and often don't accept the responsibility they should. Many don't pay attention to their dog, and many have no idea what constitutes proper behavior, or what a dog may be signaling to another dog. Some defend their dogs when the animal exhibits poor or inappropriate behavior. Some overreact to a normal interaction, in which one dog discourages the attention of another. Occasionally, some owners use parks as babysitters, even leaving their dogs unattended while they shop. And most owners have far less control over their dogs than they believe!

Educating owners is a tough job. Many believe firmly that they are socializing their dogs in the proper way, and don't like suggestions that they limit dog park time or monitor their dog and others. Teaching them what good play looks like is a first step, and empowering them to actually interrupt poor interactions is a necessary second step. Often, people don't want to offend other dog owners, so they allow poor behavior to continue.

Trainers can help them learn by describing what appropriate interactions look like, possibly by narrating what the dogs are doing as two dogs play. I've found that owners really enjoy learning what good play manners are like—they appreciate the same kinds of descriptions that they hear from sports announcers during games.

Finally, some dogs should not go to dog parks. They can be too shy, too bold, too defensive, or have tendencies to guard toys and balls. Often, when consulting with clients, I ask them to consider giving parks a pass and concentrating on walks or runs, either alone or maybe with some special friends. I'm occasionally surprised by the relief these people feel when they find out dog park play is not mandatory! They thought they had to do it.

Keys to a Successful Dog Park

If you believe that your dog will benefit from the advantages of a dog park, here are some things to watch for in terms of dog park design so that you and your dog will have better odds of a successful experience:

- *Entrance and/or exit:* Double gates for safety, preferably shielded from dogs that are already in the park that you want to avoid. Two or three entrances are best. Dogs tend to gather at entrances and exits, arousal goes up, and incidents can easily occur.

- *Size:* As large as possible. At least an acre, preferably not a square piece of land, but one that is oddly shaped. Ponds or lakes are preferable (at least from the play point of view, if not from the owner's!)

- *Contour/topography:* Hillocks or trees to block dogs from racing towards each other and body slamming or muzzle bumping each other.

- *Structures:* Tough obstacle equipment, hiding places for frightened dogs, other view-blocking structures if hills and trees aren't available.

Behavioral Tips for Dog Park Attendees
Do's:

- Check out the entrance before entering to make sure dogs aren't congregating there.

- Pay close attention to your dog's play style, interrupting play if necessary to calm your dog down.

- Move around the park so that your dog will need to keep an eye on you.

- Remove your dog if the dog appears afraid.

- Remove your dog if it is bullying others.

- Respect your dog's wish to leave.

- Leave special toys at home to avoid resource guarding problems.

Don'ts:

- Allow your dog to enter the park if there is a "gang" right next to the entrance.
- Believe that dogs can "work it out" if you just let them do so.
- Congregate at a picnic table or other area and chat with dog owners who are not watching their dogs.
- Let your frightened dog remain in the park and hope things get better.
- Listen to other attendees in the park who may not understand your dog's needs.
- Assume a dog is aggressive when it is only trying to communicate its discomfort. ❖

Training Wheels™ Urban Solutions

Sue Sternberg, November/December 2003

There is a crisis in high-crime urban areas perpetuating a cycle of violence. Dogs are used as macho status symbols for young people and fighting and sparring are often the only models of human-canine interaction these kids know. Sparring and dog fighting can be found erupting in alleys, basements, and on street corners at any given time. Maulings and serious dog bites occur frequently in urban neighborhoods and these dogs are bred in proliferation.

Although the past 20 years has seen a significant decrease in the overpopulation problem due to an aggressive spay/neuter campaign, that campaign has had a limited effect with this urban population. The campaign is, and has been, highly effective in encouraging, educating, and offering low-cost opportunities for pet owners for whom the behavioral and physical benefits of sterilization are worthwhile and pertinent. For many pet owners, financial constraints prevent them from sterilizing their pets, so low-cost or free services is all they need to comply. For others, the health benefits and increased potential lifespan are the motivation to sterilize. Still for others, the behavioral benefits are useful: a decrease in dog-dog aggression, dominance aggression, and sexual frustration and arousal and other behaviors that are influenced by testosterone.

Most of these motivations are completely off-target for urban youth, who breed dogs for their toughness, aggressiveness, and size. The numbers of unwanted fighting dogs, litters of macho breed-types, and dominant-aggressive dogs is large, and are filling up city animal shelters across the nation. Bred, trained, and raised for dominance and aggression, these unwanted dogs are euthanized or held interminably in shelters since the possibility for successful rehabilitation and ultimate re-homing of these dogs is so remote.

Creative community outreach is desperately needed in our urban areas. New programs to find ways to encourage spaying and neutering as well as programs that provide positive role models for young people and their dogs are crucial.

Training Wheels™ Urban Solutions

Training Wheels offers programs to break this cycle by:

- Providing positive role models for adolescents;

- Encouraging alternative dog sports that are exciting, compelling, and competitive rather than violent and harmful;

- Developing positive relationships in the community to intercept and influence current and future generations.

Who can serve as the model for the humane treatment of people and animals in the community, if not the local animal shelter?

The Adolescent Alternatives Program

The Adolescent Alternatives program was created by Jane Kopelman in November, 2001 to involve at-risk teens in the Training Wheels program as an alternative to incarceration. The goal is to give them the opportunity to learn animal handling and dog training skills, and basic, humane care, allowing them to go back into their neighborhoods and help people and pets work toward a more humane community.

Participants in the program are given the opportunity to learn reward-based training methods by pairing them with shelter dogs. They learn how to achieve desired results without the use of force or intimidation. The kids learn how to develop empathy with people by building patient and compassionate relationships with dogs. By learning to work with dogs using positive reinforcement, they also learn to communicate with people in positive, non-judgmental ways.

The program offers short-term residential stays in the dormitory area of the Rondout Valley Animals for Adoption shelter. Each day, under supervision, they feed, bathe, exercise, and train shelter dogs. They are immersed in the daily life of the shelter, and participate in special programs and various dog sport workshops. Regular Training Wheels trips into the community are made and participants receive experience working within the community. These kids take the skills they have learned training dogs and share them with pet owners in need of help. The program also sends participants to workshops on all aspects of dog training, including tricks, musical freestyle, Frisbee™, agility, and shelter dog training.

It is the goal of the program to instill compassion, commitment, and confidence in the youth who participate, offer them skills and knowledge they can use forever, and inspire other kids in their neighborhood.

The Lug-Nuts™ Program

Most urban dog fights are not organized by professional dog fighters, but rather by kids spontaneously sparring their own pet dogs. Breeding their dogs and selling the puppies, along with winning casual street corner fights, can be profitable and compelling for urban teens.

Most young people in urban areas have few role models for positive, healthy, constructive interactions with dogs. Often, the only "sport" these kids see is dog fighting or sparring. Weight pulling has all the elements of dog fighting—the excitement, the competitiveness, the machismo, the thrill—but none of the violence, bloodshed, or cruelty. The Lug-Nuts program is an antidote to dog fighting.

Lug-Nuts is an inner city program that organizes and hosts informal weight-pulling contests. Plastic children's snow sleds (often pink!) are loaded up with bags of dog food. These have known weights and also make great prizes afterwards. Dogs are hooked up to the sled with a dog-sled gang line and wear padded pulling harnesses. The most gifted dogs at weight-pulling are the "muscle" and "bull" breeds and their mixes. There are no age limitations and no prior training is needed. A dog cannot be forced to pull. A good relationship, a strong bond, and a strong dog are often all that is required. Hot dogs are offered as lures for owners to encourage the dog to move forward. In the first round, the dog is hooked up to the sled with very little weight and pulls from the start line to the finish line to get used to dragging a sled behind him. The first round continues as more and more weight is added. Weights are determined by using the ratio of the dog's weight compared to the top weight he pulled in the first round. Promising contestants are asked to hang around for the second and final round.

Cash prizes (and pet supplies) are offered for first, second, third and sometimes fourth place. Cash prizes are doubled if the winner is sterilized, and access to free spaying and neutering is offered. So far, in all but one contest, the second place winner was already fixed, and the second place winner won more cash than the first place winner.

Contests are held once a month, and a top-pulling dog then has the potential to make more money at a career in pulling than he might if he were used for breeding or fighting. And none of the dog's machismo is lost.

History of Lug-Nuts

Lug-Nuts was first introduced in New Haven, Connecticut in the summer of 2002, and has been held on a fairly regular schedule at Marcus Garvey Park in Harlem in New York City. There has been interest from shelters and dog trainers in every part of the country to implement this program.

These are just a sample of small miracles that have occurred:

- Alberto Bolinas, the owner of a young red Doberman, seen in a video tape of the New Haven weight pull, has since attended, with his entire family, a dog training course offered free to the community by one of the volunteer Lug-Nuts trainers. On the day of the weight pull he was adamant about using his dog for stud. After the course, he is now "considering" neutering.

- We met the winner of the first Harlem weight pull when we pulled up to the park and he was in the background, smacking and yelling at his pit bull puppy. We ignored his actions and focused on helping another owner train his older pit bull. We used reward-based training techniques, and gradually the young man previously seen yelling and hitting his puppy moved closer to the training session. After working his puppy and instantaneously getting a "sit" and a "down" on nothing but hand signals, the owner asked how we did it. We shared the secret of good, positive dog training: *treats*. We did not see him again until a few months later for the weight pull. While trying to convince him to enter his pit bull, the owner casually reached into his pocket, which was filled with jerky treats, and lured and rewarded his dog to pay attention and stop barking at another dog.

- After a cancellation in the series due to a missing park permit, the winner of the last weight pull—a young male with a huge, fighting-cropped, intact male pit bull—contacted our shelter (a long-distance call) to inquire when the next time the shelter was coming down to do another weight pull.

Each miracle speaks to the success of Lug-Nuts and its ability to make a connection between the community and the animal shelter, to provide a motivation and a model for humane care, spaying and neutering, and having a positive, fun, and lasting relationship between people and their dogs.

The Skyscrapers Program

Dog sport instructors and competitors have a lot to offer young people. The dog world is in the midst of a positive reinforcement renaissance and never before have there been so many humane, inspiring, fun, and effective dog trainers. There can be a significant ripple effect when these talented trainers teach group classes and pass on their techniques to students and their dogs. Dog sport instructors and trainers can make amazing role models for at-risk adolescents and young people. They model humane and loving ways to interact and work with dogs and people all in the context of teaching group training classes. Our Skyscrapers Program seeks to match dog sport trainers and competitors with extra or retired fully trained dogs with at-risk adolescents in urban areas. These adolescents would work with, train, and perhaps perform and compete with these "loaner" dogs, all under the tutelage of these reward-based trainers. In small group workshops, the trainers reveal ways to experience the frustration of learning and teaching a dog, and ways to cope with these feelings.

While catch and retrieve is the most common event, and the easiest for beginners, the most spectacular and fun to watch is canine Frisbee freestyle. This event consists of a timed routine choreographed and performed to music. The routine is a presentation of tricks that involve many different types of throws and catches. Some of the more spectacular tricks involve the dog leaping off the leg or back of the thrower and catching a flying disc that is tossed high in the air for the dog. The tricks one sees in freestyle are only limited by the creativity of the performers. In the Skyscrapers Program, skilled professional competitors coach the kids and help them create and polish their own routine set to the music of their choice.

Calling All Dog Trainers!

We are looking for:

- Any trainer, instructor, or dog sport competitor (disc, agility, or musical freestyle) who might be interested in participating in any of these programs;

- Anyone who might have (or know of a student with) an extra already-trained, retired, or "loaner" dog for one of the participating youths to borrow for the class.

- Specifically for instructors who use reward-based training methods with the dogs as well as their human students.

Participating teens will have gone through a screening and orientation process before entering the program. Interested trainers and instructors will also need to go through a screening and orientation process before entering into the program.

For more info on these programs, e-mail Sue Sternberg at info@suesternberg.com and include "TW Urban Solutions" in the subject heading. ❖

Providing for Your Dogs When You Are Gone

APDT Legislative Action Committee, September/October 2003

In our homes the dogs are part of the family, but the IRS will not allow us to claim them as dependents. Courts regard dogs as property with no legal rights; dogs can neither sue nor be sued. Access to the courts is not particularly problematic for the dogs themselves, but can become an issue when we humans are providing for pet care. Under the laws of all 50 states, a dog may not inherit directly. We cannot leave our money to our dogs, and if we attempt to do so the courts will invalidate the will and split the money up according to state laws of inheritance.

So how do we insure that our dogs do not end up at a shelter when we die? First, have a will drawn up by a local attorney. The will should clearly identify the new owner for the dogs and to whom money will be left to cover the cost of caring for the dogs. You should consider the cost of food, veterinary care, toys, outings, and treats. Write up a biography on each dog that includes a copy of their training plan and little tidbits that might not be obvious, such as the fact that a sing-song repeating mantra of "Rachel is a good girl" will keep a dog who hates having her nails done sit quietly for the procedure. This is also the place to make a "living will" for each dog, spelling out your wishes about quality of life issues. For example, do you want any illness aggressively treated as far as possible? Under what conditions would you euthanize an ailing dog? It is vital that you insure the person taking in your dogs knows your expectations concerning the dogs' care. "My kids will take the dogs" does not constitute designating a new owner, and "treat them well" is not providing the information the new owner needs to help the dogs cope with their loss and make the adjustment to a new home.

You should also have a *power of attorney* to give the new owner access to the dogs and funds while the will is in probate, or in the event you become incapacitated and unable to care for the dogs. A will is read only upon your death, but what if you have a heart attack or fall into a coma? Without a power of attorney it is possible the dogs can end up anywhere, even at a local shelter.

It may be possible to leave funds *in trust* for your dogs, depending on the laws of your state. States that have adopted trusts are Alaska, Arizona, Colorado, Florida, Iowa, Michigan, Montana, New Mexico, New Jersey, New York, North Carolina, Oregon, and Utah. Three states (California, Missouri, and Tennessee) have laws that recognize trusts for pets but do not provide for their enforcement if the trustee decides not to implement them. A trust is funded with either money or property, with the proceeds to be used by the designated trustee for the care of the dogs. There are costs associated with administering a trust due to accounting and other paperwork requirements. Some states will honor trusts where money is left for the care of a pet, others will not. Assuming your state recognizes pet trusts, an attorney will advise you how to avoid the pitfalls in drafting a trust, such as violating the rule against perpetuities (setting the trusts up with a limited time span). As dogs cannot enforce the terms of the trust, you may need to appoint another person to insure the terms of the trust are carried out. An additional consideration is what happens to the balance of the trust when the dog dies. Should the money go to the trustee, or to someone else?

The critical consideration in all of the above is the new owner, for the new owner acquires all your rights as a dog owner, including the right to euthanize the dog. Unfortunately trainers know all too well how difficult it can be to find someone both willing and able to take in a well-behaved and healthy dog, so finding homes for our aging dogs and our "project" dogs can be very challenging. If one cannot find a friend, relative or fellow trainer, there are special services run by various organizations that agree to provide care for your pet in return for a donation. It is up to you to insure that your dogs have the same standard of care after your death that they enjoy now. ❖

Resources

The best resource is a consultation with an attorney familiar with the law in your state to insure that your wishes are clearly expressed and that your will, trust, power of attorney, or some combination of the three, meet all legal requirements. You will truly be able to rest in peace knowing your dogs are well provided for.

For Further Reading

All My Children Wear Fur Coats by Peggy Hoyt (Legacy Planning Partners, LLC; 2002)

Perpetual Care: Who Will Look After Your Pets If You're Not Around by Lisa Rogak.(Litterature, 2002)

Animal Care Organizations

Some local organizations have programs set up to help find loving homes for deceased members who contributed to their organizations. Veterinary colleges are offering these types of programs—in exchange for a donation they give veterinary care and keep the dog in a home-like setting. There are also private organizations which will provide the dog a home upon your death. You can locate information on all of the above options at www.furr-angels.com/planpetfuture2.htm.

ASSOCIATION of PET DOG TRAINERS

Shelter Dogs

Working or volunteering in a shelter environment is an important way for a dog trainer, or future dog trainer, to develop a wide range of evaluation and training skills. Sue Sternberg, who contributed several of the articles in this section, gives you practical information on how to work with shelter dogs for your mutual benefit. Learn how to "read" dogs so they can be handled safely, how typical shelters operate, about employment opportunities for trainers in shelters, and how to deal with the difficult issue of euthanasia.

The Rescue Dog

Sue Sternberg, March/April 2002

While teaching an inducive retrieve clinic a few years ago, I was working on advanced retrieving problems with dogs who were already retrieving. One student, a woman with a Standard Poodle, was trying to keep her dog from rolling the dumbbell in his mouth when presenting it during the sit-front. To gauge the extent of the problem, I first asked the woman if the Poodle already had his CDX.

"Oh heavens, no!" she replied. "This is a rescue dog!" When I asked her to explain the relationship between the dog being adopted and not yet earning his CDX, her response was indirect. She said that the dog was not paying attention to her in the ring, and that he was having problems with a reliable retrieve.

I wondered if, perhaps, the previous owner had beaten the dog with a Max 200 dumbbell when he peed on the rug. Or maybe, I thought, the dog had been abandoned and left to starve in an obedience trial "Open Level" ring. What was the woman implying? That, given the right circumstances, the dog would be retrieving reliably and already have not only a CDX, but probably an OTCH? That purchase from a reputable breeder at the age of eight weeks, a promising puppy aptitude test score, and the perfect home environment would make all the difference?

"Rescue" Does Not Mean "Problem"

I once had a conversation with an instructor—a Rottweiler breeder, incidentally—at a dog training camp in which I was enrolled. Because I arrived at her camp with a mixed breed dog, I suppose she assumed I had rescued the dog (or maybe she knew my involvement in the animal shelter world). At any rate, she began a conversation about rescued dogs. She said that she, too, had a rescue dog—one she had bred a year ago that she knew immediately was a problem. She told me that the pup had been mouthy and growly and downright aggressive from the start. She had expected to get the puppy back and, indeed, the buyer returned the pup after only a few weeks.

This breeder sighed and told me she kept the puppy because, after all, what else could she do? She described the dog's temperament as aggressive toward her, and as very aggressive and lungey toward strangers. Yes, she continued, this was her little rescue because of all its behavior problems.

I was stunned. Why should "rescue" be synonymous with "problem"? Why should a rescue dog automatically be assumed to be a difficult dog?

I hate the term "rescue dog." Technically, it should refer only to a search and rescue dog. So I don't refer to my dogs as rescues, even though I may have adopted or found them. After all, they need homes, not rescuing. And I don't cut my dogs any slack for having been adopted or found. Nor do I blame every training, performance, or behavioral problem on suspected prior abuse.

Don't Overestimate the Influence of Background

I have met countless hand-shy and easily spooked dogs with no prior history of physical abuse. I have met dogs of all ages who were owned by convicted animal abusers—owners captured on film or witnessed by passersby while being abusive, or those who confessed to kicking and beating their dogs—and those dogs were neither hand shy nor foot shy. Nor did they exhibit any fear or aggression issues whatsoever. They had the same ratio of sweet, trusting, and gregarious temperaments versus dominance-aggression and fear-based aggression issues as dogs raised in kind and caring homes.

Good and bad dogs, confident and fearful dogs, aggressive and affable dogs come from shelters as often as from reputable breeders. And they are as likely to be strays as pet shop purchases. Rescuing is not an excuse for poor temperament, behavior problems, fear responses, or unsuccessful performance. Rescuing—meaning adopting—is a choice.

Don't Assume That Issues Exist

The owner of an adopted dog is no more or less altruistic than one who purchases a puppy from a good breeder. The rescuer—whom I prefer to call the adopter—chooses to partner with a particular dog. He or she can choose a difficult or long-term problematic dog or a super pet. Either way—and with no excuses—the choice moves the action forward. The only objective, regardless of behavior, temperament or motivation, is to begin the fun and challenge of training and working with the dog.

Too many trainers say things like, "I would rather start with a puppy instead of rescuing because I don't want to have to iron out any issues before getting down to competition training." Why assume that issues exist? Why not evaluate and select a dog without issues? Why should adopting or "rescuing" be characterized only as a big-hearted person taking on the long-term project of a problematic dog? A dog is only pathetic or pitiful or a victim if treated as such.

Do You Just Want To Rescue Something?

A few years ago, my shelter received an urgent phone call from a local rescue group. A white German Shepherd, chained outside her entire life, had been left in the back yard when the owners moved and had almost starved to death. Because of our facility's reputation for personal attention and extensive training, the group wanted to send this dog to us for care, rehabilitation, nursing, and, ultimately, adoption. We accepted.

The dog who arrived a few days later was a robust, outgoing, cheerful, tennis ball-loving purebred. She was friendly, sweet, and remarkably heavy for a starved dog. I'm not certain if the rescue group put all the weight on her or she hadn't been starved to begin with, but there was nothing pathetic about this dog. To the contrary, she was lovely to look at, had an outstanding temperament, and was highly adoptable.

Within a few days of her arrival, we received a phone call from a woman interested in adopting her. The woman had heard from the rescue group about the dog's plight, and she was appalled by the situation. She was able to offer the dog a good home, complete with a huge fenced yard, another dog to play with, people around almost all day, and no financial concerns whatsoever.

We brought the dog out into our shelter's front yard when the woman arrived the next day. She had made all sorts of preparations—including the purchase of high quality, calorie-dense food and nutritional supplements, and a transition schedule that restricted visitors and minimized loud activities in her home for the next few weeks.

The woman was visibly surprised and disappointed at the dog's healthy appearance. In fact, when we handed her the tennis ball, she looked at the dog and questioned if we had brought out the correct animal. Finally, after a weak comment about the dog being thin, she left alone. She didn't want a happy and optimistic dog in her life. She had wanted to rescue something. (We eventually adopted the dog, without a story attached to her, to a wonderful shepherd-loving and active couple.)

That woman's goal was to save a needy, helpless animal. And that's one of my goals as well, or I wouldn't have a shelter. But my biggest goal is to make everyone happy—both dogs and people. I want people to seek out my shelter for the same reason they go to a reputable breeder: to get their dream dog. It's all a matter of choice, no strings attached. ❖

Becoming a Shelter Dog

Sue Sternberg, Published in three parts, July/December 2001

PART I

It takes all the behavioral and training knowledge I can muster to get through each day at my shelter, Rondout Valley Kennels. My staff and I face never-ending responsibilities, decisions, and choices in all areas of the business—administrative, service, training, and direct care—but the most critical area is the care of our shelter dogs. We dedicate countless hours to getting to know each dog, providing a loving shelter environment, assessing the need for training, and trying to maximize the likelihood of his or her adoptability into a suitable home.

Every day is gratifying, yet humbling. Every day I find my beliefs about the behavior of dogs and humans reinforced, yet challenged. The more I work with shelter dogs, the more I realize that each dog's experience is unique...and each dog and owner has a story to tell. I would like to share some of these stories with you, not because they are extraordinary but because they are important. They remind us that dogs do not control their own destinies, and that we humans, who do hold control, can either acknowledge or ignore the opportunity to do right by them.

What My Shelter Looks Like

Before I introduce you to my shelter dogs, I want you to picture their environment. Our shelter is quite small, with only ten runs/rooms. During the spring and summer, our canine head count may be as high as 20 to 25 when we're boarding two dogs per kennel and perhaps holding some dogs in the boarding kennel (which is a separate facility on the property). In the winter, our kennels are usually much emptier, but it depends on how many adoptable dogs we bring in from outlying high-volume shelters. As I write this article, it's March and we are relatively empty.

The indoor portion of each kennel is a unique prototype design: a tiny wooden room, a glassless window and Dutch door facing the aisle, and a high window and a guillotine dog door to the rear that leads to a traditional chain-linked concrete outdoor run. Our kennel design has been phenomenal in lowering the dogs' stress levels and reducing indoor barking almost completely. Because we add an old, soft, cozy, overstuffed (donated) chair to most rooms, the dogs already accustomed to a home environment experience much less of a jolt coming into our shelter, and most dogs who have never lived indoors in a home acclimate easily to their homelike kennels.

We cannot, of course, guarantee that every dog will adapt comfortably to shelter life. Even in my shelter—where we provide incredible care, a homelike physical environment, behavior modification programs, training, playgroups, and an abundance of affection— dogs occasionally deteriorate emotionally, behaviorally, and mentally.

Not-For-Profit Decisions

While most of our shelter dogs are looking for homes, we occasionally accept boarders on a short-term, temporary basis. Such was the case with two dogs and two cats who were surrendered to us because their owners were forced to leave their former residence and take up temporary residence in a trailer park that didn't allow pets.

I was raised to believe that surrendering family pets because of relocation shows a lack of commitment and responsibility, and that belief has stayed with me into adulthood. But the truth in this case is that the family is just as loving, caring, committed, and responsible as I am. However, they are facing hard times. With two dogs, two cats, three kids, and limited finances, the task of moving from one rental to another is difficult. The family cannot live in their car, nor can they afford to board their pets while in limbo.

We are holding their pets while the owners make a last-ditch effort to find housing. And we'll absorb most of the costs (although the owners donated $25 toward upkeep) because we care about these animals, and we believe their best chance for a loving home is to remain with their original family.

Each abandoned and surrendered dog who comes through our doors may cost us hundreds of dollars in sterilization, vaccinations, and heartworm screening and prevention. Each effort to assess a behavior problem, provide basic training, and screen a potential adoptive family takes significant manpower, both volunteer and paid. As a shelter owner, I must regularly make decisions that reflect the value of a dog's life in terms of doing what's right, not what's cost effective.

Our Training Wheels™ Program

I've written in another article about Training Wheels, our mobile outreach program that helps us intervene with local pet owners needing assistance in keeping, caring for, or giving up their pets. This program is an integral part of our shelter services because it helps meet needs not often provided by conventional shelters. Within the limits of staff availability and sponsor support, Training Wheels gives us a chance to help people with free dog training, vet care, supplies, and rehoming. We visit people in apartments and trailer parks, at malls and in rural areas, all to reach a population unable or unwilling to come to us. This is shelter work outside the shelter walls.

Being a Shelter Worker Versus a Dog Trainer

When I'm working in my shelter, I assess each dog in terms of how he may behave with his next owner. As I try to identify the needs, problems, and issues he may face in his next home, I likewise try to determine the level of commitment and follow-up behavioral care his new owners will need to provide. In this context, I am wearing my shelter worker hat, not my dog trainer hat.

If I were evaluating this situation strictly as a dog trainer, I would most likely have access to the owner. Consequently, I would probably be able to obtain information on the owner's willingness, commitment, time availability, and likelihood of follow-through with the dog. And yet, to some extent, I must juggle both roles. As a shelter worker, I am aware that even the best shelter environment is not as desirable as a loving home. As a trainer, I recognize the importance of improving the dog's behavior—thereby increasing the likelihood of adoption—before the shelter's inherent conditions and physical environment have a negative effect. It's an ongoing challenge.

PART II

I want to introduce you to my shelter dogs—the ones who are staying with us at Rondout Valley Kennels as I am writing this article—because their stories offer valuable insight to everyone who trains and works with dogs. These stories defy the myths that all shelter dogs are alike, that all shelter dogs have been abused or are untrainable, or that all of them can be successfully rehomed. These stories remind us that each dog is unique, and that we do a great disservice if our attitudes and actions do not take each dog's individuality into account.

A Brood of Great Pyrenees

Four of our runs are filled with a delightful brood of Great Pyrenees: three ten-week-old pups and two adults. Their owners were local AKC breeders who needed to make a sudden cross-country move and whose efforts to sell the entire kennel as "breeding stock" were less than successful. The owners called us and we suggested they call a breed rescue organization, but they said they didn't have the time to deal with that. So we immediately took the five remaining dogs they hadn't been able to sell.

Thankfully, these dogs have superb temperaments—gentle, sweet, mildly submissive, very mellow, and people oriented. All of them are ideal family pets.

They will cost us hundreds of dollars in sterilization, vaccinations, and heartworm tests and medications. We will call Pyrenees Rescue to ask for a contribution to some of the spaying/neutering costs. We will also ask that organization to send us any approved adoptive families on their waiting list.

Three Shepherd Mixes

In the next kennel are three nine-week-old black and tan shepherd mix puppies, surrendered by a family who placed the rest of the litter on their own.

When litters such as this one are surrendered, we pay to have the mother dog spayed. We recognize that it doesn't make sense to take the puppies if the mother is just going to produce another accidental litter in six months.

Moose, a Pit Bull Mix

In an adjacent kennel is Moose, a six-month-old male pit bull mix. Moose was transferred here from a shelter that was concerned about his possible deterioration in the limited environment of their kennels. Moose had arrived at the original shelter as an infant with his littermates, along with a purebred pit bull mother who exhibited serious dog-dog aggression issues.

Moose, who has been with us for four weeks, has been a delightful guest. His skills with other dogs are outstanding, and he has assisted me many times when I have evaluated and worked with private behavioral clients and their dog-dog aggressive dogs.

Moose can appease, calm, and cajole almost any other dog to play. He is gentle, affectionate, and adoring of young children. Training him is a pleasure because he is easy to motivate and exudes a calm, low-key intensity. He is doing very well due to his busy schedule of private lessons, group agility classes, dog playgroups, toys, chewies, and human affection.

Unfortunately, Moose has been passed over on our shelter's Web site that profiles our adoptable dogs because he is listed, truthfully, as a pit bull mix. And people who visit our shelter looking for pets dismiss him because of his "pitty-ness." Nevertheless, Moose is an ideal family pet.

Michael, the German Shepherd

In the next run is Michael, a three-to-four-year-old purebred German Shepherd Dog who was brought in by the local animal control officer as an unclaimed stray. Michael, who has been with us about two weeks, is a physically and temperamentally sound GSD. All he needs is some basic training.

Lucy, the Pit Bull Mix

Sharing Michael's run is Lucy, a six-month-old pit bull mix who came in as a rescue and has been here almost a month. Her story is complicated. Lucy first came to our attention when our Training Wheels program received a report of a chained puppy. When we went to the house on a cold winter day to investigate the report, no one was home. However, we found a pit bull mix puppy chained to the outside of the garage with the garage doors closed. She appeared to be about five months of age.

The puppy growled at us in fear, but when I finally made friends with her, she was excited to play and she leapt up at my face in greeting. We left a bag of dog food and a note for the owner, offering to help with free training, vet care, supplies, and rehoming if necessary.

The puppy's owner called us that night in tears. An ex-boyfriend had given her the puppy, but she was ill and unable to care for a pet. We sympathized with her about her illness and being left alone to care for a dog. Although she was reluctant to surrender the puppy, she agreed to do so.

At the shelter, we allowed Lucy a few weeks to settle in, fatten up, socialize with people, learn how to learn, learn a few cues, and play with other dogs. We were encouraged that Lucy had come to us at a fairly young age because surrendered young pups have a much greater chance than older dogs in regard to successful rehabilitation, socialization, and behavior modification. There is simply less time for neglect, reinforcement of bad behaviors, bad habits, or bad experiences to set in.

About three weeks after Lucy's arrival, she was temperament evaluated. Despite the boost that our Training Wheels program gives surrendered dogs, Lucy tested borderline for food bowl aggression and quite high for rawhide aggression. She was tense around her food bowl and was overstimulated by food, which may have made her great fun to train but it also meant that she was a risk if there was enough food for her to covet and guard. She occasionally "freaked out" with strangers, suddenly lunging at them through the window of her kennel or while on leash. Being coprophagic, she once defecated in the front of her kennel and then guarded it as someone tried to clean it up. Her reactions, as I had observed the first day I met her, went from zero to one hundred in a split second and were quite intense, especially for such a young dog. Despite being affectionate, fun loving, silly, and endearing, Lucy was volatile.

At the tender age of six months, Lucy is already so far along in the sequence of "how to get strangers to back off" (e.g., sudden lunging/growling at their faces) that the outcome is not optimistic for rehoming. Until Lucy reaches the age of two or three, every encounter with a stranger must be carefully crafted to ensure that she is "working" and not "off duty." Every approaching stranger needs to be instructed not to make direct eye contact initially, not to approach frontally, not to reach over and pet Lucy until she is comfortable or in a non-fearful emotional state, and not to walk or run by suddenly unless Lucy's owner/handler can prevent her from lunging. In short, Lucy requires an intensive, ongoing behavioral modification program of desensitization, counter-conditioning, and follow-up—a tremendous amount of time and effort.

Because of Lucy's fast reaction time, sharp mind, high prey drive, and athleticism, she also requires appropriate and ongoing activity outlets such as agility training, trick training, tracking, or advanced obedience. If she were rehomed with a professional or hobby dog trainer, she might have more of a shot at success. Belonging to the average pet owner—with a real life, a real schedule, and a real family—Lucy doesn't stand much of a chance. And at this point, I would never recommend that she live with a family that includes children.

So Lucy is our most challenging guest at the moment. Even as we continue to assess her strengths, weaknesses, and needs, she is being impacted by shelter life. Our team of shelter workers is concerned about the following issues:

- In our shelter, Lucy will encounter a daily barrage of strangers as people come looking to adopt a pet.

- Lucy will be kenneled in a small space, with limited options for backing away to create more distance from scary strangers. We expect that she will quickly opt for lunging, barking, and hitting the front of her kennel. (She already lunges occasionally, thereby practicing her aggression.)

- With repeated practice, Lucy will increase in both the frequency and intensity of her lunges.

(continued)

- Lucy could be moved out of the public adoption wing and into an area where only staff is allowed, but then no one would be able to view her to consider her for adoption. Keeping her in the restricted area until she is "cured" would mean keeping her for at least two more years.

- If she stays in the adoption wing, we recognize that no reasonable person would want to meet or adopt a pit bull mix who is charging aggressively at the front of her kennel. And too, her aggressive behavior is likely to contribute to the public's perception that pit bulls are mean and scary.

What is the fate of Lucy and the other dogs in our shelter? Stay tuned!

PART III

When I started writing this three-part article, it was late winter—historically the best time of year for shelters because it's when our dog population is the lowest and we can devote maximum attention to our residents. As I sit here writing, it's mid-July and the height of the season for unwanted pets. Not surprisingly, our shelter is filled to capacity.

As promised, this final section will follow up on all the dogs I introduced above. You'll get no false happy endings or overly dramatic stories, just a glimpse into real life at a shelter.

The Shepherd-Mix Puppies

The three shepherd-mix puppies were all adopted within the first weekend. When I made my follow-up calls for this article, I was only able to contact one of the three families.

In this case, a young girl answered the phone. When I identified myself and asked if I could speak with her parents, she said her mother would call me back. I, being a cynical shelter worker, immediately assumed they didn't have the puppy any longer (which meant they had breached their contract to return the dog to us no matter what).

I asked the girl, "Do you still have the puppy?" "She's right here sitting with me," said the girl. And then she volunteered that they had named her Valentine, that she was very big, all black, and looked just like a black Lab. I felt guilty for having doubted the family.

Michael, the German Shepherd Dog

Michael was the stray, adult male purebred GSD who had entered the shelter in late November. He was finally adopted in early February by a couple who had been searching the Internet for a GSD. They traveled six hours from Rochester, New York, to meet him.

Michael was an easy keeper who did not need a lot of extras to keep him sane and emotionally and behaviorally healthy. His only flaw when he came to us was lack of training. So we taught him to offer a sit when on lead, to face whomever he was with, and to lie down on a hand signal. Although he learned the skills quickly in early December, we did not consistently enforce them.

When the Rochester couple came to see him, they were blown away with delight by his training. They loved Michael and spent about an hour visiting with him, both indoors and outdoors, before signing the adoption papers. They told me that their last dog, who was trained with traditional methods, had been compliant but unenthusiastic. So they saw Michael's joy and responsiveness as magic! They were quickly convinced that reward-based training is superior to traditional training when teaching skills to a dog.

During my follow-up call, I learned that Michael's new name is Rusty. He is doing well in his new home, and the owners really love him. When I pushed for more details, however, the woman finally admitted that they were still having two problems with him.

My heart sank, and my adrenaline started spurting. Had some hidden aggression shown itself?

But no, the problems were of my favorite variety. Rusty gets carsick, and he occasionally has loose stools. Imagine the worst behavior problem with a new dog is carsickness! So we talked about appropriate solutions, and the owner was very responsive.

The final thing these owners were concerned about—rather, they were both pleased and perplexed—was that Rusty doesn't bark at strangers or people passing in front of their house. Although his behavior wasn't a problem, they were wondering when he would feel confident enough to protect his home and territory. I assured them that eventually he would probably exhibit some guarding behaviors. Secretly, I was relieved that he hadn't yet done so. Maybe his is not the sort of temperament a GSD breeder would want, but it is exactly the kind of temperament that I believe makes for an ideal pet.

The Great Pyrenees

After I wrote Part II, we took in the last two Great Pyrenees pups that the breeder hadn't been able to sell. We used the Internet to find adopters who were looking specifically for Pyrenees, rather than waiting for random adopters who might fall in love with the novelty or look of an uncommon purebred without knowing anything about the breed.

The oldest of the family, a five-year-old bitch named Lilly, took the longest to place but found a wonderful home in mid-February. A single woman traveled almost six hours from Annapolis, Maryland, and adopted Lilly immediately. All the others, except for one ten-week-old puppy who was adopted locally, went to people who had been waiting for a Pyrenees. The adopters hailed from Somerset, New Jersey (three hours away), Windsor, New York (two hours away), Rome, New York (five hours away), North Bennington, Vermont (four hours away), and Duchess County, New York (one hour away).

All the Pyrenees adopters with whom I did follow-ups were quite pleased with their dogs, reporting that the dogs were large, loveable, sweet, and doing well. The locally placed Pyrenees puppy had completed the full six weeks of our free puppy class, and she was doing splendidly.

Moose, the Mostly Pit Bull

Having entered the shelter system with his mother and litter at the age of four weeks, Moose finally got the home he deserved after eight months of waiting. His long wait was due entirely to the fact that he is mostly pit bull.

As I discussed above, Moose had a wonderful temperament and we gave him a lot of training during his stay. He even participated in our shelter's Christmas party agility game, where the dogs had to pull their handlers across the start line in a wheelchair to earn the right to go off lead and run the course. Moose, who loved to pull on leash and run agility, was a star.

In February, a family with three young children fell in love with Moose and adopted him. Although they had never owned a dog before, they knew many nice pit bulls and weren't bothered by the fact that Moose was mostly pit bull.

When I called Moose's family, they told me that his new name was Duke. Aside from not being able to leave Duke home unsupervised because he liked to chew, they adored him. The mother said that Duke's favorite person was their 11-year-old daughter and that Duke slept in her bedroom every night. This story is the sort of adoption that makes all the stresses of sheltering worthwhile.

Lucy, the Pit Bull Mix

And I euthanized Lucy, the pit mix whom we had identified as being highly aggressive toward strangers.

We worked with her until the beginning of March (four months total), but the incidences of her lunging, growling, snapping, food guarding, and coprophagia continued despite all our efforts. We finally determined that the odds of the average person successfully managing her into adulthood without being bitten were far too poor.

Before we euthanized Lucy, we gave her the royal treatment: extra exercise/play times outside, extra treats, toys, chewies, the softest quilts and comforters, canned dog food, and table scraps. On the way to the vet, I took her through the drive-through at McDonalds, where she got McNuggets and a couple of hamburgers.

And then I held her while the veterinarian delivered the lethal injection. With a sudden overdose of anesthetic, death came quickly.

As For Euthanasia...

Euthanasia is, each and every time I witness it, a profound and disturbing act. Although we all understand euthanasia at the shelter, not everyone feels comfortable with it. Certainly, individual kennel staff will fall in love with particular dogs and have an extra-hard time saying good-bye to them. That's the irony of it. The best staff is caring, loving, sensitive, and emotional people who often have the most trouble with euthanasia.

What we must come to grips with is the fact that not all dogs are behaviorally adoptable. If we accept that premise as fact, then the two remaining options are euthanasia or permanent kenneling. Neither is an easy choice. ❖

Learning to Read Dogs

Sue Sternberg, January/February 2003

A Worksheet for Trainers Observing Dogs in the Shelter

Many trainers are reluctant to go to a shelter to learn more about dogs because they assume that without a mentor or supervision, they will not be able to learn anything by themselves. This is not so, and the best arena for learning to observe dog behavior will be missed. I have designed a worksheet to accompany trainers and aspiring trainers into the shelter. It contains practice exercises and a series of activities to help you become a more acute observer.

There is also the mistaken belief that in order to learn anything, you need to know why dogs do what they do, or what each behavior and signal means. Ultimately, the meanings will be important to acknowledge, but the most useful information comes from being a keen observer of the details.

Make four copies of the worksheet and then go to your local shelter and offer to volunteer to walk dogs, or just visit with them. There is no need to present yourself as a trainer with something to offer the shelter; rather it is simply best to offer to help with the dogs, get them out, let them have some exercise. Our goal is to soak in what these dogs can teach you, not to attempt to teach the dogs or the shelter anything (although that is a worthy cause for another time).

Take a walk through the kennels. Select four available dogs for your lesson. You will be taking each one out on lead, one at a time, to the same location and will do the same activities with each dog.

By comparing four dogs, you will have the opportunity to see a range of behaviors, responses, and postures. It is in the differences between the dogs that you will begin to understand the intensity and seriousness of each behavior.

Equipment You Will Need:

- A 6-foot cotton, nylon, or leather noose lead or snap lead (thread the clip through the handle loop so that it creates a noose lead).

- An indoor room or hallway NOT in the kennels.

- A chair for you to sit on.

- A pen or pencil.

Parts of the Dog to Watch:

- Eyes

- Ears

- Tail carriage

Things to "Feel" From the Dog:

- His strength on leash.

- How quickly he begins using his mouth on your skin (gets "mouthy") and how hard and on what body parts he aims

- How good or poor are his physical boundaries when he physically interacts with your body.

- How hard or gently he jumps up on you, or how hard or gently he uses his toenails.

Task #1

First contact begins with you extending your hand out towards the dog, making soft eye contact with the dog, and babytalking and sweet-talking the dog. If/when the dog sniffs or interacts with your hand, move your hand three inches to the left, remain for three seconds, then move your hand six inches to the right, remain for six seconds, then move your hand twelve inches down. Continue sweet-talking the dog the entire time.

Eyes:
    Big, round, hard, forward _____
    Soft, squinty_____
    Pupils: dilated_____ light reflects out/marbled_____normal pupils_____
    When do eyes harden _____
    When do eyes soften_____

Ears:
    Forward, tight_____
    Back, tight_____
    Alert, erect_____
    When do ears relax backwards _____
    When do ears go up or move forward_____

Tail Carriage:
    High (above the plane of the dog's back)_____
    Level_____
    Low (below plane of dog's back)_____
    Tucked_____
    When does tail raise? _____
    When does tail lower? _____
    When does tail wag? _____
    When does tail stop wagging?_____

Task #2

Remain neutral and nonresponsive at all times (never let the dog know you are a trainer, do not try to train, reinforce, punish, or in any way influence the dog's behavior. Just sit back and enjoy the ride).

- Gently lasso your noose lead over the dog's neck and keep a steady, but mild tension on the lead at all times. Do not jerk, pop, or slacken the lead.

- Find an indoor area or room away from the kennels and other dogs. Even a hallway will do, with minimal to moderate people traffic, but minimal to no dog traffic.

- Arrive at your indoor destination and stand and ignore the dog. Check your watch and time for 60 seconds.

How long before the dog initiates soft, warm, affectionate contact with you? Such contact means the dog will turn to orient toward you, his eyes will be soft, pupils will be normal and not dilated. _____

Does dog sustain soft, affectionate contact? Yes_____ No_____

Does dog sustain soft, affectionate contact for more than 50 percent of the 60 seconds? Yes_____ No_____

How long before dog makes hard or aroused or attention-seeking contact? (eyes will be big and round and hard, pupils dilated)._____

Is hard contact sustained? For how long at a stretch?_____

Does dog make significant social contact with you at all in the 60 seconds? Yes_____ No_____

Does he remain tense, tail may be tucked, dog remains out of reach, and unmoving, fearful? Yes_____ No_____

Does dog seem distracted/environment-oriented? Yes_____ No_____

Eyes:

Do eyes soften when/if dog makes social contact with you? Yes_____ No_____

Ears:

Do ears relax backwards when dog makes social contact? Yes_____ No_____

Do ears remain plastered back throughout? Yes_____ No_____

Do ears remain erect, tense forward throughout? Yes_____ No_____

Tail Carriage:

Does tail come up during 60 seconds? Yes_____ No_____

Does tail lower during 60 seconds? Yes_____ No_____

Does tucked tail relax during 60 seconds? Yes_____ No_____

Does tucked tail remain tucked during 60 seconds? Yes_____ No_____

Dog's Physical Strength:

On a scale of one to six, with one being soft and gentle and tender, and six being rough and painful, please rate the dog: 1 2 3 4 5 6

Task #3

After 60 seconds, lean over only enough to reach the dog, and stroke the dog along its back, starting at the back of the neck, slowly running your hand down to the base of his tail. Stand up, then slowly lean down and repeat two more times.

It is important to remain detached and as unemotional as you can be here. By this point, many of you will be emotionally attached to the dog, or already "in love," and you will cease to be a careful observer, and instead, answer from your heart and emotions. Pretend you are an aerial observer and be completely objective. In between each stroke, does the dog:

A. Turn to orient towards you, and approach closer than where he was before you touched him?

B. Remain neutral and remain in the same general area he was before you touched him? Yes_____ No_____

C. Move farther away from you, or shake as if re-adjusting his coat hairs? Yes_____ No_____

Mark down A, B, or C for the dog's response after each stroke—a total of three times.

Response after first stroke: A B C

Response after second stroke: A B C

Response after third stroke: A B C

Can you see the whites of the dog's eyes? Yes_____ No_____

If so, count how many times during this particular exercise? _____

Does the dog turn, either slowly or quickly, to orient its mouth or muzzle toward your stroking hand? _____

Does the dog "mouth" that hand? Yes_____ No_____

Task #4

If there is a chair or a seat, sit down for 30 seconds.

Does dog orient to you within five seconds, come over, ears back, eyes softening, and make soft and affectionate contact? Yes_____ No_____

Does dog not orient to you at all within 30 seconds? Yes_____ No_____

Task #5

After 30 seconds, stand up, and call and cajole the dog over to you, by patting your legs encouragingly, and make smoochy sounds, and speak to the dog in baby-talk. When and if the dog comes to you, immediately begin petting it with both hands, in such a way as to mildly overstimulate it, and get excited with your voice and stroking. Without physically restraining the dog or using a short lead to keep the dog close to you, do your verbal and enticing best to keep the dog interacting and in touching physical contact for 30 seconds. (Use your watch to time this—30 seconds is actually a lot longer than you would imagine.)

Does dog become "mouthy?" How many times do his teeth touch your body? On what parts of your body does he "mouth?" _____
Does dog NOT become "mouthy?" Yes_____ No_____
Does dog lick? Yes_____ No_____

Eyes:

Do eyes soften when/if dog makes social contact with you? Yes_____ No_____

Ears:

Do ears relax backwards when dog makes social contact? Yes_____ No_____
Do ears remain plastered back throughout? Yes_____ No_____
Do ears remain erect, tense forward throughout? Yes_____ No_____

Tail Carriage:

Does tail come up during 60 seconds? Yes_____ No_____
Does tail lower during 60 seconds? Yes_____ No_____
Does tucked tail relax during 60 seconds? Yes_____ No_____
Does tucked tail remain tucked during 60 seconds? Yes_____ No_____

Task #6

Return the dog to its kennel, pulling it in ahead of you, close the kennel door gently on your hand (which is still holding the leash, which is still attached to the dog.) When the dog turns around in its kennel, hoping to exit again, pull the lead toward you, creating enough opposition so that the dog balks back to the rear of the kennel.

While he is leaning back, suddenly reach in and pull the noose lead off his neck, before he has time to try to escape.

Give the dog 60 seconds to settle back into his kennel.

Task #7

Stand facing the kennel, as close as you can get. Keeping a completely neutral expression, (neither threatening nor friendly) make sustained, direct open eye contact with the dog, and continue staring as you count (one Mississippi, two Mississippi, etc.) After the third second, lean forward one inch at every subsequent second.

Eyes:

Hard, big, round? Yes_____ No_____
Soft, squinty? Yes_____ No_____
Pupils dilated? Yes_____ No_____
Pupils normal? Yes_____ No_____
Pupils marbleized/reflecting light? Yes_____ No_____

Ears:

Are ears up, tense, forward? Yes_____ No_____
Are ears plastered back? Yes_____ No_____
Do ears come up or retract back at any time? Yes_____ No_____
When? _____
Do the dog's eyes soften as his ears go back? Yes_____ No_____
Do the dog's eyes harden as his ears go up? Yes_____ No_____
Do the dog's pupils dilate at any point? Yes_____ No_____
Do the dog's pupils retract at any point? Yes_____ No_____

Tail Carriage:

Does dog's tail come up during this? Yes_____ No_____
When? _____
Does dog's tail lower during this? Yes_____ No_____
When? _____

General Observations:

Does dog lunge forward at you? Yes No After how much time? ___
Does dog avert eyes? Yes_____ No_____ After how much time? _____
Does dog offer any appeasement gestures? (licking, curling body into a cashew, circles away, smile, lifting one hind leg, rolling over, etc.?) _____

Okay! Well done. Repeat the above with all four of your chosen dogs.

Think of your role as Columbo, the trench-coat wearing, cigar-smoking detective. Your job is to collect evidence, and to make observations and form questions. Eventually, you will be the master of observation and detailable to figure out whodunit. But for now just train your eye to observe each dog in its entirety. ❖

The Safety SCAN

Sue Sternberg, November/December 1999

Okay, trainers, since I now have many of you ready to go into your local shelters, I know you are worrying about reading/handling the dogs and about your own safety. It's a good thing to feel that way. Anyone without a fear of some dogs is in for a hideous lesson.

SCAN is an overused-yet-handy acronym to learn some skills in observing and reading unknown dogs before handling or interacting with them in any way.

S = Sexually Mature/Intact

Dogs over a year of age are more capable of intense or severe aggression, more likely to have experience biting, and more likely to be adept at biting than juvenile dogs or young puppies. If you don't know a dog's age, you'll just have to eyeball the dog and take your best guess.

Intact or sexually mature dogs (both male and female) need to be handled with more caution than juvenile or neutered dogs because testosterone can exaggerate aggression. It is a "Sue Sternberg Belief" that even sexually intact females need more cautious handling because, in general, people who own bitches and have been through a heat cycle usually keep them more at arm's length than juvenile or spayed females. The average intact female shelter dog was probably not a family companion, but more likely an outdoor or penned-up dog, which suggests that she was less exposed to handling and pushing and is more accustomed to getting her own way or being left alone. This type of background can result in a dog who is not accustomed to close, physical contact with people and a home life.

C = Cautious

Dogs who remain cautious or uncomfortable with you or their environment, even after a few minutes of initial contact, are stressed. The more stress a dog experiences, the lower his threshold for aggression. A dog should start to form some bond with you if you are gentle and non-confrontational in the first few minutes, and he should start to relax or look toward you for security and comfort. Nervous dogs might lean against you, move closer to you, or snuggle their rears toward you as they use you to gain enough confidence to look out at the rest of the scary world. A nervous dog who remains aloof to you is not a safe dog to handle.

A = Aroused

Dogs who are in a constant state of agitation or arousal, or dogs who appear hyper, unfocused, unsettled, or reactive should be handled with extreme care. An aroused dog may appear friendly, excited, or even happy—for example, tail wagging quickly and broadly, grinning, and panting—but watch for dilated pupils ("black upon black" pupils) and a furrowed brow.

Think of the Seinfeld television series: the Kramer character was aroused and Jerry Seinfeld was more calm. A friendly dog may wag his tail broadly; pant; usually nudge you for attention; make sustained physical contact; or make direct, sustained, squinting, soft eye contact. An aroused dog will often wag and pant, but he will not seek out or make any gestures or offers of sustained physical contact. The aroused dog may jump up on you to get a better view of things up high or behind you. The aroused dog may bark at you for attention but not want any petting in return.

N = No Signs of Friendliness

Watch out for the dog who shows no overt signs of friendliness. A dangerous or volatile dog may not look/act aggressive or fearful in any way but still lack any normal friendly signs. The behaviors a dog is lacking are often as significant as the behaviors he is exhibiting. A dog who appears aloof, distant, unconnected, or independent has lower thresholds for aggression because he has no buffer zone of affection and attention to protect him from something unpleasant or unwanted you may do to him or with him.

Don't make excuses for particular breeds or breed mixes, saying that these breeds are "supposed to be aloof or suspicious at first." I don't care if the shelter dog is a Golden Retriever or a Chow Chow who is lacking signs of friendliness and coming across as aloof. Either way, the dog has little use for my friendship at first and, therefore, is much more likely to be intolerant of any mistakes I might make in handling (or even intolerant of anything the dog perceives as unpleasant). Since the dog is unknown to me, I cannot be sure if something as benign as putting him back into his kennel could be perceived as unpleasant and provoke his aggression.

Another "Sue Sternberg Belief" is that many breeds described in breed standards as "reserved with strangers," "aloof with strangers," "suspicious at first with strangers" tend to be the breeds with the highest levels of aggression. This is because they have limited "buffer zones" before they resort to biting people. All people are strangers to dogs until they become familiar. Why on earth do we need dogs who are reserved, aloof, or suspicious of people?

Do's And Don'ts

Here are some tried and true do's and don'ts for safe handling of unknown dogs, whether they are in shelters, on the streets, or in your classes.

Do's —

- Do use a gentle, steady pressure with the lead. No yanking or sudden pulls.

- Do be big, be neutral. It works with bears in the wild, and it works with dogs in the shelters. Keep your balance, and don't let a dog surprise you or pull you over.

- Do wear non-slip shoes and comfortable clothing with nothing too loose or jangling. Tie your hair back and avoid dangling jewelry.

- Do be prepared, be aware. Move deliberately and confidently and gently and slowly.

- Do let the dog make the first contact and come to you, instead of initiating and going to the dog before he may want you, need you, or like you.

- Do love dogs, but respect dogs.

Don'ts —

- Do not make direct eye contact. Dogs will read your eye contact as a threat or a challenge... and neither is good news.

- Do not think you need to dominate or show the dog who's boss. This approach only serves to make the bossy dogs angry and the fearful dogs defensive. Remember: Be big, be neutral.

- Do not take a dog by the collar if he gets loose in the kennels. Instead, use a leash to catch him. If the dog is fence fighting, noose leash the dog and slowly pull him away from the other dog. Remember: High levels of excitement and arousal can trigger aggression.

- Do not punish/discipline/correct a shelter or unknown dog, not even by popping or jerking the leash. You could get corrected with a bite.

- Do not go in the cage/kennel run with a dog who still has his food bowl, a dog who is eating, or a dog who didn't initiate first contact.

- Do not go into the kennel space with a dog if you are alone in the kennels.

- Do not put your face near a dog's face, particularly any dog with a SCAN you feel puts you or anyone at risk.

- Do not grab a dog or pull a dog by his collar or scruff to move him. Instead, use a leash.

From my experiences and travels, shelter dog populations near large urban areas and on the East Coast are more dominant, aroused, and dangerous than shelter dog populations in the central and south central United States. Safer, younger, and more friendly and submissive dogs are more likely to be found in animal control facilities than in no-kill or limited-access facilities where the dog populations tend to level out with older, more difficult-to-adopt dogs. I'm basing these observations on my temperament evaluating and handling of large numbers of dogs in all types of shelters all across the country since 1994.

Even if all you do is go into the shelter once a week and observe the dogs in the kennels, you will learn a tremendous amount. And remember: Friendly, loving, affection-seeking shelter dogs are the safest to handle. ❖

Determining Canine Age

Sue Sternberg, January/February 2000

Being able to accurately determine the age of a stray or unknown dog is beneficial for both trainers and shelter staff. First of all, a dog's accurate age assessment is needed before evaluating his temperament and behavior and certainly prior to handling. Why? If you are going to approach and fondle an unknown dog and the dog is going to be aggressive during this event, you are more at risk for damage from a mature adult dog (two years or older) than if the dog were an adolescent or puppy. That's not to say that all mature adult dogs will bite you if you approach and fondle them. But aggressive mature dogs are more apt to do damage than aggressive younger dogs. The same holds true for sterilization. Testosterone is responsible for exaggerating aggressiveness. I would rather approach and pat a neutered male dog than a sexually intact male dog. That's not to say that all intact males are going to bite, but rather that the bite's severity is likely to be worse from intact males than from neuters. For me, the same holds true of females, even though I am aware that females can have lots of testosterone, and sometimes spaying a female and taking away her estrogens can leave only her testosterone.

The reason I am more wary of mature, intact, unknown female dogs is because I believe that mature intact females (who typically go into heat every six months for three to four weeks) are probably kept less as indoor family companions. Dogs with this profile are more likely than spayed females to have been kept at arm's length for at least three to four weeks every six months, and they are probably kept fairly distant from lots of close indoor contact and handling. So I am especially cautious in handling sexually mature intact dogs *and* bitches.

Yet I don't care to grope a three or four-year-old stray male Chow Chow to find out if he is neutered or intact. And I especially don't care to look in his mouth and check his teeth to figure out his age! The best way to gauge overall age and sexual status in stray or unknown dogs is to exercise your overall, gut-level intuition (first impressions). Start by eliminating all the ages the dog couldn't possibly be. This sounds silly, but once you state and eliminate the obvious, you can narrow down an accurate age assessment.

Questions to Ask Yourself

- Is he too young to be adopted/bought/sold, meaning under six to eight weeks?
- Is he under six months? At less than six months, the puppy will still look out of proportion, his ears and joints will appear too large for the rest of him, etc.
- Is he over six months, but under a year? His chest may still be scrawny and his ribs are unlikely to have sprung, he will most likely lack any firm, hormonal muscling, he may still have a puppy coat, etc.

• Is he an old dog? Is his muzzle very grey, is his spine boney and arthritic, is he losing muscle tone in his hindquarters, does he have heavy calluses on his elbows, does he have multiple scars or old nicks/bumps/warts, etc.?

If you're not sure of the answer and cannot figure out the dog's age, err on the side of making the dog older rather than younger. You should handle an older or mature dog with much more caution; therefore, if you're not sure of the dog's age, it is safer to assume he is mature rather than juvenile because, hopefully, you will treat the mature dog with respect.

Teeth: Your Guide To Age Via Dentition

Teeth are another way to assess age. Puppy teeth are, in general, less bright white than adult/permanent teeth. Puppy teeth are to skim milk as adult/permanent teeth are to half & half. Puppy teeth are sharper tipped than adult teeth. Adult/permanent teeth have rounder tips.

The front cutting/nibbling teeth are called the incisors. The vampire-type fangs are called the canines. The big "plaque magnet" teeth in the way back top and bottom are called molars, and the in-between, shark-like teeth are called pre-molars.

Eight to eleven weeks. Puppies at this age will have a full set of puppy teeth. The closer in age to eight weeks, the closer together the incisors will be. The closer in age to four months, the farther apart the incisors will be.

Twelve weeks to four months. Puppies at this age will still have all puppy teeth, but the incisors will be more and more spread out. The closer in age to four months, the more space there will be between the incisors.

Four months. Puppies at four months will still have all puppy teeth, but the front two incisors will be loose or already replacing. The canines will still be "skim milk" puppy teeth.

Four to five months. Puppies at this age will have adult permanent incisors, but the adult incisors will be very spread out.

Five months. I call this the "nub" age. Puppies at this age will have adult/permanent canines just crowning ("nubs") with the half and half color; the adult/permanent incisors will be half and half in color, flush, even, and tucked close together; and the end incisors will be smaller than the adult/permanent canines.

Six months. The canines will be halfway down. At this age, the canines are just longer than the end incisors.

Seven months. The canines may look all the way dropped, but actually are only 3/4 of the way down. The seven-month-old mouth is a joy to behold. Teeth will never look this good again. The dog's breath will never smell as fresh!

Eight to ten months. The canines have dropped further, and the overall mouth is less pristine than at seven months.

One year. Every tooth is in, fully descended, big, and powerful. The teeth should still be relatively clean, although their condition varies—by breed and geographic area—in terms of early staining and tartar. Some breeds (sighthounds and toy breed types) have notoriously awful teeth. At this age, there will not be any wearing or flattening on the ends of the incisors or canines, except in the case of German Shepherds and Border Collies, who will have already broken off half their teeth fetching rocks and croquet balls.

One to three years. There should be relatively little flattening of the incisors.

Three to five years. There will be some flattening of the incisors in dogs with level or scissor bites.

Five to eight years. There will be significant flattening of both upper and lower incisors. You will see overall subtle yellowing of all teeth (half & half with a teaspoon of molasses) and overall general wearing of pre-molars. There will likely be significant tartar buildup on upper molars. Some teeth will likely be chipped.

The best way to learn about determining age in dogs is to go to an all-breed conformation trial and look at dogs, make a guess yourself, and then ask the owner or handler for the dog's actual age. Most conformation dogs are very familiar with having their teeth examined and exposed for viewing. Explain to the handler/owner/breeder what you are trying to learn and ask if he or she might show you the dog's teeth.

The more you look, the better you'll get at assessing age. Learn by studying dogs and puppies whose birthdates are known, and you will get good at determining the age of unknown and stray dogs.

Good luck, and remember to wash your hands between dogs and before eating! ❖

The Deterioration of a Shelter Dog

Sue Sternberg, January/Febuary 2001

I can think of very few situations in which to house a dog that are less humane than a shelter. The shelter environment is intensely overstimulating and detrimental to a dog's long-term behavioral, mental, and emotional health. I have met some long-term shelter dogs (dogs whose stay exceeds two weeks) and "lifers" who have simply lost their ability to calm down.

The Highly Aroused Dog

One of the most disturbing elements of the long-term shelter dog's environment is the constant, elevated state of arousal. The aroused dog usually has trouble maintaining weight. He is well muscled, however, due to repetitive movements such as spinning, pacing, circling, bounding, and rebounding off the walls of his kennel. His pupils are almost constantly dilated, and he exhibits a furrowed brow and a bug-eyed look. He seems unsettled, jittery, and hyper. He will likely be the dog who barks loudly and rhythmically in excitement.

High arousal is a downward spiral for the shelter dog. The more aroused he gets, the less of an adoptable impression he makes on the public, thereby ensuring a longer (and, hence, more arousing) shelter stay.

Human Interaction and Arousal

When do shelter dogs see and interact with people during their stay at the shelter?

- At feeding time.
- When the kennels are being cleaned.
- When the dogs are moved into the outdoor portion of their kennel runs.
- When volunteers walk the dogs.
- When the public comes to view the dogs.

On a scale of 0 to 100—with 0 being brain dead and 100 being so aroused that an aneurysm is imminent—how does each of the above activities rate on the scale of arousal? Each activity rates 110+.

Doing Nothing

Shelter routines condition a dog to associate the presence of humans with a state of intense arousal. Yet the single best thing we can do to prepare a shelter dog to get adopted is absolutely nothing.

When a volunteer comes to my shelter, my first response is to think of an activity to do with a dog. Out of habit, I suggest a walk or a training exercise. Instead, I should have the volunteer take the dog out of the kennel run and do absolutely nothing.

Think about it. Most of a dog's time alongside her owner at home will be spent doing nothing, so that is what a shelter dog needs to learn to do. The most life-saving activity for a long-term shelter dog is a non-activity.

The Nothing Exercise

Go into the kennel area and select a highly aroused dog. Slip a lead on the dog and take her out to any quiet indoor area. If there is no quiet indoor area, a bathroom will do.

Give the dog a very specific and limited amount of leash to pull on (three feet is perfect). You should sit, but let the dog pace, wander, stand, whine, bark, or roll over. Ignore the dog completely—do not even make eye contact—and say nothing. Be very specific about the leash length. Do not allow the dog to yank your arm or pull out a few more inches of leash. Turn your face away and pull down subtly on the lead if the dog tries to jump toward your face or onto your lap.

At some point—maybe 20 minutes or longer—the dog will lie down, sigh, and settle down. Count off three seconds after she has settled, and then bend down and stroke her down her back, speaking quietly and soothingly as if you were talking to a child in a library. Your touch should be firm and confident, like a one-directional massage.

As soon as you pet her, she will probably break position and become aroused and active again. This is to be expected. Immediately withdraw your attention, stroking, and eye contact. Ignore her, and she will settle down much more quickly this second time. Once she is settled, begin once more to quietly speak to her and stroke her back.

Even though your inclination may be to ignore the dog when she settles—because, after all, won't you be ruining the moment of quiet?—remember that the dog is learning how to handle human interaction calmly. If you give her no attention for being aroused, she will quickly learn to maintain her calm mood while you stroke her.

After a few days of these lessons, the dog can be asked to settle down for longer and longer periods of time without attention. Let her settle for a few moments, and then release her for a potty break, a training session, or a walk in the exercise yard.

Be aware of the important role you can play in the life of a long-term shelter dog. Reinforcing her high arousal and overstimulation will get her ignored. Helping her learn to be calm and peaceful will result in dog activities and rewards…and may get her adopted. ❖

Do Shelters Need Behavior Departments? A Case Study: The Michigan Humane Society

CJ Bentley, September/October 2004

Take a walk through your shelter's dog kennel area. Is it full? Unfortunately, the answer to that question is undoubtedly "yes." But take a closer look. What's interesting is how it's full. Years ago, shelters were overcrowded with litters of unwanted puppies. Today, for many shelters, the overcrowding is due to adolescent and adult dogs, not puppies.

The implications of this trend are immense. Unwanted puppies are typically victims of people not willing to spay or neuter their pets—sadly, they come into life homeless. Unwanted adolescent and adult dogs are another story because these dogs were wanted once—taken home by families—and then for some reason, these same dogs became unwanted. Why? For many dogs, the reason is "bad behavior."

For shelters, it is important to look closely at how we accomplish our mission. Many of us are very good at tugging on people's heartstrings. It's an important part of what we do and, thankfully, it works. People respond in times of need and in cases of cruelty. We are getting better and better every day at highlighting the need on the front end…but what happens after the animals are adopted? What if the dog doesn't meet the new owner's expectations? What if the kitten doesn't understand what "new furniture" is?

The Michigan Humane Society

In 1996, the Michigan Humane Society (MHS) decided it was time to bridge the gap between placing animals in homes and keeping them there. Acknowledging "bad behavior" as an underlying cause for many relinquishments, the organization formed a committee to investigate the possibility of creating a behavior department.

"Our committee's goal for the behavior department was multi-faceted," stated Beth Chamberlain, CPDT, who is the program's manager. "We researched other programs and realized this was something the animals in the community could benefit from." The committee's first step was to establish core goals:

- To improve the bond between people and their companion animals, thereby reducing the number of animals surrendered and improving the animals' quality of life at home.

- To place safe, friendly animals up for adoption—helping to ensure that animals remain in their homes and dispelling the public's impression that shelter animals are "damaged."

In late 1996, the committee made its presentation to the MHS Board of Directors and, with funding from the Oliver Dewey Marcks Foundation, the Pet Education Center (PEC) was born. "We were excited about the prospect of curbing the number

228

of dogs relinquished to shelters," says Petra Pepellashi, long-time MHS Board Member. "Looking back, there were some stumbling blocks we hadn't anticipated, but that's to be expected with any major undertaking. Today, the PEC is a vital resource within the organization."

The Pet Education Center

The PEC has two main functions. Internally, the department works with on-staff evaluators to monitor temperament testing procedures. This temperament test for dogs has been in place since 1997 and is constantly being honed and updated. "The temperament test is an invaluable tool in helping us place temperamentally sound dogs up for adoption," states Chamberlain. "The results of the temperament tests are also made available to potential adopters. This helps the people understand the dog a bit better and aids our staff in helping to make the best dog-family match."

At this time, a temperament test for cats is being developed and the PEC is in the process of conducting its first research study on fearful dogs. The PEC also manages an in-shelter dog training program that is staffed and coordinated entirely by volunteers.

The PEC is also very involved in community outreach. Course curriculums have been custom-developed for over nine different dog obedience classes including an outdoor class, a modified agility class, and a class for small dogs only. Classes run five evenings a week and Saturdays during the day. There are five different locations (two are in-shelter).

"We differentiate our program from other local training schools by focusing on training good manners as opposed to strictly obedience," said Chamberlain. For example, PEC students learn how to prevent behaviors like door dashing, jumping on visitors, and counter surfing while learning how to walk nicely on a leash, come when called, and go to your place. Class attendance has grown from a few hundred students in 1998 to close to 1,000 in 2003.

"We've seen hundreds of success stories over the years," adds Chamberlain. "When a student comes to class frustrated beyond belief and leaves proud of their dog…that's what it's all about. It is not uncommon for us to hear, 'If it wasn't for you guys, I wouldn't have kept my dog. You taught me so much!'"

PEC obedience classes are taught by staff instructors and highly trained volunteers. The current core of PEC volunteers numbers over 70. There is an extensive training program in place for both trainers and instructors and an instructor certification program is in the works. "Our volunteers are some of the most dedicated people you could ever meet," says Chamberlain. "Many of them have been with us since the start of the PEC program."

The PEC also provides behavior consultations for dogs with aggression issues or separation anxiety. There is a fee for the service, although special consideration is given to MHS adopters. "We strive every day to be more responsible for the animals we put up for adoption," adds David Williams, MHS Director of Operations. "Anyone who adopts from us and requires a consultation within the first month of living with the animal receives a free consultation." Thankfully, according to Williams, the special service is rarely needed.

The PEC also manages a Behavior Help Line. This service is staffed by volunteers and provides free help via phone for questions regarding basic behavior problems. "We're able to help folks with questions on cat behavior, dog behavior, bird behavior, and other small animals as well," says Bonnie Braund, Behavior Help Line Coordinator. "Our staff is trained to know who can be helped over the phone and who requires a referral to one of our other services." Last year alone, the Behavior Help Line took over 1,000 phone calls.

So, do shelters need behavior departments? The Michigan Humane Society would answer with a resounding "yes." Will there be roadblocks? Will there be some resistance? Very probably. In fact, the PEC is currently contemplating a program that could help other shelters learn from their experience. Because in the end, it's the animals who benefit. And that's what it's all about. ❖

Some Thoughts on Euthanasia

Sue Sternberg, March/April 2001

During a recent Web surfing expedition, I came across an animal shelter's Web site that was advertising a large mixed breed dog for adoption. The dog had come into the shelter as a stray at the age of one year, and was still awaiting a home at the age of ten. I wondered, not for the first time, if it was humane to keep that dog alive in a kennel for nine years.

Dogs live in the moment. That is one of their best qualities—their spontaneity, their in-the-moment zest for life. They neither dwell over the past nor daydream of a better future. Is it humane to watch a dog in a shelter bound and rebound off the walls of his kennel every day (or spin in his own excrement) while we, his caretakers, daydream of a better future for him in a home?

How Do We Define Emotional Health?

Shelters and kennels are architecturally designed to hold lots of dogs for short periods of time, not lots of dogs for long periods of time or indefinitely. Nevertheless, we are keeping dogs alive for longer periods of time. We may have agreed not to euthanize the dogs, but what provisions have we made to ensure that the dogs remain sane? Has anyone identified the minimum requirements for the emotional health of dogs in shelters?

Considering a dog's emotional health suggests that we need to ask ourselves about the dog's quality of life. Quality of life issues cover a myriad of concerns, including but not limited to the following types of questions:

- Aren't we responsible for more than just the dogs' physical health, nutritional requirements, fresh water, and a clean, sterile kennel?

- What about leash walks? How many leash walks per day should be the minimum requirement for dogs in shelters?

- What about petting? Should there be a "touching" or "stroking" daily requirement?

- What about toys? Bedding?

- What about peace and quiet time?

- Should a dog be kept alive regardless of physical pain, suffering, disease, aggression, severe separation anxiety, and obsessive-compulsive disorders until a natural death occurs?

- Should a dog be kept alive indefinitely, no matter how he or she adjusts to long-term shelter life, until either a natural death or an adoption occurs?

- What behaviors or physical ailments make a dog "unadoptable"?

Evaluating the Shelter Dog

Two questions should be asked of every dog awaiting adoption in every kennel in every shelter in this country. The questions deal with the two most important issues pertaining to euthanasia: quality of life and behavioral adoptability.

1. Is this dog a better dog today—behaviorally, mentally, and emotionally—than he was yesterday?

2. Is this dog a better dog today—behaviorally, mentally, and emotionally—than he was the day he came in?

If the answer is not yes to both questions, I believe the dog is better off euthanized. And I don't believe the decision hinges on opinions, policies, emotions, or feelings about euthanasia.

The Controversy of Euthanasia

I recognize that euthanasia is a controversial, highly emotional issue. But after traveling to shelters across the country for the last seven years, I believe that not one temperamentally adoptable dog would need to be killed because of a lack of space or time. Too many shelters are holding aggressive and dangerous dogs interminably, while just around the corner another shelter euthanizes dozens of highly adoptable dogs for lack of cage space.

The decision to euthanize must be made in the best interests of the dog. He is living in the present. It is a human's responsibility to make sure the dog is not living in what the dog would consider hell. It is selfish to keep a dog alive if he has deteriorated emotionally or behaviorally, or if his mental health is gone. It is unfair to offer to the public a dangerous dog or one who will be a behavioral nightmare for life.

I have been assisting with, performing, injecting, holding, comforting and making decisions so others can euthanize for more than 20 years. My most recent experience with euthanasia was as profoundly disturbing as my first. And yet, when I repeatedly see dogs living a hellish existence in shelters with virtually no hope of an eventual adoption, euthanasia sometimes seems to be the more humane option.

While my mission in life is to prevent the euthanasia of any "adoptable" dog in a shelter due to lack of space or time, I also care passionately about preventing the adoption of dangerous dogs and stopping the torment and torture of interminably or permanently kenneled dogs. ❖

ASSOCIATION of PET DOG TRAINERS

Working with Veterinarians

Veterinarians can be important allies of dog trainers. Vets see behavior problems daily but often lack the time or expertise to resolve them. Because it is the vet who frequently is first approached by an owner with questions when problems arise, the trainer who has a good relationship with a vet can turn a problem into a referral. Some larger veterinary operations use the services of a dog trainer more directly—in fact many vet techs are dog trainers who work with clients in a clinic environment. This section includes a range of articles including how to get more referrals from vets, operating vet-sponsored training classes, and dealing with behavior issues in vet clinics which dogs often perceive as stressful environments. It also has an excellent article to help you understand lab reports because many behavior problems are medical problems in disguise.

Veterinary Referrals: A Trainer's Best Friend

Nicole Wilde, September/October 2003

When dog owners are in need of obedience or behavioral help for their fur-kids, they want someone they can trust. So whom do most dog owners turn to for a referral? Their veterinarian.

Referrals from vets are invaluable to trainers. In fact, veterinarian referrals alone can account for a large percentage of one's income. And these referrals offer not only quantity, but quality. When potential clients have been referred by a veterinarian, there is already a certain level of buy-in; after all, they already trust their veterinarian's judgment. And owners who spend money at a veterinarian's office are less likely to balk at your training rates than those who do not. Compare the veterinarian-referred potential client with one who has found your ad in the phone book and is comparison shopping; in the latter case, there will be more selling required to get the job.

So how does a trainer go about getting veterinarian referrals? By establishing a relationship. First, grab a phone book and make a list of the veterinarians in your area. Now you have a few options:

1. Call each office. Ask whether they can recommend a trainer. If they say no, tell them that's great because you *are* a trainer, and would like to know to whom you can speak regarding setting up an appointment to introduce yourself. If they already refer to another trainer, ask whether it is an exclusive arrangement. If not, ask whether they would be open to meeting with you.

2. Visit each office. Notice whether other trainers' brochures are displayed. If there are a few, getting in might be as simple as introducing yourself and asking whether you could put yours up as well. While some offices are very picky about who they refer to and will require you to be interviewed by the office manager and/or veterinarian, others will simply give permission to display your materials.

3. If you feel uncomfortable visiting or calling, send a letter of introduction to each veterinarian's office. Keep it brief and pleasant. List a few credentials, and tell them what you can do to benefit their clients. Finish by saying you will call to follow up, and do so.

4. Bring a dog in for an exam, and strike up a conversation while you are there. This also affords an opportunity to speak directly with the veterinarian.

If a veterinarian currently refers to another trainer, make a note of it and check back in a few months. Circumstances change and persistence pays off.

Once you have arranged an appointment to meet the office manager or veterinarian, arrive promptly and dress neatly. Bring a brief resume outlining your experience and credentials. Include any community work with local shelters, rescue groups, schools, or others. Answer questions patiently and pleasantly, even if you feel you are being put on the defensive. There is one veterinarian who now refers to me, who was very cautious when we first met and all but cross-examined me. It turned out the last trainer he had referred to had badmouthed him all over town (not too bright a business move), and consequently, it took me a few months to gain his trust. Another veterinarian at first had doubts about referring to a female trainer, especially regarding aggression issues, until he began to receive consistent positive feedback from his clients.

Explain to the veterinarian and staff how your services can benefit their clients. For example, puppies they refer to you will be much easier to handle during exams. (If they distribute "puppy packets" to new clients, you could suggest your brochure be included.) Clients whose dogs have behavior problems will remain clients, thanks to your intervention, allowing the dog to stay in the home. Many veterinarians are relieved to have someone knowledgeable to send training and behavior issues to.

There are other ways to establish a relationship with a veterinarian's office, other than directly soliciting referrals. You could ask whether they would like to offer a group class to their clients, such as a puppy socialization group, or basic obedience class. Many veterinarians like being able to offer comprehensive services. You could offer free lectures for owners on subjects such as caring for a new puppy, housetraining, etc. Brief one-topic handouts the veterinarian's office can distribute are another way to get your contact information out there. Ask what the veterinarians would like their clients to learn about.

Once you have a foot in the door and are receiving referrals, it is important to maintain the relationship:

1. Be diligent about restocking advertising materials. There is one veterinarian's office that refers to me that used to refer to another trainer as well. A few months back they said, "If he does not bring more brochures in pretty soon, we are not going to refer to him any more"—and they don't.

2. The front desk is where you will get most of your referrals, so be pleasant and maintain your relationship with the receptionists. If they are not busy, stop and chat when you come by to restock. Bring small tokens of appreciation now and then—donuts, bagels, cookies. I have worked at a veterinarian's office and trust me, a little tasty reinforcement goes a long way!

3. Give holiday gifts to the veterinarian and staff. Be creative so your gift stands out. For example, buy each staff member a pair of movie tickets. Last year I gave each person at one veterinarian's office a small photo frame with paw prints on it, and a personalized gift to the veterinarian reflecting her favorite breed.

4. Send thank you notes periodically, naming recent referrals. For example, "Thank you for referring Maxine and her Bichon, Beau. (Or list them if there are many.) They are doing wonderfully and I appreciate your entrusting your valued clients to me." Send reports on serious behavior issues that have been referred as well.

(continued)

5. Do not step on veterinary toes! If your clients have questions that are more medical than behavioral, refer them back to the veterinarian; and never directly disagree with advice the veterinarian has given.

The veterinarian's office should soon begin to receive rave reviews about your services, perpetuating further referrals. After a while, once the veterinarian is comfortable with you, you could even ask for a testimonial to put on your brochure or web site. A veterinarian's public endorsement will generate even more clients for you. ❖

Alerting Your Clients to Potential Behavior Problems

Valerie Barrette, July/August 2002

During my more than 20 years of work in the veterinary field, my primary responsibility has been client education. When a client comes in with a pet, I review the pet's record to be sure that all appropriate procedures and preventions have been recommended. I advise new kitten owners about feline leukemia testing. I counsel people with outdoor cats about the need for leukemia vaccinations. I recommend heartworm testing and preventive medications for all dogs. And I explain to the owners of unspayed dogs that spaying reduces the risk of mammary cancer and minimizes the potential for uterine infections.

Our clients rely on veterinary staff to advise them of potential medical problems and preventive options. If we don't take that responsibility seriously, we can risk the health of our patients and strain their caretakers' trust in us. It is our job—not our clients' job—to try to figure out the health issues and concerns relevant to their pets.

When we recommend a procedure, we need to clearly communicate the cost, time, and risk so that each client can make an informed, educated decision. We also need to be careful to not alienate the client who declines our recommendation. Ultimately, it is the client who decides what's best for his or her pet.

Be Alert To Behavior Health Problems

While we work hard to be proactive about a dog's physical health, are we doing the same for his or her behavior health? Are we preparing owners for potential problem behavior and giving them appropriate preventive strategies? Are we recognizing "red flag" warning signs and alerting the owner to them?

Most of the time, the warning signs of potential problem behavior may be easy to overlook. So let's consider several scenarios in which the behavior is less than optimal. As you read each case, think about what you would have done in that situation. Have you witnessed or been involved in similar situations? How did you react?

Case Scenarios of Problem Behavior

Case #1. An eight-week-old pup tries to climb her owner's shoulder when you enter the exam room. The owner may dismiss the behavior as a normal puppy response, but you know better. Time and time again, you have seen puppies like this grow up to be shy, fearful dogs. Some of those dogs will bite out of fear, and a few will become impossible to handle.

So do you nod and commiserate with the owner, or do you gently explain that fearfulness now can translate to fearfulness later?

Case #2. Years ago, I entered the clinic's waiting room to greet a client and his two nine-week-old puppies. He sat on the reception sofa with a growling puppy on either side of him. "Look, they're already protective!" he exclaimed, grinning in delight.

Oh, boy. With some counseling, the client learned that his puppies' behavior was not protection of him, but defensive aggression brought on by fear. With a strategy in place, he began to work with the pups. Now, years later, these dogs come into the clinic wagging their tails.

Case #3. A client brings in a three-month-old puppy for vaccines. While in the waiting room the pup lunges and barks incessantly at every dog she sees. The owner jerks on the leash and loudly scolds the puppy. At one point, he grabs the puppy and forces her on her back, inviting the owner of a nearby dog to bring his dog over for a sniff. As he holds down the frantically struggling pup, he comments on his puppy's dominance.

Will you help this owner see that his methods stand a good chance of making the puppy's behavior much worse? Can you provide him with sound strategies to help his puppy become more comfortable in the presence of other dogs?

Case #4. I remember a client who came to the clinic with a recently adopted rescue dog and her two young children. During the visit, I observed the dog repeatedly trying to avoid the children. They pursued the dog in fascination and, whenever they could corner him, the dog would stiffen and avert his face. While nothing about the dog suggested overt aggression, I was uncomfortable. I discussed my concern with the owner, who became a little defensive.

While the dog was on the exam table eating cookies, I moved my hand to about a foot in front of the dog to brush a piece of cookie toward him. He immediately hunched and hovered over the food. I pointed out this behavior to the owner, who rationalized that the dog had been rescued, had probably experienced hunger, and had no doubt been abused in its previous life. (I'm not sure where the abuse theory came from, but it seems every rescue dog has one.)

The warning flags turned into a danger siren for me when I took the dog's temperature. I had a staff member restrain him, which was hardly needed. I withdrew the thermometer, the helper stepped back, and, as I turned back to the dog, he whirled and did a machine-gun triple bite up my arm. No punctures, but I sported bruises of many colors for weeks.

The owner viewed the biting as evidence of the dog's awareness that I didn't like him and, therefore, he didn't trust me. After I told the owner that I had grave concerns about this dog living with her children, I suggested professional intervention and then shakily left the room. I hope, for the sake of those children, that I was wrong.

Educate, Educate!

Recommending reputable trainers is a start in the direction of proactive behavior health, but not all owners seek the help of trainers. If a client doesn't perceive a problem, he or she is unlikely to look for a solution. For example, my clients frequently describe problem behavior such as jumping and pulling on leash, yet they remain oblivious to signs of handling intolerance.

The most significant proactive step—and the one over which you have the most control in the veterinary clinic—is client education. Be alert to opportunities to teach both physical and behavior health education, keeping in mind that your approach and format will be dictated by clinic policy and your individual ability to communicate with each dog owner. Take one day and one client at a time. A small effort can result in a huge benefit for dogs and the people who love them. ❖

Starting a Veterinary-Sponsored Puppy Program

Valerie Barrette, Published in three parts, July/December 2001

PART I

It's late morning at your veterinary clinic, and Mrs. Jones is at the front counter paying her bill. Wiggling at her feet, alternately tugging at her pants leg and stalking an unsuspecting bug, is Spencer, her Sheltie puppy. Spencer, who has already been seen by your staff for vaccinations and a recent sock-eating adventure, was treated today for a scratch to his eye after wandering out the front door and discovering the neighbor's cat.

"He's adorable!" exclaims the receptionist as she leans over the counter in time to see the bug become part of the food chain.

"Yes, and it's a good thing," replies Mrs. Jones. "Sometimes his cuteness is the only thing between him and the street!"

Mrs. Jones turns serious. "I need to get him trained. He runs out the front door every morning when I leave it open for air. He knows he's not supposed to because I've caught him once or twice. But if I turn my back…oh, and once he's out, you can forget about catching him. And he's starting to chew on all my teddy bears. And when do these pups get housetrained? I keep finding spots all over the house."

"Well, puppies certainly are a challenge," muses the receptionist as she glances at two phone lines on hold. "Do you want to schedule your next appointment now? He'll need to come back in four weeks for his 16-week booster."

Mrs. Jones replies, "No, I'll call you once I know my schedule. Honestly, it seems like I'm always coming or going. Can you recommend a puppy class that's close by?"

"No, I don't know anyone close," says the receptionist. "Here's a card for a puppy school in Orangevale. Some of our clients have gone and they enjoyed the class. Can I help you with anything else, Mrs. Jones?"

"Orangevale! Oh boy, that's a twenty-minute drive!" Mrs. Jones exclaims. "I was hoping for something really close. Well, that's too far. I guess Spencer and I will muddle through on our own. I'm sure it's just a matter of time. Thanks for all your help."

The receptionist picks up the phone and waves good-bye. Mrs. Jones moves toward the exit door, unaware that she is leaving behind the tattered remains of the tassels that adorned her shoes. Have you ever wondered how often your clients leave your clinic with their puppy questions and issues unresolved? And how many of those puppies lose their homes because simple management techniques were not put into place? Or base their decision to attend a puppy class on convenience of location?

Structured or Drop-In Classes

If your clinic held a puppy class, would your clients come? The decision to host a veterinary-sponsored puppy class needs to be a careful one. You must determine whether your class will have a structured format or will be hosted on a drop-in basis.

Will there be a charge, or will it be complimentary? Will the class be open only to your clients?

One benefit of a structured class is that it tends to run more smoothly. You have an idea of how many puppies to expect so that you don't become overwhelmed. The drawback is that some puppies will lose out, such as when the class has already started and the next one doesn't start for some weeks.

Rotating Topics

If you choose to rotate topics—perhaps addressing one primary and one secondary topic each week—a client could sign up at any time. In a four-week class, for example, your primary topics could be housetraining, play biting, destruction, and socialization. Your secondary topics could be basic commands such as sit, down, come, and walk nicely.

The drawback of a rotating schedule is that reviewing last week's topics might be confusing to an owner attending the class for the first time. You might want to include a "freestyle" period each week in which the participants can work individually on topics of their choice while you circulate among the group, offering suggestions and encouragement.

Complimentary or Fee Based

Should you charge for your puppy class? Consider that a complimentary puppy class is an impressive offering that presents your clinic in a favorable light. It also gives you a chance to promote your services and supplies. That said, many people don't appreciate the value of a free class and you might find yourself playing to a solo audience. So one compromise between paid and free classes would be to offer a prepaid puppy package that includes discounted vaccines and puppy training classes.

Your decision to offer the class exclusively to your clients or open it up to the public will most likely be determined by space availability and the number of puppies you feel comfortable working with. In addition to needing a safe, secure area for young puppies, you will need to provide your clients with thoughtful, sound advice on a variety of puppy-raising issues.

PART II

Holding puppy classes at your clinic has its pros and cons. Unless your clients are very savvy, most of them bring their puppies into your clinic only for vaccines, exams, nail trims, etc. So it is only a matter of time before most puppies develop a reluctance to enter the door. To their way of thinking, pulling into the parking lot and walking through the clinic's front door results in a less-than-desirable outcome.

Not so for the puppy who also attends puppy school at your clinic! He comes charging in the front door, happy and excited. He's too busy looking for his friends to worry about why he's at the clinic. And if you've done your job right and introduced fun handling exercises on the exam table during your class, that happy-go-lucky, thrilled-to-be there mentality will carry on into the exam room.

High Standards and Expectations

The drawback of hosting classes at your clinic is the immense responsibility of making the experience not only fun and educating, but also safe. You know that your veterinary clinic waiting room gets more than its share of exposure to disease. And, as veterinary personnel, you know that there is no mystery to killing viruses if you use the proper products and techniques.

However, your clients will hold you to the highest standards. If Fluffy gets sick, you can bet that suspicious eyes will be cast in your direction regardless of the fact that Fluffy goes to the groomer for baths once a week and lives with a family of runners who cruise the neighborhood and local parks on a daily basis.

When I first started holding puppy classes, I used our clinic reception area one night a week for puppy class. In addition to disinfecting the floors, I washed and scrubbed the walls to a height of four feet. I also cleaned the inner and outer portions of the entrance and exit doors, as well as the doorknobs and windows. I think the clinic was disappointed when I opened up my own training facility because someone else had to take over the weekly deep cleaning!

Vaccinations and More

In addition to making your class safe for the puppies, make sure that the puppies themselves are safe for the class. Current vaccines are a critical step in protecting the puppies from a variety of diseases.

Keep in mind that an unvaccinated puppy can be a threat to other puppies. For example, it is possible for an unvaccinated puppy to be exposed to the parvovirus, incubate the virus, not show any clinical signs, and yet shed the virus in his stools for months. Puppies also need to be free of parasites, both to prevent infecting other puppies and to help protect their own immune systems. Instruct your clients to leave unwell puppies at home, but encourage them to attend the class themselves to keep current with the material.

Risks of Undersocialization

While there is no argument that puppies—with their immature, inexperienced immune systems—are at greater risk for exposure to disease, raising puppies in restricted environments creates "plastic bubble" dogs who are unable to adjust to normal facets of their world. And while many owners would suffer a shy, fearful dog in order to keep her safe, most are not prepared for the inevitable onset of aggression as the unsocialized dog matures and tries to keep herself safe in a strange land.

You must educate your clients about the balancing act of socialization and protection. Don't discount their concerns. Help them develop strategies that get the puppy out into the world, but at a safety level that is comfortable for the owner. As a veterinary staff member, you are in a perfect position to take the mystery out of diseases like parvovirus and kennel cough. Understanding the symptoms and how these diseases spread can help your clients develop sound socialization strategies.

Secure the Exits

Another safety issue is door security. If your clinic has door levers rather than knobs, examine them closely. Is it possible to disengage the lock just by hitting the lever? A door that opens inward is not a real problem; if the door opens outward, on the other hand, you could lose a puppy.

Setting up a barrier, such as an exercise pen, can create a double-lock system. Teaching your puppy owners to knock before entering the classroom door can help ensure that all puppies are secured.

PART III

If you are new to the training game, consider enlisting the services of an experienced puppy class instructor. You can then observe firsthand her methods and techniques, as well as how she fields questions about common puppy problems. Listening to her observations as puppies interact will help you to get a finer sense of social play, in addition to learning when it may be necessary to intercede.

It is also time for you to hit the books. As veterinary personnel, your clients will view you as the expert. Don't disappoint them, and don't sell them short. And don't rely on techniques you used ten years ago to train the family dog. Throw away that outdated book on dog training; if the author has evolved over the years, he or she should have an updated version.

Keep in mind that today's training methods—such as those using lures and rewards—are much more dog-friendly than older methods using pinch collars and choke chains. If you're working with a large dog who is difficult to control, for example, a more humane alternative to a pinch collar is a halter that uses leverage rather than tracheal pressure. It's a brave new world, and you need to join it.

Reference Book Recommendations

I want to recommend four good reference books. These are not the only books you should read; however, I feel that these four will give you the most comprehensive orientation to dog behavior and training:

The Culture Clash by Jean Donaldson (James & Kenneth Publishers, 2005) will give you a no-holds-barred, straight-to-the-point education on dog behavior. Who dogs are and why they do the things they do are key points in this book (and no, it's not about dominance). You should read this book cover to cover. The information on socialization alone is worth its weight in gold.

Excel-Erated Learning by Pamela J. Reid, PhD (James & Kenneth Publishers, 1996) discusses the science of learning. Don't expect it to be a dry read, however. Lots of analogies and examples are used to make the learning simple and fun. The table of contents in this book is to die for.

Don't Shoot the Dog by Karen Pryor (Bantam Books, 1999) provides you with real-life examples and applications of learning principles.

And, finally, *The Handbook of Applied Dog Behavior and Training, Volume I*, by Steven R. Lindsay (Iowa State University Press, 2000) has pertinent information regarding the effect of age on learning in the chapter titled "Development of Behavior." This is essential reading for anyone working with puppies.

Puppy Age and Class Curriculum

The age range of the puppies in your class will determine your curriculum. If your goal is to work with young puppies (eight to twelve weeks), your clients will want to know about housetraining, play biting, and destruction. They will be worried about jumping and coming when called. You, on the other hand, will be worried about socialization and resource guarding.

The owners of puppies sixteen weeks and older generally want obedience topics (sit, down, stay, etc.). Many of these owners may believe that obedience training will affect issues such as barking and destruction, so you will need to address those topics.

If you are planning to offer a play session, the age range becomes especially important. I don't recommend mixing puppies under 10 weeks with puppies over 16 weeks. At 16 weeks and up, puppies are much more excitable and uninhibited, in addition to being very competitive. Also, don't plan on your play session being a free-for-all. In the four years I have been running The Right Steps, I can count on one hand the times I have been able to combine the entire class in play.

Puppies Have Different Comfort Levels

In addition to differences in physical size and play style, puppies may have different comfort levels. One puppy may come into your class never having seen another puppy since he left his littermates. Another may regularly play with dogs much larger than he. Turn these two loose at the first play session, and you're going to have a problem.

Be prepared to separate your puppies into groups if needed. At my training facility, I have the luxury of numerous exercise pens and eyebolts in the wall. However, when I was using the veterinary clinic's lobby, I would station the owners to act as goalies. They got pretty good at it! While on-leash socialization is not my favorite method, it beats having a worried puppy harassed and pursued.

The larger the play group, the better the chance you will find appropriate matches. One class structure that has worked well for me is to schedule two classes around a play session. Some of your students will come to the class and then stay for the play session. Others will come first to the play session, and then stay for the class. This makes it possible to keep your class size small.

Know Your Limitations

Be realistic about what you can handle. If a student has a problem with a puppy and you're not sure of the solution, enlist the advice of an experienced trainer. (Most trainers would be thrilled at the opportunity to establish a working relationship with a veterinary clinic.) Continue to educate yourself by reading and attending seminars. Never stop reviewing and improving your class. Talk to other trainers. Ask questions. Join the APDT. ❖

Fear and Aggression in the Veterinary Waiting Room

Valerie Barrette, Published in two parts, November 2000/January 2001

PART I

"One's up!" announces the receptionist over the clinic intercom, indicating that the first of your afternoon appointments has arrived. As the technician in charge of exam rooms for the day, your job is to get vital statistics (temperature, pulse, heart rate, and weight) and patient history before the doctor goes into the room.

As you enter the waiting room to get the chart, you hear an explosion of movement and sound. A large dog lunges forward while barking hysterically, backs up and fights his leash like a bucking bronco, and finally comes to rest behind his owner, peering out at you and growling softly. Do you always have this effect on animals?

If you have worked in the veterinary field for any length of time, the above scenario is not new to you. For most dogs, the vet clinic is an environment of unwanted handling, unpleasant or uncomfortable procedures, and owner separation. With the exception of some of the extremely social breeds (who consider even a thermometer in the rear a social event), most dogs develop an array of avoidance and escape responses when faced with a vet clinic's front door. It's a small wonder that any dog walks willingly into our little shop of horrors!

So here's the deal. Like it or not, dogs who visit the vet are going to be subjected to all the indignities a veterinary visit entails. And, like it or not, you are going to have to deal with unhappy dogs in the future. Is there a way to keep you and the rest of the staff safe, get the job done, and not make uncooperative dogs harder to handle next time? Let's explore that possibility by first addressing how to get the dog from the waiting room into the exam room.

Aggression as an Emotional State *and* a Strategy

Keep in mind that fear is an emotional state. Just as with humans, intense fear causes rational thought and common sense to fly out the window. Fear-based behavior can be very frustrating for owners who think that everything will be fine if their dogs will just sit and stay. When unsuccessful, owners often resort to aggression—such as jerking and punishing their dogs for making a scene—which does nothing more than elevate the fear level of already panic-stricken dogs.

Dog aggression is a strategy. Many dogs who exhibit aggression in the veterinary environment never exhibit it anywhere else. A fearful dog, on a leash and in a building, is running out of strategies.

If you feel that a dog owner needs assistance in addressing the dog's behavior, you can help him or her locate a trainer by contacting The Association of Pet Dog Trainers at 1-800-PET-DOGS or www.apdt.com.

A Secure Collar

Before you bring the dog into the exam room, make sure he cannot slip back out of his collar. If he tries and is successful, it will be much harder to get him to move forward the next time. If you must, you can give the owner a kennel lead. If possible, have the owner tighten the flat collar so that, if the dog fights, he'll be fighting with the back of his neck and not choking. Choking an already fearful dog will raise his defense response to a new level. Also, make sure the dog is not on a pinch collar. In a nice way that doesn't make the owner defensive, explain that you don't want to add pain to the picture. In a nice way, don't give the owner a choice. That pinch collar will get you bitten.

Labels Don't Help

Labels such as "unsocialized" or "dominant" are not terribly helpful. We must deal with the situation at hand. Correcting or otherwise threatening the dog will only increase his motivation to defend himself. The first step is to stop taking the dog's behavior personally. The second step is to forget everything you ever read about alpha rolls and scruff shakes; they won't help you and will most likely get you bitten. The third step is to actively involve the dog's owner in the process. Owners of aggressive dogs tend to feel very embarrassed, believing that no one likes their dog. They bear the responsibility (not always fairly) for how their dog behaves and can't understand how their beloved pet can be so "bad." You should describe to owners the best techniques (as discussed here) to use in dealing with their dog's fear.

Body Language Makes a Difference

Be conscious of your body posture and position as you have the owner bring the dog into the room. Don't expect the dog to be able to walk past you, and don't try to make friends. He would much rather be ignored. If he will eat tossed treats, that's great...but don't count on it.

Go only as far into the waiting room as needed for the owner to see you, and then turn your back as you escort the dog and owner into the exam room. Keep your body turned away or to the side as the owner brings the dog in. If needed, leave the room by way of the inner door until the dog is inside and the door is closed.

When dealing with aggressive dogs, never try to appear tough or dominant. To the fearful dog, you will be terrifying. To the offensively assertive dog, you are a challenge.

Your goal should be to appear as neutral and non-threatening as possible. You can accomplish this by avoiding a direct, confrontational stare. Fast or excessively slow movements, as well as a towering, threatening demeanor, can literally make the dog's hair stand on end!

(continued)

PART II

So here we are... a dog owner, a veterinary technician, and one quivering, growling mass of dog confined in a small exam room. The game plan calls for you, the vet tech, to sidle up right next to this dog (why don't they make stethoscopes just a little bit longer??) and listen to his heart rate and breathing. Then you expect this dog to willingly turn his back to you and stay still while you insert a lubricated thermometer into his rectum and take his temperature. Right. This dog was not born yesterday. He's been here before. He's *ready*.

The Old Way Was Traumatic

When I started working in this field 18 years ago, I would go into the exam room, muzzle the dog, struggle with him while I got his vital signs, take the muzzle off, and then re-muzzle him when the doctor was ready. A dog who struggled was treated as if he was simply refusing to obey. We would actually command the dog to stay, not understanding that he was fighting for his safety. The veterinary visit was traumatic, especially if the dog had also waited a lengthy time in the waiting room.

The New Way Is Less Stressful

Now we know better. We know that reducing a dog's stress increases her tolerance, and we can take specific steps to make the veterinary visit less stressful for the dog:

- Set the appointment for early morning or early afternoon (before the clinic has a chance to get behind schedule).
- Work with the owner to minimize both the owner's and the dog's tension.
- Shorten the time the dog must spend in the exam room.
- Use muzzles that fit properly.
- Let the dog see his owner during the exam.

Talk With the Owner/Watch the Dog

Spend some time talking to the owner about why the dog is at the clinic. While you are talking, quietly observe the dog from the corner of your eye. Is he sniffing in your direction? Wandering around? Does he eat the cookies you've tossed onto the floor?

The stressed dog stays in his corner, either staring directly at you or trying to hide his head. He makes no effort at all to greet you or observe the environment. As Sue Sternberg would say, he shows no overt signs of friendliness.

Leave Your Emotions at the Door

If this dog is not interested in getting to know you, you are starting at ground zero. Making smoochy noises or approaching the dog and extending your hand for a sniff could very well earn you a bite. This isn't the time to try to make friends. You have a job to do, and part of that job entails humanely handling the dog in a manner that won't make him more fearful in the future. So leave your own emotions at the door.

Muzzle the Dog

Let the owner know that you will need to muzzle the dog for the exam. Explain that the muzzle will allow the doctor to expedite the exam and get the dog out of the clinic sooner.

Make sure your clinic or hospital carries a wide selection of muzzle sizes. A good muzzle fit can make all the difference. Unless I feel the owner is at risk, I will have the owner muzzle the dog. I estimate the size of the neck plus a little extra to make it easy for the owner to put on the muzzle. The moment I hear the click of the snap-lock, I step in, slip on the kennel lead, and tighten the muzzle. (*Four Flags Over Aspen* has muzzles for both short, squatty-nosed dogs and long, snippy-nosed types.)

If possible, have the same team members work with this dog during every visit. It is possible for a dog to acclimate to those team members over time. He may not like what you are doing—and you'll probably still need to muzzle him—but familiarity may eventually diminish that "added panic" component that tends to give the struggling dog super-human strength.

Let the Dog See the Owner

To minimize the dog's panic and struggling, I try to position the owner so that the dog can see him or her. To maintain control of the dog in this position, I generally use a kennel lead to ensure that the dog won't back out of his collar, but I also keep a couple of fingers or my thumb under the collar to prevent it from tightening. If I lose hold of the dog with my arms, I can always remove my fingers so the collar tightens. I unhook the leash so that the owner doesn't inadvertently choke the dog.

Support the Owner

Veterinary visits can be difficult for the owner who is trying to equate her growling dog who must be muzzled with the sweet, loving pet she sees at home. Coach the owner on what you want her to do during the exam. Involve her. Tell her that she can't scold or console the dog and that her communication must be in the form of upbeat stories or funny jokes.

I frequently recommend to owners that they sing "Happy Birthday" if their dog begins to struggle. While I've never had an owner initiate the song, I have had plenty of experiences where an upset, teary-eyed owner starts to laugh when I launch into "Happy Birthday." Is it my imagination, or has the dog relaxed just a bit because the owner is more relaxed? It's worth a try. ❖

Diagnostic Lab Work: A Primer

Karen Overall, May/June 2004

Veterinarians, like human doctors, are more often schooled in the abnormal than the normal, but a large part of how we recognize abnormal involves deviations from expectations. The first sign that any client or veterinarian has that the animal is "not feeling well" is behavioral. Clearly, although all conditions present to the veterinarian with behavioral changes, not all problems are behavioral. Specialists in any field often develop tunnel-vision because they expect to have patients referred to them who are afflicted with a condition in which the specialist is interested. In human medicine, where patients can talk, this is not a huge concern, although all of us have stories about missed medical opportunities. If the specialty is a purely visual one, we have a greater chance of identifying the concern even in the absence of speech: most of us are able to recognize skin loss or broken limbs.

In the case of behavioral conditions where evaluations depend on discrete observations and enhanced observational and history-taking skills, the judicious approach is to ask whether the condition is primarily medical or fundamentally behavioral. In behavioral medicine we are challenged by the fact that all behavioral signs are non-specific and can be shared by medical and behavioral conditions. Furthermore, medical/physical problems can involve or develop behavioral aspects (e.g., fear in a dog with a broken back), and behavioral conditions can have primarily physical manifestations (e.g., lick granulomas).

The keys to sorting out this mess are: (1) history; (2) physical examination; (3) laboratory evaluation; and (4) direct observation accompanied by more history. Because it's the aspect least familiar to trainers, the following discussion will explain why laboratory evaluations are important and what they could mean. It is really important that we all remember that improvement in a problem dog's problematic behaviors is a function of partnership and teamwork: the vet, the veterinary technician, the trainer, the client, the human and canine family, and the patient.

Importance of Baseline Data

The baseline data required for a decent laboratory evaluation include heart rate, respiratory rate, temperature, complete blood cell count (CBC), a complete chemistry panel, a urinalysis and, often, a complete thyroidal evaluation. These parameters often covary, i.e., changes in one can mean changes in another, so all interpretation must occur in the context of the entire set of results, along with the history and physical signs.

Non-specific signs of inflammation include increased heart rate, increased temperature (and we must remember that excited dogs and young puppies have increased body temperatures), and changes in white blood cell (WBC) count. Increases in heart rate and respiratory rate can be associated with illness, but also with pain, anxiety, fear, heat, etc. If inflammation is present, it's usually a bacteria or a virus and results in increased neutrophils, particularly the reactive type (polymorphonuclear neutrophils (PMNs). This is common when animals have foreign bodies, gastrointestinal perforations, skin infections, etc.

Of course, these conditions can be secondary to behavioral complaints, hence the need for a full history. Immunosuppressant conditions (e.g., autoimmune conditions, parvo virus, some cancers) often result in decreased WBC counts, temperatures, and low platelet counts. The WBC and platelet responses are often due to a suppressed or less active bone marrow. Low thyroidal values can also often look like this immune-mediated response, but they can also be the result of stress or of some concomitant infection. This is one reason why a rush to treat a dog with thyroxin replacement on the basis of mildly low thyroidal levels may not be rational.

Different types of poisonings can cause neurological behaviors that look behavioral and they can sometimes be detected in the CBC. One example of this is lead poisoning, which can change shapes and patterns of red blood cells (RBCs). Canine RBCs do not have nuclei. When we see nucleated RBCs in a smear of blood on a glass slide when examined microscopically, we have to ask why baby or immature red cells are being released from the marrow. Many neoplastic conditions can affect the marrow and also be associated with odd behavioral changes.

The Chemistry Panel

The chemistry panel is performed for two reasons. First, this is the series of tests that—with the urinalysis—evaluates liver and kidney function. These two organs metabolize food and drugs, and help maintain suitable levels of just about every chemical necessary for life. They also insure that we can package, transport, and dispose of wastes or substances we cannot use. Protein, believe it or not, is often considered a waste, and dogs that have impaired ability to use and clear protein can develop hepatoencephalopathy, a condition where they act demented, frantic, aggressive, and wholly atypical. A very low protein diet allows these dogs to revert to their normal, happy selves.

Second, because we may be using psychotropic medication as part of a treatment plan for animals with behavioral problems, we need to insure that the liver and kidneys are functioning and can metabolize these drugs, and we need to ensure that if the dog is taking any other medication there is unlikely to be any adverse inter-drug responses. Many people feel that dogs with behavioral conditions are usually "healthy" and, therefore, pre-medication laboratory evaluation is not necessary. I wholly disagree with this view and I think that it represents a less than optimal practice of medicine. While we likely take blood too often from humans, we also likely don't take it often enough in dogs. All dogs should have at least annual blood work. They cannot tell us when they feel ill, and so conditions that can be evaluated by laboratory means may go untreated until they have worsened considerably. Also, if the dog does have an adverse reaction to the medication, how are you going to know if the alterations in laboratory values are the result of or indicative of the reaction, or if they preceded it, and the impaired function was made worse by the drugs? Simply, unless you are omniscient—and I am not—you cannot know. So, I always want lab work. That said, there are two cases in which I will forgo such tests: the dog is sufficiently aggressive that no one can safely obtain a sample; and/or if the clients are really broke and the choice is labs or drugs in a healthy-appearing young animal. In both cases I make sure that clients know that I view this as a sub-optimal but somewhat rational course, given the circumstances, and that I want them to be particularly vigilant.

Liver Enzymes

That said, some lab values are more informative than others in behavioral conditions. Increased serum levels of enzymes may reflect increased activity of liver enzymes (ALT, AST, ALP, GGT) associated with many medications (including those used to treat epilepsy) and may not be associated with clinically significant liver disease. Activity of liver enzymes in circulation is affected by their intracellular location, their baseline intracellular activity, their tendency to leak from the cell if membrane permeability increases, and their serum half-life.

ALT [alanine transaminase aka alanine aminotransferase] is considered liver-specific in the dog and cat, and its immediate release follows hepatocellular injury or altered membrane permeability. A 50% or more increase in ALT can be seen in acute liver disease, but small increases are often seen in dogs as a result of microsomal enzyme induction. Treatment with some anticonvulsant medications can be associated with a four-fold increase in serum ALT concentrations, and treatment with glucocorticoids (e.g., steroids) may result in 3-5-fold increases in concentration.

AST [aspartate transaminase aka aspartate aminotransferase] has high concentrations in multiple organs in the dog, but hepatic AST is associated with mitrochondrial membranes and cytosol. Increases in serum AST concentrations can be associated with any factor that alters membrane permeability, including microsomal enzyme induction commonly associated with medication. For dogs with naturally developing liver disease, increases in AST activity are more sensitive than increases in ALT activity.

ALP [alkaline phosphatase] increases are the most commonly noted one in routine laboratory evaluation in ill dogs. ALP in dogs has a high sensitivity but low specificity (e.g., many falsely leading elevations). In dogs, elevations are commonly due to isoenzymes associated with exogengous corticosteroid (e.g., prednisolone, megace, et cetera) and to elevation associated with induction by medication, including those used to treat behavioral problems. In acute canine hepatic disease ALP increases 2-5 fold over baseline, overlapping the 2-6-fold increases that can be seen in chronic administration of anticonvulsants.

GGT [gamma-glutamyl-transferase] is important in foreign compound detoxification, among other functions. Substantial increases are commonly associated with either cholestasis or pancreatitis. Microsomal enzyme-inducing drugs (barbiturates, TCAs, gluocorticoids, etc.) may stimulate GGT in a similar fashion as ALP in dogs.

The preceding discussion should make it clear why routine labs can be useful. The thyroid evaluation issue is trickier.

The Role of Hypothyroidism

Hypothyroidism has been postulated to be associated with fear and/or aggression in dogs and with sudden shifts in these behaviors. Hypothyroidism has been reported to account for 1.7% of canine aggressive behaviors. Dogs with hypothyroid-associated aggression may not show the other classical signs of hypothyroidism such as a poor hair coat, lethargy, or weight gain. Aggression is gradual in onset and triggers can be inconsistent. Appropriate thyroid screening should be part of a minimum database on an aggressive pet to rule out thyroid related diseases; however, caution is urged in over-interpretation of data, given the relative rareness of the condition.

It's important to realize that the estimated incidence of behavioral problems is considerably greater than that of hypothyroidism. Also, the age of onset for hypothyroidism overlaps that for the development of most behavioral conditions in dogs (~12-24 months of age). These data are important because they show that while behavioral and thyroidal conditions may be co-morbid, the patterns involving age of onset strongly suggest that any rule postulating a causal association may be overly optimistic.

Although there have been anecdotal suggestions for the use, either alone or in combination, of thyroid supplementation for the treatment of canine behavioral conditions, there is currently no good rationale for supplementation with exogenous thyroxin in the absence of specific behavioral clinical signs and aberrant levels or response of compounds that tell us more about thyroidal function (e.g., serum thyroid transthyretin) in pets with behavioral problems. Such cavalier dispensation of potent medication is particularly problematic given the wide range of breed-specific reference ranges for T3, T4, free T3, and free T4. Resting free T4 levels, if grossly low, may provide a rough gauge to thyroid function since free T4 is less likely than total T4 to be affected by non-thyroidal illness or by drug therapy.

Most accurately measured using dialysis methods, low free T4 concentration combined with an increase in thyroid releasing factor (TRF) is consistent with a diagnosis of hypothyroidism. In the absence of both clinical signs of hypothyroidism (obesity, seborrhea, alopecia, weakness, lethargy, bradycardia (low heart rate), and pyoderma (skin infections)) and low (not low-normal) free T4 (or the equivalent TSH-stimulation test result), there is no rational or competent reason to treat dogs with behavioral or any other diagnoses with thyroxin. There may be a small population of dogs for which this generalization might prove false in the future, but they will be rare. These dogs, if they exist, may have anxiety conditions that are affected by cholecystokinin [CCK], a gastrointestinal hormone that acts in the brain (CCK-B) and in the GI tract (CCK-A). In male rats, CCK-A (alimentary) receptor stimulation inhibits TSH secretion at the level of the anterior pituitary.

This is not to say that dogs with thyroid disorders do not alter their behavior; they do, but the behavioral changes are non-specific and should not be confused with a behavioral diagnosis. There may be non-responders to anti-depressant and anti-anxiety medication in the canine population that are analogous to non-responder conditions seen in the human population. If so, supplementation with thyroxin in addition to the antidepressant and/or anti-anxiety medications may help. However, most single-mechanism (i.e., thyroid) hypotheses for the underlying cause and treatment of complex behavioral phenomena like aggression and fear are simplistic and invariably wrong. In this case, supplementation is not benign, and executed in the absence of a diagnosis is a poor reflection on the practice of medicine.

Glossary

Alimentary - Of, relating to, or functioning in nourishment or nutrition.[1]

Alopecia - Baldness; hair loss. [1]

Anterior - Situated before or toward the front; situated near or nearer the head.[1]

Barbiturates - A drug with sedative and hypnotic effects. Barbiturates have been used as sedatives and anesthetics, and they have been used to treat the convulsions associated with epilepsy. [2]

Bone marrow - The inner, spongy tissue of large bones where red blood cells, white blood cells, and platelets and made. [2]

Bradycardia - Abnormally slow heartbeat. [2]

Cholecystokinin (CCK) - Hormone released in the small intestine; causes muscles in the gallbladder and the colon to tighten and relax. [2]

Cholestasis - Accumulation of fluid and products from the bile ducts.[3]

Co-morbid - The coexistence of two or more illnesses.

Concomitant - Accompanying, attending. [1]

Corticosteroid - Potent anti-inflammatory hormones that are made naturally in the body or synthetically for use as drugs. The most commonly prescribed drug of this type is prednisone. [2]

Cytosol - Fluid contents of the cell in which cell components and chemical and enzymatic factors are found.

Dialysis - The process of cleansing the blood when the kidneys are not able to filter the blood. [2]

Enzyme - Any of several complex proteins that are produced by cells and act as catalysts in specific biochemical reactions. [2]

Exogengous - Caused or produced by factors outside the organism or system.[1]

Glucocorticoid - A compound that belongs to the family of compounds called corticosteroids (steroids). Glucocorticoids affect metabolism and have anti-inflammatory and immunosuppressive effects. They may be naturally produced (hormones) or synthetic (drugs). [2]

Half-life - The time required for half of something (as atoms or a drug) to undergo a process. [1]

Hepatic - Pertaining to the liver. [2]

Hepatocellular - Pertaining to cells in the liver.

Hepatoencephalopathy - An encephalopathy (brain disorder) that is associated with increased protein-driven nitrogen; the increased protein is a result of the inability of the liver to break down protein into its component parts and use these. Afflicted dogs stagger and act unpredictably because the way they see and interact in the world is impaired.

Hypothyroidism - Underactive thyroid activity. [2]

Immunosuppression - Suppression of the body's immune system and its ability to fight infections or disease. [2]

Inflammation - Characteristic reaction of tissues to injury or disease marked by four signs: swelling, redness, heat, and pain. [2]

Intracellular - Inside a cell. [2]

Isoenzymes - A subtype of enzyme that comes from a specific part of the body (e.g., from the muscle compared with the liver), helping the clinician to localize the area afflicted that is producing abnormal enzyme levels.

Lick granulomas - Sores that dogs induce on their body, usually their limbs, by licking.

Megace - **Megestorel acetate** - a long acting corticosteroid.

Microsomal Enzyme Induction - The process by which the liver enzymes degrade or process medications. These enzymes are not always active, but are induced by exposure to the drug. Most metabolism is associated with the cytochrome P450 system, and the extent to which any human or dog is capable of metabolizing a drug may depend on the form of cytochrome P450 enzymes that they have, which is genetically determined.

Mitochondria - Parts of a cell where aerobic production (also known as cell respiration) takes place. [2]

Neoplastic - Relating to tumors; new growths of tissue serving no useful purpose in the body. [1]

Neutrophils - The larger and physiologically most numerous class of infection-fighting white blood cells, characteristically even more numerous in generalized bacterial infections. Segmented neutrophils are the larger and physiologically most numerous class of infection-fighting white blood cells, characteristically even more numerous in generalised bacterial infections; segmentation signifies cell division, so a high segmented neutrophil count implies vigorous response. [2]

Nuclei - Plural of nucleus: a mass of gray matter or group of nerve cells in the central nervous system. [1]

Pancreatitis - Inflammation (pain, tenderness) of the pancreas which can make the pancreas stop working. Inflammation of the pancreas, often causing destruction of pancreatic and other abdominal tissues due to the escape of pancreatic enzymes. [2]

Parvo Virus - Both a class and a specific virus in dogs that is immunosupressive and causes fulminate diarrhea, usually bloody. Puppies often die from this, but adult dogs can recover with supportive care. The parvo vaccine is considered one of the core vaccines in the new vaccine protocols, meaning it should be kept routinely up to date. Parvo outbreaks are common in crowded environments in hot weather (e.g., cities) and some breeds are more susceptible than others.

Pituitary - Gland in the brain that secretes hormones and regulates and controls other hormone-secreting glands and many body processes, including reproduction. [2]

Platelet - Cells found in the blood. [2]

Prednisone - Belongs to the family of drugs called steroids and is used to treat several types of cancer and other disorders. Prednisone also inhibits the body's immune response. [2]

Psychotropic - Acting on the mind.

Pyoderma - Skin infections.

Receptor - A molecule inside or on the surface of a cell that binds to a specific substance and causes a specific physiologic effect in the cell. [2]

Red Blood Cells (RBCs) - Cells that carry oxygen to all parts of the body. Also called erythrocytes. [2]

Seborrhea - A accumulation of scales of greasy skin, often on the scalp. Dandruff. [2]

Serum - A clear fluid that separates when blood clots. [2]

Serum Thyroid Transthyretin - Hormone that allows thyroid compounds to move into and out of cells and so affect the metabolism of other cells.

Steroids - Any of numerous organic compounds, including cortisone, estrogen, and testosterone, each of which has many effects on the body. [2]

T3, T4 - The two thyroid hormones that are routinely measured as a gauge of thyroid function. T4 is the more sensitive measure, but must be interpreted in the context of thyroid stimulating hormone (TSH) levels.

TCAs - Tricyclic Antidepressants - A class of medication used to treat anxiety and depression in humans and animals that primarily work by affecting levels of two neurotransmitters: norepinephrine and serotonin.

Thyroid - A gland near the windpipe (trachea) that produces thyroid hormone, which helps regulate growth and metabolism. [2]

Thyroxin - Hormone produced by the thyroid glands to regulate metabolism by controlling the rate of oxidation in cells; "thyroxine is 65% iodine." [2]

TSH - Thyroid Stimulating Hormone - The hormone that acts in a thermostatic fashion to tell the thyroid to make more hormone and when to stop making hormone.

White Blood Cell - Blood cells that engulf and digest bacteria and fungi; an important part of the body's defense system. [2] ❖

Sources

[1] *The Merriam-Webster Dictionary*, 1997.
[2] www.hypodictionary.com, Medical Dictionary
[3] Medline Plus, www.nlm.nih.gov/medlineplus/ency

Behavior-Induced Euthanasia

Valerie Barrette, March/April 2002

Anyone who works in the veterinary field is familiar with the scenario: the family dog lying on the hospital's best blanket, the box of Kleenex readily available, the family gathered around. As the graying muzzle and tired eyes turn away from offered cookies, and hands large and small anxiously stroke and soothe, you exchange glances with the veterinarian. You say a silent prayer to the euthanasia gods that this one goes smoothly, and that your own eyes remain dry enough so you can perform your job. As the beloved dog slips away, you pass the doctor a stethoscope and get in return an empty syringe. You leave the room in the midst of quiet sobs, silently thankful that the owners were able to make this difficult decision. A splash of cold water on your face, one last wipe of your eyes, and you enter the next room to greet another owner and her new puppy. And the day goes on.

Sometimes, though, it's not so simple. Sometimes the dog being euthanized isn't old or sick or otherwise suffering. Sometimes the owner's reasons for euthanasia are much more complex.

Behavioral Intervention

A recent call from a local veterinarian prompted the topic for this article. The veterinarian was frustrated with recent occurrences of owners requesting euthanasia for aggressive behavior in their dogs. She was trying to determine how to gauge the situation. If the owner pursued help, was there a reasonable chance of success?

It is a difficult situation. Frequently, by the time the owner makes the decision to euthanize, the problem behavior has gone on so long that all the owner feels is a sense of relief. It can be difficult to redirect this owner into problem solving. In addition, only a thorough consultation can determine the extent of the problem and the prognosis. By this point, many owners are reluctant to spend the time or the money. I have lost count of the times I have been told by owners that I am their last hope, when I should have been their first.

Proactive Planning

Behavioral issues—ranging from incomplete housetraining to aggression—can frequently be the cause of an owner "souring" on his or her dog. While we want to question the reasons why an owner requests euthanasia, we need to be cognizant that many factors may have played a part in the decision.

The time to approach the issue of euthanasia with your clients is not when they walk into the clinic for that final appointment. Get together with the doctors in your clinic and determine a course of action. When an appointment is made for euthanasia, there is no reason why the owner can't be gently questioned as to the reason. Many owners offer it themselves.

If the reason is behavioral, perhaps you can have one of the veterinarians call the owner back. A housetraining, anxiety, or aggression issue may have a medical basis. It may be possible to point the owner in the direction of assistance from a behaviorist or behavior counselor. Or, in some cases, you may want to ask the owner to consider surrendering the dog to the clinic. In general, many owners are unaware of the incredible resources at their disposal.

It is important to keep your finger on the pulse of your client's relationship with his or her dog. While it is common to ask about the dog's recent health when an annual exam is performed, are we also asking about behavior? Owners frequently mention problem behavior to veterinarians and their staff, but are we listening? And, more important, are we helping?

Determine Your Clinic's Policy on Euthanasia

Your clinic should set a policy regarding the euthanasia of healthy dogs. Even if your clinic decides on a "don't ask, don't tell" position, at least the staff knows the game plan. Remember that the inevitable delay that occurs as the clinic tries to make a decision on whether or not to honor the owner's request doesn't help anyone. I realize that there are truly uncaring people out there, but most owners requesting euthanasia for their dogs agonized over the decision—and the disconnect you are seeing may be simply a coping mechanism.

Follow the Laws

Be aware that when owners decide to euthanize a dog for aggression, it is usually due to a recent aggressive encounter. Be sure to determine whether an actual bite has occurred because you may need to take certain actions as required by local law. The dog may need to be quarantined and the euthanasia delayed until the quarantine period is over or, in some areas, the dog can be euthanized immediately if appropriate authorities then conduct a brain necropsy.

Endnote

I am fully aware that the term "euthanasia" denotes mercy killing and is, therefore, inappropriate within this article's context. "Put to sleep" (or worse, "PTS") is a euphemism that isn't much better. "Execute" may be a more accurate description; however, it is not my intent to judge the owners who make these decisions. It is my wish to help you educate them. ❖

The Business of Dog Training

While you may not think of it this way, professional dog trainers are business people. Business people who don't know how to run a business successfully will not be much help to their clients over the long run if they go out of business. While working for someone else may be an acceptable alternative, running your own dog training business is viewed as the ideal situation for many people in the field. In this section you will be asked to step out of your training persona and put on your business hat to learn about subjects like management techniques, employee relations, liability insurance, along with marketing and promotional activities. Remember, doing what you love—training dogs—will likely be dependent on your business acumen.

Starting Your Own Dog Training Business

Susan Smith, September/October 2002

Because most dog trainers tend to be softies about dogs, we often overlook the practical aspects of running a business. If you're thinking about starting a dog training business, you'll want to take the time to assess what you need and where you're going. Remember: The greater your financial success, the more people you'll reach and the more dogs you'll help!

Here are some "insider" tips that have worked well for me and many other dog trainers.

Getting Started

Visualize your business and what you want to be doing in five years. Your vision should be the foundation of your business plan. Your vision can change, but you need goals to help you get started.

As a new business owner, you'll be faced with a myriad of practical and legal decisions. What type of business will you be—a sole proprietorship, a partnership, or a corporation? Will you be selling just services, or both services and products? Will you need a business license? A sales tax account? Should you buy insurance? Should you have clients sign liability waivers? When do the Yellow Pages come out? The choices you make in these and related areas are critical to the success of your business. Research your options, including the pros and cons of each, and ask for help when you need it.

Image and Marketing

Many people will benefit financially from investing in a good publishing/graphic design software program to help create a unique business image. You can use the software to design your own business cards, brochures, postcards, and Web site (and many programs even include templates for the creatively challenged). Before you buy software, though, consider your aptitude, interest, and hardware capabilities. If writing and designing marketing materials isn't for you, you may want to hire an expert for these tasks.

Create at least one brochure outlining your various services and costs. In addition, you'll save time by having a flyer for each question you are routinely asked. All your brochures and flyers should include your name, logo, phone number, and Web site address. They should all be complementary in color, style, and layout. Nothing looks shabbier than a bunch of hodge-podge flyers from different sources. Use high quality paper for your brochures and have them professionally folded (this is very inexpensive and well worth the cost).

A Web site, while optional, can be helpful if you do it right. It can serve a variety of purposes, including the following:

- Provide information about you.
- Provide overviews and tips on various topics (such as how to housetrain a dog).
- Give class descriptions, times, and locations.
- Provide enrollment forms.
- Keep former clients aware of your services by sending a periodic newsletter.
- Keep track of data.

An excellent reference book for marketing your services is Lisa Wright's book, *How To Market Your Dog Training Business* (Dog Trainers Marketing Resource Center, 1997). Also, I strongly suggest that you set a firm goal of having three referring vets and three referring rescue groups within your first two years of business. These people can keep you busy!

Equipment

A computer is essential. You will save hours by using e-mail rather than the phone, and you'll save money by designing your own marketing materials. A combination fax/scanner/copier/printer will meet many of your communication needs—and take up very little room in your office. Before you buy any office equipment, though, identify your needs and then do some research and comparison shopping. You probably don't need a state-of-the-art computer with a huge hard drive if you'll use it only for basic word processing and your database. Similarly, you probably do want a stand-alone fax machine if you anticipate sending and receiving dozens of faxes each day.

A separate phone line with an answering machine will add to your professional image. Your message should give helpful information about your business, your hours, when you will get back to the caller, and instructions for skipping your introductory message (e.g., "Press *1 to bypass this message").

You'll also need a way to keep track of appointments. I use a Week-at-a-Glance diary, but I know many people who love their Palm Pilots. Your method really doesn't matter, as long as it works.

Client Relations

Professionalism is very important. Returning phone calls and e-mails, doing what you say you will, and following up with clients will go far to earn you a good reputation and recommendations from clients and veterinarians. Use your day planner, wall calendar, or personal digital assistant to make notes of things you need to do.

Refunds can be problematic. Everyone has his or her own policy, usually based on experience. Put your refund policy (e.g., for classes) in the information sheet that your clients fill out and sign. Consider using or creating a client information sheet that includes "conditions of enrollment" such as policies on aggressive dogs, training methods, disruptive behavior, refunds, and liability waivers.

Mental Health

To avoid burnout, you should set aside at least one day a week when you do not have classes or appointments and don't even answer the phone. You need time to re-group, be with your family, and play with your dogs. Don't let yourself get to the point where you can't enjoy your business because you're too busy or too exhausted.

Employees

Employees mean more administrative responsibilities for you, and you must decide if that is what you want. It may be difficult to know when to add an employee to your operation, but you can help make the decision easier by looking at the financial pros and cons.

Let's look at a typical case scenario. You charge $75 an hour for private lessons, and you're thinking about hiring a receptionist at $10 an hour (which is really $12 when you add 20 percent for hidden costs). Would hiring this employee be a good financial move? If you currently spend two hours a day on the phones but could fill that time with private lessons, you'll gain $114 a day even if your receptionist spends three hours doing phone work. Sounds good...as long as you actually teach two more hours of private lessons each day the receptionist works.

Or let's say you teach two one-hour classes per night, but you actually work 3 hours each night. If you teach alone, you can handle six students in each class. Each student pays $12, so your gross income is $72 per class (or $144 per night) and your gross hourly rate is $41.15. If your receptionist is also your assistant trainer, the two of you can handle 10 students in each class—for a gross income of $240 per night. After you pay your assistant $42 for 3 hours of work, your gross income for the evening is $198, or $56.58 per hour. That's a $15.43 increase in your hourly wage. Is it worth it to hire an assistant? Probably yes, as long as you actually get four more students in each class. You should also factor in the time spent in teaching your assistant, expecting that there will be a greater investment of your time at the beginning as you train him or her.

Conclusion

For most of us, dog training is a serious business with a financial bottom line. If you want to join the ranks of dog trainers who are self-employed small business owners, you need to do your homework. Read everything you can—not just about dog training, but about owning a small business. Talk with people who have taken the plunge, and find out what worked for them and what didn't. Work on achieving a balance of visionary dreams and realistic expectations. Learn from your mistakes, celebrate your successes, and always keep an open mind about what you can do to improve your business. Welcome, all of you newcomers, to an exciting, rewarding profession! ❖

When To Ask for Help

Susan Smith, September/October 2002

As a rule of thumb, think about the business-related task you want to accomplish and what needs to be done to accomplish it. If you feel comfortable with and capable of doing it yourself, great. If not, save yourself some frustration and hire an expert.

Remember that if you try to do something yourself and aren't able to get the job done, you'll have spent valuable time, money, and effort—and you may end up hiring an expert anyway!

Here are just a few of the areas in which you'll want to decide whether or not to get expert help:

Attorney. If you have any questions about the safety of your business, your liability, or your personal assets, consult a business attorney. If you want to do something more complex such as incorporate, buy a facility, or even rent a facility, you might also want the advice of a business or contract attorney.

If you need basic forms (such as client contracts), keep in mind that many generic legal forms are available for little or no cost (e.g., most office supply stores carry forms software and hard copy forms, and the Internet is also a great resource). Remember, though, that every state has its own laws and conventions; a contract drawn up in California may not hold water in Louisiana.

Bookkeeper/Accountant. Depending on the volume of your business, you may be able to do your own bookkeeping in just a few hours a month. With the availability of software programs such as Quicken and QuickBooks, it's easier than ever to track your income and expenses. Regardless of the format you use, however, consider taking a course in bookkeeping (not accounting) so you have a basic understanding of the double-entry system.

Although doing your own books gives you a great feel for your business, you might want to hire a bookkeeper if your time is limited and/or you have no aptitude for or interest in numbers. A good bookkeeper will keep you aware of your financial picture and let you know how your money is being spent.

Depending on your situation, it makes sense to hire an accountant to do your taxes. Although software programs such as TurboTax are popular—and many people find them excellent—an accountant can give you individual attention and advice. Tax laws change every year, and an accountant can help you get the maximum allowable deductions for your business.

Design. The design of your business cards, flyers, and brochures projects your professional image. If you are comfortable designing your own collateral materials, that's great; however, get expert help when you need it. For instance, consider hiring a Web design expert for your business Web site. Lots of people can put together a simple Web site, but an expert can include features—such as automated forms, renewal notices, and payment and data collection options—that will help minimize your work load. Before you sign on the dotted line, however, ask to see samples of the expert's work.

Other areas in which you may need or want assistance include office support, custodial services, marketing, expansion, and retail sales. Remember that your needs will change as your business grows—and, most likely, your own time will become more valuable.

Figure out what you want to accomplish, and whether or not you can do it efficiently and effectively. Taking the time to assess your needs and skills will help you determine when to hire professional help. ❖

Dog Training Isn't Rocket Science—But It's Close!

Audrey Schwartz Rivers, September/October 2004

I've held four different careers in my life—journalist, corporate marketer, NASA spokesperson and now, dog professional. Students and novices frequently ask me for advice about how to undertake careers in these respective fields. Interestingly, the answers I give for each profession, albeit with some obvious technical peculiarities, tends to be similar. With nearly 30-years cumulative experience in communications, public relations, and "rocket science," I offer the following advice to beginning trainers.

Read...Read...and Read Some More

- Read everything you can get your hands on about your chosen field—books, consumer and professional publications, research journals, email groups, and web sites.

- Read every dog training book you can find, including both traditional and positive trainers, to compare and contrast methods.

- Check out "dog training for kids" books as they provide simple illustrations that you and, most importantly, your clients can grasp.

- Read books by other animal trainers for ideas that may be applicable to dogs, such as:

  - *The Education of Koko* by Francine Patterson and Eugene Linden.

  - *Next of Kin* by Roger Fouts.

  - *Lads Before the Wind* and *On Behavior* by Karen Pryor.

  - *The Alex Studies* by Irene Maxine Pepperberg.

  - *When Elephants Weep* by Jeffery Moussaieff Masson.

  - *The Parrot's Lament* by Eugene Linden.

  - *The Others: How Animals Made Us Human* by Paul Shepard.

  - Anything by Jane Goodall, Stephen Budiansky, and Marc Bekoff.

- Read books about human behavior including Carl Jung, Erik Erickson, and, yes, even Dr. Phil!

- Read books on management and creativity:

  - *Flawless Consulting: A Guide to Getting Your Expertise Used* by Peter Block.

  - *Managing Change* by Robert Heller.

  - Anything by Roger Von Oech.

- Read what your clients read, especially the classic fiction stories about dogs (because they all want a "Lassie"):

- *Call of the Wild* and *White Fang* by Jack London.

- *Beautiful Joe* by Marshall Saunders.

- *Lassie Come Home* by Eric Knight.

- *Shiloh* series by Phyllis Naylor.

- *Old Yeller* by Fred Gipson.

- *Where the Red Fern Grows* by Wilson Rawls.

- Anything by Albert Payson Terhune, James Herriot, or Richard Adams.

• Read *Walden* and the essay *Life Without Principle* by Henry David Thoreau, which teach nothing about dogs but everything about living well.

Go Where the "Big Leaguers" Play

• Listen to acknowledged experts in the field. Attend their seminars, read their books, network with them, and watch them work.

• Join national and local professional organizations (like APDT). Attend meetings and conferences regularly.

• Volunteer for "grunt work" at agility events, obedience trials, flyball tourneys, Rally-O, "mutt strutts," and other dog events.

• Find a dog that impresses you with both skill and temperament. Inquire about its trainer and the methods used.

• Get a mentor. Get a nemesis. You'll learn as much from each.

Practice...Practice...Practice

• From all your research and observations, select the methods you think will work well for your vision, goals, and ethics as a dog trainer.

• Practice methods that do no harm to you, your clients, or animals—with the knowledge that you *are* a beginner.

• Keep a sharp eye out for what works and what doesn't for you, your clients, and their animals. Understand the reasons why.

Shake Yourself Up Whenever Possible

• Investigate trainers who propose radically different dog training methods. Take the ones that bother you and try them at least once (as long as no person or animal is harmed). Discard the ones, after hands-on experience, that still make you feel uncomfortable, but always understand *why* they do.

• Experiment with "in vogue" training methods and equipment. Do they work for you? Continue until you understand why or why not? Decide whether to stop using the latest training "fad" and go back to your favored practices—or shelve the old and plunge into something fresh.

- Never take someone else's word on what is right or wrong in dog training, or life in general. Do your homework and make an informed judgment based on what is appropriate for *you*.

- Always reserve the right to change your mind.

Empower Failure

- Learn the difference between learning to fail and failing to learn. Humans never would have walked on the moon if we did not blow up a few rockets first.

- Examine your assumptions constantly. Know how fact, opinion, and intuition differ and which you can trust.

- Realize you do not know it all and do not be afraid to say so. The life you save may be your own.

Follow Your Heart

- Discover what aspect of dog training you enjoy most and focus on that.

- Take methods, ideas, and activities that feel best and excite you most. Practice them religiously

- Stop when your training, business, career, or interest becomes a chore. Your apathy negatively affects all around you, especially emotionally sensitive dogs.

- Think of possibilities. What if the "Pet Psychic" really can communicate with animals?

- Reinvent yourself frequently. And if you do that, you can reinvent the world as well. ❖

Understanding Your Costs and Pricing Your Services

Dan McNally, September/October 2002

The accounting side of business is typically not a dog trainer's favorite subject. Most of us decided to pursue the profession of dog training because we like working with dogs, not because we are enamored with numbers. If we wanted to deal with numbers, we would have gone into accounting, right?

Wrong. A dog training business is exactly that—a business. And part of running a business is figuring out how much to charge for your services, what discounts to offer (if any), how to keep track of expenses, how to increase profit margins, etc. Decisions about pricing, budgets, and overall costs might be a "non-fun" aspect of dog training, but they are just as important as the training itself. If you cannot make enough money, you cannot afford to train dogs. Consequently, you may not be able to help as many dogs simply because you are better at dog training than economics.

Deciding what to charge for your training involves many factors—such as what services you offer, what the market will bear, and whether or not you will travel to appointments. You also need to consider your expenses, your tax liability, and your investment of time.

What Will the Market Bear?

One of the first factors you need to identify is how much people will pay for your services. Prices for most products and services will be generally higher in large, metropolitan areas and lower in small, rural areas. But, even with that guideline, setting your prices is not as easy as setting prices for products in the highly visible retail market, where you can visit a number of stores and do a quick comparison of an identical item's cost. Dog training services vary greatly in regard to content, length, materials, degree of owner involvement, and format (e.g., group class, individual class, board and train). So you need to be honest with yourself about what you are offering compared to what others are offering.

Ask yourself some basic questions:

- What are other trainers charging?

- What are they offering for that price?

- Do they offer more than I do?

- Do they offer less than I do?

- How do my services compare to the other trainers in the area?

It may seem appealing—and a good idea, especially at first—to lower your prices to get more business, but you need to be careful. Although lower prices may very well result in more business, you may end up working more hours and earning less than you need or want. After you have assessed your skills and services in comparison to others, be sure to not sell yourself short. Too many part-time trainers do not charge what they are really worth, which can be a major factor in why they are training dogs part-time instead of full-time. This under-pricing is also, in some trainers' opinions, part of the reason our professional services are sometimes undervalued in the market-place. Remember that you are a professional offering a professional service, so charge for it accordingly.

Price Ranges for Your Services

Using information from other trainers across the country, I have compiled a list of different types of training services and price ranges for each. As you research local market rates and carefully assess your skills and services, the price guidelines given below may help you set or change your own rates.

Group Classes

Group classes have a fairly standard structure in regard to popularity, duration, and price. They can easily be broken down into a cost per week that you can multiply by the number of lessons in your program. For example, if the average rate for an eight week class in your area is $80, the weekly fee is $10. So a comparable price for a six week class would be $60. In general, group class prices average between $10 and $20 per hour per student.

Private Classes

Too many trainers tend to set prices for private classes that are too low. Think about how much your time is really worth in a group class. If you run a group class by yourself and if your average group class is six students at $10/hour, that works out to $60/hour for your time. Private lessons generally average one-and-a-half to four-and-a-half times the weekly fee per student, or $15 to $60 per hour if your group rate works out to $10 per hour per student.

There are two basic ways to set up private lessons. You can charge by the hour or charge for a pre-determined group of private lessons. The advantage of offering private lesson packages is that your clients are more likely to return because they have made a greater financial investment.

Special Services

Special services such as aggression and behavior modification training should be charged according to the trainer's expertise and skill level. Many trainers do not offer these types of services, which means you are more valuable if you do offer them. Specialty training costs average from zero to three times the private class rate i.e., $60 to $180 per hour if your private class rate is $60.

Travel Time

Do not discount your driving time if you provide in-home private lessons. You could be training dogs instead of driving, so don't give that time away. Travel charges average one half to 1.5 times the hourly lesson rate i.e., $30 to $90 per hour if your private class rate is $60. Alternatively, you could charge the client a mileage fee (typically $0.30 to $.0.35 per mile).

Board and Train

Board-and-train services can be provided for a set fee (for a certain training level) or a daily fee (until the dog is trained to an expected level). Each option has advantages and disadvantages.

If you charge a set fee and the dog trains very quickly, you need to put out less effort for the same fee. If the dog takes longer than expected, however, you need to expend more effort for the same amount of money.

Charging on a daily basis can also be a double-edged sword. On one hand, the owner can get just what he or she needs and not have to pay for more. On the other hand, if the dog takes a long time to train, you run the risk of appearing as though you are gouging the customer for more money.

Board-and-train prices generally average two-and-a-half to five-and-a-half times the average boarding rate for your area

Supplies and Retail Sales

The basic rule of selling retail is to never buy the items at retail prices—and, if you have to pay retail, look for a better deal. Many suppliers offer wholesale prices or volume discounts (typically six to twelve or more of the same item), either as part of their advertised pricing or upon request. Some suppliers also offer a discount to APDT members. It never hurts to ask for a discount, and you may be surprised at the size of the price break you are offered.

Buying in volume will work to your advantage in the long run, even though you may have to limit your inventory due to your budget. Offer your clients the best equipment and supplies available, and build up your inventory as you can afford to do so.

To set prices for retail items, check out the prices for identical or comparable items at your local pet supply store. Some trainers charge the same as pet stores, and some charge a little less. Depending on the state you live in and how you buy your retail stock, you may have to add sales tax to the price. Be sure to check with an accountant regarding the sales tax laws in your state. If there are no comparison prices, the average mark-up is 50 to 100 percent of your cost.

Calculating the Cost of Running Your Business

The profitability of your business is impacted by your gross income, expenses, taxes, and number of work hours. Let's look at each component individually and then apply our knowledge to a case scenario using Sue, a mythical dog trainer.

Gross Income

Your gross income is the amount of money you are paid to perform services before you deduct expenses and taxes. In Sue's case, she offers an eight-week group class that meets once a week at a cost of $80 per student. She teaches four of those group classes each week, with eight students in each class. So she has a total of 32 students who each pay $80, for an income total of $2,560 every eight weeks (or $1,280 per month). Sue's gross monthly income of $1,280, divided by the 16 hours she spends teaching each month, works out to an hourly rate of $80. Sounds pretty good for Sue, doesn't it? But let's look further.

Expenses

This area is a really big deal! You need to make enough money to cover your expenses, or you cannot survive economically. If you're not aware of all your costs, you may end up wondering why there doesn't seem to be much left over at the end of the month.

Basic costs include, but are not limited to, the following categories:

- **Continuing education/professional affiliations**—Books, videos, seminars, APDT dues, etc.

- **Insurance**—liability, facility rental, homeowners, and auto.

- **Licenses**—business license, kennel license.

- **Marketing and promotion**—design and printing of brochures, business cards, flyers, and other collateral materials; advertising (Yellow Pages, newspaper ads, Web site).

- **Mortgage/rent/utilities**—for home office, business office, training site

- **Office equipment and supplies**—computer hardware and software, printer, fax, phone, camera, and video equipment; paper, pens, three-ring binders; postage.

- **Professional and support services**—lawyer, accountant, bookkeeper, administrative assistant, custodian.

- **Training equipment and supplies**—course handouts; toolbox of toys, leads, clickers.

- **Transportation**—car or van maintenance and repairs; gas.

Let's look at some conservative, yet realistic, monthly expense figures for Sue's business (note that figures have been rounded to the nearest dollar):

- **Continuing education/professional affiliations**—$6 for APDT dues ($75/year) and $75 for continuing education ($900/year).

- **Insurance**—$25 for liability insurance ($300/year); $15 for rental insurance ($180/year).

- **Licenses**—$4 for business license, kennel license ($50/year).

- **Marketing and promotion**—$150 for advertising; $30 for brochures ($360/ year); and $10 for business cards ($120/year).

- **Mortgage/rent/utilities**—$300 for training room rental ($3600/year); $50 for training room utilities ($600/year).

- **Office equipment and supplies**—$10 for cleaning supplies; $5 for postage to mail confirmation letters to students. ($180/year).

- **Professional and support services**—$20 for an accountant ($240/year).

- **Training equipment and supplies**—$20 to print class handouts; $80 for class supplies ($5 per student for clicker, treats, etc.) ($1200/year.)

- **Transportation**—$40 for gas ($480/year).

Sue has a total of $850 per month in expenses.

Taxes

Let's not forget Uncle Sam. For most people, the federal tax rate is 15 percent. Additionally, if you are self-employed, you must pay 15 percent in self-employment tax (this is your Social Security payment). And you may need to pay state and local taxes, too. In Sue's home state of Pennsylvania, for example, state income tax is two percent and local income tax is one percent. Add that up and she's looking at a 33 percent tax liability.

You want to take all the deductions you are entitled to take. If you use a percentage of your home as a training area, you may be able to deduct that percentage of your mortgage and utilities as a business expense. Be aware, however, that any business use of the home higher than five to ten percent may increase the likelihood of an audit. I currently use 25 percent of my home for business purposes, and *I have* been audited. Keep all of your records in order, just in case!

If you use your dogs regularly in your training business, you may be able to deduct their expenses as well. I use my personal dogs for demonstrations, public appearances, to test other dogs, to help socialize other dogs, etc. I am allowed to deduct all my costs for food, veterinary care, and other dog-related expenses for my personal dogs.

Any questions you may have regarding allowable deductions should be directed to your accountant. Having an accountant prepare your taxes is a good idea. He or she will know which expenses are allowed and which are not—and will be of invaluable help if you are audited.

Your Time

Your time counts. *All* your time. You'll want to keep track of all your time because it will help you determine your hourly wage.

Let's assume that, for each of Sue's four classes per week, she spends a total of one hour driving round-trip to the training center, getting ready for class, and cleaning up after class. She also spends four hours per week making phone calls and working on class handouts. So every month she spends 16 hours teaching classes, 16 hours driving and being at the training center, and 16 hours doing prep work. She is devoting 48 hours per month to her dog training business.

Putting It All Together

After you deduct expenses and taxes from your gross income, are you making as much as you want or need to make? Here's how to calculate your real (net) income:

- Figure out your gross income (how much you're getting paid before taxes, expenses, and other deductions).

- Figure out your expenses (and be sure to include all the costs of running your business).

- Figure out your tax rate (Sue's tax rate is 33 percent).

  The basic formula looks like this:
  (Gross Income - Expenses) - Tax Rate Percentage = Real Income.
  In Sue's case, we're looking at the following figures for each month of work:
  ($1280 - $850 = $430) - (33% of $430, or $141.90) = $288 per month.
  And when you divide $288 by the 48 hours Sue works each month, her hourly rate is $6. It doesn't seem like much now, does it?

Increasing Profits

Sue could obviously use a few more dollars in her pocket at the end of the month, and there are various ways to achieve that goal. Sue could consider one or more of the following options:

- Raise her prices.

- Increase her client base.

- Lower expenses.

- Offer more varied programs.

- Find more effective, lower-priced advertising.

- Buy from lower-cost suppliers.

- Train out of her home.

Now that Sue has actual numbers at her disposal, she can begin to make choices that help increase her income and allow her to move toward becoming a full-time dog trainer.

Are you ready to do the same? ❖

The Perils of Pricing Private Training Sessions

Wendy van Kerkhove, September/October 2003

Dan McNally has written an excellent article (see above) on understanding our costs and pricing our services. After rereading the article, I decided to write a complementary piece.

My intention was to write about the issues I struggle with when accepting a private client. First was my inability to manage the client throughout the process efficiently without spending many extra hours on the phone or behind the scenes troubleshooting their problem. Second is the fact that at times, I feel almost mercenary in accepting my client's money. After six article revisions, however, I had a moment of epiphany. My problem is not about client management! It is about my pricing structure and not having a respectable understanding of the value of my time. Yikes!

Determining a Pricing Structure

I charge $75 per hour for private sessions. How did I arrive at that figure? It was the average rate charged by other local trainers and half the hourly rate of the veterinary behaviorist in town. Using this method to determine my hourly rate was *just plain irresponsible*. Ultimately, calculating this rate should involve determining how much money I need to earn each week and how many hours per week I can work. Then there is the consideration of incurred expenses.

When I charge my hourly rate, it is only for the face-to-face time that I spend with the client. However, for each of those hours, there is time spent talking to the person before they become a client. Once I am hired, there is time spent considering the specific issues, developing a treatment protocol, coaching the client through the process, and of course, time traveling to and from the appointment. If the dog has some tricky issues, the amount of time I can spend considering how to fix it can really add up. Once the treatment plan is given to the client, there are often questions as the person implements each step. A client may call me numerous times between each appointment for advice.

If I am going to only charge for "face time," then I must make sure that what I charge for each of those hours covers *all* of the hours spent working behind the scenes. It is imperative that I know the average amount of time spent for each client and the average amount of time I spend traveling to and from each appointment. Only then can I figure out what to charge per hour when we actually meet. I grossly underestimated this calculation. Keep in mind that this calculation only considers my time, not any other expenses that I might incur, such as advertising, printing, postage, paper, and liability insurance. These expenses must be considered when I determine my annual earnings goal.

Thus what I originally perceived as poor client management was not that at all. Part of delivering good service involves being a good coach, offering encouragement along the way, and keeping the client on track. If this takes three hours of my time for each hour that I spend with them, so be it. My goal, however, is to be paid for my time, knowledge, and effort.

Pricing and Guilt

The next problem was more insidious than the incorrect pricing of my services. In a word, it is about guilt. I deal with owners whose dogs have allegedly shown aggression to other dogs. Often, it is evident that in all probability the person is completely overreacting to and misinterpreting their dog's behavior. A combination of poor leash handling skills and a nervous, uneducated owner is really at the crux of the problem. Most of these clients do not understand dog social interactions and do not realize their dog, in all probability, only wants to go and greet the other dog, not tear his head off. When dealing with these clients, I often find myself thinking that taking their money to show them that their dog is fine is wrong.

Well, I am over this now. Why? For two reasons: first, because time is money, and I invested time and effort in this client. Second, because the client is usually overjoyed to see that his dog might be okay. I had to do a paradigm shift when dealing with these types of situations. Just because the dog is ultimately fine, the owner still needs to learn how to interpret his dog's actions and how to handle his dog in a variety of situations when the dog is on leash. Dog training is, after all, human training.

The most important lesson that I have learned from this is that time is a limited and valuable resource. Calculating what my time is worth, and making sure that I am fairly compensated, will keep me in business and allow me to continue to help clients in need. It is not my place to judge which clients truly need my help—that is a decision for the client to make. ❖

Liability Protection

Doug Johnson, September/October 2002

With all the hats we wear as dog trainers, it is easy to forget about the legal aspects of operating a dog training business. And, even if we think about that area of our business, many of us don't have the resources and time to analyze all the legal issues involved in training dogs.

This article provides you with an overview of liability protection as it relates to dog training. There are three general areas to consider: entity formation, insurance, and waivers.

Entity Formation

There are three basic types of business entities:

- Sole proprietorships (which operate as DBAs or "doing business as" entities)

- Limited liability companies (LLC)

- Subchapter S corporations

There are several considerations when determining which entity to use including tax consequences and setup/maintenance. Of lesser consideration, but still important, is the available body of relevant statutory and case law.

Proper entity formation generally protects you from personal liability for business-related debts. With that in mind, nobody in the dog training business should be a sole proprietorship/DBA. Although DBAs cost the least amount of money to start because they usually do not involve drawing up legal documents, they offer no protection from personal liability.

A much better option is the limited liability company (LLC) because it does what its name indicates: it limits your personal liability. Most states now allow LLCs to be formed by only one person, so if that is the case in your state, then all you need to do is file Articles of Organization.

Corporations are extremely statutorily driven and their bylaws must include a multitude of legal requirements, so you'll probably need the assistance of an attorney if you choose to incorporate your business. The primary benefit of becoming a Subchapter S corporation is that you pay no corporate income taxes; however, you may be required to pay state income taxes.

Insurance

Insurance is actually more important than any other aspect of your business. You must have insurance if you are going to train dogs! Entity formation will not protect you from suits brought under actual or perceived negligence.

Waivers

The definition of negligence and the validity of waivers you might ask a client to agree to will vary by state. You want to make sure your waivers will stand up in court. Even states with an exculpatory bar (i.e., being without fault, blame, or responsibility) usually have an analytical process to determine if the waiver language is valid.

In Kentucky, for example, the test analyzing a waiver would look at the following information:

- Voluntary signing of the release.

- Equal bargaining power of the parties.

- Public interest in the activity.

- Recreational nature of the activity.

- Knowledge and familiarity of Plaintiff with activity.

The bottom line is that waivers should be drafted or at least reviewed by an attorney. The review isn't to ensure that you aren't waiving too much; rather, it ensures that you are waiving everything you can. If it's illegal or too exculpatory, let the other party prove it.

Consider the liability waivers of huge businesses, ski resorts, and theme parks. They don't say, "Our state laws say we can't waive willful or wanton negligence, so we'll leave that out." They waive everything on earth and in the stars, and they do it for a reason: to cover themselves in all imaginable situations. You should do the same.

Conclusion

No matter what type of dog training you do, you can't afford to be without liability insurance. Along with good insurance, you should set yourself up as a proper limited liability entity and use waivers for all training. ❖

Internships: Training the Trainer

Mardi Richmond, Published in three parts, September/October 2002

PART I

Internships? Instructor courses? Dog training schools? Options abound for learning the art of professional dog training. But which options should new trainers consider? And how can experienced trainers help? Can assisting new trainers benefit a training business? Or will it simply create more competition in an already competitive field? This article explores these questions and provides thoughts for trainers who are considering participating in or offering an internship program.

A quick survey of any group of professional dog trainers will reveal the multitude of ways people learn the art of dog training—and the skills needed to teach dog training to others. With choices that include informal apprenticeships with local trainers, reading books and self-study, working in shelters, and formal apprenticeships, internships and schools, there is no single path for a newcomer to follow. For those of us who are new to training as a profession, muddling our way through the options—and evaluating each one— can be a truly daunting task. As one new trainer described it, "You need the drive of a Border Collie and the tenacity of a pit bull just to figure out how to learn this trade."

Because the APDT continues to push for professional standards, some of the vagueness and uncertainty is dissipating. Opportunities such as the Certified Pet Dog Trainer Program (CPDT) help clarify the skills needed and valued within the profession. As trainers take advantage of certification, the career path will undoubtedly become clearer and increasingly formalized. This has become a critical time for trainers, new and experienced alike, to evaluate the pros and cons of the various options available for training the trainer. Several of the most valuable options fall into the category of internships.

Internships Defined

The term "internship" is used broadly to describe a variety of training opportunities. In fact, when I surveyed trainers and training schools, the use of the term was so varied that it was difficult to pinpoint a single definition. An internship generally refers to the opportunity for a newer trainer to work under and learn theory and technique from a more experienced or master trainer. Internships most often provide some type of formal instruction, coupled with hands-on practice. They can be long term, such as apprenticeships, or short term, often labeled instructor training courses. Programs offered through training academies or schools may also be considered internships.

Long term internships. Long term internships are very closely related to apprenticeships. One trainer who has worked with new trainers both as apprentices and interns said that the only real difference in her mind is that an intern starts off with some experience in dog training, where as an apprentice generally has no experience.

Long term internships can be informal arrangements or formalized programs. Like apprenticeships, they provide new trainers with a foundation of experience. An informal internship may be offered as a work exchange, for example, where the intern assists with classes or provides other support services in exchange for being taught the business. In formal programs, a trainee may pay a set fee to intern with a master trainer for a specified number of hours, days, or weeks. Fees for formal programs generally range from several hundred to several thousand dollars or more, depending on the length of the program.

Short term internships (a.k.a. instructor training courses). Instructor training courses are generally a short term "crash course" type of internship. Best suited for trainers with some experience, instructor training courses usually range from one to two weeks. Costs vary, but average from $100 to $150 a day. Instructor training courses and internships often offer the opportunity for people to train, however briefly, with some of the most respected trainers in the industry.

Training academies and schools. A cross between long term internships and short term internships, training academies and schools often provide foundations in both learning theory and hands-on experience. A good option for trainers with little or no experience, they provide a more extensive foundation than may be gained from one or two week programs. They are also a good opportunity for trainers who have gained knowledge through more casual avenues, such as self-study, to formalize their education. Academies and schools generally range from six weeks to six months and can cost thousands of dollars.

Internship Pros and Cons

Working long term with an experienced trainer—especially one whose philosophies and methods align with yours—provides the ultimate opportunity for any new trainer. Long term internships and apprenticeships can provide in-depth exposure to all aspects of the training business. Unfortunately, many novice trainers do not have access to a top quality trainer who is willing to take on an intern or apprentice. For those of us who do not have an experienced trainer in our neighborhood, the intensive short courses and dog trainer academies offer reasonable alternatives.

One to two week programs are a good option for trainers who need to continue working while learning new skills. A trainer can take a defined period off work—vacation time from his or her day job, for example—and attend for one or two weeks, which may be more realistic for trainers who are already running their own training business. In addition, the short courses allow trainers, both new and experienced, the chance to study with people they might otherwise not have the opportunity to learn from.

Longer internships through academies or schools, those that run from six weeks to six months, will obviously provide more in-depth experience. However, they may be less of an option for people with financial, family, or community responsibilities that limit their ability to leave work or home for long periods.

One important note: Programs with defined timelines, whether one week or six months, may get a new trainer started and provide continuing education for an experienced trainer. But they are only one piece of larger education. It can take three years or longer of intensive study and practice to become a good novice trainer. It can take ten or twenty years to gain the experience needed to be a master trainer.

More for Your Money

Advantages and disadvantages also arise between formal and informal opportunities. For example, one of the questions when considering an informal internship or apprenticeship is: Will a new trainer appreciate an opportunity for which he or she is not paying a fee?

Informal internships certainly can be successful. At one time or another, many well-respected trainers worked with more experienced trainers in an informal setting. An informal internship can provide a win-win situation; the student can learn skills needed to become a trainer, and the teacher can gain valuable assistance with classes or other business tasks. But informal training opportunities with well-respected trainers are not easy to find.

PART II

Searching for an Internship Program

An Internet search of dog training internships, instructor courses, academies, and schools will provide you with a multitude of internship options. Some offer wonderful opportunities. From others, you will want to run away—and fast!

How will you know the difference? Ask the following questions:

1. Do the training methods and philosophy of the trainer or program match your own? Ask specifically about the teaching methods. Listen for what is *not* said, as well as what is said. Quiz the trainers on how they would train a specific behavior or how they would handle an uncooperative dog. Ask for recommended reading lists or examples of their written materials.

2. How much will it cost? What exactly will you get for your money? Program fees vary, but most average $100 to $150 a day. Ask if the fees include books, supplies, and other learning materials? How about time working with dogs? Time working with people? Are there any extras or hidden costs?

3. What topics will be covered? What specifically will be taught? Will you be getting in-depth information? Be careful of programs that promise more than seems reasonable for the length of the internship.

4. How much time will the program demand? Instructor courses can run from one week to eight weeks or longer. While you are doing the internship, will you continue to work and meet other demands in your life? Will that be realistic?

5. Will the program offer hands-on training? Will you have the opportunity to work with a variety of dogs and/or people through this program, or will you be primarily observing?

6. Will the trainer be available to answer questions after the program is completed? While it is not realistic to expect long-term mentoring from a one-week class, the trainer should be available to answer questions about topics covered in the course.

7. How will this program fit into your overall learning and educational experience? Will this particular program provide you with the type of educational experience you need right now? Is the information at the appropriate level for you? A program could be too basic or too advanced.

8. If you are considering a long-term internship, do you think you and the trainer are a good match? Do you think you'll be able to take instruction from this person? Do you like his or her communication style? For a long-term program, it is especially important to take your time to find a trainer you respect and who respects you. If you are unsure of a program or person's credentials or qualifications, consider the following:

- Ask people you trust. Do they know of this program or trainer? What have they heard? Do they think it will be a good match for you?

- Talk to people who have gone through the program (the trainer may give you names of people who have completed it). You might ask about an alumni list or e-mail list so you can do your own research.

- Call the Better Business Bureau in the city in which the program is offered. Find out if there have been any complaints filed. Check with other unaffiliated sources such as the local humane society or a local veterinarian.

PART III

Launching an Internship Program

If you would like to launch an internship program, here are some questions you should ask yourself:

- What do you hope to gain from offering an internship program? Income? New employees? Expanding your reputation? Promoting humane training methods?

- What will you offer an intern? What are your areas of expertise? How will you build a program around the things that you know and do best?

- How much time and energy do you want to invest in the program? Will spending time on internships detract from other aspects of your business or personal life?

- Would you prefer to work one-on-one with new trainers? Or would you be more comfortable providing group instruction? Each has its advantages. Working one on-one with a new trainer gives you the opportunity to share in-depth information and to really get into the nitty-gritty of training in a way that is difficult in a group environment. Group classes, however, can help you reach a greater number of people.

- Given the amount of time you want to invest, how many interns can you realistically serve? Will you offer ongoing support to those who study with you? If so, how will you provide that support and how will it affect your time in the future?

- What specific services or learning experiences will you offer interns? The clearer you are about what you are offering, the more likely that your interns will receive the education they expect—and the more likely they will be happy with the experience.

- How will you decide who will be eligible for your program? Will you screen potential interns? What if you end up working with an intern who does not have the ability or talent for the job? How will you handle it? How will it reflect on your internship program or on you as a trainer?

- How will you measure success? Will you give written tests? Evaluate practical or hands-on skills? Ask for pro-gram evaluations from your interns?

- How will you bring students into your program? How will you advertise or spread the word about the program?

Teaching others requires a real commitment. When you are charging people to train with you as interns, you must provide them real value for their tuition fees. Keep in mind that you will need to teach people not only how to make dogs perform desired behaviors, but also the how and the why of dog learning and behavior.

Formal programs, whether long-term internships or short-term courses, may afford additional advantages. A formal program may be better defined, covering specific aspects of training and the business of training. The new trainer will have an idea of what he or she will gain from participating. In addition, the fees charged provide the master trainer with financial compensation in exchange for time and expertise.

Master Trainers Wanted

Let's face it, those of us who are new to training simply couldn't do it without the help of those of us who are more experienced. We need master trainers—people with experience, knowledge, and the ability to communicate both—to teach the profession of dog training. But aside from helping new trainers, taking on interns may offer additional benefits for the master trainer.

Sharing your knowledge and skills with other trainers is a powerful way to promote humane training methods.

Teaching new trainers can also help you become fired up about training. The enthusiasm of new-comers is contagious. Successful short course internships can bring in income and help build your reputation. If you charge for long-term internships, you will benefit both from a financial perspective and because the personalized attention of your interns will provide your students with a better class experience. And, if you are interested in expanding your business, interns give you a pool of quality people to consider for future hire.

Will training others create undo competition in an already competitive profession? Many trainers believe there is plenty of room in the dog training community for more good, positive trainers. It is possible that training trainers in your immediate community can lead to some competition.

But they can also create demand. The more trainers who provide humane training options, the more the general population will look for positive trainers.

Offering internships can be good for a training business, for the field of humane dog training, and certainly for the new trainer seeking guidance. ❖

Special thanks to Pat Miller, Peaceable Paws Dog and Puppy Training; Valerie Pollard, Valerie Pollard Dog Training; and Margaret Hughes, Magohn's Positive Paws Dog Training for their feedback, thoughts, and insights in preparing this article.

Thinking about Adding Board and Train To Your Services?

Dan McNally, September/October 2004

What is board and train? It is keeping your client's dog, training the dog, and then returning the dog to the owner. There are some things to consider if you are thinking about adding board and train to your training programs.

Although some trainers are of the opinion that board and train does not work, as someone who does it, I can tell you that it does work as long as the owner continues your training at home. Problems occur when the behaviors are not trained well enough or practiced, and the owner does not understand what they need to do to maintain it.

Some things work well on a board and train basis and some things may not work so well. New behaviors generally transfer easily to the owner. Issues that are a product of the dog/owner relationship can be more difficult to address on a board and train basis. Issues like loose leash walking, separation anxiety, and resource guarding do not always transfer well. Although these things may not transfer well, you can still teach new things like heel, giving up objects, and being alone strategies that can be incorporated at home to continue working on those problems.

The most important part of board and train is when the owner picks the dog up. Unless the owner completely understands what you have done and knows how to continue the training at home, the dog will likely regress to where it started. It is also important to offer follow up lessons as the owner needs them.

When the owners drop their dog off, I give them all of my training information so they can go over it while their dog is here, making things easier for them to understand when they pick up their dog. During my pick-up session, I go over everything I did with their dog and make sure the owner understands what I have done and is able to work their dog themselves.

Why Use Board and Train Over Private Lessons?

Training is a mechanical skill that some owners do not possess. Board and train can give them a big head start as they can skip the beginning steps of the training that they may have problems with, whereas they can handle the maintenance part.

Some owners really do not have a lot of time or the consistency to train their dog. Some owners are at their rope's end with their dog and just getting the dog out of the house for a few weeks can do wonders to help them reset the relationship and like their dog again. Another reason I often hear for wanting board and train is because the owners are going on vacation and need to board the dog anyway.

Set Up

A board and train set up can be anything from dogs being in a large, traditional kennel to a trainer keeping one dog in their home for training. Personally, I feel the most efficient way of doing a board and train is to replicate a normal home life as much as possible.

You need to decide what you will train while you have the dog. What behaviors will you want to install, to what degree, and how long will it take you to finish the training? It can be designed as one program for a specified length of time or more than one program with different lengths of time and with different expectations. There can be different programs for specific issues like housetraining.

Other Considerations

There are a few other things to consider if you want to offer a board and train program. If you intend to have the dog in your home, do you have the room for another dog for a few weeks, including room for a crate if you need one? Is your house set up to easily allow access to the outside for potty breaks or a fenced yard for exercise or the time to walk an extra dog?

Having a board and train dog interact with your own dogs can do wonders for socialization, provided your own dogs do not have dog issues. However, if there are too many dogs coming in and out of your house, it might burn out your own dogs as far as them not wanting to interact with other dogs as much as they used to.

You may need to obtain a kennel license. In some states you need to obtain a kennel license even if you only have one dog stay at your home for one day. You also need to see if your liability insurance will cover a client's dog in your home.

What to Charge

Board and train services can be provided for a set fee (for a certain training level) or a daily fee (until the dog is trained to an expected level). Each option has advantages and disadvantages.

If you charge a set fee and the dog trains very quickly, you need to put out less effort for the same fee. If the dog takes longer than expected, however, you will need to put more effort out for the same amount of money.

Charging on a daily basis can also be a double-edged sword. On the one hand, the owner can get just what they need and not have to pay for more. On the other hand, if the dog takes a longer time to train, you run the risk of the appearance that you are gouging your client for more money.

According to a pricing survey I conducted with trainers, board and train prices generally average two-and-a-half to five-and-a-half times the average boarding rate for your area. ❖

Dogs in Day Care: Who Are the Best Candidates?

Danette Wells, January/February 2002

Editor's note: Dog day care owner and operator Danette Wells drew on her own experiences and also conducted an informal survey of dog day care centers to compile information for this article. The day care facilities she surveyed ranged from small centers with 12 dogs to large centers with 70 dogs.

Dog day care is not appropriate for every dog. While it provides a valuable service, day care can be detrimental to some dogs because of its high-stimulation, high-stress environment. Thus, it is important for day care owners to understand the limitations of the day care environment and which types of dogs are the best candidates. This basic knowledge, accompanied by appropriate screening, knowledgeable staff, and owner education, will help ensure the safety and happiness of the participating dogs.

As we make generalizations about dog behaviors and breeds—not only in this article, but in our daily work with dogs and in discussions with others—we should make note of and recognize their limitations. Generalizations are helpful, but they are not adequate substitutes for hands-on observation and assessment of a particular dog. Just as there are exceptions to every rule, there are undoubtedly dogs who break the mold of their stereotypes.

What's Good About Dog Day Care?

- **Learning socialization.** Young dogs (under two years of age) can develop excellent social skills and manners. Some breeds that typically exhibit dog-dog problem behavior—such as Shar Peis and Chow Chows—benefit greatly from day care if introduced to that environment at four to six months of age.

- **Learning appropriate play.** I have seen exuberant dogs learn to tailor their play (literally lying down) in order to play with a smaller or shyer dog.

- **Getting exercise.** Regular exercise can help minimize normal but unwanted behaviors such as jumping, chewing, barking, and digging. An added benefit is that clients generally pick up a calm, manageable dog from day care, rather than coming home to an overexcited dog who has been understimulated all day.

What's Not Good About Dog Day Care?

- **Limitations on control of the dogs.** The dogs' human supervisor at the day care has no real physical control over the dogs. The supervisor can use voice control and water squirt bottles, but both methods may be ineffective and may only temporarily halt unwanted behaviors. The human supervisor must also be adept at using positive reinforcement methods.

- **Potential loss of clients.** Day care is not appropriate for every dog, which can be a difficult position to explain to a prospective client. The hard part is not the loss of business, but the sense of having failed both the dog and the client.

- **Overstimulation.** Some clients do not want their dog to rest at all during the day (people want the most for their money!), but dogs do need rest time. My facility includes a separate "quiet room" with crates and beds that dogs can always access. Some dogs will nap on their own, while others need structured "time outs."

The Screening Process

Prior to acceptance to my day care, all dogs must meet certain requirements—including being spayed/neutered, being vaccinated according to veterinarian specifications, and not being toy or food protective to an unmanageable extent.

All the facilities that responded to my survey do some type of evaluation, but the extent varies from a phone interview with a trial visiting day to extensive evaluations and trial periods. I conduct an evaluation in which I meet with the dog during off-hours so he or she can become acquainted with the environment without being bombarded with the other attendees. I also have at least one other non-threatening, well-socialized dog present to get an idea of the prospective dog's reactions to others.

During the evaluation, I use basic cues to assess the dog's level of training. Although I do not require basic training of my day care dogs (nor does any facility I surveyed), the following cues are helpful for the dog to know:

- **Wait.** There is a picket fence enclosure inside the front door of my facility where the dogs must sit and wait when first entering the day care. When your ten best dog pals are clamoring inside for you, sitting and waiting is not an easy task—but the reward is exceptional.

- **Leave it.** This cue is helpful in numerous situations, especially in fight prevention. Often I can spot a dog do what I call "tailing"—constantly following another dog, sidling up to him or her, hovering, striking dominant postures, etc. Simply saying "leave it" to a dog who understands the cue has prevented many tailing incidents from escalating.

- **Out/drop it.** One of my regulars is a dog so responsive to this cue that I always hope she's the dog who ends up with the "whatever" in her mouth. On cue, she consistently drops any item from her mouth (including food), whether or not she is surrounded by other dogs.

- **Stay/quiet.** The dog's responsiveness to these basic cues would make the lives of day care owners much less stressful!

(continued)

Good Candidates

Dogs do well in day care if they generally fit the following profile:

- They are under two years of age; or they are well-socialized, easy-going adult dogs who like to play.

- They often belong to the family of sporting breeds (retrievers, spaniels, pointers, etc.). Sporting breeds—who tend to be friendly, social types with high exercise requirements—seem to adapt most easily and benefit the most from the day care experience. Sporting types can be hyperactive, however, so rest periods are essential.

  - They have had some basic training and are familiar with basic cues.

Poor Candidates

My survey elicited varied responses regarding which types of dogs—as characterized by breed, age, personality, etc.—tend to do poorly in day care. A summary of those characteristics is as follows:

- **Herding breeds.** These dogs, who typically require structured activity, tend to spend the majority of their time at day care trying to control the other dogs' activities. Herders also have a tendency to be overly protective of toys. In general, there is usually too much chaos in this environment for the herding dog.

Note: Several survey respondents indicated that age, not breed, seems to play the biggest role in a dog's acceptance of the day care environment. I agree with that observation, having experienced that many "difficult" breeds, namely working breeds (e.g., Mastiffs, Rottweilers, Huskies) and some non-sporting breeds (e.g., Chow Chows, Shar Peis, Shiba Inus) do well when started in day care at a young age.

- **Dogs with high arousal tendencies.** Pit bulls, Rottweilers, and some terriers (and mixes thereof) seem to be the best examples of this type of dog. These are the dogs who go after anything in their path when there is any type of disruption in the environment, namely entrances or exits of any other dog or human. Some of these dogs do well if removed (crated or put in another room) when someone new comes into the environment.

I have had success with some of these dogs if they know (and follow consistently) a "leave it" cue. If not removed or strictly voice controlled, these dogs can get "amped" and the result is usually high-arousal, redirected aggression toward the closest dog. You do not want these dogs in this environment unless your day care staff is experienced.

- **Dogs with toy or food guarding tendencies.** While friendly competition and games of chase with toys are normal and fun, it is imperative that no dog is protective to the point of fighting over a toy or food.

- **Intact males or females**. Be cautious about males who were neutered late, usually after maturity (between two and four years of age). These dogs tend to behave like intact males and have trouble or start trouble with other males (whether neutered or intact).

- **Dogs with true separation anxiety.** Many owners of such dogs think the solution is to expose the dogs to other people and dogs when the owner is away. This doesn't work. These dogs are usually attached to a specific person and, consequently, still display severe anxiety in day care (panting, pacing, whining, etc.). They cannot be consoled or distracted by other people or dogs. They seem blind to the activities around them and are usually focused on finding an escape route.

- **Some older dogs.** For some older dogs, the day care environment is too stressful. If there is a separate space/room for these dogs to get away from the younger dogs, many do well. The question here is: Does the dog enjoy this environment, or is he or she at day care simply to relieve the owner's guilt? Keep in mind, however, that many older dogs do really well in day care. They are relaxed, play games with the other dogs, and have fun. Such dogs are a much needed asset in regard to fairly and appropriately correcting younger dogs and teaching them good dog skills.

Tips for a Successful Day Care Environment

Here are some general suggestions concerning the day care's operation:

- **Gather and use information from the owner.** Since many dogs know different words for different actions, it is important to have each owner document his or her dog's cues and descriptions on the day care application—and for the day care supervisor to know those cues.

- **Encourage participation in obedience classes and other types of training.** We offer obedience classes and private training at our facility, and I strongly urge my clients to attend at least the basic obedience course. There is an obvious difference between dogs who are worked on a consistent basis and those who are not.

- **Maintain a well-educated staff.** It is extremely important to have a staff knowledgeable in dog behavior, especially canine body language. Dog play can sometimes look extreme, even violent to people who are not familiar with normal dog behavior, and I've seen people intervene at inappropriate times. I have seen people reprimand and even correct an older, higher-ranking dog from disciplining a younger (usually adolescent) lower-ranking dog, thereby confusing both dogs. I have seen very few actual fights where blood has been drawn, but I have seen hundreds of episodes of normal canine spats or what I like to refer to as a dog getting "told off" by another dog for his inappropriate or rude behavior. Staff members must be able to tell the difference between normal and inappropriate (or potentially dangerous) behaviors. It is simply not enough just to have a love of dogs; the staff must understand them.

And here are some suggestions regarding the dogs:

- **Accept dogs of varied ages.** A playgroup with only ten-month-olds would be a disaster. Older, higher-ranking dogs (who are well-socialized and fair) are needed to dole out corrections when necessary. They do a much better job of effectively and appropriately correcting than any human I've ever seen.

- **Accept both males and females.** The only serious fights I have seen in this environment have been male/male or female/female. Scuffles and fights generally occur among dogs close in status (age, size, and sex) or when a persistent lower-ranking dog is constantly testing a higher-ranking dog for position and will not back down when corrected.

- **Implement a policy of nap times.** Some dogs will become tired and cranky (and less tolerant of others) unless crated for a nap. Almost all of the surveyed day care facilities used "time outs" of various lengths (depending on the dog) to calm the dogs and curb unwanted behaviors.

- **Establish a policy of maximum attendance.** For most dogs, attending day care two or three days a week is optimal. More than three days is simply too much stimulation for most dogs. Varying the dog's activities with leashed walks or shorter off-leash exercising on non-day care days seems ideal for the majority of dogs.

- **Separate dogs into smaller groups as needed.** Most facilities have 10 to 12 dogs per human supervisor. Try to separate dogs by temperament, personality, and activity level, rather than by size. ❖

Marketing Basics

Valerie Barrette, September/October 2002

You got into this business to work with dogs, because you like dogs and you want to help people like their dogs better. Toward that end, you spend time getting yourself better educated by attending seminars, reading books, and discussing ideas and techniques with other trainers.

But how do dog owners discover you so they can hire you? It's time to take off your bait pouch and put on your marketing hat!

Even if business is pretty good, you still need to put a lot of energy into marketing. Why? Because the people you are helping now won't always need you. Sure, they may refer you, but relying on past client referrals only is a risky venture if you are trying to make a living. You need to get your name out there.

Who Is Your Target Market?

Can you describe your target market? Obviously, the average dog owner needs to know about you. But is that where you are going to spend your marketing time and dollars—notifying dog owners of your existence? The dog owner who sees a newspaper article or advertisement may not need your services now. And if he needs you in the future, will he remember your name?

Your marketing efforts will be better served by targeting the pet industry: veterinarians, groomers, and the nice man who sells the dog food. Your information onslaught has a much better chance of being remembered by a pet professional who can recommend you with authority. The best type of referral is multiple: first the veterinarian gives your card to someone, then that guy sees your flyer at the feed store, then his tennis coach mentions that his puppy is currently in your class and doing great. You're practically a shoo-in!

So what are the marketing tools available to you? There are many, ranging from cold calls, direct mailings, flyers, and Yellow Pages advertising to public speaking and writing articles that set you up as an expert.

Yellow Pages Advertising

People looking for service providers use this resource regularly. Yellow Pages advertising requires that you have a business line, and that your existing personal line can be converted to a business line if needed. You pay an initial set-up fee, higher rates than for your personal line, and your outgoing calls may be metered. A business line entitles you to a single line listing in both the White and Yellow pages, as well as a listing in Directory Assistance (411). A larger ad can be obtained for an additional fee.

Flyers/Signs

Posting flyers can get your name in front of the public. Placing flyers in areas frequented by dog owners works the best, although locations where people linger (e.g., waiting areas, laundromats) are also good. Keep your flyers updated and neat, and always ask the business owner's permission to post them. If you send flyers as part of a direct mail campaign, you can get your information out to veterinarians and other pet professionals without spending time and legwork placing them at those locations yourself.

Cold Calls

While walk-in cold calls are a great way to make eye contact with people, it is difficult to gauge whether your arrival is convenient. The groomer who is trying to get a dog done for an early pickup, or the veterinary staff that is trying to cover lunches while surgeries are performed, may be less than thrilled to see you. Bringing cookies or the makings of root beer floats can certainly help thaw the ice, but calling ahead and making an appointment may be a better recipe for success.

Public Speaking/Article Writing

If you offer free seminars on housetraining or write an article for the local paper on choosing a puppy, you can set yourself up as an expert. Speaking at a local dog club or running an "Ask the Trainer" booth at the yearly Adopt-a-thon can also provide you with free publicity and establish credibility. Be sure to request an acknowledgment from the organization to keep in your portfolio.

Web Site

A well-organized and maintained Web site can function as your brochure. Prospective clients can view upcoming classes and schedules, as well as learn about your training style and services. Having information available on common dog training issues, a list of recommended reading, and a link to your e-mail address make a Web site a low-cost way to market your business. ❖

How an Urban Legend Can Jumpstart Your Business

Teoti Anderson, September/October 2004

Have you heard about those famous cookies? They're an urban legend…some say it all started with Mrs. Fields™, some say Nieman-Marcus™. The story goes that a woman visited a restaurant and loved the cookies so much, she asked for the recipe. The employee said she could share it for a fee.

The fee seemed reasonable, so the woman gave the employee her credit card, and she received the coveted recipe. When her credit card bill came, she was appalled to realize she had misunderstood the amount—by several decimal points! So in a rage, she decided to share the recipe with the world, in retaliation for what she thought was an inflated price.

The story is a myth. But the cookie recipe? It's delicious! What does this have to do with dog training? Well, you'll discover that when it comes to drawing attention to your business, people respond just as well to cookies as your canine clients do!

Feed Them and They Will Come

Reward-based trainers know that food is the fastest way to a dog's brain. Food is also an excellent lure for veterinary support staff and the media—all important people who can dramatically increase your business. The difference is the timing. With dogs, you reward the behavior. When marketing to people, sometimes you have to give the reward first to get the behavior!

Who do you think the veterinary receptionist will remember best? The trainer who comes in, tacks a flyer on a bulletin board and leaves? Or the one who drops off a warm batch of fresh-baked cookies for the staff…then personally hands her a stack of business cards? Cards that she'll happily hand to clients who ask for a dog trainer recommendation!

It sounds simple, but it's a powerful marketing technique often overlooked by trainers. We're the first to pack our pockets with a myriad of treats for the finickiest of our canine clients, but we never think to "treat" the people we need to improve our business.

Take the media, for example. I used to work in radio, and each year the morning personalities would joyfully announce the launch of the annual Girl Scouts' cookie drive. They would rave on and on, lovingly describing each tasty treat. All free advertising for the little girls in green. How did those smart young ladies get such a valuable, cost-effective ad campaign? They brought backpacks full of cookies each year to the radio station! The disc jockeys found it easy to extol the virtues of the cookies—especially since they were chomping on them behind the microphone.

Here's an insider tip: disc jockeys are not the highest rung of the radio ladder. The salespeople are—they make money off of advertising sales, which pays the bills. While most radio listeners think their local personalities are basking in the glory of fame, they often don't get the respect they deserve at the station itself. But they're the ones who are the voice of the station—the voice that can reach your potential clients!

Bring the morning on-air folks a basket of cookies, along with a thank you note for keeping you company on your morning drive and a brief write-up about your business. Who knows? They may even invite you to sit in on a show sometime!

The next time you're trying to get media coverage for a special event, try the same technique at your local television stations. Sure, you can fax them a press release, but it'll get lost in the piles of press releases that litter the newsroom. Instead, buy a new, large dog bowl. Fill it with fresh cookies, and wrap it in colored cling wrap (you can get different colors at the grocery store these days). Use bright ribbon to attach a cover note and your press release to the package—and you've just created a simple lure to grab a reporter's attention!

Recipe for Success

Now you've got to keep their attention with effective marketing communications. Most importantly, why should they pay attention to you? Always remember—the answer to that question does not begin with you—it begins with your audience.

You may be the most educated, experienced trainer in your area, but what does that mean to a reporter or a client? You can roll out your credentials like slides from summer vacation, but you'll lose your audience if you don't introduce, early on, what's in it for them. Will they care if you were valedictorian of the Imperial Dog Trainer's Academy of Famousness class of '02? Only if you tell them up front that you can help stop their puppy from peeing in the house! Always focus on what your audience wants—and then how you're the best trainer to give it to them.

When You Have to Make Substitutions

What if you're not a baker? Find a local bakery or doughnut shop to keep you in supply. Fill those promotional dog bowls with candy and you'll still be a hit! Other popular bowl fillers are pens and notepads featuring your logo and contact information. At vet's offices, clients are always walking off with their pens, so receptionists often appreciate a new supply. And if it ends up in the pocket of a puppy owner, that works just fine!

What if you're not a good writer? Hire someone who is, because your marketing materials can make or break your business. If you have a tight budget, check the local journalism college for advertising students eager to add to their portfolios. Consider hiring an editor if you write your materials yourself—typos and grammatical errors in your communications do not leave a good impression!

Presentation is Everything

You wanted to learn more about your profession, so you joined the APDT. Want to learn more about writing and marketing? Check out your local university or community college for courses. There are also government educational resources for small businesses—try visiting www.sba.gov. And when you start attracting clients in droves and the media is beating down your door, don't forget to mention the APDT! ❖

Creating a Web Site for Your Dog Training Business

Stacy Braslau-Schneck, September/October 2004

It's the 21st century, and more and more people are searching the Internet to find information, products, and services. You want potential clients to find your business, and be motivated to hire you.

A web site is cheap, effective advertising. Web hosting (getting someone to display your web page on the Internet) can cost as little as $20 per year or may even come free with the e-mail address you already have; registering a domain name (www.yourname. com) is as low as $10 per year, which is cheaper than most Yellow Pages listings. A web site can be very effective as well. About 40% of my clients find me through web page searches, and about 90% of my clients find out my class descriptions and schedule through my web site schedule and even register on-line, saving me hours of telephone and mailing time. (Of course, I live in the heart of Silicon Valley. As we say in cyberspace, YMMV—your mileage may vary!)

The web is an easy way to exchange information. At the very least, your web page can provide a lot more information than a simple brochure or flyer can. Your site can display your most current schedules, prices, and policies. At its best, your web page can be interactive, allowing your potential clients to send you their information as well.

What Your Web Site Should Include

At the very least, a simple web page acts as a flyer or brochure—it provides a description of your services and contact information. Additionally, a web page can display your current class schedules and prices (but you should only post this information if you know you can keep it current—potential clients will stay away if they only see classes that have already started). All advertising is created to encourage potential clients to take some action, and a web site is no exception. A good web site will motivate potential clients to sign up for your classes or services.

Your web site should definitely include a clear description of your services and prices, and should clearly lead to the next step you hope your visitors will take, whether that is calling you, e-mailing you, printing out a form to mail in, or filling out a form on-line. Remember that this is the World Wide Web, so be sure to include your city and state/province/country clearly in your contact information! Because my web site is easy to find, I regularly get inquiries from people who are in other states or even other countries.

Your web site is no good if visitors can't read the information you provide. Avoid background colors that are too bright, lettering that doesn't contrast well with the background (dark print on dark background, or light print on light background), very fancy font styles, and small print. If your web site has more than one page, provide clear navigation—make sure it is easy to go from one page of your site to another and back again.

In my opinion, good web sites also avoid:

- Too many graphics (they are slow to appear on your client's computer).

- Animated graphics (one small one might not be too distracting).

- Music (some of your clients may be "surfing" from work and don't want to announce that they are doing so!).

- Too many navigation buttons (they get overwhelming).

- ALL CAPITAL LETTERING (it looks like you're shouting, or don't know how to use capitalization).

- Big blocks of text (small chunks of writing and lots of white space is easier to read).

- Abbreviations, lingo, and acronyms (your clients might be intimidated).

- So much at the top of a page that your clients have to immediately "scroll down" to get to what they wanted to see.

- Long introductory pages (clients will have to read a lot or "click through" several pages before they get to what they want).

For more ideas on what not do do, see "Web Pages That Suck" at www.webpages-thatsuck.com.

Also, be sure to respect the copyrights of text and images—do not copy wording from any published source, including other web sites, and do not use images that you do not have express written permission to use. There are many sites that provide free dog and training graphics, but make sure they are available for commercial use. Professional APDT members are allowed to use the APDT logo on their sites. (Please contact the business office for guidelines.)

If you have a logo or some favorite pictures but they are not in digital format, it is easy to take them to a copy shop and get them scanned.

Some of the best marketing strategies include some "freebies." On the Internet, instead of pens or magnets, your best freebie is information. For example, my web site lists all dog events in our general geographic area, and it has become well known for this resource. I also provide about a dozen short training articles dealing with frequent problems, like housetraining and barking.

(continued)

Constructing Your Web Site

You can easily create a static, non-interactive, one-page web site with any modern word-processing program (such as Microsoft Word or WordPerfect). Create the page as you would any flyer (though it can be longer than one page) and then look under the "File" menu for a command like "Save as ... web document/HTML" or "Publish to HTML" or the like. It will vary for each program.

For an interactive web site (one with hyperlinks to other pages within your site, links to other sites, interactive e-mail addresses, or interactive forms), you can use a web-publishing program like Microsoft FrontPage (FP) or DreamWeaver (DW). FP lets you easily create professional-looking web sites with consistent-looking graphics, navigation buttons, backgrounds, and fonts (but in my opinion adds a lot of extra, unnecessary coding that will take up a lot more space on your host server). DW is slightly more difficult to learn from scratch but in my opinion is easier to work with once you have a little more knowledge.

Of course, you can also hire someone to create a web site for you. There are thousands of professional companies, charging around $100 and up. Or, one of your friends—or their kids—could probably create a basic one for you!

Once you have created a web site, there are still at least two more steps: publishing it to the Internet, and making it possible for your potential clients to find it.

Hosting Services

A file saved on your computer isn't accessible to your potential clients searching the web for you—you need to "publish" your page to a computer system that makes its pages available to the web. To publish your page, you'll need to find a "host server." If you have an e-mail address, whoever provides your e-mail service may also be able to host your web page (possibly even for free, though there is usually a charge for commercial sites, including any that promote a business or sell a service). There are thousands of companies who will provide hosting services; you don't even need to be in the same geographical area. Shop around for prices and services—make sure they are easy to contact and work with.

You don't need to have your own domain name to have a web page, but it will be easier for potential clients to remember "DogTrainingByFred.com" than "http://www.hosting servername.com/~username/dogtraining/index.html." Once you've chosen your domain name and checked to see that it is not already in use, you can register the name of your choice through a "registrar" company. Often the host server will provide registration services for you. If not, you can find a registrar through www.internic.com.

Your web site host will provide instructions for publishing your web site (in other words, how to get the document you created from your computer to one that will allow it to show up on the Internet). Most hosts will have a page that indicates how to load files from your computer; or to use an FTP program to "upload" files.

Search Engines

Once your web site is available on the Internet, you'll need to get people to look at it. Most potential clients looking for services like yours will be "surfing the net" through the use of search engines (like Yahoo, Google, or my favorite, Dogpile.com). Search engines list web sites through one or both of two methods: they either accept listings of sites from you, or they actively search the web for new sites.

For the sites that accept listings from web site owners, you can either tell search engines about your site yourself—a tedious process that can save you some money— or you can pay for a service to submit your site for you. Also, some search engines will let you pay them additional fees to list your site within the first few listings. Each search engine's homepage will have some indication—usually near the bottom of its page—of how to "add a site," "list a site," "add a listing," etc. Click on that link and follow the instructions.

However you choose to get your site listed with search engines, you'll want to make sure that those engines will be able to register your site correctly. Search engines use a particular type of coding called "Meta Tags" to categorize web sites and match them to search inquiries. You add "Meta Tags" to your web page document that allows you to describe and list key words about your site. The description is the line that you see showing up in the search engine, and the key words are the ones that allow the search engines to find it.

Make sure that you choose your Meta Tags with care. Try to think how your potential clients might look for your business via the Internet, and be sure to include their search terms among your key words. For example, mine includes "dog, dogs, training, obedience, puppy, puppies" etc., as well as my city and local towns. You might even want to include common typos and misspellings like "puppys." Your description should clearly communicate that your service is what your clients need. Meta Tags need only be on your home page, but any pages with special information (like a page on barking) might have special additional keywords (bark, quiet, barking, speak, shush, hush, etc.).

Additional Points

Like any other piece of advertising, you want to consider what you include in your web site. One way people will evaluate your web site is the quality and quantity of links your site has to others. In my opinion, too many links, or links that are not organized well, will give people a bad impression. Don't have links to trainers or products that conflict with your training philosophy and will give the wrong impression of your work. Equally bad are links to sites with irrelevant content. In other words, don't have links from your professional business site to your favorite TV show fan page, outside hobby, or personal "vanity" page. You will not find a link from my business web site to the page that shows pictures of my adorable newborn daughter, or to the site that describes my fascination with medieval Jewish history in Spain.

Be sure to give each page a title, like "Dog Training by Fred - Home Page" and "Class Schedule - Dog Training by Fred." Leaving "Page 2" or "Untitled Document" looks very unprofessional!

You can get more "traffic" by joining a "web ring," a series of sites linked together through a common theme (such as obedience training, or a specific breed). However, if the other sites in the ring are of low-quality, or promote training methods you don't agree with, it will reflect badly on your site.

Don't forget, you can make money (just not a lot of it!) through affiliate programs. In these programs you promote merchandise sold through a separate company that you have made an agreement with, and when visitors to your site buy something through their site, you are sent a referral fee. Check to see if your favorite dog-related web sites have affiliate programs that you can take advantage of. ❖

The Write Stuff: Launching Yourself Into A Freelance Career

Arden Moore, September/October 2003

Imagine making a living writing about your passion: dog training and behavior. Imagine paying the monthly mortgage from checks received for writing magazine articles and books. Imagine having to turn away some writing offers due to the abundance of assignments that regularly come your way.

Why imagine? This can be a realistic scenario for you—if you take the right steps. Four years ago, I left the stable, secure, get-my-paycheck-every-two-weeks world of newspaper reporting and in-house book publishing to become a full-time freelance writer. I relocated from Philadelphia to San Diego, bought a home, wrote 11 books, and became a regular contributor to several pet and health publications.

You can make a living as a freelance writer, but you need some tools. The first is attitude. Adopt a big dog attitude—be confident and calm. As dog trainers, you are the teachers of owners who look to you for guidance in developing solid relationships with their canine pals. What you demonstrate in your classes can be put into words in the form of handouts, booklets, magazine articles, newspaper columns, and books.

The second tool: start small but think big. Do not attempt to write the definitive book on dog training as your first writing venture. Do not try to woo a major book publisher in the beginning. Instead, look at the smaller markets such as your local newspaper (small dailies or weekly newspapers are the most receptive) and dog-related newsletters. You may need to write your first few articles for free, but the payoff is having published articles to show to editors of publications that do pay. Build up your portfolio before approaching the mid-range and major writing markets.

The third tool: create a Web site. Editors want answers fast. They do not like to spend a lot of time waiting. They need a stable of dependable writers. In pitching story ideas to editors, it is far better to put your writing samples and your dog training talents on a Web site for them to view than to have them wait to receive copies of your work by snail mail. When I launched my freelance career, I hired a web master to create my Web site and got many writing jobs because the editors could immediately check me out on my Web site.

The fourth tool: unleash your creativity. The world of pet writing is not limited to just dog-specific publications such as *Dog Fancy*. Offer to team up with an animal behaviorist or veterinarian to co-author an article for a parenting publication. Contact your local veterinary school to see if you can write an article in their newsletter. Seek out Web sites that feature pet articles. Write a small training booklet that you can distribute to local animal shelters or at pet expos. Ghostwrite an article or book for a top name in the pet world. Usually these individuals have a lot to say, but very little time to sit down and write books.

The fifth tool: be organized. Set up a home office and hone your computer skills. You need to establish an accounting system that works for you. Some like computer programs such as Quicken, while other freelancers prefer maintaining their monthly finances on paper in ledgers. Build a directory that contains experts, dog owners, and key people from pet companies. Maintain separate folders for each writing assignment. Most importantly, create an ideas folder. When you get an idea for a story, jot it down. And do not forget to get business cards and stationary with your letterhead.

Will you get rich from writing? Who knows, but the best writers are those who enrich the lives of others through their words.

Terrific Writing Resources

Here are some helpful sources to launch your writing career and hone your writing skills:

- National Writers Union (www.nwu.org) is a professional writer's organization. This group has an excellent resource book called *Freelance Writers' Guide*.

- The latest annual edition of *Writer's Market*, which lists contact information for more than 8,000 books and magazines. You can borrow a copy at the library, or invest in your own book by ordering through www.writersmarket.com or at a local or online bookstore.

- The Dog Writers Association of America (www.dwaa.org) is a "must" group to join if you plan to write on canine topics. This group sponsors annual writing contests and touts the work of its members.

Arden Moore's Top 10 Author Traps To Avoid:

1. **Assuming that you know what the focus of the assignment is.** When you pitch a story to an editor—or an editor contacts you for an assignment—listen carefully to what the editor wants addressed. If your editor wants you to focus on five specific, practical ways owners can reduce separation anxiety in their home-alone dogs, do not turn in an assignment that describes the physiological and physical theories behind separation anxiety without offering take-home tips.

2. **Being high-maintenance to your editor.** Do not bombard your editor with phone calls or e-mails for every minor question. Editors are very busy individuals who seek writers who can address minor problems on their own. They quickly learn to identify demanding, time-draining writers and steer clear of them.

3. **Setting unrealistic writing deadlines.** Take into account the time you may need to thoroughly research a magazine article or book when negotiating your assignment's deadline with your editor.

4. **Writing in isolation.** If you plan on writing a puppy school article, visit a class in your area to be able to add some color and description to your assignment. Do not try to write stories by merely sitting in front of your keyboard in your home

office or without conducting telephone interviews. Attend pet conferences and local animal humane events to mingle and gather story ideas.

5. **Exceeding the word count.** You may think your story merits 5,000 words, but your editor assigned 2,000 words. Editors must take into account the entire publication. They dread having to chop stories that come in double or even triple the word count.

6. **Locking into a writing style not appropriate for your audience.** Writing in a chatty, conversational style may be ideal for a publication aimed at new dog owners, but not for a scientific publication aimed at veterinary researchers.

7. **Failing to do your homework on writing fees.** Find out what the publication pays for story submissions and do not demand double the customary rate. Editors must adhere to monthly budgets.

8. **Committing typos and misspellings.** Before you turn in your assignment, wait a day and then read your document with fresh eyes. Use the spell check option on your computer. Check and re-check the spellings of names cited, even simple ones like John Smith. One source I interviewed spelled his name "Jonn." Editors do not like receiving what they term "dirty copy"—filled with grammatical mistakes.

9. **Selecting the wrong experts to cite.** You may be on friendly terms with your local veterinarian, but if the assignment calls for you to interview experts on the latest advances in treating heartworm disease in dogs, do your research and find leading researchers at veterinary universities. Your readers deserve the best in each subject area.

10. **Ignoring the writing contract.** Some publications pay upon acceptance; others pay when the article is published. Some publications offer a modest kill fee if the story is not used; others do not. Some publications demand all rights to your article while others only seek first-rights so that you as the writer can re-claim this work after it has been published in that specific magazine or book. Lesson: read the fine print. ❖

Behind Every Successful Writer is an Excellent Editor...or Two or Three

Terry Long, November/December 2003

Have you ever noticed how book authors often mention editors high on their list of acknowledgements in thanking people who have contributed to their books? Experienced authors know what neophytes often learn the hard way: Knowing how to work well with editors is the key to successful publishing.

In her acknowledgements in *The Other End of the Leash* (Ballantine Books, 2002), Patricia B. McConnell, PhD, writes, "I am equally grateful to my editor, Leslie Meredith, whose belief in the book has always been stalwart, and who was invaluable at many stages of the writing." Suzanne Clothier, in *Bones Would Rain from the Sky* (Time Warner, 2002), writes, "Many thanks to my editors, Jackie Joiner and Jessica Papin, for their support. To all at Warner Books, my thanks for working so diligently to polish up Bones and dress it in its Sunday best. With so many talented people dedicated to this task, *Bones* cleaned up right nice ..."

McConnell and Clothier are each gifted writers. And yet they recognize the integral role an editor plays in ensuring their works are the best they can be—before they reach the general public. If you aspire to write professionally about dogs and dog training, recognizing the different kinds of editors and how to build successful relationships with them can be the difference between having editors and publishers pursue you, and getting those dreaded rejection letters.

Know Thy Editor

Choosing an editor, or understanding how to work with a particular editor of a magazine, depends on the kind of editing you need. In her role as managing editor of *Clean Run: The Magazine for Dog Agility Enthusiasts*, Kathy Keats focuses on establishing the overall vision for the magazine, soliciting article ideas, and choosing writers. She also checks articles for technical accuracy, but she has additional editors at her disposal who help with editing for clarity, grammar, etc. Contrast this with Nancy Kerns, editor of *Whole Dog Journal*, whose job is all-encompassing. Kerns identifies topics, assigns articles, writes some articles herself, takes most of the photographs, and is responsible for editing, proofing *and* layout and production. Understanding the role played by the editor with whom you will be working will help you, the writer, tailor your interaction to make their job easy (and that's a sure-fire way of making an editor want to work with you again in the future!)

Know Thy Publisher

If it is a book you want to publish, it pays to do your homework about the various publishers who publish and/or sell books about dogs and dog training. Dogwise's Charlene Woodward suggests, "Authors should know what a publisher does, which topics they've done in the past, where their current interest lies. Authors need to do their homework and be knowledgeable about the publisher before contacting them. For example, Dogwise doesn't publish breed books. We concentrate on publishing or selling books that focus on improving the way people train." (For information about publishing through Dogwise go to www.dogwise.com and click on the "Publishing" tab at the top of the home page.)

Understanding what a publisher actually does is equally important. Gone are the days when publishing houses provided a full range of services from editing to promotion. According to Woodward, "Many new authors think that a publisher will take a rough draft, whip it into shape, and do all the marketing and promotion. It just doesn't work that way at most publishers. And, if the author is a good writer, we can proceed to a contract much faster."

A Cooperative Effort

So let's say you want to get some articles published in a magazine. *Clean Run's* Keats has these tips for prospective authors: "The main thing is to be willing to work with the editors. Editing is part of the publishing process. There is no such thing as a perfect article. Working together will usually produce a piece better than either the editor or the writer could have done by themselves. If writers do not want to have their piece changed at all, they should be clear about that up front because it is not the norm and will probably impact whether or not the editor is willing to use the article. Fortunately, most of the people I have dealt with have been very open minded, and we end up with a superior article that both the writers and editors are thrilled with."

While *Clean Run* has several people handling various aspects of producing the publication, *Whole Dog Journal's* Kerns is busier than the proverbial one-arm paperhanger. She says, "In the last two weeks of the month, I have to focus all my efforts on the issue at hand, and spend all my time in front of the computer editing, writing, scanning photos, and laying out the magazine. I can barely speak to people on the phone, and the mail stacks up!" Kerns offers the following advice to those wanting to leverage their writing talents: "Because I have so many balls in the air, I really value the writers who produce copy that is pretty darn good on the first draft; I simply don't have time to work with writers who turn in work that has to be completely overhauled from top to bottom. If an article comes to me needing major revisions, or lacking lots of crucial information, it may well be the last time I can afford to work with that writer."

The Ideal Writer

When asked what her dream writer looks like, Kerns mused, "My perfect writer has writing experience (journalism preferred), is at least peripherally involved with some aspect of the dog world (i.e., already knows dogs and some of the issues important to dog lovers), and appreciates WDJ's aesthetic," she notes. "The best writer in the world won't do me much good if she promotes compulsion-based training or strongly believes that all dog foods are created equal. Of course, a writer doesn't have to agree with everything in the magazine, but if she is opposed to much of what *WDJ* espouses, she'll have a hard time using the voice and tone I want. In contrast, if she is already a fan of positive training and has an open mind regarding complementary healthcare methods, we'll have no trouble communicating." Kerns adds, "The more writing experience someone has, the better. Many people are sensitive to every little cut and revision to their work early in their writing careers, and they may even need to talk about it—my worst fear! I need authors who are professional and who understand that the article has to serve *WDJ*'s purposes first and foremost."

Book publishers such as Dogwise have their own version of what constitutes a dream writer. Woodward's dream author is an expert in the field, a good writer, understands the value of submitting his/her ideas for peer review, is well-versed about the literature available on the topic, is capable of self-promotion (such as presentations at APDT, doing the seminar circuit, etc.), and has a good balance of being humble and yet confident in their knowledge or expertise. "Enthusiasm to support their ideas helps a lot, too!" says Woodward.

Options for the Non-Writer

So what should a person do with extensive subject matter expertise, but less than stellar writing skills? Consider the following:

- Hire a writer who will turn your ideas into winning prose.

- Write a draft, and hire a professional editor to polish it.

- Contact the publisher or editor and ask if they work with people like yourself.

As Kerns says, "If someone's information is important enough, or impossible to get elsewhere, I'll put a lot of my own resources of time and attention into helping them 'write' an article. Sometimes this means completely reworking a rough draft they have written, or adapting a speech they gave into an article, or simply interviewing them on the phone and then writing the article for them. Compensation, in this case, is generally not an issue; I do most of the work, and they get all the credit—and publicity for their businesses."

Dogwise's Woodward agrees: "My worst nightmare is that I'll reject the next *Gone with the Wind* so I always encourage inquiries into what Dogwise is looking for. Good ideas shine through bad writing. Even if we don't publish it, we may sell it! Generally, though, if someone has a good idea, but isn't a great writer, they should find someone to help do the writing," Woodward emphasized, adding, "People with good ideas need to reach out to freelance writers to help them put their ideas down on paper. Many, many publishers these days want a well-developed manuscript before a contract will be signed."

Teaming up with photographers and/or illustrators can also position an author for a more successful relationship with publishers. "Authors who can provide their own good-quality photos and illustrations are a real plus for publishers," noted Woodward. "The additional cost of artwork can make a niche project like a dog book too expensive; therefore, both big and small publishers often require the author to provide photos illustrating the book. The good news is that the author has more control over what goes into the book. 35mm color photography burned to a photo CD is the safest way to go unless the photographer has excellent-quality digital images, and 35mm is easier for the graphic artist to manipulate."

Choosing a Professional Editor

If you choose to work with a professional writer and/or editor, be clear about the services you need. Judith Engstrom, a professional writer and editor (and former *APDT Chronicle of the Dog* copy editor) from Sequim, Washington says, "Decide what you need most when you hire a professional editor. Some editors, myself included, can do organizational critiquing and let you do the rewrites, or we can do it all, i.e., reorganization, editing for grammar and punctuation, down to the nitty-gritty proof-reading of the final product. An author needs to be clear at the outset about their needs or a lot of time and money can be wasted."

Whether your goal is to become a full-time freelance writer, write the occasional magazine article, or publish a book, an editor—or two or three—may well play an incalculable role in your success. Knowing how to leverage others' editorial talents is your first step. ❖

Resources

Clean Run - The Magazine For Dog Agility Enthusiasts
Clean Run Productions, LLC
Kathy Keats, Managing Editor
35 North Chicopee Street
Chicopee, MA 01020
800-311-6503
Outside the U.S.: 413-532-1389
24-hour fax: 413-532-1590
info@cleanrun.com
www.cleanrun.com

Dogwise
Charlene Woodward, Publisher
701 B Poplar
Wenatchee WA 98801
800-776-2665
charlenew@dogwise.com
www.dogwise.com

Whole Dog Journal

Nancy Kerns, Editor
1175 Regent Street
Alameda, CA 94501
510-749-1080
nakerns@aol.com

For subscription information, call Belvoir Publications' customer service at 800-424-7887 or see www.whole-dog-journal.com.

So You Want to Enter the Lecture Circuit

Donna Duford, September/October 2002

Seminars and workshops are a great way to impart information and share techniques. Dog trainers are eager to learn and soak up well-presented material. If you think you would like to get your feet wet as a presenter, here are some tips:

- Be professional. Be organized, start and end on time, and dress and speak in a way that shows respect for your profession and your audience. Professionalism lends credence to everything you say and motivates listeners to pay attention.

- Balance lecture with activity. If you are giving a hands-on workshop, offer a combination of training, lecture, and non-dog exercises. If the seminar is not hands-on, include demonstrations and interactive games. People get tired of too much sustained activity but fidgety after too many hours of straight lecture.

- Move around. Help your audience stay focused by moving around and using visual aids.

- Provide and announce breaks. When people know when the breaks are, they can relax and focus on the seminar. For a full-day seminar, a 10-minute break each hour is a great structure.

- Plan for afternoon sleepiness. To help your audience stay awake after lunch, make your first afternoon session interactive or include lots of demonstrations or videos.

- Test the equipment. Make sure everything is in working order. Faulty or missing equipment can really dampen a presentation for both the audience and the speaker.

- Use evaluation forms. Give your audience a simple evaluation form so they can provide feedback about your presentation. Evaluations enable you to assess your audience's interests, get positive reinforcement for your work, and improve your seminars.

- Have a contract. If someone is sponsoring the seminar, prepare a written agreement. Be sure to include what you will provide (e.g., services and materials), what the sponsor will provide (e.g., setup and advertising), your fee, who will pay expenses, and a cancellation policy.

Setting Fees

Setting fees can be a daunting task. Your fees should take into account not only your presentation time, but your preparation time as well. Prep time includes creating lecture notes, videos, slide presentations, handouts, phone time and e-mail with the sponsor, marketing, and travel time.

You might want to itemize all your expenses and time involved in giving a seminar, and then base your fee on those calculations. If you are an independent contractor, remember to figure taxes and liability insurance into the equation.

Enjoy!

Even though you need to take care of all the logistical details involved in giving a seminar, one of the most important things you can do as a presenter is to share your passion. Passion is infectious and inspiring. ❖

Structuring Your Presentations

Nina Bondarenko, November/December 2002

As a presenter at the APDT annual conference in the Catskills in September 2001, I was delighted to be able to meet and work with positive dog trainers who were dedicated to continuing education. I appreciated their enthusiasm, their passion, and, most of all, their feedback on my workshops and lectures. Their thoughtful evaluations have been invaluable in helping me hone my speaking skills and aspire toward ever-higher standards of professionalism.

If public speaking on any topic is to be successful, it requires knowledge of both the subject matter and the audience. Just as importantly, it requires skill in the areas of presentation style and format. This article offers some guidelines on presentation—the art of knowing which format to use and how to present information in the most effective, engaging way.

Lectures

Many speakers prefer to impart information in a lecture format: a standard sequence that includes an introduction, explanations, examples, and a conclusion. This format often works well, especially if considerable amounts of factual, theoretical, and statistical information are being offered and the audience is likely to want to take notes. You'll want to provide good handouts, however, so that the audience isn't forced to write furiously to keep up with you.

One challenge with this format is that it is best suited to a short session because the information can be "dry," and people's attention spans vary greatly. Another challenge, from the presenter's perspective, is that handouts require considerable preparation and transport. If your preparation time is limited or you're unable to carry large quantities of your handouts with you (e.g., if you're lecturing abroad), the lecture format may not work for you.

Question-and-Answer Sessions

Sometimes the best way for people to receive information is through Q&A sessions that follow a basic structure. You begin the session with an outline of points to cover, and you address each point while seeking and responding to questions from the audience. As the audience participates, you gain insights about their backgrounds and experiences and, thus, can customize the session to meet their needs and interests. The primary challenge with this format is that, no matter how adept you are at guiding the subject matter in the desired direction and answering people's questions succinctly, there's a risk that a subtopic or single audience member will dominate. You must ensure that the main points of the session are covered, even if questions move the session away from planned structure. Your audience expects to hear certain information, and you need to meet that expectation.

Audiovisual Aids

Perhaps the best approach for sessions that contain both theoretical and practical aspects is to use videos or slides. For many presenters, however, time factors and restricted resources can make videos difficult to prepare. Videotaping specific behavioral scenarios requires not only that dogs, videographers, and video equipment be available, but also that the dogs display the behavior in a venue that can be documented. As many trainers know, the owners of dogs with behavioral difficulties want the problems resolved; they are usually not interested in waiting for the trainer to videotape the session.

If you use videos, particularly those that demonstrate problem behaviors, include a written disclaimer (and also announce to the audience) that the videotaped dogs are individuals and not meant to represent the behavior of the breed as a whole. Recognize that your audience, particularly if it is comprised of non-trainers, may be protective of and sensitive about perceived criticisms of a particular breed.

Live Models

One of the best ways of demonstrating a theory or technique is to use live models. It is easier for people to see how something works if you can make your point with dogs and people in action. This approach, however, requires the use of assistants who can effectively manage the dogs. You want to avoid situations in which your demonstration dogs behave so poorly that they distract the audience and disrupt the flow of the presentation. Using live models works best if the presenter imparts all factual and theoretical information before introducing the dog or dogs. With that preliminary background and knowledge, the audience can get the most benefit from the live demonstration.

Conclusion

One integral component of successful public speaking is imparting information in a format that complements the content, the speaker, and the audience. Know your subject matter thoroughly—and become comfortable with various presentation formats—including lectures, Q&A sessions, the use of audiovisual aids, and live demonstrations. Get to know your audiences' interests and levels of expertise so you can adapt your presentation as needed. Your goal is a solid, well-organized delivery that delivers the promised content in a professional manner. ❖

Final Thoughts

To end this volume we turn to three subjects that are of vital importance to all professional dog trainers. No group as diverse as this will always agree on techniques and philosophies—unanimity among a large group of bright people should not be expected. Donna Duford recognizes this and makes a plea for trainers to engage in healthy disagreement, to be respectful of others, and to back up arguments with evidence, not emotion. Sue Sternberg takes a thought-provoking look at "The Future of Dogs" asking what will the world of pet dogs look like if the only dogs that are reproducing are purebred show dogs and urban macho dogs? The last word belongs to Michael Baugh whose wonderful essay "You Saved a Dog's Life Today" should resonate with all dog trainers. What can be more rewarding than to know that your work has saved a dog's life and brought happiness to people?

Us and Them

Donna Duford, May/June 2001

Although the APDT is a young organization, it seems at times that we are really two groups: Us and Them. I expect it is an inevitable stage of a growing organization. When I think about the complexities of it, I am astounded.

Here we are, a newly formed professional group serving a profession that has deep roots and people who are accustomed to being autonomous. We have members who are novices, as well as many who have been in the field for the better part of a lifetime. We come from a myriad of backgrounds, academic and practical, and many of us are solidly entrenched in our ideas, views, methods, and prejudices. We are passionate people and, when we come together as a group, there is bound to be disagreement, not to mention posturing, rank classification, and a bit of leg-lifting. This does not mean we cannot get along, however we may need to reframe our expectations of each other to do so.

Shortsighted Interpretations

When we are exasperated by and judgmental of our colleagues, it is often due to unmet expectations, coupled with our tendency to interpret each other's motives. One of the by-products of being deeply committed to a training philosophy is a tendency to hold other people to the standards we set for ourselves. When others don't measure up, it is easy to be judgmental.

We are equally judgmental, or perhaps more so, when we fall into the trap of interpreting other trainers' motives. We see a trainer do something we don't like, and we form an opinion about the trainer. We enter into discussions with trainers whose methods differ from our own, and we condemn them as stupid, unyielding, or cruel. This tendency, although common and understandable, is a limiting, short-sighted practice. When we judge each other, we cut off the possibilities of learning from each other and of improving our profession as a whole.

Let's consider two typical trainer scenarios, typical reactions to them, and common truths regarding motives (see Figure 1 below).

For each of these scenarios—as well as most others we observe in our work—we can assume the worst about each other, or we can assume the best. It is our choice. Perhaps we should sit back, look at the big picture, and keep in mind that we are all on the same team. Although our techniques and methodologies may differ, we share a love and passion for dogs and training. We also share common goals—among them to improve the lives of dogs and the people who love them.

Debate and Critical Thinking

At the heart of dog training exists some basic truths. One of them is that, regardless of our training methodology, we all strive to do what we think is in our clients' and their dogs' best interests. No one in this business is striving to do a sub-standard job.

We all want to use the best, most humane and effective methods available. We may not agree about what those methods are, and that is where things get interesting.

The reason for so much disagreement regarding training methods is in part due to the fact that we don't have answers to questions regarding the efficacy, speed of acquisition, and reliability of various techniques. We are just scratching the surface of these areas with scientific research and it will take some time before results are available.

In the meantime, we possess two valuable tools—debate and critical thinking—that can help answer these questions. When we enter into dialogue with other trainers, we have the opportunity to challenge each other and tease out the very best techniques. The more we engage in thoughtful debate, the more we poke holes in theories and methods, the fewer holes those theories and methods will have. Only those that stand up to scrutiny will prevail—survival of the fittest, so to speak.

Healthy Disagreement

The fact that we disagree can be beneficial to us all. When we debate, though, we must be careful to resist the temptations of defensiveness and judgment. Instead, we need to think critically and stay on task, discussing only the merits of the techniques and not the intelligence or integrity of the trainer who uses them. We must separate our feelings about the training from those about the trainer.

If you proclaim that physical corrections make aggression worse, for example, back up your statement with evidence, either anecdotal or scientific. If your statement is based on the fact that physical punishment makes you uncomfortable, your argument has no foundation. "I dislike physical punishment" is a far cry from "Corrections make aggression worse." If you think training with food is a waste of time and not reliable, explain why you think so. Make sure you have something tangible with which to back up your claim. Have you tried the technique or at least observed it before coming to a conclusion, or is it merely an impression based on supposition?

When discussing techniques with colleagues, we must stick to what we know and avoid making decisions based on emotion. If we are going to debate, we need to do it well, arguing relevant points and avoiding personal attacks.

The APDT is dedicated to education. Let's educate each other with the same thoughtful approach we use in training. Challenge each other, and do it with respect. If we get embroiled in the game of discerning each other's intentions and passing judgment, our passions get the better of us and we create rifts where we need bridges. We have so much to learn from each other, Us from Them and Them from Us.

(continued)

Figure 1

Trainer Scenario	Assumptions	Actual Motives
Joe Hangman uses force to treat aggression. When a dog aggresses toward other dogs, Joe strings up the aggressive dog.	• Joe is cruel and abusive. • Joe doesn't know what he is doing. • Joe is macho. • Joe is a terrible person. • Joe is a bad dog trainer. • This training will make the dog worse.	• Joe finds this technique very successful. • Joe wants to give his client quick results. • Joe is working hard to save the dog's life and keep it in its home.
Sally Feedsalot uses counter-conditioning to treat aggression. When a dog-aggressive dog sees another dog, Sally gives the aggressive dog a treat.	• Sally is a wimp. • Sally doesn't know what she is doing. • Sally is all fluff. • Sally doesn't know how to do real training. • Sally is unrealistic. • This training will not solve the problem.	• Sally finds this technique very successful. • Sally wants to give her client quick results. • Sally is working hard to save the dog's life and keep it in its home.

❖

The Future of Dogs

Sue Sternberg, July/August 2003

Are pet dogs heading for extinction? The pet dog, not a breed but a temperament, is disappearing. Soon I think they will be extinct. Our plan for the future of dogs is similar to President Bush's plan for the environment—we are kind of okay for now, but what will it be like in 20 years? There are two fatal flaws in our plan, and they are on a colliding trajectory. We are near interception, at which point we will have effectively eliminated all suitable pet dogs.

"Pet" Overpopulation?

The shelter world is responsible for one fatal flaw. For the past 20 years, we have promoted an intense spay/neuter campaign to remedy the overpopulation problem. It has been a very effective campaign and the numbers of dogs euthanized in shelters has dropped dramatically. The numbers of litters of puppies entering the nation's shelters has dropped significantly in many urban areas.

While unwanted litters are an indicator of overpopulation, adolescent and adult dogs entering shelters indicate more of a problem of unwanted dogs with behavioral problems. Our assumption that we had one huge "pet overpopulation" problem is inaccurate, and maybe was so even 20 years ago. We have a "unwanted pet overpopulation" problem and an "aggressive dog" overpopulation problem. Although we are sterilizing the pets, we are not, for the most part, sterilizing the aggressive dogs.

Just the way the sound of a rewinding cassette tape accelerates as it nears the end, I think "pet overpopulation" is nearing that end. We have reduced the numbers of dogs euthanized in overcrowded shelters through spaying and neutering. The last of these sweet, wonderful, and appropriate family pet dogs fill up the rural shelters in the southern U.S., the southern plains states, and other very rural regions (Tennessee, Kentucky, Oklahoma, and Alabama to name a few). Many, sometimes most, of these pet dogs are euthanized due to the low number of adopters compared to the high numbers of family pet dogs. While in the more urban parts of the country, and the entire northeast, our ratio is the opposite. We have a much higher number of great families looking to adopt than we have adoptable family pet dogs. By contrast, in the more rural and remote areas of the U.S., most dogs are not sterilized due to lack of education and financial constraints. Therefore, when you educate them and offer free surgery, compliance is very high. On the other hand, our current spay/neuter campaign is completely ineffective against the remaining owners with unsterilized dogs. These include almost all intact dogs in urban areas and in the northeastern U.S. Imagine driving into the Bronx and pulling up alongside a group of macho teenagers with a couple of pit bull terriers. You recommend neutering because:

- It is healthier for dogs and they will live longer, healthier lives.

- In male dogs, the risk of prostate and testicular cancers is virtually eliminated with early neutering.

- Breeding a litter is really not a money-maker. By the time a breeder gets done with all the medical screening for hereditary problems, money will be lost, not earned.

- It helps control the overpopulation problem.

- It can help with certain behavior problems, such as dog-dog aggression and dominance.

Are any of these reasons even remotely pertinent or useful or motivating for these kids? These urban macho dogs (mostly pit bull, Rottweiler, and Chow Chow purebreds and mixes), found in every inner-city neighborhood in this country, compete neck and neck with the high-end show dog breeders, contributing to the unsterilized and growing aggressive dog overpopulation. These urban muscle dogs are the breeding stock of many, if not most, future dogs. And there will continue to be a disproportionate increase in the numbers of these dogs (since the current spay/neuter campaign is useless against them) while there will be a decrease in the number of pet dogs (since these are all effectively being sterilized). This is a frightening future when at the same time the shelter world is concerned primarily with "numbers"—trying to increase adoptions while lowering euthanasia numbers. A noble goal on paper, but when you include the actual dogs, there are big problems.

I grew up in New York City, and when I was 15 years old, I had my own dog-walking/sitting business. There was one dog in particular I really liked—his name was King and he was a young, coyote-sized mixed breed with frizzy brown hair, like a Chesapeake Bay Retriever. King was an unneutered male owned by a single man. I did not think about this or notice it. I would walk the dogs in my care to a small park, where a bunch of other dog owners would congregate. One day, someone at the park asked me what kind of a dog I would get when I grew up. I proudly told them that I was planning to get one of King's puppies. I relayed what King's owner had so proudly told me, that he was going to one day let King mate and sire puppies.

In an instant, everyone in the park turned to face me, and they quite forcefully told me how it was bad that King was to be bred, it was awful he was intact, and it was irresponsible of King's owner not to neuter him, and even more irresponsible to breed him. I was so embarrassed, and felt so horrible that I somehow betrayed all my dog friends by unknowingly supporting such a terrible plan. I was humiliated. I had no idea. I had never been educated on the subject of spaying and neutering, or overpopulation.

We always had dogs while growing up, but they were females, and spayed before their first heats. They were not spayed for any moral reasons, but rather to avoid the mess of bloody heat cycles.

Since my initiation, I have been part of that wall of shelter people who condemn breeding, abhor the sight of testicles dangling on any male dog, become enraged at the sight of an unsterilized mixed breed, and secretly (although we are supposed to be okay with the reputable breeding of purebreds) hate just as much the sight of an unsterilized purebred.

Our mantra in the shelter world is "Spay/Neuter." Even purebreds—anything with testicles makes us furious. "Pet overpopulation," "too many," "not enough homes"—those are the issues in the shelter world. And although the system was set up so that only reputable breeders should breed, we secretly believe that no one should breed. We feel breeding and making more dogs is competing for the finite numbers of good homes that we want for our shelter dogs, and ultimately any puppy brought into this world was one less home for one of ours, and thus meant more euthanasia. I strongly believed that anyone breeding a litter had a duty to come to the shelter and rescue or adopt and place privately the very same number of new lives they had brought into the world, or they were a morally bad, unethical person.

I can remember when the San Mateo, California breeding ban took effect. The shelter world was triumphant and thrilled, while breeders everywhere were incensed and felt threatened. The shelter world thought it was a major step in the right direction towards ending the needless slaughter of dogs in shelters, and those in the breeding world felt a dangerous trend taking effect. Leave the future of dogs to most shelter people, and all dogs would be sterilized until there were none.

So the basic plan in this country for the future of dogs rests in the hands of the purebreds. The plan further narrows the ideal down to "reputable" breeders. What is the definition of a "reputable" breeder? A reputable breeder:

- Does not breed the bitch at every heat cycle; only one litter every other cycle to give her time to recoup.

- Screens carefully for genetic health problems.

- Takes deposits and has most of the puppies already sold or spoken for before breeding a litter.

- Sells "pet quality" puppies with limited registration to ensure that they will be sterilized.

- Carefully scrutinizes puppy buyers, and sell puppies only to worthy and savvy owners.

Can "reputable" breeders influence the overall dog population? Are they, with such sound practices, producing the dogs for the future? And how many "reputable" breeders of any breed do you know?

Breeding and Temperament

The most voluminous producers of purebred dogs are high-end show/conformation breeders—breeders who boast "over 60 champions." These breeders have such large numbers of breeding stock that they house their dogs in outside kennels. These dogs are, at best, rotated into the breeder's home every so often and are relatively un-known behaviorally to the breeder. By definition, a kenneled dog cannot be "bred for temperament," other than to select for a temperament that would make the dog win in the show ring. Breeders often cannot judge the dominance levels of their kennel dogs, since dominance and dominance-aggression reveals itself most commonly in the home, where the dog is comfortable and settled. They breed primarily for physical traits that make ultimate show dogs, and those not of that physical quality get sold as pets. All the qualities of temperament necessary to live successfully in a home with a family would be unknown and ignored. What kind of temperament does it take to win in the show ring? What kind of temperament does that top winning stud dog have? A dog that at the end of an exhausting weekend of trotting around the ring in front of a crowd, and can still hold his head up high, carry his tail up, and strut around the ring telling the judge that he should be chosen as the winner. This kind of attitude, in the same dog in a home with a family, would in all likelihood be too self-assured, too cocky (pardon the pun), too independent, and too dominant to be a safe or ap-propriate pet. Soft, sweet, family-type pet temperaments do not make it in the show ring, despite good conformation.

Dominance and high arousal make a top-winning champion and many show dogs are bred to produce more champions.

Breeders themselves often cannot judge "good" temperament. Their experience, expertise, confidence, and often dominant nature around dogs can mask the true, underlying, raw nature of their dogs. A breeder who is "good with dogs," and handles and trains dogs well usually sees their own dogs only through their own eyes and actions. This means the breeder will likely get responses from their own dogs that would be way too dominant and aggressive when placed with the average family. A lot of temperament and behavior problems can be hidden and covered up by good timing, expert handling, and early intervention into the sequence of events preced-ing aggression. A breeder may live for years with her dogs, and never experience any aggressiveness, whereas the same dog in the average, inexperienced home could be seriously aggressive.

Because they have large numbers of breeding dogs in their kennels, and have many litters every year from different bitches, they can provide a puppy buyer with an immediate sale. No need to wait for a litter to be planned and executed and born and raised for eight weeks. A puppy buyer can usually purchase a puppy anytime they are ready. For the average puppy buyer, the convenience and immediate gratification of being able to purchase a puppy right away will steer most of them to these high-end show dog breeders, and not toward the reputable breeders where they might have to wait a few months before getting a puppy.

Breeding and Health

Once a breed is acknowledged as a breed, the gene pool effectively closes. Under the section on health problems common to Boxers, from the book, *Boxers for Dum-mies*, cardiomyopathy is mentioned:

"Cardiomyopathy is progressive deterioration of the heart muscle. It is frequently undetected, because dogs may not show any signs of the disease for years. As many as

80% of Boxers may be affected with cardiomyopathy or are carriers of the condition, which causes the affected dog to have an arrhythmia (irregular heartbeat). Although many dogs are without symptoms, some may have episodes of fainting or collapse, weakness, and occasionally heart failure. Death often occurs from an inability to control irregular heart rhythms and is usually sudden." (From *Boxers for Dummies*, Richard Beauchamp, IDG Books Worldwide, 2000, p. 116)

That leaves 20% of the population of Boxers as breedable. With a closed gene pool, that leaves an even smaller population of Boxers with whom to breed to try to eliminate cardiomyopathy.

And I pulled this interesting statistic off the Internet from a *Review of the Epidemiology of Cancer in Dogs* by Todd Bessinger: "Purebred dogs are twice as likely to get breast cancers than mixed breed dogs of the same age." There is no theory as to why; it is just an interesting statistic.

At the height of popularity of the Shar-Pei, I spoke with one veterinarian in Queens, New York, who said he was able to hire two extra veterinarians with the extra money he made and clients he received with Shar-Peis riddled with chronic health problems. In the health section of the book *The Chinese Shar-Pei*, (Ellen Weathers Debo, TFH, 1986) it talks about demodectic mange, which is a proliferation of a skin mite in which "The Shar-Pei is plagued." (p. 86) Equally as tempting, is their tendency towards rectal prolapse, "characterized by a small or large red mass that is inflamed (even bloody) which protrudes from the anus." And if that were not enough, the book recommends that owners "Keep a careful watch on your dog's eyes…Eye entropion, sadly, is a very common problem in the Chinese Shar-Pei. It is an in-rolling of the eyelid (either top or bottom, although frequently, both eyelids are involved). These in-rolled lids bring the eyelashes into direct contact with the cornea and cause great discomfort, making it necessary for the animal to blink constantly. Entropion afflicts other breeds, but in Shar-Peis it is caused primarily by the excess wrinkling on the face and around the eyes." (p. 83). The book warns prospective owners of some of the delights unique to the breed:

"The Shar-Pei's mouth also needs special attention. Those individuals with large, fleshy mouths, whereby even the lips have folds, need special care. Food gets trapped between those folds and becomes rancid, producing a foul odor." (p. 83). With a closed gene pool, can we, or are we, effectively improving or eliminating health problems in a breed? It hardly seems so.

The Next Generation

In 20 years, what dogs will be available for the next generation to own? Only purebreds, since we deem mixed breeds surplus, and recommend sterilization across the board? Only the urban macho dogs? Only show dogs? I am at the point where I fret each time I make the spay/neuter appointment for every sweet-tempered family pet that comes into my shelter. I look at these wonderful dogs, usually structurally flawless, healthy despite inadequate care and nutrition, low thresholds for aggression of any kind, and I feel defensive. It feels almost like racial prejudice to me. We exclude these ideal dogs from breeding while, just because they are purebred, many (quite frankly) hideous dogs continue to be perpetuated. ❖

You Saved a Dog's Life Today

Michael Baugh, May/June2001

I got in my car and shook off the cold of late fall in Ohio. I was still jumpy from the high of working with an excellent dog. I was euphoric. And I began to cry. One by one, the names were coming to me. I thought of every trainer I'd ever met, every trainer I'd ever read, every trainer who gave a workshop or sat on a panel I'd attended, every trainer who was kind enough to let me observe a class or a consultation. I remembered each name. And with each one, I thought, "Thank you. You saved a dog's life today."

Keefer was my first dog-on-human aggression case. I thought I was a fool for taking it. Normally, I would have turned it down. That's easy to do, by the way. You just say, "No, thank you. I don't really like dogs who bite." But this time I said I'd help. What the heck! There was a time when the idea of standing in a park in a blizzard, cheering because my dog went poopie, seemed pretty absurd. I'm flexible.

The first call came from a local rescue group who had placed Keefer three years earlier. The owners were ready to surrender him because he had bitten their daughter's friend in the face. My eye twitched just thinking about it.

The next call was from the owner, a wonderful woman who had never really wanted a dog. Still, she took on the task of fixing the problem for the benefit of her family. God bless her.

"No, we never expected Keefer to bite. No, he's only done it once. Yes, it only happens in the home. Yes, he even cornered a guest in the bathroom once. And oh, he's growled and barked at strangers from the very first week we've had him."

I was in their driveway on the mobile phone. "I'm going to ring the doorbell and pretend I'm just a regular visitor. You handle Keefer as you normally would. After that, we can chat and talk about treatment." Oh, it sounded so simple. Elegant even.

Solon, Ohio, is a suburb of fetching homes with smart landscaping, large lovely porches, and welcoming doorways with charming leaded glass. So when Keefer threw himself against the front door, the window refracted his snarling face into a hundred horrifying images. I felt naked with my meager hot dog treats. I rode a wave of nausea that I feared might end in an embarrassing bout of submissive urination.

"Hi, I'm here to help with Keefer."

I guess that's when I heard the first friendly voice whispering in my ear. It was a trainer wiser and more experienced than I who reminded me how appropriate and normal it was to be afraid. Then there was another trainer who reminded me to breathe. Deeply. And then another whose book I clutched in my hand. "Before we start, I'd like to offer this to you on loan. It's the most human-friendly dog book I've ever read. Start with the chapter on fear and aggression."

Things moved quickly. I was handing out information so fresh in my brain I could still remember where it came from. Every name. That woman from the East Coast, telling me it was okay to make mistakes. Recover. Move on. I cracked a joke and we were laughing. I was being clear. They were asking questions. This was making sense.

They brought Keefer out again. Don't forget about barrier aggression. "Just let him go," I suggested. "It's okay."

I taught them a verbal bridge reinforcement. The son was dishing out treats and saying "Yes!" every time Keefer gave him attention. I was four feet away, yawning. The trainer whispering in my ear had an accent.

In a while I was tossing treats to Keefer. "Yes!" And handing them to him. "Yes!" And getting sits and downs and stands. "Yes! Yes! Yes!"

The mom was surprised by Keefer's new attitude and asked me why he was so anxious around strangers. I started to answer when a trainer tapped me on the shoulder. Let's just fix the behavior. "It's really hard to say," I said. "He's been practicing acting a certain way when new people come into his space. Now we're just going to teach him a new way to act. And, at the same time, we're going to show him that strangers coming over always means good things are in store for Keefer." And I sneaked a little pet under Keefer's chin. "Yes."

We were about halfway through our session when the dad offered up the one sentence that made my heart stop and the room spin. He said it in front of everyone. He said it as clearly and calmly as if he were offering me a glass of water.

"You know, you're Keefer's last hope."

There in that frozen moment was Dr. Ian Dunbar. I was in Houston at the APDT conference, and Dr. Dunbar was on the verge of tears. He was telling us how our work could mean the difference between life and death for a dog. Every time we interact with a client, imagine that we're holding a syringe of Euthanol in our hand. Alienate the client, and we risk the client giving up on the dog. Treat the client with respect, share our knowledge, and the syringe is cast aside. And, said Dr. Dunbar, imagine five syringes of Euthanol every time we interact with another trainer. If we fail to treat each other as professionals, we not only lose the opportunity to educate each other but we put the dogs at risk. If we open our doors, share our hearts and minds, and connect with humans and the dogs, one of those five syringes is cast aside.

I remembered every trainer I'd ever met. I remembered every trainer's book, workshop, and panel. I remembered every trainer kind enough to let me observe his or her skill and talent.

Before I left, I gathered up every gift every trainer had ever offered me. Together, they had paved the way for this turning point in Keefer's life. Together, the family and I agreed on a plan of action. We looked for trouble spots and vowed to keep thinking. Progress was at hand. Keefer pushed out a deep sigh. Could he have known?

Mom, Dad, Son, and I made plans to meet again in a week. I passed once more through the welcoming doorway and chuckled at the leaded glass. Cold wind hit me with the sure promise of winter on the way. Keefer brushed up against my leg. He'll see another spring.

I hugged the dog who just two hours ago was screaming for a piece of my face. "Yes." ❖

Contributors

Teoti Anderson, CPDT owns Pawsitive Results, LLC in Lexington, South Carolina. She serves as the APDT President and is the author of *Your Outta Control Puppy; The Super Simple Guide to Housetraining*; and *Quick and Easy Crate Training*, which earned a 2005 Maxwell Medallion in the Dog Writers Association of America competition.

Marian and Bob Bailey are two of the most well-known applied behavior analysts. Sadly, Marian passed away in 2001. She was one of B.F. Skinner's early undergraduate and graduate students, held a doctorate in psychology and was a university professor for almost 20 years. Marian and her first husband, Keller Breland, were the first people to apply operant conditioning commercially.

Bob, who holds degrees in chemistry and biology, pioneered operant-based animal training methods in free-environment and production settings. He began training in the late 1950s and was a pioneer in the open ocean use of dolphins as the Director of Training for the U.S. Navy.

The Baileys trained over 15,000 animals representing more than 140 species in the past 50 years. Among these are numerous dogs for commercial, research, and military applications. Large segments of their work have involved releasing trained animals (both birds and mammals) in environments that were sometimes hostile and always distracting.

Melissa Bain, DVM Diplomate in American College of Veterinary Behaviorists, is a veterinarian specializing in treating behavior problems in animals at the University of California-Davis School of Veterinary Medicine. She is also involved in research and in teaching veterinary students. She can be reached at mjbain@ucdavis.edu.

Valerie Barrette, CPDT has worked as a veterinary support member for over 20 years. She runs The Right Steps, a canine behavior counseling service specializing in puppy socialization and agility classes.

Jim Barry, MA, CPDT, CDBC teaches training classes and offers private instruction and behavior consultations in Rhode Island and Southeastern Massachusetts. Jim is a Certified Pet Dog Trainer and a certified member of the International Association of Animal Behavior Consultants. For more information, visit www.ridogguy.com .

Michael Baugh, CPDT owns North Coast Dogs Ltd. in Cleveland, Ohio. He's a full-time trainer and a graduate student in community counseling at John Carroll University. You can contact Michael by e-mail at michael@northcoastdogs.com.

CJ Bentley, CPDT is the Manager for the Michigan Humane Society Pet Education Center (PEC). The PEC offers group training classes, private lessons, behavior modification programs and operates a free Behavior Help Line. MHS is a non-profit organization that operates three open-admission shelters with full-service veterinary clinics, is the home of Animals Planet's "Animal Cops: Detroit" series and touches the lives of over 50,000 animals per year.

Jodi Brunson (Binstead) originally became a member of APDT in 1995 and served for several years on the Ethics Committee. Her dog training career began 22 years ago. In 2003 she moved to Oregon and spent a year training Police and Narcotics dogs. She offers private behavior consultations and competitive obedience.

Nina Bondarenko is Program Director for Canine Partners, www.caninepartners.co.uk. She gives seminars to police forces in the UK and Europe on positive and behavioral training techniques and runs courses in dog behavior, domestic animal training, assistance dog training, puppy assessment, and training. A judge of Schutzhund trials, she has trained dogs for security, SAR, film and TV, sheep and cattle, agility, obedience, tracking, and carting. She can be reached at ninadogs@gmail.com.

Stacy Braslau-Schneck, CPDT, CAP2 the director of Stacy's Wag'N'Train, which offers group classes and private lessons for pet dog owners in San Jose, California. As a graduate student in Hawaii, she trained bottlenose dolphins at Kewalo Basin Marine Mammal Lab while exploring the limits of the "creative porpoise" for a Master's degree in psychology. She can be reached at stacy@wagntrain.com.

Ali Brown, M.Ed., CPDT lives in Neffs, Pennsylvania. She has a BS in Psychology and earned her MEd in Human Development/ Behavioral Science. She is the author of *Scaredy Dog!*

Mel Bussey, CPDT, CDBC has been training professionally for over five years. She is the owner of Training Tracks Learning Station in College Corner, Ohio, where owners learn how to use positive reinforcement effectively to train their dogs and to modify behavioral problems. She is a current member of the APDT Board of Directors and a volunteer trainer at the Humane Association of Butler County.

Jean Donaldson, CPDT, CDBC instructs at The San Francisco SPCA Academy for Dog Trainers www.sfspca.org/academy and is the author of *The Culture Clash*; *MINE! A Guide to Resource Guarding in Dogs*; and *FIGHT! A Guide to Dog-Dog Aggression*.

Donna Duford, CPDT is an internationally known dog trainer, behavior counselor, and instructor, and one of the highest-rated speakers at APDT conferences. She is the author of *Agility Tricks for Improved Attention, Flexibility, and Confidence*. She can be reached at k9dancer@aol.com.

Dr. Ian Dunbar is a veterinarian, animal behaviorist, and dog trainer. He has written numerous books and videos and hosted the popular British television series *Dogs With Dunbar*. He received his veterinary degree and a Special Honors degree in Physiology and Biochemistry from the Royal Veterinary College (London University) and a doctorate in animal behavior from the University of California-Berkeley. He is a member of the Royal College of Veterinary Surgeons, the CVMA, the Sierra Veterinary Medical Association, the AVSAB, and the APDT—which he founded. Dr. Dunbar is currently Director of the Center for Applied Animal Behavior in Berkeley, CA.

Joan Guertin is a Charter member of APDT proudly possessing membership # 46. Joan's purpose in life is to better the relationship between man and his best friend, the dog, and to promote responsible dog ownership philosophies. To that end she constantly works to find gentler, kinder, more positive methods to enhance the learning at both ends of the leash. Her website is www.joanguertin.com and she can be reached at jbguertin@aol.com.

Beverly Hebert is a freelance writer and pet dog trainer in Houston, Texas. Through her business, Holly's Den, she offers puppy preschool, basic obedience training, and private behavioral counseling with the goal of fostering peaceful pack living for humans and their dogs. She is the author of the *Holly's Den Behavior Modification Training Guide for Reactive and Aggressive Dogs* and she can be reached at monty@hollysden.com.

Doug Johnson, who has been training dogs professionally for over 15 years, specializes in aggression cases. He has trained dogs for the US Department of Defense, the British Royal Air Force, and HM Customs (British). He is also a practicing attorney in Salt Lake City, Utah.

Emily Keegans lives in Seattle and is the owner of Lupa Dog Training, offering private lessons, Tellington TTouch, and behaviour counseling. Emily teaches classes for the Humane Society for Seattle/King County and DogSports Northwest.

Trish King, CPDT, CDBC is the Director of the Animal Behavior and Training Department at the Marin Humane Society in Marin County, California, and the author of, *Parenting Your Dog* (TFH Publications), drawing on her experiences as a parent as well as dog owner. She established the Canine Behavior Academy at the Marin Humane Society for trainers, which covers training theory and techniques, handling dogs, and teaching people. She has presented at several well-known venues, including the APDT Annual Educational Conference and Trade Show, Humane Society of the United States, and the American Humane Association.

Lynn Loar, PhD, LCSW is a social worker who teaches at-risk families to clicker-train dogs as part of abuse prevention treatment. She is the president of the Pryor Foundation (www.Pryorfoundation.org), an organization devoted to promoting the study and applications of marker-based shaping to influence human and non-human animal behavior. She is the co-author, with Libby Colman, of *Teaching Empathy: Animal-Assisted Therapy Programs for Children and Families Exposed to Violence* (Latham Foundation). Lynn can be reached at l.loar@comcast.net.

Terry Long, CPDT is a professional writer, dog trainer, and behavior counselor in Long Beach, CA. She is the former managing editor of *The APDT Chronicle of the Dog*, current editor of *The APDT Chronicle of the Dog's* "On Behavior" column, and authors *Dog World Magazine* "About Agility" column. She can be reached through her Web site at www.dogpact.com.

Dan McNally, CPDT, CDBC is a professional, full-service dog trainer and the owner/operator of the Spring Canine Academy in Sinking Spring, Pennsylvania. He currently serves on the APDT Board of Directors and was the past Chair of the APDT Legislative Affairs Committee.

Karen Overall, MA, VMD, PhD Diplomate, American College of Veterinary Behaviorists, ABS Certified Applied Animal Behaviorist, Center for Neurobiology and Behavior Psychiatry Department, Penn Med Translation Research Laboratory, 125 S. 30th Street, Philadelphia, Pennsylvania 19104; overallk@mail.med.upenn.edu. Karen is the author of *Clinical Behavioral Medicine for Small Animals.*

Paul Owens, CPDT is author of the book and DVD *The Dog Whisperer*, director of Raise with Praise, Inc., and founder of Paws for Peace, a children's violence-prevention program   He can be reached at info@raisewithpraise.com.

Sue Pearson, MA, CPDT has a graduate degree in education and is owner and training director for SPOT & CO. in Iowa City, Iowa. Pearson has been teaching classes for pet dog owners for nearly 20 years. She has been a speaker at APDT Annual Educational Conferences, was a member of the American Humane Association's task force for humane training, and served for four years on the APDT Board of Directors.

Janine Pierce runs J9's K9s in Granada Hills, California. She can be reached at her Web site, www.j9sk9s.com.

Mardi Richmond, MA, CPDT is a writer and trainer living in Santa Cruz, California. She is also the co-author of *Ruffing It: The Complete Guide to Camping with Dogs.*

Michelle L. Douglas (Romano), CPDT, CDBC owns and operates The Refined Canine in southern Connecticut. She has been training dog owners since 1997. The Refined Canine offers group classes, private lessons, and behavior modification programs. Michelle has been featured in *The New Haven Register* and *The Connecticut Post* newspapers, has been a guest on Pet Talk on Southern Connecticut Cablevision's channel 12, and most recently, the Chaz and AJ morning show on 99.1 FM WPLR.

Terry Ryan, CPDT, CDBC is a "train the dog trainer" expert who holds trainer classes and workshops all over the world. Terry is the author of *Coaching People to Train Their Dogs, Outwitting Dogs*, the *Sounds Good* sound desensitization CD series as well as several booklets. She can be reached via e-mail at teryan@olypen.com.

Veronica Sanchez, Med, CABC-SAC has worked as a pet dog trainer, an elementary school teacher, a Hispanic Parent Liaison, and a Dual Language Specialist. Currently, she trains pets and service dogs in Northern Virginia. Veronica can be reached at koberle@cox.net.

Audrey Schwartz Rivers founded and serves as executive director of PetShare, a 501(c) nonprofit that provides animal-assisted programs and humane education to at-risk children in Houston, Texas. She can be reached at asrivers@petshare.org.

Pia Silvani, CPDT, CABC is Director of Training and Behavior at St. Hubert's Animal Welfare Center, Madison, New Jersey. She developed a behavior department and conducts private consultations specializing in aggressive and anxiety-related problems for dogs and cats. She has spoken at various conferences and forums internationally and routinely consults with shelters to assist them in improving and expanding their programs. She recently completed a "virtual reality" training DVD and her newly published book *Raising Puppies and Kids Together – A Guide for Parents* was voted one of the top three parenting books in the 2006 Franklin D. Roosevelt Awards for Journalism.

Susan Smith, CPDT, CDBC, CTC was named APDT Member of the Year in 2004. She founded the PositiveGunDogs e-mail discussion group which promotes positive reinforcement training for bird dogs. Sue regularly contributes to *The APDT Chronicle of the Dog*, has been published numerous times in newspapers addressing behavioral and training issues, and has written for *The Bark* magazine. Sue lives in Austin, Texas and is developing a series of courses and marketing materials for use by professional trainers. She can be reached at her Web site www.raisingcanine.com.

Sue Sternberg is a lecturer, shelter owner, trainer, author, and creator of the infamous "Assess-A-Hand." Sue is the author of *Successful Dog Adoptions* and *Great Dog Adoptions: A Guide for Shelters* as well as several booklets, videos and training tools. She can be reached at Rondout Valley Animals for Adoptions, 4628 Route 209, Accord, New York 12404, or at sue@suesternberg.com

Diane Sullivan, CPDT is the owner of Good Dog Training & Doggie Resort in Rio Rancho, New Mexico. She can be reached at gooddogtraining@qwest.net.

Wendy van Kerkhove, CPDT, CTC is a graduate of the San Francisco SPCA Academy for Dog Trainers. She resides in Minneapolis, Minnesota and has her own business, Fresh Air Training. Wendy teaches "off leash only" obedience classes, runs Pint Sized Play groups for small dogs, and runs growl classes. She also offers private training to owners of dogs with aggression issues towards other dogs. She can be reached at wendy@freshairtraining.com.

Danette Johnson (Wells) is a Licensed Veterinary Technician in the state of Washington. She has been training and working in animal hospitals and shelters for the past 12 years. She has owned and operated her own dog training facility and day care center, Dog's Day Out, for the past six and a half years. Danette is a licensed CGC evaluator for the AKC as well as a Delta Society Pet Partner's (animal-assisted therapy) Instructor.

Nicole Wilde, CPDT runs Gentle Guidance Dog Training in Southern California. Nicole is the author of five books including *So You Want to be a Dog Trainer*; *It's Not the Dogs, It's the People! A Dog Trainer's Guide to Training Humans*; *One on One: A Dog Trainer's Guide to Private Lessons*, and her latest book, *Help for Your Fearful Dog*. She co-stars in the DVD *Train Your Dog: The Positive, Gentle Method* and is also the editor of the "Member Profile" column in *The APDT Chronicle of the Dog*. Nicole presents seminars nationally and internationally, including at the annual APDT Educational Conferences. She can be reached at phantmwlf@aol.com.

Mychelle Blake, MSW, CDBC has served as Managing Editor of *The APDT Chronicle of the Dog* since the 2003 January/February issue. She also serves as Editor-in-Chief of *Animal Behavior Consulting: Theory and Practice*. She has written articles for *The APDT Chronicle of the Dog* and other publications. She specializes in working with rescued and shelter dogs and has created several "head start" programs for volunteers at shelters. She served as past Chair of the APDT Legislative Affairs Committee.

Abbreviations

CPDT Certified Pet Dog Trainer. Granted by the Certification Council of Pet Dog Trainers. For more information on certification or locating a certified trainer to go www.ccpdt.org

CABC and CDBC Certified Animal Behavior Consultant and Certified Dog Behavior Consultant. Granted by International Association of Animal Behavior Consultants, www.iaabc.org

CAP1 and CAP2 Competency Assessment Program Level 1 and Level 2. Granted by Kay Laurence (UK), www.learningaboutdogs.com

CTC Certificate in Training and Counseling. Granted by San Francisco SPCA Dog Training Academy, www.sfspca.org

Index

From Dogwise Publishing, www.dogwise.com, 1-800-776-2665

BEHAVIOR & TRAINING

Aggression In Dogs: Practical Mgmt, Prevention & Behaviour Modification. Brenda Aloff
Behavior Problems in Dogs, 3rd ed. William Campbell
Brenda Aloff's Fundamentals: Foundation Training for Every Dog DVD. Brenda Aloff
Bringing Light to Shadow. A Dog Trainer's Diary. Pamela Dennison
Canine Body Language. A Photographic Gd to the Native Language of Dogs. Brenda Aloff
Clicked Retriever. Lana Mitchell
Dog Behavior Problems: The Counselor's Handbook. William Campbell
Dog Friendly Gardens, Garden Friendly Dogs. Cheryl Smith
Dog Language, An Encyclopedia of Canine Behavior. Roger Abrantes
Evolution of Canine Social Behavior, 2nd ed. Roger Abrantes
Give Them A Scalpel And They Will Dissect A Kiss DVD. Ian Dunbar
Mastering Variable Surface Tracking, Component Tracking (2 bk set). Ed Presnall
My Dog Pulls. What Do I Do? Turid Rugaas
New Knowledge of Dog Behavior (reprint). Clarence Pfaffenberger
On Talking Terms with Dogs: Calming Signals, 2nd ed. Turid Rugaas
Calming Signals: What Your Dog Tells You, DVD. Turid Rugaas
Positive Perspectives: Love Your Dog, Train Your Dog. Pat Miller
Right on Target. Taking Dog Training to a New Level. Mandy Book & Cheryl Smith
The Face In The Window:
A Guide To Professional Dog Walking And Home Boarding. Dianne Eibner
Therapy Dogs: Training Your Dog To Reach Others. Kathy Diamond Davis
Training Dogs, A Manual. Col. Conrad Most
Training the Disaster Search Dog. Shirley Hammond
Try Tracking: The Puppy Tracking Primer. Carolyn Krause
Winning Team. A Guidebook for Junior Showmanship. Gail Haynes
Working Dogs (reprint). Elliot Humphrey & Lucien Warner

HEALTH & ANATOMY, SHOWING

An Eye for a Dog. Illustrated Guide to Judging Purebred Dogs. Robert Cole
Annie On Dogs! Ann Rogers Clark
Canine Cineradiography DVD. Rachel Page Elliott
Canine Massage: A Complete Reference Manual. Jean-Pierre Hourdebaigt
Canine Reproduction and Whelping, A Dog Breeder's Guide. Myra Savant Harris
Canine Terminology (reprint). Harold Spira
Dog In Action (reprint). Macdowell Lyon
Dogsteps DVD. Rachel Page Elliott
Performance Dog Nutrition: Optimize Performance With Nutrition. Jocelynn Jacobs
Puppy Intensive Care: A Breeder's Guide To Care Of Newborn Puppies. Myra Savant Harris
Raw Dog Food: Make It Easy for You and Your Dog. Carina MacDonald
Raw Meaty Bones. Tom Lonsdale
Shock to the System. The Facts About Animal Vaccination... Catherine O'Driscoll
The History and Management of the Mastiff, 2nd Ed. Elizabeth Baxter & Pat Hoffman
Work Wonders. Feed Your Dog Raw Meaty Bones. Tom Lonsdale